Olga Tufnell's 'Perfect Journey'

Olga Tufnell's 'Perfect Journey'

Letters and photographs of an archaeologist in the Levant and Mediterranean

Edited and introduced by

John D.M. Green
and Ros Henry

First published in 2021 by
UCL Press
University College London
Gower Street
London WC1E 6BT

Available to download free: www.uclpress.co.uk

ISBN: 978-1-78735-904-8 (Hbk.)
ISBN: 978-1-78735-905-5 (Pbk.)
ISBN: 978-1-78735-906-2 (PDF)
ISBN: 978-1-78735-907-9 (epub)
ISBN: 978-1-78735-908-6 (mobi)
DOI: https://doi.org/10.14324/111.9781787359062

Contents

List of figures

List of maps

Preface

When Olga Tufnell wrote the words 'a perfect journey' in a letter to her mother she was describing her first excursion to the Middle East. These three words would also be a good description of her life.

Olga Tufnell came from a privileged background and had little formal education. There was little indication during her youth to suggest the direction that life might lead her in. One of her greatest attributes, however, was a love of adventure for its own sake. This, combined with the happy chance of coming under the influence of Flinders Petrie, the great Egyptologist of the day, would lead this young woman to participate in excavations in Palestine and eventually make a major contribution to the archaeology of the Near East and Eastern Mediterranean. Her published reports on ancient Lachish (Tell ed-Duweir),[1] where she spent some of the most crucial years of her life, are lasting testaments to her scholarship and dedication, as well as to the memory of the expedition's director, James Leslie Starkey.

These letters home show the foundation of that process and the beginning of her lifelong commitment to archaeology. The period from 1927 to 1938 saw the start of many friendships and professional relationships with well-known archaeologists and prominent persons. The letters give a contemporary view of life and times in an excavation camp and its setting from the archaeological, social and political perspective of the day, illuminated by Olga's own youthful enthusiasm and keen sense of humour. They illustrate the preoccupation of the time with biblical archaeology in Palestine, especially the sponsor Sir Charles Marston's hopes for Tell ed-Duweir; and Olga's references to biblical sources, including asking her mother to send out her Bible to enable her to check them.

Although surveys and excavations in Palestine had been carried out from the second half of the nineteenth century, archaeology was in a state of relative infancy compared to Egypt. Following the First World War, with Palestine under a British Mandate, interest in the geography, culture and heritage of the region greatly expanded. It seemed that many great discoveries were yet to be made. There were fewer restrictions than in Egypt, and local labour was relatively inexpensive. This fashionable cause attracted finance from institutions and private individuals, facilitating large-scale excavations, within which Olga Tufnell was to play a small but significant part.

To some extent, Olga's letters reflect a typically British attitude towards Palestine in the Mandate period, one that today might be viewed as colonialist or orientalist, affected by the biases and prejudices of the society she was born into. At the same time, they reflect a paternalistic (or perhaps maternalistic) approach in that she took her own practical steps towards assisting and improving the situation for 'native' people, especially through the camp hospital, which provided basic medical care to many local Bedouin and anyone else who needed it. Her rapport and good relations with almost all the people she came into contact with illustrate her generosity of spirit and openness. The letters give a sense of life in a period of unrest, although often such references are muted, perhaps as she did not wish to cause alarm to family back home. They give an impression of the manner of travel in more spacious days: trains across Europe, steamships across the Mediterranean and expeditions in the open touring cars of the day (with their unreliable engines). Olga was an avid traveller, noticing all about her and making friends wherever she went. Above all the letters reflect Olga's personality, awareness of her surroundings and ability to understand and communicate, helping to explain the transition she made from untrained amateur to acknowledged scholar.

Ros Henry was first made aware of these letters by Heather Bell, late librarian of the Institute of Archaeology in London, to whom Olga had left a vast amount of material and which Heather in turn had handed over to the Palestine Exploration Fund.[2] Olga herself had begun to transcribe some of these handwritten and fragile letters to preserve them as a record, perhaps with the intention to create a memoir. Years later it was suggested to Ros that she continue transcribing and editing them as they might be suitable for publication under the auspices of the Palestine Exploration Fund.

Ros was pleased to do this, as she remembers Olga with great affection – having met her in 1955 by walking into the old Institute of Archaeology in Regent's Park, armed with a degree in history and a short typing course. Ros asked Kathleen Kenyon (who had dug with her aunt at Wroxeter) if anyone needed an assistant, and was introduced to Olga. Luckily, Olga was in need and immediately set Ros to work proofreading

Lachish IV, dividing up Fosse Temple material for museum collections around the world (they had had to wait a long time) and sorting sherds from bags unopened since the 1930s with the soil still on them.

Ros was later encouraged to work on Olga's letters by many people, including Roger Moorey, for whom Vronwy Hankey and Ros had written an obituary of Olga for the journal *Levant*. Practical difficulties prevented work on the letters until Jonathan Tubb, then Assistant Keeper at the British Museum and Chairman of the Palestine Exploration Fund, very kindly made copies available so that she was able to work on them at home. It was in 2007 that Jack Green, then at the British Museum, offered to assist in further editing the letters and chapter introductions, selecting photographs and providing archaeological input where necessary, and helping to bring this volume to fruition. Jack and Ros both thank the many people and institutions who have helped to make this happen as listed in the acknowledgements.

Acknowledgements

The authors thank many people for their help and encouragement, specialist advice and access to libraries, archives and images. We apologise for any omissions. They include: Rupert Chapman, Felicity Cobbing, John MacDermot, Casey Strine and the staff of the Palestine Exploration Fund; Peggy Drower (Mrs Hackforth Jones), Michael Macdonald, Ginny Mathias and the late Rachel Maxwell-Hyslop; Sarah Micklem (great-granddaughter of William Nevill Tufnell), Cathy Warwick (great-niece of Olga), Wendy Slaninka (granddaughter of J.L. Starkey) and John Starkey (son of J.L. Starkey); Stephanie Boonstra, Josef Mario Briffa, Ian Carroll, Yosef Garfinkel, Anna Garnett, Lois Hall, Maarten Horn, David Jacobson, Billie Melman, Peter Parr, George Parris, Michael Peleg, Barbara A. Porter, Joan Porter McIver, Kay Prag, Isobel Thompson, Jonathan Tubb, Rachael Sparks, Amara Thornton, Myriam Upton and Catriona Wilson. Thanks also to the staff of the Wellcome Collection, including Helen Wakely and Andreann Asibey. We also thank Yannis Galanakis, Thomas Kiely, Anthi Papagiannaki, Emily Teeter, Anja Ulbrich and Donald Whitcomb for confirmation of details on site names and maps, and David Ussishkin, Yosef Garfinkel and Abigail Zammit for information and sources related to Lachish. Thanks to Matthew Adams and Sarah Fairman for access to the library of the W.F. Albright Institute, Jerusalem, and to Carol Palmer and Firas Bqa'in for access to the library of the British Institute in Amman of the Council for British Research in the Levant. Thanks also to the staff of the American Center of Research, Amman and its Library.

Thanks to Matthew Amyx for proofreading and making edits to the transcribed letters. Thanks to Leslie Schramer of the Oriental Institute of the University of Chicago, who created the maps. J.D.M. Green is grateful for research funds from the Oriental Institute, University of Chicago, which supported a research visit to the Palestine Exploration Fund archives in 2015. For introducing us to UCL Press, we thank Carly L. Crouch, former Chair of the Palestine Exploration Fund Publications Committee, for proposing this volume to Lara Speicher, Head of Publishing at UCL Press. We thank Lara and colleagues at UCL Press for their patience and support, especially Robert Davies for his excellent editing and proofreading, and Jaimee Biggins and Alison Fox. We also thank the two anonymous reviewers for their helpful insights, suggestions and corrections, which have been integrated into the volume. Lastly, we are grateful to Olga Tufnell for writing these letters in the first place. We are glad to make them available to a wider readership.

A note on the letters, photographs and illustrations

The letters and many of the photographs presented in this volume come from the Olga Tufnell archive at the Palestine Exploration Fund (PEF), London.[3] This selection of letters was written mostly to her mother (often on a weekly basis) and occasionally to her father and others. Notes on some letters indicate that they were intended for reading aloud to friends or relatives, occasionally with Hilda Petrie while she was in England. Parts marked 'private' or 'not for publication' were clearly not intended to be shared. Whereas the letters to her mother are filled with references to people, places and events, the few letters to her father often allude to nature, wildlife and the potential for hunting or shooting. She also wrote newspaper articles for publication in the *New York Herald* and the *Daily Telegraph* on the subject of the excavations, drafts of which were sent home and are incorporated here.

The documents presented in this volume continue to be of value for researchers in a range of fields, and it is hoped that this resource can continue to be mined for future studies in archaeology and cultural heritage, social history, gender studies, tourism and heritage studies, traveller biographies and Middle Eastern studies. Those interested in the history of archaeology, historical geography, the history of the British Mandate in Palestine or studies related to the British Empire may also find this volume of interest. A key strength of the letters is that they provide personal viewpoints and responses to people and places, as well as a background to 'dig life' and perceptions of archaeology.

Wherever possible, we have attempted to identify the people and places mentioned in the text and in photographs, and to provide contextual information wherever relevant to guide the reader if they wish to further their research. The photographs are useful as a dated record of sites, landscapes, people and ways of life. Although many have been published before, a significant number are presented here for the first time. Some images provide unique viewpoints and information about the preservation and/or restoration of sites.

Some opening and closing remarks and passages have been omitted (shown by an ellipsis), and corrections to obvious spelling errors and minor changes to punctuation have been made to improve the overall readability and consistency of the text. The specific year of some of the letters was not given but it has been possible to put them into good chronological order, and dates in letter headings are standardised for ease of reference. Insertions in square brackets fill in additional information relating to names abbreviated to initials, or modern spellings of place names. Notes elaborate on specific terms, foreign words or explanations. Olga's own spellings, which can be inconsistent or abbreviated, are followed here for the sake of accuracy. There are frequent variations and inconsistencies in her spellings of Tel or Tell (artificial mound), or Wady/Wadi (river valley), as well as specific place names.

The photographs bring Olga's letters to life in many ways, and may be useful to current and future researchers. Many come from the Olga Tufnell archive and were scanned by the Palestine Exploration Fund from negatives and prints, including from her photo album. It is not always possible to determine if a photograph in Olga Tufnell's photo album was taken by her, and if known, the photographer is cited. Labels accompanying groups of Olga's photographs and negatives in the PEF archive may be brief (e.g. 'Cyprus' or 'Diabolical') or give a general idea of the location and/or year the photograph was taken. Other archival sources include the Wellcome-Marston Expedition Archive, also known as the Lachish archive, the British Museum's Department of the Middle East, the Wellcome Library, the Institute of Archaeology and Petrie Museum at UCL, the Starkey family collection and collections of Tufnell family descendants.

The letters are helpful in identifying and contextualising people, places and events in the photographs, although it was not generally possible to match specific photographs mentioned in (or sent with) the letters to those found in the PEF's archive. Chapters 2 and 4, for example, are sparse in terms of Olga's own photographs. Attempts were made to include images related to the time, place and content of the letters, and individuals mentioned in them, as well as filling in gaps not covered in the letters. Lastly, biographical entries are provided in endnotes for individuals mentioned in the letters where they initially appear, and a list of the principal persons associated with Olga's archaeological work is given below. The biographical index lists occurrences of names in the letters, which will prove useful for those carrying out biographical research.[4] The index of places relates to places featured in the letters, rather than in introductory text and footnotes. Though not exhaustive, it focuses on the places which Olga Tufnell saw, visited or wrote her letters from.

Maps included in this volume refer to places mentioned in the text. Map 1 shows principal places visited and ports and cities encountered during periods of travel, including the route taken during the overland motorcar journey in 1933 (Chapter 7). Maps 2–4 feature places in Egypt, Palestine and Cyprus mentioned in the letters. A photograph of Olga's sketch map of southern Palestine (Map 5) includes roads and sites referred to in many of the letters home. A few of Olga's own sketches have been scanned directly from the letters and included in the volume.

List of principal persons

The people listed below played an integral role in the archaeological expeditions in which Olga Tufnell participated, and are by far the most frequently mentioned individuals in the letters of 1927–38. For a full index of the appearance in the letters of these and other people, listed by date of letter, see the biographical index. Endnotes with short biographical summaries are available for listed individuals at the point of their initial appearance in the letters.

Colt, Harris Dunscombe (Jr.), 1901–73

American, resident in England and United States. Archaeologist, philanthropist, collector and student of the engraving arts. First participation in excavations in 1922 at the Roman site of Richborough in Kent. Colt joined the committee of the British School of Archaeology in Egypt as representative of New York University in 1931 and was a supporter of Petrie's excavations in Egypt and Palestine. He worked with J.L. Starkey at Tell ed-Duweir as expedition co-director in 1932, withdrawing in 1933 to lead his own excavation at the sites of Sobata (Esbeita) and Nessana, the latter of which yielded important Byzantine papyri. Married Teresa Strickland in Malta. Established the Colt Archaeological Institute and its publication series.

Harding, Gerald Lankester, 1901–79

Student of Margaret Murray who conducted archaeological fieldwork with Petrie at Tell Jemmeh, Tell Fara and Tell el-'Ajjul, and with J.L. Starkey at Tell ed-Duweir (Lachish). Chief Inspector (later Director) of Antiquities, Transjordan and Jordan, 1936–56. Founded the journal *Annual of the Department of Antiquities, Jordan*. Worked with Père de Vaux at Qumran on the Dead Sea Scrolls and retrieved and published Safaitic inscriptions from the Jordanian desert. Expelled from Jordan in 1956 with other British personnel. His cremated remains were buried at

Jerash, Jordan, in 1979. Commonly referred to as 'Mr H.', 'H.' or 'Gerald' in Tufnell's letters.

Inge, Charles Hamilton, 1909–74

Archaeologist and administrator. Following initial participation at Samaria, Inge joined the Expedition at Tell ed-Duweir in 1932. Following the murder of J.L. Starkey in 1938, Inge took over as Director of the Wellcome-Marston Expedition to Tell ed-Duweir (Lachish) in its closing months. Alongside Olga Tufnell, he assisted in the publication preparations for the Fosse Temple volume (1940). After marrying, Inge went to British-controlled Aden during the Second World War, becoming Director of Antiquities. He participated in Wendell Phillips's excavations at Qataban, Yemen, in the early 1950s. He remained in Aden as an 'Information Officer' until his retirement, apparently not returning to archaeology.[5] British personnel left Aden in 1967. Upon retirement, he settled in Salisbury. Referred to mostly as 'Charles' in Olga Tufnell's letters.

Marston, Sir Charles, 1867–1946

Industrialist, philanthropist and author. Founded Villiers Cycle Components in 1898 to provide components for his father John Marston's factory, developing Sunbeam racing cars and motorcycles. He supported many excavations including those of Kathleen Kenyon at Uriconium in Shropshire, and John Garstang at Jericho. In 1933 he funded J.L. Starkey's expedition to Tell ed-Duweir (Lachish) jointly with Sir Henry Wellcome and Sir Robert Mond. On Wellcome's death in 1936 he became responsible for a half share of the expenses. Interested in religion from a Christian fundamentalist viewpoint, Marston authored several books on biblical archaeology. President of the Philosophical Society of Great Britain from 1942. Knighted in 1926, made Knight of the Order of St John, 1943. Fellow of the Society of Antiquaries.

Petrie, Sir William Matthew Flinders, 1853–1942

Prolific Egyptologist and archaeologist who made significant advances in archaeological fieldwork methods, recording, surveying and publication for Egypt and Palestine, 1880s–1930s. Established first systematic stratigraphic excavation of an archaeological mound at Tell el-Hesi, Palestine, in 1890. Edwards Professor of Egyptian Archaeology and Philology at UCL, 1892–1933. Founder of the British School of Archaeology in Egypt in 1905. After a career largely in Egypt, Petrie undertook a series of excavations of archaeological sites in Palestine in the 1920s and 1930s, including Tell el-'Ajjul, Tell Jemmeh and Tell Fara. Died and buried in Jerusalem. Referred to as 'P.', 'F.P.' or 'Prof' in Olga Tufnell's letters.

Petrie, Lady Hilda Mary Isobel, 1871–1957

Née Urlin. Irish Egyptologist and wife of Flinders Petrie (married 1896). Artist, copyist, surveyor and registrar for Petrie during his fieldwork, accompanying him on almost all of his archaeological expeditions in Egypt and later in Palestine in the 1920s and 1930s. Played a significant role in excavations and surveys of important sites in Egypt, especially Abydos. Worked as secretary and fundraiser for the British School of Archaeology in Egypt, 1905–47. Died in London. Referred to as 'Lady P.', 'H.P.' or occasionally 'M.P.', probably meaning Madam Petrie, in Olga Tufnell's letters.

Richmond Brown, Ralph, 1904–75

Assisted Flinders Petrie at Tell Far'ah (South) and Tell el-'Ajjul, 1930–2. Photographer for the Tell ed-Duweir (Lachish) Expedition, 1932–7. Served in RAF Intelligence in the Second World War. Research Assistant for the Department of Antiquities, Jordan, 1946, assisting with the excavation of the Dead Sea Scrolls at Qumran. Fellow of the Society of Antiquaries, 1953. Referred to as 'Brown' or 'Ba' in Olga Tufnell's letters.

Starkey, James Leslie, 1895–1938

Introduced to archaeology as a student of Margaret Murray. Excavated at Qau, Egypt, with Petrie, 1922–4. Expedition Director at Kom Washim, Egypt, University of Michigan, 1924–6. Assisted Petrie at Tell Jemmeh, Tell Fara and Tell el-'Ajjul, Palestine, 1926–32. Led the Wellcome-Marston Expedition to Tell ed-Duweir (Lachish), 1932–8, including discovery of the famous 'Lachish Letters' in January 1935. Fellow of the Society of Antiquaries. Murdered in Palestine, January 1938. Known as 'Les' to family and close friends, and often referred to as 'S.' or 'Starks' in Olga Tufnell's letters.

Starkey, Marjorie Rosaline, 1899–1952

Née Rice. Known by family and friends as Madge. Wife of J.L. Starkey (married 1925) and accompanied him on several expeditions, including to Karanis, Egypt, from 1924, and Tell Fara and Tell ed-Duweir (Lachish) in Palestine. The couple took their three young children (John, Mary and Jane) along on most of the expeditions. Mrs Starkey did not accompany the final expedition to Tell ed-Duweir, 1937–8. While not actively participating in archaeological fieldwork, she assisted the camp and helped with cleaning and 'waxing' skulls from the cemetery excavations. Widowed in 1938 on the murder of her husband. The Starkey children were supported with an award from King George VI following her husband's death.

Strickland Colt, Teresa (Terry), 1903–55

Née Strickland. Niece of Sir Gerald (later Lord) Strickland, Governor of Malta; cousin of Mabel Strickland. Born and raised in Malta, and married Harris Dunscombe Colt Jr. there in 1927. She kept her family name when married, though is referred to in Olga Tufnell's letters throughout as 'Colt'. Participated with her husband in Petrie's excavations in Palestine, 1930–2, and in Starkey's excavations at Tell ed-Duweir (Lachish), 1932–3. Worked from the United States for the British War Relief Society for Malta during the Second World War, decorated in 1946.

Notes

1   Tufnell et al. 1940; Tufnell 1953, 1958.
2   Acquisition recorded in 1987.
3   The Palestine Exploration Fund was founded in 1865 and is the oldest organisation in the world created specifically for the study of the Levant, the southern portion of which was conventionally known as 'Palestine'.
4   Biographical entries are derived from varied sources and for the sake of brevity they have not been systematically referenced. Resources include obituaries and articles in the journals *Palestine Exploration Quarterly* and *Levant*, Olga Tufnell's own writings and interviews, Bierbrier 2019, and the following online resources: *Breaking Ground: Women in Old World Archaeology* (http://www.brown.edu/Research/Breaking_Ground/introduction.php), edited by Martha Sharp Joukowsky and Barbara Lesko; *Trowelblazers* (http://trowelblazers.com); and *Filming Antiquity* (http://www.filmingantiquity.com).
5   Olga Tufnell interviewed by Jonathan Tubb, British Museum. Transcript of audiotaped interview, *c.* 1985.

References

Bierbrier, Morris L. 2019. *Who Was Who in Egyptology*. London: Egypt Exploration Society.
James, Frances W. 1979. 'Petrie in the Wadi Ghazzeh and at Gaza: Harris Colt's Candid Camera', *Palestine Exploration Quarterly* 111: 75–7.
Starkey, James L. 1933. 'A Lecture Delivered at the Rooms of the Palestine Exploration Fund, on June 22nd, 1933', *Palestine Exploration Quarterly* 65: 190–9.
Tubb, Jonathan N., ed. 1985. *Palestine in the Bronze and Iron Ages: Papers in Honour of Olga Tufnell*. London: Institute of Archaeology.

Tufnell, Olga. 1953. *Lachish III: The Iron Age*. London: Oxford University Press.

Tufnell, Olga. 1958. *Lachish IV: The Bronze Age*. London: Oxford University Press.

Tufnell, Olga. 1982. 'Reminiscences of a Petrie Pup', *Palestine Exploration Quarterly* 114: 81–6.

Tufnell, Olga, Charles H. Inge and Gerald L. Harding. 1940. *Lachish II: The Fosse Temple*. London: Oxford University Press.

Ucko, Peter J., Rachael T. Sparks and Stuart Laidlaw. 2007. *A Future for the Past: Petrie's Palestinian Collection. Essays and Exhibition Catalogue*. Walnut Creek, CA: Left Coast Press.

von Harten, Marjorie, and Marston, Melissa. 1979. *Man of Wolverhampton: The Life and Times of Sir Charles Marston*. Cirencester: Coombe Springs Press.

Weir, Shelagh. 1989. *Palestinian Costume*. London: British Museum Publications Ltd.

Maps

Map 1 Map of Europe and the Mediterranean, including Egypt, with harbours, major destinations and route of the 'Diabolical Strength'. Prepared by Leslie Schramer after H.H. McWilliams, *The Diabolical* (1934).

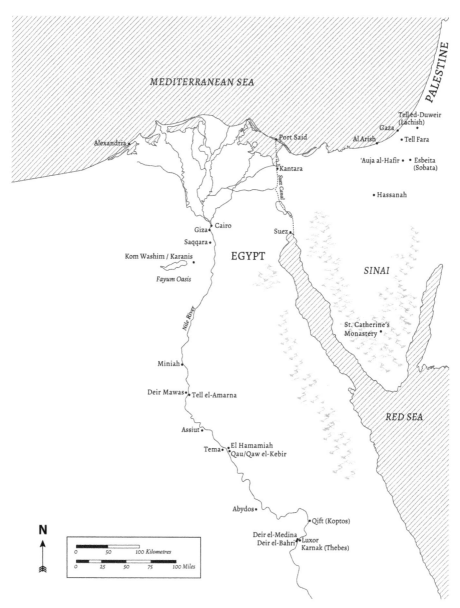

Map 2 Map of Egypt with principal sites mentioned in the letters. Prepared by Leslie Schramer.

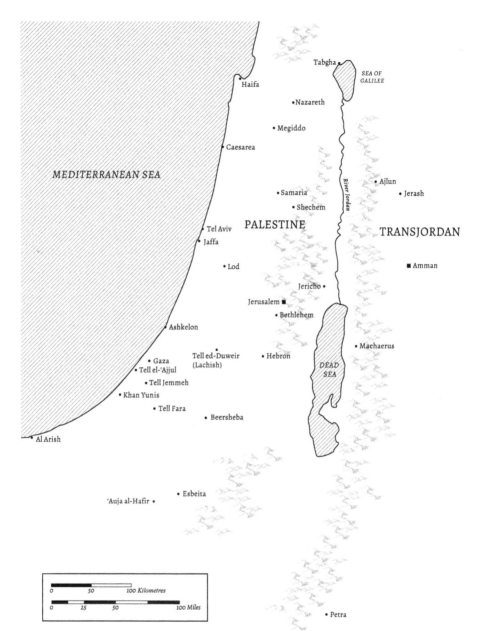

Map 3 Map of Palestine and Transjordan with principal sites mentioned in the letters. Prepared by Leslie Schramer.

Map 4 Map of Cyprus with principal sites mentioned in the letters. Prepared by Leslie Schramer.

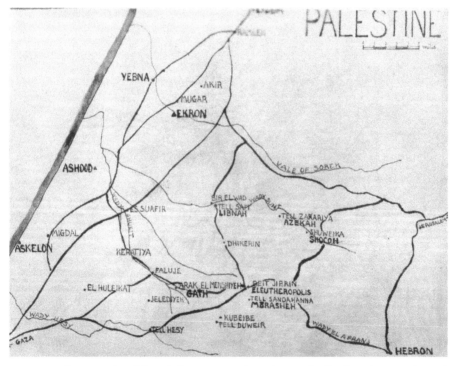

Map 5 Photograph of hand-drawn map by Olga Tufnell, showing roads and principal sites in southern Palestine. Olga Tufnell archive, Palestine Exploration Fund. Courtesy of the Palestine Exploration Fund.

1
Introduction

Olga Tufnell was born in 1905 and grew up at Langleys, a country house and estate at Great Waltham, Essex, England – the home of her grandparents. As a member of the wealthy and influential Tufnell family, Olga was born into privileged surroundings. Her childhood and education, however, were not as conventional as might be expected for someone of her family background. On the contrary they were full of change, travel and new experiences. Her father, Beauchamp le Fevre Tufnell, was the fourth son of William Nevill Tufnell of Langleys, an estate the family had acquired in 1710 (Figure 1.1). It was bought by Samuel Tufnell, a local man, a lieutenant in the Foot Guards and a Member of Parliament. He remodelled the original Elizabethan house, transforming it into the splendid Queen Anne mansion that still stands today (Figure 1.2). His architect was a William Tufnell (relationship unknown), hereditary architect at Westminster Abbey, and the gardens were laid out and planted by Charles Bridgeman, gardener to Queen Anne and famous for the gardens at Stowe House in Buckinghamshire. The Tufnell family provided a number of High Sheriffs for Essex over the centuries, and were much attached to the land and developments in farming. They also had interests in banking through Sparrow, Tufnell & Co., founded in Chelmsford in 1803 and later amalgamated with Barclays Bank.

Beauchamp, Olga's father, settled at Little Waltham Lodge near Langleys (Figure 1.3) after serving in the army. The Lodge was a substantial country house – seven bedrooms, a coach-house and several acres – and here he was content to live a country life with his wife, Blanche, and their three children, Gilbert, Olga and Louis, breeding game birds for the estate and other shoots and teaching his children to fish and ride. Langleys was a magical place for Olga; she spent much of her time playing in the woods and beside the watermill on the river Chelmer, which ran through the estate, and in the house itself running along the

Figure 1.1 Men of the Tufnell family at Langleys, undated. Courtesy of Sarah Micklem.

Figure 1.2   Olga Tufnell's grandparents' golden wedding anniversary at Langleys, 1911. Six-year-old Olga is in the car on far left. Courtesy of Sarah Micklem.

Figure 1.3   Little Waltham Lodge, Essex, 2011. Photograph by Ros Henry.

long gallery that spanned the whole of the upper floor. It was altogether a happy time.

But the country idyll was not to last; Blanche was a very different character from her husband. Daughter of a banker with American interests and an American wife (also called Olga), she had a cosmopolitan outlook, a fondness for travel and artistic leanings, and was a good amateur pianist (Olga remembered sitting on the piano while her mother played). Blanche had been brought up in the more sophisticated surroundings of fashionable seaside society. Sidholme, her home near Sidmouth, Devon, was a large Victorian mansion furnished in opulent style, complete with a spectacular music room with its own organ where musical soirées were often held and Paderewski had played. In addition, Blanche's mother had married again after the death of her husband, this time to a German scientist, A.F. Lindemann, with whom she had four more children, one of whom, Frederick Lindemann, later became Lord Cherwell, the distinguished physicist and confidant of Winston Churchill.[1]

In 1912, when Olga was seven, Blanche, perhaps tiring of country life, took her and her younger brother Louis to live in Belgium, where Olga was sent to boarding school at the Pavillon St Paul near Bruges, and Beauchamp retired to lodgings. Two years later, when war was imminent, Blanche moved back to Kensington, London. Olga was first sent to Miss Roberson's Private Classes for Girls in South Kensington, and then despatched to live at Easton Lodge, home of the notorious Daisy, Countess of Warwick, to share a governess with Mercy, the youngest daughter.

At Easton Olga came into contact with an exotic lifestyle. Daisy, friend of Edward, Prince of Wales, was an extraordinary woman, fond of extravagant parties and musical entertainments but also an ardent philanthropist and socialist. One of her projects was an underwear shop in Bond Street employing girls who would otherwise have had to work in factories. Besides having a passion for animals – she kept her own private menagerie – she was a keen follower of the Warwickshire Hunt. H.G. Wells was a neighbour, often producing plays at the house, and Elinor Glyn, the romantic novelist, was a frequent visitor. It would have been impossible for Olga not to have absorbed some of her eccentric hostess's ideas on the importance of a broad outlook on life, especially for women.

By 1918 Olga was again at boarding school – at New Hall, Chelmsford, a Catholic convent. Letters to her mother from school describe how she often spent leave weekends either at Langleys with her grandparents or at Easton, one describing the Armistice celebrations.[2]

In 1921, after a brief spell at the Italia Conti stage school in London, Olga went back to Miss Roberson's and took the Oxford Local Examinations, failing to pass mathematics, which meant an overall fail. As art was her favourite subject she was then sent to the English-Italian School in Florence for six months, lodging with a cousin, Bertha Penrose, who ran a boarding house for young ladies, taking them on cultural visits and providing opportunities to paint at a nearby studio. Olga's passport photograph from that time shows her with plaited hair (Figure 1.4). Olga describes her life there in a letter to her grandmother: the food ('chilly macaroni and mashed potato, tea also sketchy'), friends she has made and, as a sign of her now grown-up status, the fact that she is going to put her hair up.[3] There seems to have been no suggestion of Olga being presented at Court: the Tufnell family were landed gentry, not aristocracy, and it would not have been in Olga's mother's character to suggest it (nor, it would seem, in Olga's). By the same token, Olga was unlikely to fall in with the excesses of the 'Bright Young Things' of the

Figure 1.4 Olga Tufnell's passport photograph and signature, 1921. Courtesy of Cathy Warwick.

Figure 1.5 Olga Tufnell in evening dress, undated. Courtesy of Cathy Warwick.

day with their exotic parties in London and weekends in the country.[4] Her formal portrait photograph seems somewhat at odds with her character and style (Figure 1.5).

Introduction to archaeology

In 1922, Blanche found something for her to do. This was a sensible move whether Blanche was aware of it or not; the national census of 1921 revealed the huge demographic disparity between men and women following the ravages of the First World War. There was considerable public debate and social controversy as women increasingly took up employment in spheres that had been male-dominated. Olga's forthcoming occupation was both entirely suitable and unlikely to cause comment. Blanche was a great friend of Hilda Petrie, the wife of Flinders Petrie; Hilda and Blanche were members of the Czech Society of Great

Britain, travelling about together a good deal and organising tours to Czechoslovakia. Hilda suggested that Olga might like to help the Petries with their annual exhibition of finds from excavations, at University College London. Olga was already aware of the exhibition, having seen it in 1921 after she had returned from Italy; she formally joined the Petries in July 1922.[5] The role entailed sending out notices and appeals, labelling objects, taking visitors around and selling Petrie's books. Olga was happy to carry this out and was given the title of Assistant Secretary to the British School of Archaeology in Egypt, without typewriter or telephone;[6] and, as she said in later life: 'I went for a fortnight and I stayed for ten years!'[7] 1922 was an exciting year in archaeology as Howard Carter had just discovered the tomb of Tutankhamun in Egypt. Though she was not interested enough (by her own admission) to attend any lectures, except a few by Flinders Petrie, Olga amused herself by piecing together First Dynasty objects discovered in a drawer in the Edwards Library (UCL).[8] She gradually became fascinated with the subject. She wrote to her grandmother in 1923 about her work, how the exhibits fresh from Egypt had to be 'unpacked, sorted, cleaned and mended in some cases, arranged and finally catalogued in a very short space of time'. She also found time to attend Royal Society *conversaziones* with Petrie, went to hear Paderewski play and had her portrait painted.[9] Another letter to her grandmother in 1924 describes the current Petrie exhibition and gives an account and sketch of his early attempt at stratigraphy, showing his method of dating pottery by carefully recording the different levels at which it was found.[10] Life passed pleasantly in this way for the next five years; Olga was paid £3 a week, which, considering she lived at home, was quite generous.

In 1927 came the great opportunity. Petrie had decided two years previously to leave Egypt and resume excavations in southern Palestine. He still needed a small party to finish copying tomb reliefs, paintings and inscriptions at Qau el-Kebir in Egypt, and then to go on to join the main expedition at one of the many archaeological mounds[11] in Palestine, Tell Fara (now known as Tell el-Far'ah (South)). He invited Olga to join the group, as she had first passed his acid test of stamina and frugality, thus becoming a 'Petrie Pup'.[12] This of course she was happy to accept, as it exactly suited her adventurous spirit. In November she set off for Egypt, travelling with Myrtle Broome (a former student of Margaret Murray) by train across Europe, by boat from Marseilles to Egypt – 'a first glimpse of the Nile' – and finally to camp, where she found herself lodged, unusually but excitingly, in a tomb. As she writes in one letter, it was 'a perfect journey' (21 November 1927).

Figure 1.6 Olga Tufnell (second from left) with Flinders Petrie and Hilda Petrie (centre), G.L. Harding (far left), J.L. Starkey and D.L. Risdon (right), undated. Starkey family collection. Courtesy of Wendy Slaninka.

Olga moved on from Egypt to the main expedition at Tell Fara, joining its other members (Figure 1.6). Petrie himself was absent in London that year, leaving J.L. Starkey in charge. Olga soon proved invaluable as general assistant, supervising workmen, drawing and recording, in charge of first aid and at the same time struggling to learn to speak Arabic (Figure 1.7). She reminisced in later years: 'We were all in different sections of the cemetery and met each other for coffee and at the end of the day but nobody told anyone what to do.'[13] Later Petrie was to show his appreciation of her by asking her to contribute a chapter in his excavation report *Beth-Pelet I*.[14]

After two seasons, Olga left the Tell Fara camp in late 1929 for a season of several months in Cyprus; she later said that she was very tired and needed a change of scene.[15] A letter from Petrie to her mother shows that he had tried to get her included in the Megiddo excavations with Philip Guy but no space was available.[16] It may be she needed a rest, or that, devoted as she was to Petrie, some time away from Lady Petrie, whom she found difficult, would have been good. At any rate, she spent the season not only drawing objects for the Swedish Cyprus Expedition but also enjoying herself exploring the island and competing in local gymkhanas with her pony 'Woolly'.

From amateur to experienced archaeologist

The letters in this volume continue to trace Olga Tufnell's development as an experienced archaeologist in Palestine following her time on Cyprus. Olga rejoined the expedition at Tell el-'Ajjul for two seasons (1930–1, 1931–2) as an accomplished excavator and supervisor, but in 1932 came the final break from the Petrie camp. It was a hard decision for Olga. Not only had Starkey decided it was time for him to conduct an excavation on his own, but also tensions in the camp (elaborated in the letters) had risen to crisis level.[17] Olga, much though she loved and admired Petrie, felt she must join Starkey at Tell ed-Duweir (ancient Lachish) together with her companions from the past seasons, Gerald Lankester Harding and Ralph Richmond Brown; she was by now a valued member of the team in her own right. They were also joined, as co-director and financial

Figure 1.7 Olga Tufnell and workers at Tell Fara, February 1929. From a print made by Camerascopes Ltd, labelled 'Tracing Defense of Shepherd Kings'. Original photograph by Richard St Barbe Baker. © Estate of Richard St Barbe Baker, reproduced courtesy of Hugh Locke. Digitised from original print, courtesy of Rachael Sparks.

supporter in the 1932–3 season (the first of six), by the American archaeologist Harris Dunscombe Colt Jr., who had been with them in previous seasons at Tell Fara.

In 1933 a journey home overland with Teresa Strickland Colt (Harris Colt's wife) in the truck – the 'Diabolical Strength' – was another 'perfect journey'. Often they camped along the way in wild places (even here, Olga, true to her upbringing, was careful to wash and dry her stockings on a nearby bush). H.H. McWilliams, a South African friend of Teresa's and one of the party, wrote a vivid account of the journey in his book *The Diabolical* (1934). He and Teresa, who had suggested the journey, were not discouraged by reports from members of the Royal Automobile Club in London who had undertaken the same trip. The roads and conditions were very bad indeed and the difficulties and inconveniences would require a 'spirit of adventure'.[18]

Meanwhile the Tell ed-Duweir expedition was proving a success by providing the three main contributors, Sir Robert Mond, Sir Henry Wellcome and Sir Charles Marston, with finds confirming the biblical connections they so much desired, including the famous discovery of the 'Lachish Letters'. Starkey's excavations at Tell ed-Duweir combined traditional methods learned under Petrie with greatly improved resources, almost rivalling the well-funded American expedition at Megiddo. Although some of Starkey's interpretations were later corrected and his excavation methods criticised by some, others have remarked upon the great achievements and high standards of the British expedition.[19] At a local level, relations with the workmen and the nearby villages were seemingly good, though not always entirely smooth. Olga's help with medical matters was much appreciated (Figure 1.8), her chief weapons being quinine and a thermometer.

While the Tell ed-Duweir expedition could not be seen to take political sides, the continued security of the expedition was predicated on good relations with the local Arab population, including workers from nearby Qubeibeh ibn Awad and villages around Hebron.[20] Despite her apparent innocence or naivete, and desire to keep apart from public opinion, Olga was aware of the political issues both in Palestine and in Britain, remaining well informed through newspapers and radio broadcasts. There is one short reference to Olga's support for the Arab cause found in the letters.[21] Little of her concern is expressed in letters to her mother, however, perhaps as she did not wish to overly worry her with such issues.

The camp had managed to keep itself apart from the troubled times of the Arab Revolt apart from one occasion in 1936 when Arab

Figure 1.8 Olga Tufnell administering eye drops outside the dispensary at Tell ed-Duweir. Photo by Ralph Richmond Brown. Wellcome-Marston Expedition Archive, Department of the Middle East, British Museum. © UCL Institute of Archaeology, courtesy of the Wellcome Trust and the British Museum.

'revolutionaries' had attacked it, trying to set it on fire, but leaving after beating up the men left in charge. It was all the more horrifying when in January 1938 Starkey was murdered by a gang of armed Arabs on the road to Hebron on his way to the opening of the new Palestine Archaeological Museum in Jerusalem. Olga had much to do with the arrangements for Starkey's funeral, having accompanied the body to Jerusalem. The funeral had a diverse attendance, which included many Arabs who were deeply upset. Two of the ringleaders were subsequently caught and hanged, notwithstanding fear of repercussions; there were none.

It was decided by the Wellcome trustees that the expedition should carry on until the end of the 1937–8 season, firstly under Harding and then Charles Inge, thus continuing employment for Olga and the others. Excavations would then be suspended to allow for the preparation of publications. It was impossible to return, owing to the outbreak of the

Second World War. Further information on what came next for Olga can be found in the Epilogue.

In 1983, although by this time quite frail, Olga was invited by David Ussishkin, the later excavator of Lachish, to Israel on the fiftieth anniversary of the British excavations at Lachish in 1932–3, and the tenth anniversary of his renewed excavations there. She visited the current excavations and presented her reminiscences in a fascinating and illuminating account of life on a dig in Mandate times and her thoughts and attitudes looking back (Figure 1.9).[22] She was always very gratified at Ussishkin's endorsement of her conclusions on Lachish in spite of all the advantages of modern technology at his command. This was her final visit before her death in 1985.

Figure 1.9 Olga Tufnell during her visit to Tell ed-Duweir in 1983, seated in the guardroom of the Level II gate where the 'Lachish Letters' were found. Photo by Avraham Hay. Courtesy of David Ussishkin.

Olga Tufnell in context

Class and gender

Olga's letters provide a backdrop to significant changes in society taking place between the two world wars, with relevance to social history and gender studies. Olga Tufnell can be considered an overlooked female archaeologist of her time. Although Tufnell is featured in a number of memoirs and celebratory works,[23] she has not been recognised as prominently as other female archaeologists of her time – for example, Kathleen Kenyon, Gertrude Caton Thompson or Dorothy Garrod.[24] Her story is one that should be added to the growing literature on women archaeologists of the early twentieth century who had a significant impact on the field. In many senses, like other women archaeologists, she helped to break down disciplinary boundaries, paving a way for the future.[25] Olga can be argued to have belonged to the 'second generation' of women archaeologists in Britain – following the emergence of Hilda Petrie, Margaret Murray and Gertrude Bell in the Victorian and Edwardian eras.[26] It is hoped that the presentation of these letters will help raise awareness of Tufnell's work and add to the growing literature on the impact of women on archaeology, reinserting their place within what was a male-dominated field during much of the twentieth century.

Olga was able to take advantage of living in an era of rapid social change, and she was fortunate in having the financial means to pursue her passions and interests. She was also lucky to have had an unconventional mother who herself had disregarded the strictures of her day and encouraged Olga in her career. Olga's childhood had witnessed great changes in social mobility and awareness with the arrival of the motor car, the advance of women's suffrage and the growing voice of the trade unions. The new literary style (and indeed lifestyle) of the Bloomsbury set and the corresponding departure from conventional art emphasised liberation from Victorian constraints. The First World War had changed everything, especially for women, and not least in their clothing, where 'younger women ... were abandoning their traditional whalebone corsets ... symbolic of a wider rejection of the proper goals of British womanhood'.[27] More than that, the immediate post-war period had forced a change in women's expectations. 'Surplus women', as the *Daily Express* chose to call them in the post-war period, were perceived by many as a problem, rather than as a catalyst for change.[28] A whole generation of young men had disappeared and women had not only the chance but also the necessity for making something of their lives beyond marriage and family. Even at the village level, one of the first Women's Institutes to be founded in Britain was in Olga's own village of Great Waltham in 1917 with her aunt, Mrs de Hirzel Tufnell, as president. Although she herself did not play an active part in these social changes, nor was she particularly interested in politics, she certainly took advantage of the benefits. It is worth considering that Olga's social position, networks and familial wealth made it possible for her to develop professionally in ways that perhaps not all women (or men) of the time were able to. Many women archaeologists of the time, whether self-taught or professionally trained, came from comfortable middle-class or upper-class backgrounds, were unmarried and did not have children. Olga's freedom of movement and independence allowed her to attain knowledge and skills through practice, study and the building of personal and scholarly relationships over many years.

As a woman, Olga's role as an expedition member in Palestine, and as a British subject within a British-governed land, afforded her a greater degree of freedom and status than she may have had back at home. Olga's role in the camp clinic would have made her a highly important figure to the workers and local community members of all ages and genders. As a woman with self-taught medical knowledge, she also had access to private domestic settings that would have been entirely out of reach for her male counterparts. Yet at the same time, as a British woman of authority leading groups of male workers, she would not have faced the same social and cultural restrictions as the local women around her, perhaps to the level that she would have been considered an 'honorary man'.[29] Olga's unmarried status may have been a focus of gossip for the local workers. For example, in one letter she mentions a clove necklace that she wore for a time, reporting that they were traditionally worn by pregnant women in Palestine.[30] This must have generated some amusement, and indicates a certain lack of cultural awareness about how she might have been perceived as a woman among the local Arab workers and their family members. She also refers to accompanying her male expedition colleagues to swimming pools or the sea, i.e. being present while they bathed naked – presumably an activity that would have generated gossip had it reached the camp or village. In other cases, there are insights into the awkward prudishness of male team members, such as an incident in which Oliver Myers attempted to dissuade Olga from attending an apparently risqué belly dance.[31]

There is certainly every indication that Olga had an enjoyable social life, as suggested by her optimism and good humour. Teresa Strickland Colt would not have invited Olga to accompany them on their overland trip had she not been a suitable addition to the party. There is no hint of introspection or self-analysis; Olga took a pragmatic view of life and accepted what it brought with the candour of youth. One thing lacking in these letters, however, is any suggestion of an attachment deeper than great friendship. There is not a hint of romance, and very little about her personal life. This may be accounted for by the fact that she was, in large part, writing to her mother, to whom she was perhaps cautious in expressing too much, especially as others at home would hear from her letters. She certainly had close male friendships with Ralph Richmond Brown (Ba) and Lankester Harding, which were to last a lifetime.[32] Both Richmond Brown and Harding remained unmarried throughout their lives, and there is no suggestion that Olga was romantically involved with either of them. The letters occasionally mention men who appear as escorts or travelling partners – likely to reassure her mother that she was safe and well looked after, rather than as an indication of romance. Olga remained single her entire life, which was common in her generation, which had lost so many young men to the First World War.[33]

Colonial viewpoints

From an historical viewpoint, Olga's letters are situated within the British Mandate period, which followed the First World War and collapse of the Ottoman Empire. The creation of the Mandate states of French Lebanon and Syria and British Palestine, Transjordan and Iraq was recognised by the League of Nations in 1919. The Mandates period, which continued in Palestine until 1948, can be viewed from the perspectives of both coloniser and colonised, representing a twilight era of empire and a period of nascent nationalism, demographic change and political upheaval, in which processes of nation building, insurrection and suppression were concurrent and overlapping.[34] Living during these times must have been endlessly fascinating as well as alarming. For biblical archaeologists in the Holy Land, there was always the study of antiquity to provide insulation from the politics of the present. Yet despite this distance of the past, there were no archaeologists working at this time who could truly claim to be apolitical.[35]

Olga's letters shed some light on social and political attitudes at the time, particularly from the 'coloniser's' perspective, reflecting in part the vast social, economic and cultural divides between British archaeologists and local people living and working at archaeological sites. Although she was never a director of fieldwork projects, always a humble and diplomatic figure, and was hardly ever vocal in expressing her political thoughts (at least in her letters home), Olga nevertheless carried power and influence by virtue of her nationality, connections and social class. This power differential between foreign archaeologists and the local Arab population and workforce was ultimately rooted within the political, legal, administrative and military governance of Britain over Palestine and its people, particularly its diverse rural populations.[36] These letters therefore provide a resource for a growing area of study of the Middle East Mandates, and in particular Palestine. Political and historical studies of the British and French Mandates have, for example, had an underlying aim of exploring the questions 'how did the Mandate state function, and how did societal actors interact with it, and act in it?'[37] Olga's letters, however innocent and self-effacing, provide insights into such relations and the societal networks of an individual who oscillated and negotiated her role between elite British society and the rural communities of Palestine and beyond. Olga and her colleagues were living and working in the field for several months at a time. These were by no means fleeting visits, but allowed a deepening of relationships with local people and a greater understanding of culture and traditions, as well as the learning of Arabic. This puts into context the significant investment made for fieldwork projects, as well as the efforts made by Olga to create lasting connections.

Economic and social relations were very important for the expeditions. There were underlying logistical issues of paid employment for the local labour force, as well as access to the land on which excavations were focused, the necessity to take part in festivities, celebrations and events, and the need to maintain relations with local mukhtars (village heads) and sheikhs. The presence of relatively well-resourced British expeditions within isolated rural areas must have played an important role in building and sustaining relationships with the local Arab population, not only for the expeditions, but also for the British Mandate authorities. Provision of employment for workers as well as basic medical care to workers and their families were among the contributions made by the expeditions. Still, there were clearly huge economic, educational and health imbalances between the workers and the foreign staff. Insights into the identities, role and relationships of local workers on foreign expedition projects can be gained from a study of Egyptian workers in Petrie's excavation archives up until 1924 that draws on the types of tasks assigned to workers, and the important role of these 'hidden hands', who are seldom mentioned in scholarly publications.[38] Some of Petrie's workers from Quft, Egypt, who were highly skilled and experienced in archaeological excavation, later joined him in Palestine and are mentioned in this volume alongside the names of local workers. Future studies can draw upon these references for Petrie's and other expeditions of this era.[39] Olga herself acknowledges in her final publication for Iron Age Lachish the names of some of the key Arab staff and workers from Quft and southern Palestine who contributed to the Tell ed-Duweir excavations over the years.[40] Attempts have been made wherever possible to include the names of local workers and photographs of them in this volume.

Although employment for local communities on archaeological projects might appear benign and even a form of social welfare, relations were not always positive or equitable and tensions were bubbling beneath the surface. For Tell ed-Duweir, for example, there were underlying problems between the expedition, local landowners and the British Mandate authorities concerning claims and recompense for access to land on and surrounding the archaeological site, which do not seem to have been resolved.[41] It is unclear if Olga was fully aware of the issues at hand, although she alludes to 'disputes with the landowners at the beginning'.[42]

There were also certain embedded viewpoints and attitudes that could be described today as orientalist, colonialist or racist and that would have been very widespread at the time. Olga regarded the Arabs (regardless of status) as 'natives', though in her later reminiscences she used the term 'locals'. Her recounted memories are insightful about some of the colonial attitudes of the day. Petrie and other expedition directors had initially brought workers from Egypt to dig with them in Palestine (as at Tell Fara), yet Starkey and Harding both encouraged and succeeded in the training of local Arab villagers (fellahin) and Bedouin as workers (including children) on their expedition, an initiative viewed with apparent scepticism by some at the time.[43] This seems somewhat out of step with the long history of local Arab participation and expertise as part of archaeological expeditions in Palestine during the late nineteenth and early twentieth centuries,[44] and could relate specifically to the areas where Petrie and Starkey were now engaged. Colonialist attitudes, almost parental in tone, can also be seen in Olga's reminiscences: 'there was one good thing, perhaps, that we did through having that system and employing the locals, who were then in a very poor way and had a very tiny living standard. It was lovely to see during the time that they were working for us how the small skinny boys and the pale girls who worked as our basket children grew and flourished and their faces filled out ... That was something I feel was a real contribution to this part of the world.'[45] Olga became close to many of her Arab workers, often helping them to learn English, and in turn they helped Olga with Arabic.

The relationship between Olga and the Jewish community in Palestine is also of interest. Olga mentions a visit by herself and team members to a party at the home of the Kueseviches, a long-established Jewish family in Gaza, in one of her letters from Ajjul. There were visits to Tell ed-Duweir by Jewish scholars and other important persons, especially after the discovery of the Lachish Letters. Connections with Jewish friends or colleagues, afforded through visits to Jerusalem, as well as site visits, are indicated at points in the letters. There is affectionate reference to the Hebrew scholar Harry Torczyner, who visited the site while working on the Letters, and was also in correspondence with Olga's mother. On the other hand, there were more uncomfortable moments. The short-lived stay of Michael Avi-Yonah at Tell Fara in December 1928 points to the exclusion of a Jewish team member. It is not entirely clear what transpired, as Avi-Yonah was perceived as being 'more or less a permanent fixture', yet departed the expedition after just one week. Olga wrote: 'We are not kind to strangers, I think, and the men [Arab workers] hate anyone of the Chosen Race.'[46] The occasional anti-Semitic view or turn of phrase in the letters may reflect her upbringing: anti-Jewish prejudice was part of the prevailing mindset of people of her class and generation in Britain.[47]

By the early 1930s, while living near Gaza (see Chapter 5), she became friends with a British police captain, Raymond Cafferata, and his wife Peggy, which likely gave her some additional insights into local security concerns. Within the context of the worsening security situation and responses within Palestine between 1936 and 1939,[48] Olga's letters present personal glimpses into the impact on everyday life, travel and archaeological work. The disruptions ultimately led to the dramatic murder of J.L. Starkey in January 1938, precipitating the effective end of the Tell ed-Duweir expedition and British fieldwork in Palestine. The ephemeral accounts, attitudes and responses to the security situation in Olga's letters may be of interest to those studying the Arab Revolt, colonialism and British rule, and the history of Mandate Palestine.

Archaeology

The letters presented in this volume were written at a time when British archaeologists were becoming increasingly active throughout the Eastern Mediterranean, and particularly in Mandate Palestine. The period between the First and Second World Wars saw the emergence of an internationalised 'regime of archaeology' in the Eastern Mediterranean and

Middle East, in which major new discoveries, overseen by authorities under varying degrees of British control and influence, helped serve colonialist as well as proto-nationalist narratives of antiquity and modernity.[49] While British archaeologists had already been actively involved in fieldwork and acquisition of objects in Egypt, Cyprus and Palestine during the nineteenth century and prior to the First World War, the immediate post-war period saw the emergence of British archaeological institutions in Palestine, including the British School of Archaeology in Jerusalem (1919) and the Department of Antiquities of Palestine (1920), soon joined by the Department of Antiquities in Transjordan (1923).[50] These Mandate governmental institutions joined already established institutions in Jerusalem including the École Biblique et Archéologique Française, founded in 1890, and the American School of Oriental Research in Jerusalem and the German Protestant Institute of Archaeology, which were both established in 1900. The Jewish Palestine Exploration Society was established in 1913, and the Hebrew University of Jerusalem was founded in 1918 and opened in 1925. There was also an extra-governmental organisation, the Pro-Jerusalem Society, with its diverse membership, which was founded early in the Mandate era to help conserve the Old City.[51] There were numerous amateur archaeologists, photographers and surveyors who lived at the American Colony and lent their services to archaeological projects. In short, this was a vibrant time for archaeology in Palestine, often with a focus on the archaeology of the Bible. The 1920s and 1930s have been described as a 'golden age' of biblical archaeology in terms of the scale of activity and discoveries.[52] For Olga and her colleagues, there were numerous chances to visit sites, discuss findings with visiting experts and attend public lectures in Jerusalem. As participants within this social and professional community, Olga and her colleagues were privileged to be working at important sites where discoveries were being made.

As far as Olga's letters are concerned, her visits to Egypt were relatively short and shed little light on fieldwork or museum collections, but they do serve as impressions of sites and monuments. Yet the context of the period of Olga's introduction to archaeology in Egypt and Palestine in 1927 is important, as this marks the time at which her mentor Flinders Petrie was re-establishing himself in Palestine through the British School of Archaeology in Egypt, partly because of emerging restrictions on archaeological 'divisions' in Egypt (see below and Chapter 2). The letters also shed light on a time when Petrie's methods and theories were being challenged by emerging scholars in Palestinian archaeology, such as the American archaeologist W.F. Albright.

Archaeology was still not viewed as a fully professional activity in the early twentieth century, and many fledgling archaeologists, including Olga, were gifted amateurs. She admitted that initially, neither she nor the Bedouin workers she supervised had any training, and it was all picked up as they went along – 'the blind leading the blind'.[53] Through time and skill, they achieved the professional standards of the day. Olga learned from Petrie and his students and combined these skills with observed practices that were emerging at that time. For example, the American-led excavations at Megiddo could be viewed as the most technically advanced, even if stratigraphy was still in its infancy. Some of the most important developments in stratigraphy in the pre-Second World War Middle East were introduced by the British prehistorians Gertrude Caton Thompson and Dorothy Garrod,[54] though it is unclear to what extent their knowledge and skills were exchanged with Olga or her colleagues. Other contemporaries, such as Kathleen Kenyon (who had worked with Caton Thompson), were to gain greater fame. Kenyon was to cut her teeth at Samaria in the early 1930s – making a major contribution, even if not everyone was ready for the Wheeler stratigraphic method.[55] Kenyon went on to write an important textbook on archaeological methods.[56] Alongside Sir Mortimer Wheeler, she was to bring archaeology from the amateur to the professional world.

There is relatively little detail in the letters relating to Olga's fieldwork, except for exceptional discoveries and general updates. Much of the archaeological background, including key findings season by season, can be found in preliminary and final reports (see chapter introductions and notes throughout this book). Olga's typical fieldwork season began in late November or early December, and ended in the spring in mid- or late April, which was around 20 weeks, not including holidays. This was a significant amount of time to be away from home. Including travel, it amounted to six months in a given year. There were distinct advantages to the timing, including the avoidance of the winter weather of England, as well as the searing summer temperatures of Palestine. Disadvantages included the disruptive winter rains of Palestine, which were followed by mosquitos at a time when malaria was still common. The month-long observance of the holy month of Ramadan, based on the Islamic lunar calendar, started in March in 1927, and by 1938 started in early November. This in part explains why seasons started in December for 1935–8. This would minimise the number of workers needed during Ramadan. As Muslims, workers could not eat or drink from sunrise to sunset during Ramadan, and as a result only half-days were possible in this period.

These British expeditions were also privileged to be operating within less restricted conditions in terms of acquisitions of collections compared to the late Ottoman era, for example by the process known as 'division', in which a share of the finds remained in museum collections in Palestine, with the other part being legally distributed to the expedition director or host overseas institution, sometimes resulting in the transfer of thousands of objects. The end of fieldwork, as illustrated in the letters, was marked by the creation of a division list of finds (as further digging would inevitably yield more objects). Such divisions now form the basis of major collections in overseas museums. In addition to the compiling and submission of reports, detailed inventories of objects had to be prepared and then taken to the museum in Jerusalem where they were formally divided – and then there was the packing and shipping of the material bound for England. Olga served as the expedition registrar for both Petrie and later Starkey, and worked diligently to ensure that the lists were prepared and correct. Olga also assisted Petrie in his photography, which was an important part of the process of documentation of archaeological finds.

Collections from Petrie's excavations in Palestine were also prepared for summer exhibitions in London each year through the Egypt Exploration Society, a tradition that Petrie had initiated in the late nineteenth century as a venue for his finds from Egypt.[57] The exhibits were an important part of both fundraising and raising awareness of archaeological work, alongside newspaper articles, reviews, lectures and other forms of publicity. Olga Tufnell wrote occasional newspaper articles to help publicise the Tell el-'Ajjul excavations (see Chapter 5). For the Wellcome-Marston Expedition to the Near East, philanthropist Sir Charles Marston later raised much publicity for the Tell ed-Duweir excavations through writing popular books that set out to prove the historical veracity of the Bible through archaeology (see Chapter 8). The discovery in 1935 of the 'Lachish Letters' also had a significant media impact. In addition to Richard St Barbe Baker's 1928 film *Palestine's Lost Cities* (see Chapter 3), there was also a short film documentary made for the Wellcome-Marston Expedition, entitled *Lachish: City of Judah*, made by Ralph Richmond Brown.[58] These are just a few examples of the role of media and publicity in presenting the past to public audiences.

Travel, tourism and communication

The letters presented in the volume also shed light on modes and routes of transport and communication in the period between the wars within

Europe, the Mediterranean and the Middle East, and allow consideration of the impact of travel and tourism on personal experiences, as well as the people and places encountered. Travel, as well as the transportation of mail, between London and Palestine through a combination of rail and ship could take anywhere between one and two weeks, depending on the route, connections, stops along the way and weather conditions.[59] Olga's main approach was to take a ferry from England and the train overnight across France to the Riviera, and then board a ship from Marseille to Jaffa via Alexandria in Egypt. There were several lines or services running this route, typically stopping at Naples, Piraeus, Constantinople and Jaffa. Olga sometimes took the more leisurely 'Prince Line', which connected England and Australia via the Suez Canal.

Olga's route home was typically from Haifa to northeastern Italy. Haifa was the main port for receiving goods, equipment and vehicles in Palestine, and by the early 1930s it was an important British naval port. Olga's connections with the Navy through family members are indicated in her letters, emphasising Haifa's strategic role. The fastest route home was from Haifa to Trieste, via the weekly steamer (e.g. Lloyd Triestino), where rail connections could be found to Venice, Milan and on to Paris. On her way home in 1928, Olga took a 13-day cruise in second class for the princely sum of £18 (equivalent to around £1,000 today). Stops from Haifa included Beirut, Tripoli, Alexandretta, Mersina, Larnaca and Limassol, Rhodes, Piraeus (Athens), Brindisi and Venice.

Olga's maritime travel facilitated numerous visits to archaeological and historical sites in the Mediterranean, as well as to the homes of wealthy and well-connected people. Typical stops on the way to Palestine included Naples and visits to the nearby Roman ruins at Pompeii and Herculaneum, as well as Malta, where the prehistoric site of Tarxien had recently been discovered. Malta was also an important British naval port and the location of the Strickland family home, a mansion where she was able to lunch with Kitty Strickland, niece of Lord Strickland. Olga also took advantage of visits to Athens and its Acropolis and museums, and to Crete and the Minoan palace at Knossos as well as Villa Ariadne. She also took an opportunity to visit the old city of Dubrovnik, in today's Croatia. During one journey home, she also took the opportunity to travel from Trieste to Vienna, visiting the Porada family mansion.

Although they pre-date the era of mass tourism, the letters give insights into the diversity of Olga's fellow travellers. Most were not tourists, and they were of many nationalities and occupations. Olga was always good at making personal connections and finding good travel companions, such as Myrtle Broome on her first visit to Egypt, though she was equally at home as an independent traveller who could make friends and acquaintances along the way in a variety of languages. Nurses, officials, domestic servants and missionaries were among those encountered by Olga. She also met those who were travelling overseas to find a new home, including large numbers of emigrants from Britain to Australia. By the 1930s, Olga encountered more Jewish people travelling to (and from) Palestine, particularly via Haifa. The numbers of Jewish immigrants increased in the mid- to late 1930s with the rise of Nazism and anti-Semitism in Europe.

The letters provide insights into the history of tourism during the 1920s and 1930s. The period between the wars has been termed the 'new mobility era' or the latter part of the 'post-Cook' period,[60] in reference to the travel company Thomas Cook. Tourism at this time contained elements that developed more intensively after 1950, especially in the sphere of motoring and hotels. With mass tourism still in its infancy, Olga and her friends were able to take advantage of the new opportunities afforded by the building of roads, being able to use the expedition vehicle to visit sites that few others could get to, and to stay in hotels that provided comforts away from dig life. Trips to northern Palestine were particularly popular, as well as to Damascus, Transjordan and Egypt. The seven-week journey home in 1933 by road through Syria, Turkey and Eastern Europe could be described more as adventuring than motoring, and illustrates the fluid creation of itineraries by individuals in this emerging era of travel. Cyprus was also accessible by motor car, as well as being popular for hiking and pony trekking. Olga also mentions the large numbers of American tourists visiting the Cyprus Museum in Nicosia,[61] an illustration of the impact of cruise-based tourism in the Eastern Mediterranean in the early 1930s.

Within British Mandate Palestine and Transjordan (i.e. the Holy Land), travel and heritage tourism were undergoing transformations through the growth of institutions and social and political networks that played a role in the development of sites and museums that appealed to a growing number of visitors and inhabitants. As Amara Thornton argues, the political, social and economic history of heritage tourism in Mandate Palestine can be viewed as a series of contradictions: 'a history of inclusion and exclusion, centrality and marginalization, control and repression, freedom and creativity'.[62] Pilgrimage was already a well-established, centuries-old form of religious tourism to the region, yet Palestine was now attracting a much broader range of visitors. Cultural tourism, including archaeology, was part of the stewardship agenda of the British Mandate authority.[63] Established operators including Thomas

Cook remained active in the region until the end of the Mandate period.[64] Tourism in Palestine was not immune to political differences at this time, as indicated by rising tensions between emerging Zionist Jewish and long-established Palestinian Arab tour guides.[65]

As an archaeologist, Olga indirectly contributed to the heritage tourism arena through her facilitation of divisions of excavated objects from site to museum. As described above, while the division process led to collections from those sites being shipped to London for overseas museums, equally important were the collections that remained in Palestine for display in Jerusalem, including in the newly built Palestine Archaeological Museum.[66] The objects, as well as labels and photographs of the sites displayed with them, became important reference points for British as well as other foreign archaeological missions. This can be seen as part of the colonial agenda of the time, with historical and social narratives adding significantly to the range of heritage resources available. This gave a sense of the intensity of archaeological activity, as well as the significance of new discoveries, particularly within biblical archaeology. In-person visits to as yet undeveloped archaeological sites off the beaten path, such as Tell ed-Duweir, were generally limited to specialists, officials, VIPs or personal acquaintances, rather than general tourists.

Conclusion

This introduction has set the scene for the chapters ahead in providing some of the historical, cultural and political context for the letters, which cannot just be taken at face value. Although the letters do not provide a full overview of Olga's life and work, they give an impression of an extraordinary and fulfilling period for someone with very little formal education but, more importantly, an enquiring mind. In her achievements we find her legacy. It had been, as she writes herself, 'a perfect journey', though not without its share of drama. Olga's life and work are summarised in obituaries, reassessments, dedications and in her impressive bibliography.[67] Opening up the field of study relating to Tufnell's work to include not just the archaeological sphere but also themes of travel and tourism, colonialism and gender provides an alternative set of approaches to these sources that it is hoped will be useful for further exploration and research in related archives and studies. A summary of Olga's later life, and thoughts regarding future directions, are expressed in the Epilogue.

Notes

1 Birkenhead 1961, 26–7.
2 Letter from Olga Tufnell to her mother, Blanche Tufnell (undated, 1918). From letters belonging to Cathy Warwick, Olga's great-niece.
3 Letter from Olga Tufnell to her grandmother, Eleanor Tufnell, wife of William Nevill Tufnell, 27 April 1921 (?). From letters belonging to Cathy Warwick.
4 Taylor 2007.
5 Olga Tufnell interviewed by Jonathan Tubb. Transcript of audiotaped interview, *c*. 1985.
6 See Drower n.d., 9.
7 Olga Tufnell interviewed by Jonathan Tubb. Transcript of audiotaped interview, *c*. 1985.
8 Olga Tufnell interviewed by Jonathan Tubb. Transcript of audiotaped interview, *c*. 1985.
9 Letter from Olga Tufnell to her grandmother Eleanor Tufnell, 25 June 1923. From letters belonging to Cathy Warwick.
10 Letter from Olga Tufnell to her grandmother Eleanor Tufnell, 27 August 1924. From letters belonging to Cathy Warwick.
11 An artificial mound shaped by superimposed episodes of human settlement, abandonment or destruction is known in the Levant as a 'Tell' or 'Tall' in transliterated Arabic or 'Tel' in transliterated Hebrew.
12 Tufnell 1982.
13 Olga Tufnell interviewed by Jonathan Tubb. Transcript of audiotaped interview, *c*. 1985.
14 Tufnell 1930.
15 Olga Tufnell interviewed by Jonathan Tubb. Transcript of audiotaped interview, *c*. 1985.
16 Letter from W.M.F. Petrie to Blanche Tufnell, 17 December 1929 (?). From letters belonging to Cathy Warwick.
17 Drower 1985, 390.
18 McWilliams 1934, 13.
19 Moorey 1991, 62–3; Ussishkin 1985, 213–29; 2014.
20 Tufnell 1985, 7.
21 Letter of 2 July 1936.
22 Tufnell 1985; Ussishkin 1985, 2014.
23 Henry 1985a; MacDermot 2016; Tubb 1985; Tufnell 1985.
24 Davis 2008; Edwards 2013.
25 For a range of works covering European and American women archaeologists of the first and second 'generations', see: Cohen and Joukowsky 2004; Claassen 1994; Davis 2008; Díaz-Andreu and Sørensen 1998; Hamilton, Whitehouse and Wright 2007.
26 Cool Root 2004, 22–4.
27 Pugh 2008, 2.
28 Nicholson 2007, 23–4.
29 Kathleen Kenyon's relationship with her workers at Jericho is described in this way by Davis (2008, 109). Also see Seton-Williams's comments on gender (2011, 75): she was referred to as *mudir* by her male workers (meaning a male manager or supervisor).
30 Letter of 30 November 1928.
31 Letter of 18 January 1929.
32 Dedication and acknowledgements in Tufnell 1984, iv, xiv.
33 See Nicholson 2007, which includes the story of Olga's contemporary Gertrude Caton-Thompson.
34 Schayegh and Arsan 2015; Goldschmidt and Davidson 2006, 269–90.
35 Silberman 1993, 15, cited in Green 2009, 183.
36 Miller 1985.
37 Schayegh and Arsan 2015, 7.
38 Quirke 2010; also see Doyon 2018 for more on perspectives on the Qufti workforce within and outside Egypt, and Mickel 2019 for a broad perspective on archaeological labour forces in the nineteenth-century Middle East.
39 Rowland 2014; also see Chapter 2, note 27.
40 Tufnell 1953, 9.
41 Garfinkel 2016. See also Melman 2020, Chapter 4.
42 Letter of 6 February, probably 1933.

43 Tufnell 1985, 6.
44 Irving 2017.
45 Tufnell 1985, 6–7.
46 Letters of 5 and 13 December 1928.
47 Brustein and King 2004.
48 Cohen and Kolinsky 1992; Hughes 2010.
49 Melman 2020.
50 Gibson 1999.
51 Thornton 2012b, 197–8.
52 Albright 1949; Moorey 1991, 54–78.
53 Olga Tufnell interviewed by Jonathan Tubb. Transcript of audiotaped interview, c. 1985.
54 Edwards 2013.
55 Davis 2008, 59–67.
56 Kenyon 1952.
57 Thornton 2015; 2018, 75–102.
58 Thornton 2018, n. 34; see O'Grady 2017 for a clip from the film.
59 Alternatives at the time included air travel through Imperial Airways (India Air) from the late 1920s, which reduced the journey time to Gaza to just a few days but was exceptionally expensive. The Wagon-Lits service (better known as the Orient Express) took passengers by train from London to Beirut and then by car to Haifa.
60 Middleton and Lickorish 2005, 2; Weaver and Lawton 2006, 66–7.
61 Letter of 23 February 1930.
62 Thornton 2012a, 165.
63 Thornton 2012b.
64 Cobbing 2012; Thornton 2018, 41.
65 Cohen-Hattab 2004; Irving 2019.
66 Thornton 2012b, 200–1.
67 Drower 1986; Hankey and Henry 1986; Henry 1985a, 1985b; MacDermot 2016; Magrill 2006; Tubb 1985.

References

Albright, William F. 1949. *The Archaeology of Palestine*. Harmondsworth: Pelican.
Birkenhead, Earl of (Frederick W.F. Smith). 1961. *The Prof in Two Worlds: The Official Life of Professor F.A. Lindemann, Viscount Cherwell*. London: Collins.
Brustein, William I. and Ryan D. King. 2004. 'Anti-Semitism in Europe before the Holocaust', *International Political Science Review* 35(1): 35–53.
Claassen, Cheryl, ed. 1994. *Women in Archaeology*. Philadelphia: University of Pennsylvania Press.
Cobbing, Felicity. 2012. 'Thomas Cook and the Palestine Exploration Fund', *Public Archaeology* 11(4): 179–94.
Cohen, Getzel M. and Martha Sharp Joukowsky, eds. 2004. *Breaking Ground: Pioneering Women Archaeologists*. Ann Arbor, MI: University of Michigan Press.
Cohen, Michael J. and Martin Kolinsky. 1992. *Britain and the Middle East in the 1930s: Security Problems, 1935–39*. London: Palgrave.
Cohen-Hattab, Kobi. 2004. 'Zionism, Tourism, and the Battle for Palestine', *Israel Studies* 9(1): 61–85.
Cool Root, Margaret. 2004. 'Introduction'. In *Breaking Ground: Pioneering Women Archaeologists*, edited by Getzel M. Cohen and Martha Sharp Joukowsky, 1–33. Ann Arbor, MI: University of Michigan Press.
Davis, Miriam C. 2008. *Dame Kathleen Kenyon: Digging up the Holy Land*. Walnut Creek, CA: Left Coast Press.
Díaz-Andreu, Margarita and Marie Louise Stig Sørensen. 1998. *Excavating Women: A History of Women in European Archaeology*. London: Routledge.
Doyon, Wendy. 2018. 'The History of Archaeology Through the Eyes of Egyptians'. In *Unmasking Ideology in Colonial Archaeology: Vocabulary, Symbols, and Legacy*, edited by Bonnie Effros and Guolong Lai, 173–200. Los Angeles: Cotsen Institute of Archaeology at UCLA.

Drower, Margaret S. 1985. *Flinders Petrie: A Life in Archaeology*. London: Victor Gollancz.

Drower, Margaret S. 1986. 'Olga Tufnell, 1905–1985: An Appreciation and an Assessment', *Palestine Exploration Quarterly* 118: 1–4.

Drower, Margaret S. n.d. 'Hilda Mary Isobel Petrie, nee Urlin 1871–1956'. In *Breaking Ground: Women in Old World Archaeology*, edited by Martha S. Joukowsky and Barbara S. Lesko. Available online: http://www.brown.edu/Research/Breaking_Ground/bios/Petrie_Hilda.pdf, last accessed 16 July 2020.

Edwards, Phillip C. 2013. 'Redemption in the Land of Archaeological Sin: Great Excavators in the Middle East during the 1920s', *Buried History: Journal of the Australian Institute of Archaeology* 49: 23–36.

Garfinkel, Yosef. 2016. 'The Murder of James Leslie Starkey near Lachish', *Palestine Exploration Quarterly* 148: 84–109.

Gibson, Shimon. 1999. 'British Archaeological Institutions in Palestine, 1917–1948', *Palestine Exploration Quarterly* 131: 115–43.

Goldschmidt, Arthur and Lawrence Davidson. 2006. *A Concise History of the Middle East*, eighth edition. Oxford: Westview Press.

Green, John D.M. 2009. 'Archaeology and Politics in the Holy Land: The Life and Career of P.L.O. Guy', *Palestine Exploration Quarterly* 141: 167–87.

Hamilton, Sue, Ruth D. Whitehouse and Katherine I. Wright, eds. 2007. *Archaeology and Women: Ancient and Modern Issues*. Walnut Creek, CA: Left Coast Press.

Hankey, Vronwy and Ros Henry. 1986. 'Olga Tufnell (1904–1985)', *Levant* 18: 1–2.

Henry, Ros. 1985a. 'Olga Tufnell: A Biography'. In *Palestine in the Bronze and Iron Ages: Papers in Honour of Olga Tufnell*, edited by Jonathan N. Tubb, 1–5. London: Institute of Archaeology.

Henry, Ros. 1985b. 'A Bibliography of Olga Tufnell up to 1984'. In *Palestine in the Bronze and Iron Ages: Papers in Honour of Olga Tufnell*, edited by Jonathan N. Tubb, 6–9. London: Institute of Archaeology.

Hughes, Matthew. 2010. 'From Law and Order to Pacification: Britain's Suppression of the Arab Revolt in Palestine, 1936–1939', *Journal of Palestine Studies* 39(2): 6–22.

Irving, Sarah. 2017. 'A Tale of Two Yusifs: Recovering Arab Agency in Palestine Exploration Fund Excavations 1890–1924', *Palestine Exploration Quarterly* 149(3): 223–36.

Irving, Sarah. 2019. '"This is Palestine": History and Modernity in Guidebooks to Mandate Palestine', *Contemporary Levant* 4(1): 64–74.

Kenyon, Kathleen M. 1952. *Beginning in Archaeology*. London: Phoenix House.

MacDermot, John. 2016. 'Olga Tufnell: Exploring Egypt and Palestine'. *Trowelblazers*, http://trowelblazers.com/olga-tufnell/, last accessed 17 July 2020.

Magrill, Pamela. 2006. *A Researcher's Guide to the Lachish Collection in the British Museum*. London: British Museum.

Marston, Sir Charles. 1934. *The Bible is True*. London: Eyre and Spottiswoode.

McWilliams, Herbert H. 1934. *The Diabolical: An Account of the Adventures of Five People who Set out in a Converted Ford Lorry to Make a Journey from Palestine to England across Asia Minor and the Balkans*. London: Duckworth.

Melman, Billie. 2020. *Empires of Antiquities: Modernity and the Rediscovery of the Ancient Near East, 1914–1950*. Oxford: Oxford University Press.

Mickel, A. 2019. 'Essential Excavation Experts: Alienation and Agency in the History of Archaeological Labor', *Archaeologies* 15(2): 181–205.

Middleton, Victor T.C. and Leonard J. Lickorish. 2005. *British Tourism: The Remarkable Story of Growth*. Oxford: Elsevier Butterworth-Heinemann.

Miller, Ylana. 1985. *Government and Society in Rural Palestine, 1920–1948*. Austin, TX: University of Texas Press.

Moorey, P.R.S. 1991. *A Century of Biblical Archaeology*. Cambridge: Lutterworth Press.

Nicholson, Virginia. 2007. *Singled Out: How Two Million Women Survived without Men after the First World War*. London: Viking.

O'Grady, Caitlin R. 2017. 'Sticking, Mending and Restoring: The Conservator's Role in Archaeology'. *Filming Antiquity*, https://www.filmingantiquity.com/blog/sticking-mending-and-restoring-the-conservators-role-in-archaeology, last accessed 17 July 2020.

Pugh, Martin. 2008. *We Danced All Night: A Social History of Britain between the Wars*. London: Bodley Head.

Quirke, Stephen. 2010. *Hidden Hands: Egyptian Workforces in Petrie Excavation Archives, 1880–1924*. London: Duckworth.

Rowland, Joanne. 2014. 'Documenting the Qufti Archaeological Workforce', *Egyptian Archaeology* 44: 10–12.

Schayegh, Cyrus and Andrew Arsan. 2015. 'Introduction'. In *The Routledge Handbook of the History of the Middle East Mandates*, edited by Cyrus Schayegh and Andrew Arsan, 1–23. London and New York: Routledge.

Seton-Williams, M.V. 2011. *The Road to El-Aguzein*. London and New York: Routledge.

Silberman, Neil A. 1993. 'Visions of the Future: Albright in Jerusalem, 1919–1929', *Biblical Archaeologist* 56: 8–16.

Taylor, David J. 2007. *Bright Young People: The Rise and Fall of a Generation, 1918–1939*. London: Chatto & Windus.

Thornton, Amara. 2012a. 'Editorial: Tourism as Colonial Policy?', *Public Archaeology* 11: 165–68.

Thornton, Amara. 2012b. 'Tents, Tours, and Treks: Archaeologists, Antiquities Services, and Tourism in Mandate Palestine and Transjordan', *Public Archaeology* 11: 195–216.

Thornton, Amara. 2015. 'Exhibition Season: Annual Archaeological Exhibitions in London, 1880s–1930s', *Bulletin of the History of Archaeology* 25(1).

Thornton, Amara. 2018. *Archaeologists in Print: Publishing for the People*. London: UCL Press.

Tubb, Jonathan N., ed. 1985. *Palestine in the Bronze and Iron Ages: Papers in Honour of Olga Tufnell*. London: Institute of Archaeology.

Tufnell, Olga, 1930. 'Burials in Cemeteries 100 and 200'. In *Beth-Pelet I,* by W.M.F. Petrie, 11–13. London: British School of Archaeology in Egypt.

Tufnell, Olga. 1953. *Lachish III: The Iron Age*. London: Oxford University Press.

Tufnell, Olga. 1982. 'Reminiscences of a Petrie Pup', *Palestine Exploration Quarterly* 114: 81–6.

Tufnell, Olga. 1984. *Studies on Scarab Seals II: Scarab Seals and their Contribution to History in the Early Second Millennium BC*. Warminster: Aris & Phillips.

Tufnell, Olga. 1985. 'Reminiscences of Excavations at Lachish: An Address Delivered by Olga Tufnell at Lachish on July 6, 1983', *Tel Aviv* 12: 3–8.

Ussishkin, David. 1985. 'Level VII and VI at Tel Lachish and the End of the Late Bronze Age in Canaan'. In *Palestine in the Bronze and Iron Ages: Papers in Honour of Olga Tufnell*, edited by Jonathan N. Tubb, 213–29. London: Institute of Archaeology.

Ussishkin, David. 2014. *Biblical Lachish: A Tale of Construction, Destruction, Excavation and Restoration*. Jerusalem: Israel Exploration Society.

Weaver, David and Laura Lawton. 2006. *Tourism Management*. London: Wiley.

2
Qau el-Kebir, Egypt, 1927

Now at last came Olga's introduction to fieldwork; she had won Petrie's approval in the years spent working in London as his assistant, and in 1927 was rewarded with an invitation to join his excavations in southern Palestine. First, however, there was an unfinished project in Egypt for which her artistic flair would be useful.

In 1923–4 Petrie had been engaged in recording previously excavated rock-cut tombs at Qau el-Kebir[1] in Middle Egypt, many of which belonged to high officials of the Middle Kingdom (2025–1700 BC), including the nomarchs Wah-ka ('Uakha' in earlier publications) and Ibu.[2] The village of Qau is located next to Antaeopolis, which dates from the time of the third-century BC ruler Ptolemy IV. A photograph taken some miles to the north at Assiut by J.L. Starkey gives a general sense of the landscape of Middle Egypt (Figure 2.1) – sadly, very few from Olga's photographs of this time survive. The massive Middle Kingdom rock-cut tombs were cut into the cliffs along the east bank of the Nile, with porticoes and passages leading into inner pillared halls and finally to burial chambers deep within the rock itself. Although there is every indication that the tombs were originally of the highest quality, the tomb paintings were in a poor state of preservation and encrusted with bat droppings that had to be carefully removed with damp pads of cloth. Because of the dim light, photographs of ceiling paintings were taken using an ingenious mechanism for the reflection of sunlight via the lids of biscuit tins nailed together. The tomb paintings were also copied in colour onto paper by Duncan Greenlees.[3]

Work on the tombs had ceased in 1924, in part due to the intense focus on the prehistoric Badarian cemeteries just a few miles to the north, Petrie being taken ill for some time in 1925, and increasing tensions between Egypt's Director General of Antiquities (Pierre Lacau) and Western Egyptologists over changes in the Antiquities Law placing

Figure 2.1 View of the Coptic monastery Deir al-Mualaq, overlooking the village of El-Maabda on the Nile's east bank, Middle Egypt. Photograph by J.L. Starkey, with caption: 'Maarbdah – the Deir in the cliffs from the site for the House, November 1924'. Starkey family collection. Courtesy of Wendy Slaninka.

restrictions on the divisions of finds overseas. These difficulties over the export of objects in 1925–6 impacted the activities of the Egypt Exploration Society and caused withdrawals of grants from museums that benefited from such divisions.[4]

In 1926, Petrie reluctantly chose to transfer his excavations, then on behalf of the British School of Archaeology in Egypt, to southern Palestine, partly on the basis that it was historically seen as 'Egypt over the border'.[5] The first site he focused on was Tell Jemmeh, an ancient fortress along the course of the Wadi Ghazzeh thought by Petrie to be biblical Gerar,[6] followed by excavations conducted at the site of Tell Fara (see Chapter 3).

Following the disruptions of the past few years, Petrie was still concerned with finishing his Qau project and revising copies of the wall paintings. In November 1927 Olga set off to Egypt together with Myrtle Broome to assist in this endeavour. Broome[7] was a fellow artist who had been a student of Margaret Murray in London. Well accustomed to travel, Olga revelled in the long train journey across France and transferred to one of the steamships plying the Mediterranean from port to port. Onward travel was by train from Alexandria to Cairo, then, after some sightseeing and an overnight stay in the capital, onwards to Tema via Assiut, further up the Nile. Donkeys were the main mode of transport for the five-kilometre trek to the village of Qau on the east bank.

Flinders Petrie was still in London, and the rest of the party consisted of retired naval officer Commander D.L. Risdon,[8] his wife, who Lady Petrie thought 'young and charming',[9] and Gerald Lankester Harding,[10] another student of Miss Murray; they had all been together on the Tell Jemmeh expedition. Their task was to copy the remaining tomb reliefs and paintings and then, after a month, to move on to join the main expedition at Tell Fara, Palestine. On reaching Qau, Olga stayed in an ancient tomb (Figures 2.2 and 2.3), which was quite spacious and comfortable.[11] Unfortunately, Olga's letters do not enter into detail concerning their recording methods, and no specific mention of the short 1927 season or Broome and Tufnell's contribution was made in Petrie's report.[12] The bulk of Olga's letters from Egypt instead relate to camp life and visits to sites and monuments.[13]

The final phase of Olga's brief sojourn in Egypt before her onward travel to Palestine was an active two-day visit to Luxor. This included

Figure 2.2 Uahka's tomb at Qau. Photograph published by Olga Tufnell in the *Palestine Exploration Quarterly* (1982). Courtesy of the Palestine Exploration Fund.

Figure 2.3 Photograph of one of the expedition residences at Qau (cleared-out tomb). Starkey in hat to left, adjacent to his 'office'. Note the small 'windbreak' wall on right of picture. 1922–3 season. From archives of Henri Frankfort. Courtesy of the Egypt Exploration Society.

visits to Medinet Habu, Deir el-Bahri and multiple tombs in the Valley of the Kings. Olga reports a chance viewing of Howard Carter, who had famously discovered Tutankhamun's tomb in 1922.[14] After the Valley of the Kings, Olga explored Deir el-Medineh, the Tomb of Rekhmire, the Tomb of Nobles and the Ramesseum before taking the ferry back across the Nile. Her astute and informed impressions indicate that she was not just a tourist – Olga had prepared long in advance, and was familiar with publications by prominent Egyptologists. Brief insights into her visiting experience and comments on the state of preservation or restoration of monuments are occasionally given.

The letters provide an overall sense of how Olga and Myrtle's foreign identity, knowledge and professional networks opened up many doors to new experiences, sites, monuments and interactions with local people, notable figures, tour guides and members of the Egyptian antiquities service. Their travels and experiences in Egypt were part of a well-established, romanticised tradition that had developed over many decades and grew in the years following the discovery of Tutankhamun's tomb. Tourism and archaeology were closely intertwined activities for foreign, and particularly English, visitors to Egypt.[15]

The letters in this chapter are typed transcriptions from Olga's original handwritten letters; she intended to publish them at a later date. Headings were omitted in her typed version, and have been reinserted here.

Letters of November–December 1927

[17–18 November 1927; handwritten: PEF/DA/TUF/90]

<u>1st (General News Bulletin)</u>
SS *Mariette Pasha*.
17.IX.27. [sic – 17.XI.27]

Dearest Ma,
Now you shall hear all about it. As you will have guessed from the p.cs [postcards] we are safely on board. First, the Channel crossing was really pleasant, a mild evening with lovely mountainous clouds and no wind. At Boulogne, the usual helpless smile at the douane ensured that all our belongings were marked at once. In about ten minutes we were settled in our corner seats with time left to buy a pc to send to you.

Our fellow passenger was an English 'Madame Berton', on a less generous scale. She was going to 'San Reamo' as she pronounced it and had all her provisions in a bag.

Arrived in Paris, I had a run down the platform to post your card, which had a good effect on the excellent dinner we had had just before.

We were rather dismayed when French 'toughs' came and installed themselves with us. One was less affluent than the other and had no possessions other than what he stood up in. We all dozed until after Lyon and tried to keep warm, there was snow outside and nothing to speak of in the way of heating inside. We were very sorry for the less affluent one who had no overcoat, and were even more so when he awoke from a doze to find he had passed Lyon, where, he had told us, he was stopping to 'embracez la vieille' before joining the Légion at Marseilles. However, we all became very friendly over this misfortune, and talked of life in the ranks and so on and so on. At Valence they bought bananas which were offered to us and we had chocolate all round.

We had a touching farewell at Marseilles, collected Miss B's [Broome's] box without difficulty and jolted down to the quay in a vehicle of hoary antiquity. It was a matter of a few well-chosen words to change my cabin. I have a top bunk close to the porthole in a cabin with Miss B and one other, who gets up early and goes to bed late. As we do the opposite, we hardly know she exists.

The first afternoon was gloriously sunny, and we had coasted along the Riviera, there was no doubt that it was the Côte d'Azur. That night we slept like hogs, and missed seeing Corsica. Yesterday was equally fine and slightly warmer, and we went to bed early to prepare for the events of the night.

We were awakened by appointment by a strong flow of French at 1.30, when we put on coats and wrapped up in rugs to see Stromboli. We stayed on deck an hour and a half and were rewarded by several eruptions and one real flow of lava down the side. Five other energetic novices were out too. We went down to our cabin when we were out of sight, only to be wakened again at 4.30, to be able to say that we had seen Charybdis. The straits were really narrow, we saw little but the twinkling lights of Messina and Reggio [Calabria] on each side and the larger rays from the many lighthouses, but anyhow we have seen what there is!

I had the injection this morning and we spent a lazy morning, and your sunshine was needed all the time. Now clouds have blown over and it is raining and the wind he blow.

There are only about half a dozen English in this class, as usual we all flock together and eat together at the same table. There is a Scotch Govmt nurse who was through the Palestine Campaign with Allenby[16] and has been most of the time since in Egypt, sporting and well informed with some amusing experiences to her credit.

There is an English missionary on her way to Beyrout [Beirut] for a[?] years and a friend travelling with her. If anything else exciting has happened, I haven't noticed it, so any further adventures will be recorded in the next instalment. We should see Crete sometime today.

18.XI.27

No Crete today, as we passed too far to the west. Another glorious day, spent lazily, with a little Arabic and hieroglyphics thrown in.

We are busy with preparations for landing, which we should do about 12.30 am. But everyone seems pessimistic about catching the 3 pm train to Cairo, so plans are unsettled as there is no boat train, only 17 of us travelling to Cairo. I intend to make a fierce effort to catch the earlier train, otherwise we wait till 6 pm!

We shall be sorry to leave the boat. It has been very comfortable, food excellent, and not unpleasant 2nd class.

Very best love to you all, be good and keep well.
END
NEXT INSTALMENT IN OUR GREAT CAIRO NUMBER.
Ever your loving
Olga

[21 November 1927; handwritten: PEF/DA/TUF/91]

Canadian Holiness Mission.[17]
Assiut.
21.XI.27.

Dearest Ma and all,
Well, well, I do not know where to begin or what to say first and I certainly do not know how to describe all I have seen since we landed at Alex [Alexandria] last Saturday.

That feat which had absorbed all the conversation on the boat for the last 36 hours, was accomplished very easily. Our nurse friend has a hospital orderly to meet her, and we just followed them to the customs. We had previously collected a porter who produced the luggage in a few minutes. The official just had one box open but he didn't really look inside. We then had 15 minutes to catch the 3 pm train and with an un-Egyptian quickness our luggage was heaped on a taxi and we dashed off to the station. We arrived to see the Cairo train move out, but we dashed on to the next station about 5 minutes in the car, and fell into the train at the last, complete and whole.

The next train would have been 7 pm and we should not have seen the country. This would be dull to the inhabitant[s], but to us it was full of novelty, with the gaily dressed peasants and occasional villages and minarets. Our first camel and the first glimpse of the Nile were added thrills, but soon the sun set, and at six we reached Cairo.

We were thankful to see Mr W. [Wainwright][18] on the platform, as it was unusual to catch the 3 pm, and passengers are not expected to arrive by it. He tackled our removal to the pension [guest house] in a masterly way, and he took us to our rooms in Sharia Soliman Pasha – Miss Bodmin's. There we found a cool lounge with bowls of red roses and chrysanthemums and realised we were in a thoroughly English abode. All the other residents were out and we were pleased to have 2 peaceful nights with baths, though the prices are such that we shall not go again!

Mr Wainwright called for us on Sunday morning at 9, armed with our tickets for the monuments. We walked round the corner to the museum, where we spent the whole morning. We have walked round the whole place and have an idea where things are and have seen the most favourite things. Mr Engelbach[19] took us round too for part of the time, so we were well escorted. It would be endless if I started on my own catalogue of the things there. Statues one had imagined large, are small, other things have <u>grown</u> in reality and it is strange to see the actual colours. First, we saw the gaudiness of Tut, some glorious pieces of workmanship and colouring – the gold coffin, with the modelling of the face takes one's breath away for gorgeousness. But when we saw the jewellery of the XIIth dyn. [dynasty] the Tut stuff fades into insignificance. That again is eclipsed by the Old Kingdom statuary. Nothing can compare with the Khafra statue and the Sheykh el Beled.

Mr W. [Wainwright] lunched with us and at 2.30 we went by tram to the pyramids, across the Nile, past crowded streets, and between fields of apricots and peaches, growing like apples to the very foot of the pyramids. Soon we were walking on the original pavement, where the large blocks of the original casing stone stand. To the east is Cairo, with the citadel, rising above it, built of the casing stones of Khufu's pyramid, to the south faint outlines show the pyramids of Medum. Green strips of brilliant vegetation and blue bands where the inundation still is, with palms and little marooned villages stretch out to the Mokattam hills, and as the sun sets, their faint pink lights up and the sky turns mauve and purple till the sun goes down.

Still with our perfect dragoman, we tramped round to the Sphinx, past Reisner's[20] dig [at Giza]. They are still clearing away sand near the Sphinx, and the song and chorus of the boys as they moved was a lovely sound. May we have something as melodious in Palestine!

The Sphinx was fairly disappointing. Crowds of sightseers surrounded it, and now the sand has been cleared away, large paws are revealed, which look like a photograph badly focused.

Back, thankfully, to tea at Mina [Mena] house, where I made enquiries for Auntie Gracie, who was out. The N. de G. Davies[21] were in and we had a long talk. Mrs [Davies] said she will help us in Luxor, so that will make a difference. Just as I gave up hope of seeing Auntie G. she came in, and we spoke for about 20 minutes, after which we had to catch our train. She was looking well, just in from tennis, was pleased to see me, and shall hope to see her at Xmas.

To the Pension and to bed. Breakfast at seven and Mr W. met us afterwards, took our tickets and put us on the train for Assiut. We chose a compartment with one clergyman, who, as you can gather from the address, is now our host. He got off at Miniah [Minya] and some hours later we turned up with a letter to Mrs Black, his wife, with his luggage as well as our own, to stay the night.

She welcomed us, though we must have been a blow to her, as she had to arrange a room, and there were several children ill in the house. A young clergyman drove us up to see the Xth dyn. tombs on the hill, as soon as we arrived and we saw the city beautifully from the cliff, with an unbelievable sunset of gold and purple. Then back to a pleasant room here right in the heart of the old town, which seems untouched by the West, just the Arabian nights over again. We have just had supper and prayers with the mission and so to bed. Tomorrow, an 8.30 train to Tema and then camp. There hasn't been a hitch at all so far, in fact, a perfect journey. I am beginning to get along in Arabic, it's all great fun. Please show this to Lady Petrie and anyone else who likes,

Very best love
Olga

[22 November 1927; handwritten: PEF/DA/TUF/92]

c/o P.O.
Tema
Girga Province.
Egypt!
22.XI.27.

Dearest family,
Here we are, complete with all our possessions, strange to say. We have had an exciting day. After various prayers and good wishes, our missionary took us to the station, bought our tickets and saw us off. The 6th station was Tema, we were rather dismayed to see no friendly face on the platform, so we interviewed the station master, who spoke a little English. We found it would take 4 hours to send a message to the camp.

So we decided to go there on our own. The SM [station master] chose a donkey-boy for us, and we started with 2 men, ourselves on 2 donks. and one for luggage. Through the town where all were most friendly, we must have been rather a sight, perched on our steeds, with our skirts somewhere round our necks. The luggage donkey fell twice before we reached the hill and we thought of our bottles each time! By the waters of the Nile we sat down and waited for the dahabiyeh [ferry] collecting passengers for the far bank. At last after repeated shouts it came, and we were ferried with donkeys and all to the other side and then a bit across desert and fields till at last we saw welcoming Arabs coming to us down the cliff. I recognised Uah-ka's tomb and Mohamed [el-Kreti][22] gave us a meal, so that we waited [and] rested till the others came back from work at 4.

I can't begin to tell you how wonderful it all is here – scenery, air – everything.

Now to bed, 7.30 pm and tomorrow we go to work at 6. This will be posted at Tema first thing.

All my love – this is a perfect place so far!
Olga

[24 November 1927; typed: PEF/DA/TUF/103]

We live in a very comfortable tomb on the side of the cliff, with nothing behind us but desert until you reach the Red Sea. We have a dining room and a bedroom each, with a courtyard outside, from whence one can see across Egypt, to say nothing of the stars which hang in the sky in their thousands. It is lovely to lie in bed and see them through the rock door of my tomb. You would love the birds and animals we see all the time. Plenty of camels and donkeys; the young ones are specially sweet. A jackal came into the dining room last night and nearly ate our next day's lunch; and I hear there are various foxes about. As for the birds; they are endless. I've seen storks and herons and houbous [hoopoes] already, as well as the swallows who are arriving now. Some fascinating wagtails and some little green birds with long tails and red wings, which are some kind of bee eater. Egrets are about, lovely white owls and many bats.

The inundation is over now and the crops are just coming up – barley, maize, cotton and clover seem to be the chief ones. It is funny to see ploughing going on in some fields with crops just coming up in one nearby. The ploughs are just one blade fixed to a wooden frame, which is drawn by various animals; sometimes two water bullocks, sometimes two camels, sometimes one of each, and occasionally, a camel and a donkey. This morning on our way to work (before 7) we saw a man sowing just like in a Bible picture, scattering seed just like a man in a parable and all the time, the scenes and people take one back to Bible history. Nothing seems to have changed here since then.

[25–29 November 1927; handwritten: PEF/DA/TUF/94]

c/o Post Office
TEMA
GIRGA PROVINCE
EGYPT
25.XI.27.

Darling Mummy,
[…] I am settling down to a good routine. We are called at 6 am with coffee, we dress and set off to work about 6.45 (the sun rises at 6.25). After our walk (1½ to 2 miles) down the cliff, over some fields and along a road to Hamamieh [Hamamiah], where we meet the fellahin with their camels, bullocks, sheep and goats, also on their way to work in the fields, we climb the cliff, again beyond the village and settle down in Khenty-Ka's tomb for the day. We breakfast at 8.30 and lunch at 12.15, and we close down about 4.15 to get home before sunset. When we get home, fairly weary after the climb up the cliff, I wash and make my bed, then we eat at about 6.15 and go to bed almost at once afterwards. I'm usually in bed by 8.15. Mahamed [Osman el-Kreti] cooks wonderfully and makes the tins go. His chips, and the way he roasts in a saucepan would be lessons to our good lady!

It is hot. I only need one blanket and that is often too much. As we spend all day entombed, the walk in the cool of the morning and evening is very pleasant.

Life is lovely here, we are back several thousand years, little things amuse us, the Cook steamer[23] going up the Nile today was most exciting. The best thing today was your letter and the new moon which we saw on our way home, against the setting sun.

There are pictures on all sides, chiefly biblical, it is no good trying to describe the scenery. [I]t is not so much the shapes, as the colours that defy description – never the same and including all the colours of the rainbow. The sand turns from yellow and pink to purple, there are vivid strips of jade green in the fields, and there are glimpses of the Nile in the distance.

No more tonight – this can't be posted till Wednesday.

27.XI.27

Another good day, and we are waiting very hungry for the evening meal.

28.XI.27

As you can see, the meal came, which stalled my flowing pen! The days pass very quickly, tomorrow we shall have been here a week. We hope to finish the work in a fortnight, but it may take 3 weeks. In that case we may not be in Palestine for Xmas. However any fare you may be sending will be very welcome there, Xmas or no Xmas, they say it may be cold, so though a pudding sounds impossible here, we should wolf it down out there.

We are beginning to think about a few days in Luxor, and I hope to stop for a day or two on the way up at Abydos.

I took out the camera today and took 3 snaps, hope they will come out well, shall get them developed as soon as possible and send them on.

Though it is 80° in the shade – i.e. the tomb – I am feeling wonderfully fit – eat more and more every day, and enjoy it all tremendously.

29.XI.27

[...] We have had an amusing day. The police officer here was asked to dinner and on our way home we met him in the village, where he had been recruiting. There was a most ceremonial meeting and we were invited to tea with the Omdah [village headman]. Our guest for dinner walked home with us, with his horses and policemen, so we had not time to make the contemplated preparations for the eking out of chairs and crockery. He is a cheerful little man, unusually energetic and he bewails the lack of work. He told us many amusing things, and he is very keen that we should see his men drill and parade, apparently they do musical rides on horses to Arab music, so I shall be able to tell you all about [it] after we have been at 7 on Thursday morning.

Tomorrow is Suk [market] day, this one is the first that has been observed as a holiday by us, so it will be very busy. I've got my hair to wash, and hope to take some photos, and we want to go to the limestone quarries nearby and explore the immediate neighbourhood.

Personal

I wear my jumper and skirt and the Portuguese hat all day, as well as the new shoes, which were an effort at first, but are now quite comfortable. You will be glad to hear that a [I] wear my daisy rake[?] and that my tummy is in very good order. I don't seem to mind the wandering into the wilderness a bit. These are the sort of details which you want to know I'm sure! [...]

[Undated, handwritten, follows typed version: PEF/DA/TUF/0105]

Imagine a dusty square, bounded on three sides by flat-roofed, whitewashed buildings. A shrine with a low white dome is at one corner of the open side and beyond is the desert, with the dark openings of the tombs showing in the side of the cliff.

We arrived, rather shaken, in a Ford, which had performed miracles of endurance on the way. [A]ll seven passengers were carried over ditches, dykes and doorsteps, but as the last part of the road was fairly even, we were able to compose ourselves for the military salutes, presenting of arms and introduction to Omdah and Sheykhs [elders or tribal leaders] who awaited us.

We were installed on chairs, which afterwards followed us about as they were evidently the only ones in the community of two thousand, and watched the drill and parade, which we had been invited to see.

Our friend, the Police Officer, was responsible for all this, and during the parade, he shouted encouragement and abuse to the police drilling on one side and the three soldiers solemnly drilling on the other.

The three horses of the outpost jumped, or didn't, as the case might be, the specially constructed obstacles, roughly about two foot high. And all the time we murmured our appreciation. It is amazing how he has trained these fellahin[24] to march and obey. Needless to say, the whole village was present, as it was Suk day in Qau, and afterwards, when we walked through the place we saw the market, where only meat and onions are sold.

After an inspection of the outpost building, which was spotlessly kept, and where 'Welcome' had been written in sand on the doorstep, we went on to the residence of Mohamed Hasan el Gerzawy,[25] our host.

When he took over, he had coolly commandeered the Omdah's house, as the latter was getting rather big for his boots, but I thought the Omdah even more cool, as he was charging £4 per week rent!

There we had very sweet tea and Turkish delight, and one by one the chief men of the village gathered round, including the tallest man (in the world, I think), 7ft one inch, who is the Omdah of the neighbouring village. And the chief man himself arrived in full rig on his Arab stallion, gay with coloured cloth and many tassels. He did some exhibition riding which would be hard to beat. He is 75, owns 175 fedans[26] of land worth £17,500 and still sits on the ground and haggles about onions!

Apparently a native band was on its way, it would come in five or ten minutes, and there we waited, with intervals of conversation for an hour and a half.

When it did come, it was well worth it, and we adjourned to the parade ground. The band consisted of four players, 2 playing zimmaras [flute], and the others on a large and small darabouka [drum]. As they played, they danced and hopped in front of the dancing horses, who kept time most sweetly with the music and curtsied and knelt to the order of the riders, who guided them with poles. The stick fighting came next, a most attractive display. Long sticks are flourished and curled above the fighters' heads and points seem to be scored when the sticks touch. The fellahin got excited and join[ed] in the dancing and when we left they were evidently in for a day of it. The farewells were most cordial and we are due to visit the tall Omdah next Suk day.

All flourishing here, no time for more, go I now to bed, All my love
Olga

[5–9 December 1927; handwritten: PEF/DA/TUF/95]

c/o Post office
TEMA
Egypt.
5.XII.27.

My darling Ma,
Nothing of special note has happened since my last effusion to interrupt our routine. The lower tomb is more or less finished and we are inking in on the upper one. The tombs are cut in the cliff above the Hamamieh cemetery like this:

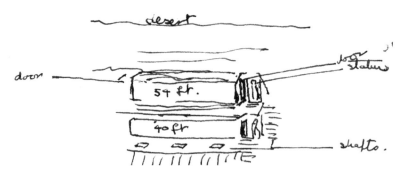

Figure 2.4 Ink sketch by Olga Tufnell of tombs cut into the cliff above Hamamieh cemetery. From letter of 5 December 1927. Courtesy of the Palestine Exploration Fund.

and it is quite a stiff climb up to them in the mornings. Ploughing is over, and the grain is coming up, in some places only 4 days after being sown, so that the paths have been done away with and we have to go round by the fields.

We have had a present of Timothy the Tortoise, presented as usual by El Gerzawy. As he only came today, we have not had a chance to get to know him well yet, but I expect we shall have various adventures with him [...]

We are all a very happy family here and seem to get on splendidly. There is no time to get bored with each other and there are always things to see and learn all round.

Mohammed [el-Kreti] and Hofney[27] who are the men with us are both splendid, they both take an interest in my Arabic and there is great applause when I come out with a new word! They are most picturesque figures in white galabiehs[28] and know their work inside out and of course they are devoted to Prof. [Petrie]

[10 December 1927; handwritten: PEF/DA/TUF/96]

c/o Post Office.
Tema
EGYPT
10.XII.27

Darling –
[...] There is something to write about tonight. We have just had an unexpected excitement.

The desert is even more lovely just now, as the moon is full, and I went for a walk, or rather a climb, up the hill.

It is all very silent, sometimes one hears the call of a buzzard or the sound of wings, and once I caught a glimpse of a dark form creeping along – a wild cat. The wadys [wadis] are very dark and the cliffs on each side tower above one, and somehow one cannot stay there for long alone! I went up the hill, and saw for miles all around: when I started to come down, it seemed darker than when I started, though there was no vestige of a cloud, and when I got back to the tomb, everyone was looking into the sky, and there was a perfectly good eclipse of the moon in progress! We watched the shadow creep over to totality and listened to the sounds from the villages below; drums were beaten and guns were fired to avert the calamity, as they believe all men will die when the moon is completely eclipsed. However, the awful moment came and went and we are still here. No lights shined from the plain, because if you have a light at these times, your enemy can come and shoot you![29]

We leave here on Thursday next, for 2 days in Luxor, (D.V. [God willing]) and shall break our journey to see Abydos. We shall be at the Thebes Hotel in Luxor, 60 PT [piastres] a day, much cheaper than most. Then on to Cairo, as arranged.

We had a visit from our friend Gerzawy late last night, he panted up the hill to ask us all if we would go to Cairo with him there and then, six in his Ford, 'to see the Mosques, the Pyramid and the Dromedaries'. He had apparently made all arrangements with his father to put us up in his house, 100 years old on the Nile in Old Cairo. It would have been a wonderful experience, but how he thought we could leap off at a moment's notice is a mystery.

However, we are spending a day with his father seeing Old Cairo. It should be a unique opportunity, as the old man is Omdah [village headman] there and keeps to all the ancient ideas and customs. He sold his daughter for £500, to a rich man, but the girl is very unhappy as she has been educated and the medieval system does not appeal to her.

Thursday 9th [sic][30]

A hot night, followed by a depressing day. No sun all day, glowering clouds and stifling. We were working at home, sticking sheets in the Great Hall of the tomb and the combined smell of rats and the trickiness of the job made us decidedly snappy. About three Hofny[31] came in excitedly to tell us it was raining and for the few moments that it lasted, we drank it in most thankfully. When it was too dark to work and the sun had set, Mr H. [Harding] and I started off to walk off our depression and the method succeeded splendidly, as it always does with me. We went straight up the hill and reached the ledge below the top without a stop; as we slowed down and began to look about us, we saw on the ledge about 15 ft above us, a huge vulture. He turned and looked at us, and after due deliberation, he took off and glided away. Evidently he thought us worthy of further scrutiny, for he turned and came slowly over our heads, so that we could see the curve of every feather and the glint of his eyes. That alone was worth climbing for. We walked along the top. The Nile and the cliffs on the other side stood out clearly after the rain, and as darkness came the desert reminded one of Dante's wilderness. The soft limestone has worn away and dark boulders lie about, some almost round, and some broken into fantastic shapes. The hills roll on like this and stretch till the Red Sea. One can understand the desperate people who die of thirst and so on, I never really believed in them before!

After sometime we came to the same wady that we walked up the other night, only we were 500 feet above, with nearly a sheer drop down. We edged our way along and after various adventures we found ourselves near the tomb and slid down to supper and bed.

Tomorrow is the last day for Christmas letters so this rigmarole must stop.

[Undated; 4–10 December 1927; handwritten: PEF/DA/TUF/104][32]

c/o Post Office
TIMA [Tema]
EGYPT.

Ya ammti mahbub! [To my beloved aunt!]
Ya ammi mahbub! [To my beloved uncle!]

It's all simply splendid here, but most un-Christmasified, so that I sit down with a great effort to wish you all the compliments of the season. The season here is perfect, fresh in the morning and evening when we have a fairly long walk to work and back. We go through the village of Hamamieh, where we are the great sight to watch and most of the village turns out! We meet the animals being driven out to graze, and the young furry camels with long, sprawly legs. There are lambs and kids with flopping ears in all good shades from black to pure white, and baby donkeys with the most engaging ways. They sometimes have patterns tattooed on the legs above the hock, which look just like gents' smart shooting stockings, and we know one donkey near here – almost white – who wears pale pink anklets and walks most gracefully in them.

As for the birds – they are endlessly fascinating – 'the father of promenading' is the friendly one and he comes right into the tomb where we work. He is really a dapper kind of wagtail, with smart black and white lines in him, hasn't he got a suitable name?

Storks are 'fathers of time' and we sometimes see them on the same spot for hours on end. There are plenty of egrets, but they haven't got any tail feathers just now. The most sensational birds in appearance are the bee-eaters – bright green to match the clover, where they wait on some stick, ready to dart at bees as they pass. As they fly there are glimpses of brilliant brown patches under their wings and they have a black streak that runs from their beaks to their eyes.

We have had plenty of adventures but you will have heard about them from Mummy. Next week we move to Palestine, via Luxor and Cairo. I shall be so sorry to leave this jolly place. We're above the dust and the smells on the edge of the cliff, with views in all directions over Egypt. It will be difficult to go back to houses and stuffy rooms!

Very best love and good wishes to you all for Christmas and the New Year.
Olga

[Undated; November or December 1927; typed]

Thomas the Turkey
The first sign I had of unusual events was when I opened my eyes yesterday morning and saw a wee white donkey looking at me through the door. As I lay on my bed, further strange sounds came to me; certain gobbles and gurgles which were never produced by any donkey. Now, you must know that animals don't get up the cliff to our tomb very easily, with the exception of jackals, a wildcat and bats, who are always about. Also, the night before, we had had a dinner party (with one guest) and had caroused and feasted until the late hour of 7.30 pm, so perhaps I was feeling the effects. Anyhow, after a time, curiosity conquered laziness and I got up, only to find that my dressing was being eagerly watched by two dark gentlemen; one in a fez, military khaki coat and galabieh, and the other draped in a checked table cloth. I cautiously completed my ablutions and came out.

There was Thomas, already at home in the courtyard, surrounded by all his admirers.

The two dark gentlemen and the donkey were only his escorts, and he was a thanks offering from our guest of the previous night. With him came a letter in these terms:

Dear Friends,
Good morning for all. I hope you will be so kind as to send me any of your newspapers.

I would be very much obliged if you could accept my photo – in both civil and military – to replace me as I could not accompany you wherever you go; as my own wish.

Thanks for your kind favour.
Remaining,
Yours truly,
M.H. El Gerzawy.

The gentleman in the fez came up to me, and it was soon evident that he wanted his photo taken. Thomas took his seat on the donkey so that his features were not lost to further generations.

All day he was tempted by small morsels; we had fears for his health when he ate a grain of rice [and] it seemed that he was going to be sick. He recovered and afterwards made a tour of the premises, including our bedrooms. As evening came, Thomas got restless; he was looking for a roosting place, and with many gurgles, he chose the kitchen roof. Our rice that night was full of small particles, dislodged by him from his perch. Next morning we bade fond farewell to Thomas, who had gained our affections, as we knew that when we returned from work, he would have gone to a better land.

The Turkey presented from Qau
Was roasted, we don't know quite how,
He was stuffed with a lot
Of what we know not
And was eaten with plenty of row.
Harding. Bk. VI. Chap. 10.V.25.

We saw our friend again that evening, beautifully disposed on a large platter. Sweet aromas were wafted on the air; perhaps we appreciated him even more with his mysterious stuffing and chips and onions. His death and embalming were worthy of record. How the process was completed we shall never know; a small primus and one super-cook and 'the help of Allah' were the only means we have any knowledge of.

Thomas may be gone, but he will never be forgotten; long after his last bone has been made into soup, we shall have sweet memories of the best turkey that ever lived.

No stone above his tomb there stands
His flesh was torn by human hands
Yet Thomas on his dying day
Did make the whole Qau party gay.
Harding. Bk. VI. Chap.10.V.26.

[Undated fragment; typed – probably November or December 1927]

It is cool, and as work is finished, it is the best time to explore the cliff. The whole side is honeycombed with tombs; large, impressive ones with huge brick causeways leading up, and pathetic coffins cut in the bare rock.

Some are falling to bits, and others have angles marked as clearly as the day they were made.

Never have I seen so many bats as we saw tonight. The air was full of the beating of wings and their frightful twitterings. They came in and out, brushing past us and hitting us in the face. The tomb was alive with the dark shapes flying recklessly. Our torch bewildered them still more, and was our only protection as we slid down the sloping passage to the tomb chamber. Once there, we could see them clinging to the walls, wings folded, ears perked and faces lifted as the light shone on them. The tomb chamber is usually just big enough to hold the massive stone sarcophagus. How these were lowered twenty or thirty feet, down narrow passages, is almost a mystery, and how they were broken into small pieces by some plunderer is nearly as incredible.

Sometimes carving can be seen, sometimes slim patterns can be traced and in Uakti-Ha's burial chamber, the ceiling is decorated with stars on a blue sky.[33]

All the elaborate arrangements for the comfort of the dead soul are wasted. Each chamber is empty and outside, exposed to the sun, are many white bones, their resting places plundered, their names lost and their identity destroyed.

After sunset, though the light is dim, shapes stand out clearly, and every stone shows.

[13 December 1927; handwritten: PEF/DA/TUF/97]

13.XII.27

Our last day here, which is sad. We were to have spent a day with the Bruntons,[34] and to have met halfway for lunch. But as the post brought no news from them, and all is finished here, we are moving off tomorrow. The itinerary is strenuous:

Get up 3 am, pack, which is a big show, as beds and all have to go, leave 5.30 am, on donkeys with chattels on camels, cross the Nile, reload onto other camels and catch train in Tema, 9.40. Arrive at the nearest station to Abydes [Abydos] about 12, spend six hours there seeing the sights, including Prof's [Petrie's] Tombs of the Courtiers and then on to Luxor, arriving 10 pm and probably thankfully, to bed at the Thebes Hotel.

After an uneventful morning, I am now sitting in a glorious wady about ten minutes from the camp, on a huge boulder, with a brilliant sky above, and the hope that I may see all sorts of birds. It is very still and crows and a flight of pigeons have already been over and the great hope is to see the vulture again.

It has now occurred to me that I never told you about our great day on Sunday.

Four of us started out bright and early about 8, to walk to the quarries on the cliffs near here. We had an intriguing walk across the desert, with our eyes glued to the ground, because at any minute, flints might appear. I found several flakes and one or two fairly doubtful flints – but it made me feel that one had really arrived. Then we saw the devastating face of the cliff, and after the usual pull up, we reached the shade of the quarries.

The face is smoothed off and great square pillars mark the entrance. Inside, the sand is a maze of tiny feet, pigeons and jackals, sometimes there was a bare human foot, and there was the unromantic trail of recent visitors, two Germans, with good stout nails in their boots. The ceiling is marked out where the blocks were to be cut, and into the distance, as far as one could see, are the square columns that support the roof. After we had rested there in the cool, we walked along the side of the cliff and saw the entrances to several unsuccessful quarries. Then, with a renewed burst of energy, we climbed to the top and came along the black-bouldered ridge toward home. I found a small calcite bead, which caused me great pleasure, only, it was Arab! There is a disappointing view from the top, just ridges of sand and black boulders. We came to the wady, where I am sitting now, which intersected our path, and made a precipitous descent. The echo is very powerful and when stones fell or we spoke above a whisper, the sound came back to us from all angles.

[…] Well, we are just beginning our last meal but one on our last night!

Very best love
Olga

[probably 15 December 1927; handwritten: PEF/DA/TUF/99]

Thebes Hotel
Luxor.
Thursday 13:XII.27 [sic, Thursday 15.XII.27]

Dearest Ma,
If I were to enter into full details of the doings of today, Baedeker would be better and more reliable. As for yesterday the itinerary as mentioned in my last was carried out. Leaving camp was fairly hectic as it was still dark and the moon our only salvation. We must have been a comic sight:

Figure 2.5 'Leaving camp'. Sketch by Olga Tufnell from letter of 13 December 1927. Courtesy of the Palestine Exploration Fund.

The pennant is composed of a fly switch and a measuring rod! However, after much cursing over loading the camels and suchlike trials, we got off. The Nile was very misty and there were masses of people waiting to cross for suk day in Tema. Two men had a row on board which nearly came to blows and at one point when the boat stuck on a bank, some men got into the water and pushed! Negotiations in the P.O. [post office] and station over in the nick of time and we got a carriage to ourselves. We cloakroomed the luggage at Baliana and got a vehicle out to Abydos. We eat [sic] our lunch in a remote sanctuary and wandered among the columns and chapels in Seti's temple. The colour is well preserved in parts and the reliefs are very fine, says I, getting into the guide book style. Stop!

We saw the Osereion [Osireon], for details ask Lady P. [Petrie] or Miss M. [Murray],[35] who first excavated it, and the much-ruined temple of Ramesseum.[36] Back to Baliana, where we enquired for the hotel. A porter said – 'oh yes. Ten minutes' walk', so off we dashed in the hope of seeing food. We walked through crowded streets with various brawls in progress and got to a picturesque tavern, straight out of Italian opera, with vines growing over trellise [sic] work on the terrace, which is on the bank of the Nile. Coffee was ultimately forthcoming after they had fetched the milk, and we dashed back to the station just in time. Luxor about ten, at last, installed here after the minimum of shouting soon after and so to bed.

We are the only visitors here, so we are well looked after. Breakfast over today, we made a B line for the Luxor temple and spent the morning there. A forest of columns, more graceful than the Seti ones in form, but still not the best that Egyptian architecture can offer. A mosque stands near the middle, and parts have been used as a Coptic church. Everywhere in these temples stones have been taken away, and re-used, upside down or anyhow on later buildings. It was pleasant to see grass and trees again. At Abydos there wasn't a blade.

After lunch at Karnak, a few minutes' walk in the other direction, we took our bearings first from the top of the first pylon and then went down and attacked the maze of colossal columns and courts. It is endless, fine work and interesting detail in many places, though it is late and everywhere a dignity and impressiveness it would be hard to beat. One court, with four delicate lotus columns still standing, has reliefs of the plants and animals that Thothmes [Thutmose III] imported after his campaigns, which are endlessly fascinating.[37] Home at sunset, having walked through the avenue of sphinxes, which seems much more dilapidated than I had expected. Saw a splendid jackal (my first) in the temple of Sekhmet.[38] Just had my first hot bath for nearly a month, which has had a 'soporific effect', like Benjamin's lettuces,[39] and so to bed.

All my love
Olga

[18 December 1927; handwritten: PEF/DA/TUF/100]

Train – Luxor–Cairo

18.XII.27.
Where did I leave off? The last instalment ended in a fade out of Karnak, I think, so that you have still to hear of 2 days' doings on the Western Bank. On Friday morning we were ferried across the river in a pleasant boat and on the other side we secured a carriage and a donkey. The former was unavoidable as Mr R. [Risdon] can't ride donkeys. First to Medinet Habu, much larger than I had expected, and a compact and decorative building. Much of the colour on the limestone carving still remains and the place gives one the impression of being more 'lived in' than other temples [Figure 2.6]. Later to the Ramesseum, quite up to all expectations, with the most perfect columns we have seen. The great relief of the Battle of Kadesh is there. Perhaps Lady Petrie will show you the pictures of all these places which will be better than any descriptions I can give. Then on to Deir el Bakhri [Deir el-Bahri], which has been one's dream of perfection. Groans and lamentations filled the air, as we drove up to a building in bright pink plaster, which would have been hooted at at Wembley. However, there was no getting away from it, and with heavy hearts we walked up the steep incline to the temple. Our spirits revived somewhat at the lovely relief of a lion on the corner of the balustrade, and when we stood in the sanctuary looking back through the gateways and across the plains to the distant hills, we felt distinctly better. Inside there are some reliefs of birds and flowers of the best period and enthusiasm was reached in the famous Punt Colonnades where the journey there and the strange things of the country are all shown in great detail.

Figure 2.6 Entrance to the small temple at Medinet Habu. See letter of 18 December 1927. Olga Tufnell archive, Palestine Exploration Fund. Courtesy of the Palestine Exploration Fund.

We could have spent hours there, every detail needed attention, all that we could do was to take in the colouring and workmanship as best we could. What had upset us was the beastly pink plaster used for the reconstructions in the 90s by the E.E.S. [Egypt Exploration Society]. It is altogether too foul, but cannot destroy the beauty of the sheer cliffs behind.

We had rather a struggle to get the equipage to take us to the Valley of the Tombs [Valley of the Kings] all in one day, but eventually we won, and were soon winding up to the wady, between steep hills. I had not realised how close all the tombs are to each other, all jumbled together in a hollow of the hills. The first person we saw on arrival was Howard Carter[40] just slinking back to his tomb after lunch.

We made straight for Seti's tomb, as we heard that the electric light stopped at one, blast it!, we had ½ an hour to spare but just when we were well entombed and were getting thoroughly excited, the lights flickered and went out, a ¼ of an hour too soon. A thoroughly Egyptian thing to do. However, we had a long and romantic wait in the pitch dark, and at last the guide brought an alarming acetylene lamp, which blew up at intervals and which was far more satisfactory to see the inscriptions by. Our Antiquities man proved to have worked for Prof. [Petrie] at the

Ramesseum so he was very pleased to see us and did us proud all afternoon. We lunched at the entrance to a late Rammy [Ramesside] tomb, and were assisted in our meal by a black hound, who gradually overcame his abject terror to the point of feeding out of our hands.

Amenhotep II's tomb is most impressive, the entrance is at the base of a sheer cliff and to get in there are masses of steps to descend and the burial chamber itself is far under the hill.

There by the light of our uncertain lamps we saw his mummy in a beautifully worked sarcophagus. I wish all the kings had been left in their tombs, they seem so out of place in museums.

Merenptah's [Merneptah's] tomb has painted inscriptions on a dove grey background, the figures outlined in strong black lines with touches of colour on dress and ornaments, a most effective way of decoration, and a change from the usual method of strongly coloured low reliefs. The lid of his outer coffin is one solid block of granite with well-carved hieroglyphs, though the lower part has been smashed to pieces by plunderers. The inner shell, which stands in the burial chamber, is a splendid piece of work. The finely moulded features in granite are meant to be seen in the darkness of the tomb and not in the glaring light of a museum.

Rammy VI tomb, just above Tut's, was not especially thrilling. In these later ones the colour is very crude and the hieroglyphs are cut to an absurd depth. We then sat on the wall of Tut's tomb and drank the best coffee I've had so far with the necessary noises of appreciation, much to the delight of our guide who had produced it. When we were ready to go, I was touched to see him high on a hill, in a row with four others, saying his prayers. So he scorned the great god Bakhshish [service payment], but we left something for him with another man, as he thoroughly deserved it.

After sunset I had my hair cut and felt quite civilized again.

On the third day, Miss B. [Broome] Mr H. [Harding] and I went off to the Western Bank by ourselves, as Mr R. [Risdon] doesn't like donks, and Mrs R. doesn't like boats. We got three splendid mokes and set off at a canter for the Tombs of the Queens. The only Queen's tomb is Nefertari, the others are princes, the most fascinating was that of a baby son of one of the Rameses. On the wall paintings he was shown as a boy of ten, though his body lying on a basket mat is that of a new-born child. The frescoes are beautifully painted, with very gay details of dress and ornaments, the blues of head dresses and so on are especially bright. The boy is shown as being introduced by his father to all the Gods, the whole is so fresh and rather pathetic.

Then over the hills on a narrow donkey path to Deir el Medinet [Deir el-Medineh]. This is a minute temple, surrounded by a high brick wall. It is beautifully preserved, a window actually remains and there are steps leading up to the roof, where the roofing blocks are still in position. Then on to the Tombs of the Nobles, where we knew the best thing of all awaited us. We saw the tomb of Senneferu, which is cunningly buried and is reached by a tortuous passage. The work is poor, the partortion [proportion?] of the figures sometimes wicked but there are many unusual details, which make it utterly charming. The wall plastering has been very roughly done, and there has been an attempt to level the ceiling. This is painted with grape vines and bunches of fruit and many different patterns, as he was the overseer of the garden of Amon. The designs on the uneven surface are so effective.

Then on to the due of the day – the tomb of Rekh ma ra [Rekhmire]. This is built on a totally different plan to the others, just a long chamber, parallel to the rock surface outside, and a long sloping passage leading inwards and widening out as it goes opposite the entrance, like an enormous T. At the far end, where the height is about 30 ft, is a niche high up in the wall. The wall surface is entirely covered with wonderfully painted scenes. All the events of daily life are shown most truthfully, and are described in lovely hieroglyphs. We were considered harmless but insane owing to the time we spent there (See Newberry's publication).[41] After lunch we browsed in the Ramesseum until it was time to meet our boat, for we were to spend two hours on the Nile and try to imagine ourselves back in the times when Iffy (the lady of our tomb at Hamamieh) drifted on the water in her boat, sniffing at Lotuses. Unfortunately we had none, but we got the atmosphere fairly well. Having left Luxor at six we are now on our way to Cairo; the less said about journeys in this country the better. My pen has run out and I've no more paper, so farewell. The days at Luxor were perfect. I've never enjoyed sightseeing so much.

Love to all
Olga.

[Undated, probably 19 December 1927; handwritten: PEF/DA/ TUF/98.2][42]

Cecil House

Dearest –
I am writing on this as there is nothing else at hand. The journey was not so bad as it might have been. We arrived here about 7.30 pm. Rather a

mouldy place, full of those English who are only seen on the Continent. But clean and good enough to sleep in. I rang up Dalton and Auntie G. This morning went to the Bank to get money and afterwards did the luggage business etc. After lunch had my hair waved to celebrate return to civilization and was called for here by the Pellys, who took me out to Gezira. This is the Ranelagh of Cairo[43] and identical in all respects, so there is no need to describe it. Enjoyed the ultra-English atmosphere for a change. They were both very well and v. cheerful. Mr D. [Dalton][44] is coming round after dinner and we may make an arrangement for tomorrow morning!

Hope to go to Saqqara tomorrow in the afternoon. We don't know if we shall get off tomorrow night, owing to the luggage, but hope so […]

I do see *Punch* as H. [Harding] gets it, also *Times* and *Lit. Sup.* [*Times Literary Supplement*], *London Ill.* [*Illustrated*] *News* and *Weekly Mirror* which I have. Other odd things at times would be welcome. Next address: P.O. Beersheba […].

Mr D. came last night and I am just off to see old Cairo with him.

[Some time later, Olga added this postscript to the letter of 18 December: 'Just before Christmas, 1927, the happy party broke up to go their separate ways. Commander and Mrs Risdon, Lankester Harding and Olga Tufnell left Egypt to start a new base with Hofni, from Quft,[45] in different surroundings and with new routines. It was the beginning of excavations on a new site, south of Gaza, living in a newly built mud house, and working among Beduin tribesmen who were as new to methods of excavation and their tasks, as the small European staff were to theirs.

Myrtle Broome, on the other hand, was at the start of the most adventurous phase of her long life. She lived for a time in an Egyptian village, coping competently with adjustments to local customs, and earning the respect and admiration of all those who knew her.']

Notes

1 Petrie 1930; Steckeweh 1936. Also see 'The Tombs of Qau el-Kebir: Background Information', https://www.ucl.ac.uk/museums-static/digitalegypt/qau/elkebirbackground.html, last accessed 20 July 2020.
2 Petrie tried to identify the tomb owners as African (Nubian) invaders, a fantastical theory that did not stand the test of time. See Petrie 1930, 12–13; Drower 1985, 360.
3 Drower 1985, 360; Petrie 1930, 1.
4 See Drower 1985, 355–7, for Petrie's role in negotiating provisions in Egypt's antiquities laws, and Dodson 1999 and Goode 2007 (Chapters 4–5) for changes in Egypt's antiquities laws and the status of museums between the world wars. Also see Stevenson 2019, 146–7.

5 'Notes and News' from *Ancient Egypt* 1926, 96; cited in Drower 1985, 364. Also see Sparks 2007 for Petrie's archaeological work in Palestine.

6 Petrie 1928, 2.

7 Myrtle Broome (1887–1978), British Egyptologist, artist and epigrapher. A student of Flinders Petrie and Margaret Murray who joined Olga Tufnell in 1927 at Qau and continued work in epigraphy and the copying of tomb reliefs with Amice Calverley from 1929. Their expeditions continued in the 1930s. Also see note 13 below on Broome's letters in the Palestine Exploration Fund.

8 D.L. Risdon (dates unknown), retired naval commander and osteologist.

9 Drower 1985, 365.

10 See the List of Principal Persons, p. xxix. For his work at Jemmeh with Petrie, see Sparks 2019.

11 Tufnell 1982, 82, fig. 2. This was also the camp of the Egypt Exploration Society's excavations at Abydos, directed by the Dutch Egyptologist Henri Frankfort since 1925.

12 Petrie 1930, 1. It is unclear whether methods employed by Tufnell and Broome at Qau in 1927 involved tracing directly from the tomb chamber walls or refining pre-existing drawings (made from photographs) in front of the original paintings, or a combination of both. For a summary of methods used in creating facsimiles at around that time, see Strudwick 2012.

13 Olga Tufnell's typescript copy made in 1984 of a selection of Broome's letters written between 18 November 1927 and 20 February 1929 entitled 'Letters from Egypt: Two Points of View' is part of the Olga Tufnell archive in the Palestine Exploration Fund. Additional information may be found in the letters of Myrtle Broome from Qau el-Kebir housed at the Griffith Institute, University of Oxford.

14 Carter and Mace 1923.

15 Lanoie 2013.

16 Sir Edmund Henry Hynman Allenby (1861–1936), Viscount, Field-Marshal, Commander-in-Chief of the Egyptian Expeditionary Force to Palestine (1917–19), High Commissioner for Egypt and the Sudan (1919–25).

17 A revivalist movement begun by American Methodists in the nineteenth century, seceding from groups formed in Canada that developed into overseas missions.

18 Gerald Avery Wainwright (1879–1964), Egyptologist. One of Petrie's assistants in Egypt, 1907–12. Held the position of Inspector in Chief of Antiquities for Middle Egypt, 1921–4.

19 Reginald Engelbach (1888–1946), former assistant to Flinders Petrie and Assistant Keeper of the Egyptian Museum, Cairo.

20 George Andrew Reisner (1867–1942), American archaeologist in Palestine and Egypt. Professor of Egyptology at Harvard University, 1905–42, and Curator of Egyptian Collections at Boston Museum of Fine Arts, 1910–42. Directed archaeological survey of Nubia, 1907–9; excavated Samaria, 1908–11, Meroë and Napata, 1916–23, and Giza, 1902–42.

21 Nina de Garis Davies (1881–1965) and Norman de Garis Davies (1865–1941), married 1907, were Egyptologists and illustrators/copyists who focused on tomb paintings. Norman recorded tombs at Tell el-Amarna, 1898–1907, and was head of the Archaeological Survey for the Egypt Exploration Fund, 1901–7. Nina settled at Thebes with Norman in 1908. She focused on drawing and copying tomb paintings, creating facsimiles for museum collections.

22 Mohammed Osman el-Kreti (also referred to as Mohammed el-Kreti and 'Othman al-Kreti' in James 1979), the Petries' cook, who had worked for Flinders Petrie since boyhood in Egypt and went on to Palestine with him. Also see reference to 'Muhammad Osman' in Quirke 2010, 84–5; Tufnell 1985, 7.

23 Thomas Cook & Son provided Nile cruises from 1869 until the 1950s.

24 Fellahin (pl.), fellah (s.): an Arabic term meaning peasant, farmer or agricultural labourer.

25 The Qau expedition's landlord.

26 Feddan or faddān: a unit of area measurement used in Egypt, Sudan, Syria and Oman. In Egypt the measurement is similar to an acre.

27 Likely to be Hofny (or Hofni) Ibrahim, one of the skilled workers from Quft, Egypt, who was to join Petrie in Palestine (Quirke 2010; James 1979); see Fig. 3.3.

28 Gelabieh: a loose cotton robe or tunic commonly worn in North Africa and the Middle East.

29 Also recounted in Tufnell 1982, 82.

30 9 December 1927 was a Friday.

31 See note 27 above.

32 Letter dated by reference to leaving for Palestine in the following week.

33 This visit to Prince Uahka's tomb was one of Olga's most vivid memories of her time at Qau, as recounted in Tufnell 1982, 82. See Petrie 1930, frontispiece, for images of painted ceiling patterns at Qau.

34 Guy Brunton, OBE (1878–1948), archaeologist and Egyptologist; a student of Petrie's, working primarily at Badari and Qau. Brunton became Assistant Director/Curator of the Egyptian Museum, Cairo in 1931. Married to Winifred, a talented artist best known for her paintings of Egyptian pharaohs and queens. See letters in Chapter 7 for further references to Brunton.

35 Margaret Alice Murray (1863–1963), Egyptologist, anthropologist, archaeologist, historian and folklorist. Studied Egyptology from 1894 at UCL, encouraged by Flinders Petrie. Excavated at Abydos and Saqqara, Egypt, 1902–4. Lecturer in Archaeology at UCL 1898–1935. Assistant Professor, UCL, 1928–35.

36 The Osireon (or Osirion) at Abydos was part of Seti I's mortuary complex. It was discovered by Flinders Petrie and Margaret Murray, who excavated the site in 1902–3; see Murray 1904. The Ramesseum, the mortuary complex of Ramesses II, was excavated by J.E. Quibell in 1896; see Quibell 1896.

37 The Festival Hall (Akh-menu temple) of Thutmose III.

38 Probably the Temple of Ptah.

39 Benjamin's lettuces as in Beatrix Potter's *The Tale of the Flopsy Bunnies*.

40 Howard Carter (1874–1939), archaeologist and Egyptologist who had worked under Petrie's tutelage at Amarna. He worked with Édouard Naville at Deir el-Bahari and later as Chief Inspector for the Egyptian Antiquities Service. He found worldwide fame after discovering the tomb of Tutankhamun in 1922 through excavations financed by Lord Caernarvon.

41 Newberry 1900. Percy Edward Newberry (1869–1949), Professor of Egyptology at University of Liverpool, 1906–49, and member of the Tutankhamun excavation team for several seasons. Also Professor of Ancient History and Archaeology at Cairo University (1929, 1933).

42 Written on reverse of letter from Charles Dalton, 'The Residency', dated 14 December 1927: PEF/DA/TUF/98.1.

43 The Gezira Club: a sporting club in Cairo established by the British in the late nineteenth century, compared here by Olga to the Ranelagh Club, a polo club in Barn Elms, southwest London (formerly Surrey).

44 Charles Dalton, British Diplomatic Corps, Cairo. Dalton composed libretti and later married the American concert pianist Ruth Lynda Deyo.

45 See Chapter 1, note 38, and Chapter 3, note 3 for references to Qufti workers.

References

Carter, Howard and A.C. Mace. 1923. *The Tomb of Tut-Ankh-Amen, Discovered by the Late Earl of Carnarvon and Howard Carter.* London: Cassell.

Dodson, Aidan. 1999. 'Protecting the Past: The First Century of the Egyptian Antiquities Service', *Kmt: A Modern Journal of Ancient Egypt* 10(2): 80–5.

Drower, Margaret S. 1985. *Flinders Petrie: A Life in Archaeology*. London: Victor Gollancz.

Goode, James F. 2007. *Negotiating for the Past: Archaeology, Nationalism, and Diplomacy in the Middle East, 1919–1941*. Austin, TX: University of Texas Press.

James, Frances W. 1979. 'Petrie in the Wadi Ghazzeh and at Gaza: Harris Colt's Candid Camera', *Palestine Exploration Quarterly* 111: 75–7.

Lanoie, Nicholas. 2013. 'Inventing Egypt for the Emerging British Travel Class: Amelia Edwards' *A Thousand Miles up the Nile*', *British Journal of Middle Eastern Studies* 40(2): 149–61.

Murray, Margaret A. 1904. *The Osireion at Abydos*. London: Egyptian Research Account.

Newberry, Percy E. 1900. *The Life of Rakhmara, Vezîr of Upper Egypt under Thothmes III and Amenhetep II (circa BC 1471–1448)*. London: Constable.

Petrie, W.M.F. 1928. *Gerar*. London: British School of Archaeology in Egypt.

Petrie, W.M.F. 1930. *Antaeopolis: The Tombs of Qau*. London: British School of Archaeology in Egypt.

Quibell, James E. 1896. *The Ramesseum and the Tomb of Ptah-Hetep*. London: Egyptian Research Account.

Quirke, Stephen. 2010. *Hidden Hands: Egyptian Workforces in Petrie Excavation Archives, 1880–1924*. London: Duckworth.

Sparks, Rachael T. 2007. 'Flinders Petrie and the Archaeology of Palestine'. In *A Future for the Past: Petrie's Palestinian Collection. Essays and Exhibition Catalogue*, edited by Peter J. Ucko, Rachael T. Sparks and Stuart Laidlaw, 1–12. Walnut Creek, CA: Left Coast Press.

Sparks, Rachael T. 2019. 'Digging with Petrie: Gerald Harding at Tell Jemmeh, 1926–1927', *Bulletin of the History of Archaeology* 29(1): 1–16. https://www.archaeologybulletin.org/article/10.5334/bha-609/.

Steckeweh, Hans. 1936. *Die Fürstengräber von Qaw*. Leipzig: Hinrichs.

Stevenson, Alice. 2019. *Scattered Finds: Archaeology, Egyptology and Museums*. London: UCL Press.

Strudwick, Nigel. 2012. 'Facsimiles of Ancient Egyptian Paintings: The Work of Nina de Garis Davies, Amice Calverley, and Myrtle Broome'. In *Picturing the Past: Imaging and Imagining the Ancient Middle East*, edited by Jack Green, Emily Teeter and John A. Larson, 61–70. Chicago, IL: Oriental Institute, University of Chicago.

Tufnell, Olga. 1982. 'Reminiscences of a Petrie Pup', *Palestine Exploration Quarterly* 114: 81–6.

Tufnell, Olga. 1985. 'Reminiscences of Excavations at Lachish: An Address Delivered by Olga Tufnell at Lachish on July 6, 1983', *Tel Aviv* 12: 3–8.

3
Tell Fara, 1927–9

Just before Christmas 1927, Olga and other expedition members made their way to Tell Fara (now known as Tell el-Far'ah (South)), Palestine (Figure 3.1). This unexcavated mound in the Wadi Ghazzeh was considered by Petrie to be the biblical site of Beth-Pelet, mainly on etymological reasoning.[1] Petrie, who had remained in London, left his assistant J.L. Starkey in charge of setting up at Tell Fara. Commander and Mrs Risdon, Harding, Mrs Starkey and Olga were joined by a team of Qufti workers from Egypt (Figures 3.2 and 3.3), and the cook Mohammed

Figure 3.1 Tell Fara with dig-house in foreground. Photograph by H.D. Colt published in the *Palestine Exploration Quarterly* (James 1979, Pl. VII, top left). Courtesy of the Palestine Exploration Fund.

Figure 3.2 Members of the Tell Fara expedition in front of the dig-house at the foot of the Tell, probably 1927–8 season. Left to right: Mohammed Osman el-Kreti (cook), Mr and Mrs Starkey, Mrs Risdon, D.L. Risdon, G.L. Harding, Sadeek in front. See letter of 26 December 1927. Olga Tufnell archive, Palestine Exploration Fund. Courtesy of the Palestine Exploration Fund.

Osman el-Kreti. As mentioned in Chapter 1, the skilled archaeological labour force from Quft was essential for the Petries' expeditions, as well as other digs in Palestine and Syria at that time.[2] As Olga later wrote, 'It was the beginning of excavations on a new site, south of Gaza, living in a newly built mudbrick house, and working among Bedouin tribesmen who were as new to methods of excavation and their tasks as the small European staff were to theirs.'[3] The site was, according to Petrie, '18 miles south of Gaza with open wilderness in between; food supply was obtained from there, while drinking water was brought 11 miles from Khan Yunis. Though there is no usual camp of Bedawy [Bedouin] in the place, the former workers of Gerar [Tell Jemmeh] flocked up and others from many miles around so that a camp was formed of about 400 men, women and children. During two years in the wilderness there was never any friction with the people, nor a single thing missing.'[4]

Olga took her share with the others in organising the workers in different areas – digging tombs at first in the cemetery, then on the Tell. There are few insights into her roles and responsibilities and the huge

Figure 3.3 Four Qufti workmen at Tell Fara in front of the dig-house at the foot of the mound. Left to right: Umbarak, Sultan Bakhyt, Hophni (Hofni in Olga's letters), Ahmad Aly. See letter of 18 December 1927 (p. 55). Olga Tufnell archive, Palestine Exploration Fund. Photo by H.D. Colt. Courtesy of the Palestine Exploration Fund.

task at hand. Olga reports on one occasion that she was in charge of 50 men and boys in one area, supported by two Qufti workers who presumably served as supervisors or foremen. The typical day began at dawn. They worked long hours, as she reports, in the field for much of the day (with a 12 pm lunch break), and after sunset focusing on drawing and other documentation tasks, working on pottery and generally clearing up. Object photography was also a task she assisted with. Olga started a clinic at Fara for the workers, primarily to provide doses of quinine as one way to manage malaria, which was still not under control at her time of arrival.[5] This served as a precursor to the clinics at Ajjul and later at Tell ed-Duweir (see Chapter 6). It seems there was scarcely a moment's rest.

In 1928 Petrie returned to Palestine to take charge, and the following year the party was joined by Harris Dunscombe Colt Jr., an American archaeologist who had worked with Margaret Murray in Malta.[6] Initially he was made welcome by Petrie, as he represented

New York University and supported the expedition with a donation, but eventually the relationship between Petrie and Colt became strained. Colt's presence acted as a catalyst in the eventual break-up of the expedition party, causing Olga to have to make a hard decision as to where her loyalties lay.

The main findings of the excavations at Tell Fara were published in two volumes.[7] This was evidently an important Bronze and Iron Age site. Findings included the Middle Bronze Age 'Hyksos' fortifications and associated buildings. The 'Hyksos' were a major focus for Petrie; this is the name given to an elite group of Levantine origin, 'rulers of foreign lands' who governed northern Egypt between the eighteenth and sixteenth centuries BC in what is known as the Second Intermediate period.[8] The Hyksos had important trading contacts between the Nile Delta, the Levant and the East Mediterranean until they were overthrown by the incoming Eighteenth Dynasty rulers of Egypt, fleeing to strongholds in southern Palestine, including the city of Sharuhen, now commonly identified with Tell Fara.[9] The Hyksos were also associated with equid burials, which Petrie excavated at Ajjul in subsequent seasons (see Chapter 5). At Fara there was also a Late Bronze Age structure, identified by Petrie as an Egyptian governor's residency from the time of the New Kingdom empire in Canaan, as well as Iron Age and Roman settlements. Several cemeteries were identified, ranging from the Late Bronze Age, Iron Age and Persian periods, including those Petrie misassigned as the 'graves of the five lords of the Philistines'. A number of early Iron II tombs (tenth to ninth centuries BC) were excavated by Olga within the 200 cemetery (Figure 3.4), and she alludes to the many skulls retrieved from them.[10]

The letters reveal very little about Olga's summer activities – yet there is brief mention (letter of 23 March 1928) of a promise of paid work for Olga for a summer exhibition of antiquities in London at UCL. This was probably an exhibit of finds from Tell Fara. The annual exhibitions raised awareness and funds for Petrie's excavations, and presumably played a motivating role in securing artefacts by formal division or partage (Figure 3.5). Such exhibits 'appealed to a London-based political, social, cultural and financial elite', yet were also accessible 'to the upwardly mobile middle classes and working classes'.[11] Public archaeology was also on the mind of Richard St Barbe Baker,[12] who arrived at Fara in 1928 to make a film – *Palestine's Lost Cities*. Petrie disapproved and thought it a waste of time.[13]

The novelty of travel and tourism is very much a theme in the letters. Olga shares her experiences of exploring Islamic Cairo, before

Figure 3.4 Olga and the early Iron Age tomb she excavated at Tell Fara. Probably Tomb 201, 200 cemetery. See letter of 30 November 1928. Starkey family collection. Courtesy of Wendy Slaninka.

Figure 3.5 W.M.F. Petrie with finds from Tell el-'Ajjul and Tell Fara exhibited in London, probably summer 1931. © UCL Institute of Archaeology.

taking rail and ferry to Palestine. Within the Levant, in addition to trips to Jerusalem for rest and recuperation as well as work on the division of finds, she travelled to northern Palestine, Beirut and Tripoli, and also to Jerash in Transjordan.

Olga's observations, interactions and embracing of Arab culture and traditions are of interest, with descriptions of a visit to a prominent Bedouin sheikh, musical and dance performances, and her acquisition of certain clothing items and accessories, including a clove necklace and a Bedouin knife. She also reports making her own 'kibber', an overcoat worn by local women, and describes the clothing and adornment of the women and girls she came into contact with. These insights can also be compared with photographs and sketches, and presumably items she collected and brought back to England, some of which are now in museum collections.[14] These observations provide rare first-person insights into local customs, though evidently through the eyes of a Western woman and traveller with a desire for understanding local traditions and lifestyles.

As in Chapter 2, the letters here are transcriptions from Olga's original handwritten letters; she intended to publish them at a later date. Headings were omitted in her text, and have been reinserted here.

Letters of December 1927–April 1929

[23 December 1927; handwritten: PEF/TUF/DA/106]

c/o Post Office
KHAN YUNIS.
South Palestine.

23.XII.27
Well, as you can see by the change of address, we are now at camp. This is what happened: We danced that night as arranged, it was funny to see English people everywhere, most of them very smartly turned out. Then on Thursday morning I went to the Museum and after I had spent some time there I routed out Mr Wainwright and he took me round. Then he had lunch with me at the Hotel. Mr Harding brought the good news that the luggage had arrived, it was arranged that we should catch the evening train here. The last afternoon, Mr W. [Wainwright] took me to the 'Musque',[15] which is the Old part of Cairo, where the market is. We wandered through narrow streets covered in by arches of material and

saw all sorts of things including strong leather shoes, [and] copper pots and pans being made. They were pounding spices in large mortars to make scent and one could smell the ingredients all down the street.

Then we went to the Blue Mosque.[16] It consists of a courtyard and several rows of columns behind, with a pool surrounded by shrubs in the middle. All round were groups of boys sitting on the ground with a teacher to each group. They were different classes, having a religious education, and the sight must have been much the same when Christ disputed with the elders in the Temple. There was one boy who stood up and talked hard and we left him at it. The mosque gets its name from the blue tiles on the walls and in the chapel of the holy man of the place, whoever he was. It was the prettiest building I've seen in Cairo.

We just looked at the Citadel, which stands above the town and where Napoleon was when he conquered Egypt. The enemy fortified a mosque about 100 feet from the citadel and they blazed away at each other at close quarters. One can still see the marks of the cannon balls. Then we went back to Groppi's and had our last civilized tea all together.

We reached Kantara at 9.30 and crossed the Suez canal in a ferry. Quite a thrill to do so, though the place is only about ½ the width of the Thames! When I gave in my passport, I was welcomed by the English officer in charge; Mr Starkey[17] had said we were coming and my name had stuck in his mind. It was a good thing, because he came to us afterwards in the buffet, where we got some dinner and asked if we had good seats. As the train was very full we hadn't done well, so he made the guard open a locked Ladies only carriage and Mrs Risdon and I had it to ourselves all night!

I slept well until five when we fell out of the train at Gaza. We left the luggage at the station and went up to the town and knocked up the only hotel. It rejoiced in the name of 'Orient Hotel' but it hardly deserved it, as the place consisted of one hall with 4 bedrooms off it, a small court at the back and nothing else. When it was light, we trapesed [sic] back to the station and waited until the customs officer deigned to appear. After much signing of forms and some routling in the boxes, we got away about ten.

After some shopping in the market, which is even more attractive than at Cairo, we chartered a car, and started off on the last lap. The car did splendidly over the desert and we arrived here to find the house built and the Starkeys waiting for us. It rained solidly that night and most of the following day, in the intervals we got ourselves settled in and are now ready to start work tomorrow – Christmas Day! Will you also send this on to Mummy, as it's part of my diary –

Very best love and New Year wishes
From
Olga

[26 December 1927; handwritten: PEF/TUF/DA/107]

c/o Post Office
KHAN YUNIS.
South Palestine.
26.XII.27.

Dearest Ma,
I think I left off at Cairo, but the sequel of the journey is recorded in a letter to Daddy, which he will send on to you. We got here at lunch time on Thursday. It was a fine day and the house is built at the foot of the Tell. There are bedrooms for Mr and Mrs S. [Starkey], Mr and Mrs R. [Risdon], Mr H. [Harding] and myself, besides 2 spare rooms (one for Mr Floyer) and also a dining room, kitchen and store room.[18]

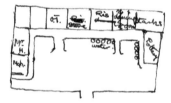

Then the Tell looks something like this:[19]

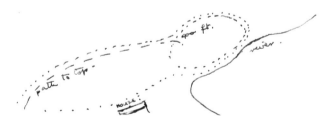

Figure 3.6 Ink sketch by Olga Tufnell of Fara dig-house (above) and Tell (below), from letter of 26 December 1927. Courtesy of the Palestine Exploration Fund.

The camels with our luggage arrived just before dark, and soon after it began to rain. Rain it did, all night and most of the next day, it was curious to see the water come down into the wady in one mass, and what had been a dry river bed, which we had crossed the night before, was soon a torrent of muddy water. We got settled in well that day and since [then] the weather has been splendid, though rather cold in the mornings and evenings. Crops are coming up everywhere, quite different to last year, they all say. Work started on Xmas morning, on the high part of the mound, and we got in a good day's unpacking and arranging as well. We were very merry in the evening, and achieved the right spirit, despite the unsuitability of the weather! We piped up the old carols and drank to the Prof. [Petrie] and all absent friends and families.

Shall miss the usual Boxing Day Theatre tonight!

Behind our house, there are valleys for a short way, and beyond flat plains. The valleys will soon be full of flowers, and the ground in front of us has already been ploughed, so that we shall have a green carpet to look at. The hills around are dotted with bedouin tents, ~~over 200~~ several hundred turned up for work the first day, they didn't take long to get wind of our arrival.

I can but repeat how much I enjoy being here, from now onwards the letters will be less voluminous, as we shall be getting down to it, and one day will be much like another. I've taken some photos of the place and will send them when they're developed. [...]

[13 January 1928; handwritten: PEF/TUF/DA/108]

c/o P.O.
Khan Yunis
S. Palestine.
13.1.28

Darling Mà,
This is Suk [market] day, so I'm settling down in the hope that I shall write you a long letter to balance yours of the 13th, 18th, 22nd & 3rd. [...]

Work is in full swing and I am out on the cemetery all day. We have now got 47 skulls and are only waiting for more to turn up to complete the round 50. There are 2 Quftis[20] and about 50 men and boys on my beat, my job is to keep the boys at it and to record anything that turns up and be on the spot generally. The Arabic moves on now that I hear little else all day, and have to try to make myself understood. You should have seen me sacking a boy yesterday, nobody was more surprised than myself. It was a fine sight; the men are very good workers and really reliable, and Mr S. [Starkey] does the rounds frequently.

The day is pretty full up, we come in for lunch at twelve till one and then carry on till sunset. After that there is drawing to be done and general clearing up until bedtime.

One bout of rain was preceded by a sandstorm, during which I appeared in full war paint, i.e. land suit and goggles. The former is rather too loose round the top of the calves, so I probably shan't wear it much.

The other day, I washed my hair and had it cut by Mrs Risdon, on the whole most successfully. I am cultivating an Eton crop, according to popular vote here.

On the 7th – the night of the full moon – we (the Starkeys, Mr H. [Harding] and myself) sallied forth to attend a 'fantaisia'. We were escorted to the tents which lie to the north of the Tell by the newly dubbed Sheykh,[21] most of the men there were either on the work or aspiranto [hoping to be]. We were installed in a row on rugs on the floor. [E]ven before we arrived we heard the familiar refrain which has been going on nearly every night. Just a few men were getting up steam, but once we were settled, many more joined in. Just a line of dark forms with the wady below and moonlit hills beyond, with one in front, generally egging them on and singing extemporary verses, bringing in our names. Steps which are more difficult than they appear to be accompany the song, and when it dies down, the 'deheyah' [*dahiyah* – dance] is started and overwhelms it.

The forms, much augmented now, bend and dip and swing, arms linked; gradually they move closer, blocking out the light, and filling the air with their strange song. So that it seems a mass of wild beasts are creeping forward. The climax comes, and the line falls back and another song is started. Sometimes a small form appears, completely draped in black. This is the 'sit' [*sitt*]:[22] she moves up and down along the line of men, [and] when she bends, the end of the line she is nearest to, do[es] so [also.] [S]he moves with perfect grace, and though she has none of the usual aids of the dancer, her performance would be difficult to beat. Even her hands are covered, but her arms are as expressive as – Pavlova's (exag[g]eration, I know, but I couldn't think of the word to follow – as) and her sense of rhythm would defeat the jaz[z] experts.

Then she was handed a sword, a long curved thing. This doubled her power, she swung and slashed it, bending down and forwards to rip up an imaginary enemy and wielding it above her head, so that it flashed in the light of the moon.

The daheyah reached a grander climax, [as] men kept pushing in to join the dancers. The audience around us got equally excited, and behind were a group of women and children, looking on. Tea was made on a Primus in front of us (the Primus was the only note which reminded us of the xxth century), the two cups which the establishment possessed were handed to us and washed afterwards for the others, the tea was good and sweet and of course we made the appropriate noises when drinking it. As I write I can hear the fantaisia in full progress over by the tents, it is lovely to feel that it was no faked up performance that we heard, but the real thing, just as they always do it.

Every day there is some amusing incident and there is plenty to keep us good and amused all day.

I would have written more, but I've just heard that the post goes at crack of dawn tomorrow.

I wish Uncle B. and Auntie D. could fly over to Gaza from Cairo and spend the day! It would do them both good to get into the sun. I only wish you were going too. [...]

Ever Yours
<u>Olga</u>

P.S. Shall get the parcel tomorrow evening, so you can imagine a most festive evening tomorrow, shall put some away for my birthday, unless the things look too good to wait!

[1 February 1928; handwritten: PEF/TUF/DA/109]

c/o P.O.
K– Yunis.
1.2.28

Dearest of Mas,

[...] Daddy's birthday letter arrived on the eve of the 26th, which was most appropriate. The day itself was as usual, we broached the cake which is v. good, like all the contents of the box.

The work is going well and we spend all our evenings keeping pace with the things as they come in drawing, recording etc. [...]

<u>Personal & Private.</u> We all get on well, as I said before. Mr S. [Starkey] is a splendid person to work under, he allows no carelessness and keeps one up to the mark, most firmly, so that I hope I shall soon come into line. I don't see much of the others during the day, as I spend it in the cemetery.

H. [Harding] is on the Tell and Mr R. [Risdon] is still surveying, while Mrs S. & R. are mostly at the house.

The food is good and wholesome and there is plenty of variety – we get fresh meat once a week, sometimes there is fish, good vegs, cauliflower, marrow, cabbage etc. and also apples, bananas, and splendid Jaffa oranges and tangerines, to say nothing of water melons. So I am not fading away, in fact I'm fatter and have a good colour, as anyone will testify.

The lavatory arrangements work well, it's a case of 'I'll take the high road and you'll take the low road', there are some encounters with natives but nobody minds.

There is a 2 minute silence 3 times a day on the work, when I blow a whistle and all the small boys yell with joy and dash off to perform in the wady, it is all very funny and friendly.

One man's head was badly smashed with a tourich [*tourikh* – hoe] this week, a large gash on his forehead which I had to dress on the spot, as best I could, though it was the sort of thing that needed stitches. He is going on well. If these people survive childhood they are tremendously hardy. [...]

[Undated letter; probably written mid-February 1928; handwritten: PEF/TUF/DA/110][23]

c/o Post Office
Khan Yunis
S. Palestine.

All is well here and things go on in the usual way. We have had 4 days of wind which culminated yesterday in a tremendous sandstorm. I was out in the cem. [cemetery] and it was blowing hard, as the afternoon wore on it got darker and darker, with ominous puffs of wind and sand. Work had already stopped in the Tell, as the wind is much stronger there, and about 4 I blew off too, we had time to collect the tools and pots and so on and started home. Suddenly everything went green, like pea soup, and I was nearly blown off my feet, luckily the wind was behind us so that we got carried homewards. One could see huge pillars of sand swirling high into the air and could feel it beating against one and could hear it making a tremendous roar.

We were glad to drop into the valley and after only a few minutes the wind dropped and the rain came down. It just seemed to fall almost in a sheet, but we were not far from the house and only got moderately damp. It rained most of the night, and there were great claps of thunder, the sun is out now and there are huge banks of clouds, so that I shall get a chance to use my new sky filter.

About midday the water came down the wady, just one solid mass, it has now spread and covers most of the plain, it is a wonderful sight, and has never been like this before. From my room I can see it and hear it as it surges past.

Ramadan starts next week, when the men eat nothing between sunrise and sunset, it sounds rather a dismal time, as they're not allowed to drink or smoke all day. We shall knock [off] at 3.30 in the afternoon then, so there may not be such a rush.

[…] I've not heard from you for some time, but expect you will be complaining of the same thing from me. There is no time for more, especially as I am to write a letter to Lady Petrie every week.

I suppose I shall soon have to think about a passage home. Should like to go to Jerusalem, then pick up a boat at Beyrouth [Beirut] and go home via Constantinople. What about meeting me in Paris and doing a few days there among the sights and shops?

[8 March 1928; handwritten: PEF/TUF/DA/111]

c/o P.O.
Khan Yunis
S.Palestine
8.3.28

Many thanks for various letters, including one, which arrived open and with nothing inside, oh! woe! Our plans are all nebulous, and I can't make any definite statement as to when we shall be leaving here. But when I do I should like to go via Jerusalem, Beyrouth, Constant., Greece and up the Adriatic to Venice, thence to Paris. This may not be a possibility, but I am writing tonight to Lloyd-Triestino for their list of sailings. What about meeting in Venice, Rome will be hot, smelly and dusty in April–May, and it's a tiresome journey all up and down the boot. Venice would be a good stepping stone for me, as it will be an effort to get back to so-called civilization. Paris afterwards would be rather fun.

My bed split all down the middle last night, as Miss Broome's did in Egypt, which is one proof of added girth and weight, then my tweed skirt which I tried to wear the other day, simply won't do up, and you remember how it was before. Altogether I'm a picture of health, no spots, no pimples, though 'tis I that say it that shouldn't, and I shall soon be emulating the Queen of Punt.[24]

[paragraph marked 'not for publication']

Life is very funny out here, I keep laughing to myself about all the things I say and do as a matter of course. The men and boys are an endless source of amusement and I think on the whole we get on well together. Mr H. [Harding] has now moved down from the Tell and is in charge of another section of the cemetery. We are hardly on speaking terms as feeling runs so high, as to who has found what. So far I'm an easy winner, as tell it not in Gath, I average four scarabs a day! [...]

[11 March 1928; handwritten: PEF/TUF/DA/112]

c/o P.O.
Khan Yunis
S. Palestine
11.3.28

My darling Daddy,
Very many thanks for your two nice long letters. I hope this attempt to answer them will be more successful than former ones, as soon as I get started, something is found, or there's a row, or somebody gets bashed with a pick, or, as you say, it's time to blow a whistle. (I was stopped here, but am now trying again an hour later.) The work is great fun and my jobs are most varied – anything from waxing a skull to administering chastisement. The whole place is a mass of flowers now, just like an old English garden on a small scale – tiny stocks, poppies, mignonette, vetch, daisies, snapdragon and so on, and any amount of red anemones. One can hardly walk on the ground with treading on something.

Last night in celebration of the Risdons' wedding anniversary, we had a fancy dress dinner, and though there were only 6 of us we spent a very cheery evening and ended up by dancing in the courtyard. We ate our much beloved Thomas II the Turkey, who was bought for Xmas.[25] He was not fat enough at the time and since then we grew so fond of him that it was all we could do to eat him. He was a friendly bird and has been known to jump onto the dining-room table during meals – little guessing how soon he would be there in earnest. He paid for his keep by laying about 20 eggs in the skullery, among the skulls, so I suppose after all his name should have been Thomasina!

I am enclosing the latest batch of photos, some of which were taken with a sky filter, so they are not so good as they might be. The next instalment will include photos of local celebrities. [...][26]

[16 March 1928; handwritten: PEF/TUF/DA/113]

c/o Khan Yunis.
Post Office
South Palestine.
16.3.28

Darling –
Just a line to tell you that all continues to go well. By the time you get this, I understand you will be having a little holiday, which I hope you will enjoy and profit by!

As I told you, I wrote for steamer sailings and the most attractive seems to be the following: Lloyd Triestino. I should go to Jerusalem and spend some days there, then pick up the boat at Haifa, then Beyrouth, Tripolis, Alexandretta, Mersina, Larnaca and Limassol, Rhodes, Piraeus, Brindisi, Venice. At each place you get time to do the sights, so I should see the Cyprus Mus. [Museum] which is important to us here owing to many Cypriote connections, and should also get a glimpse of Athens. 13 days the whole show for £18 second class. I may catch the boat on Ap. [April] 20 but probably should not be later than May 4. We can't make any definite plans for about 10 days, when we see how the new cem. [cemetery] works out.

Heavenly weather now and masses of flowers everywhere. We are having this Suk day and next week we shall have 2 days off when the Arabs celebrate their new year. We should get good chances for photos as everybody turns out in their best. We have had various visitors who upset our routine somewhat and as I write we are undergoing a visit from 2 Pal. Mus. [Palestine Museum] officials – rather gruesome!

However they will post this, so you will have something to thank them for!

P.S. I didn't give it to them, so have time to add some more [...] I have had a Bedawy head gear bought for me to wear every day. It shades the neck and is more suitable than my large hat which is unruly in the wind. Will try and send you a picture of me in the pit! [...]

[23 March 1928; handwritten: PEF/TUF/DA/114]

c/o P.O.
Khan Yunis
S. Palestine
23.3.28

My darling Ma,

Very many thanks for your last letter, I'm sorry I can't improve on my last information as to plans – but it all depends how the new cem. [cemetery] areas work out. I will wire you the date of arrival in Venice, as soon as I know.

Yesterday was the Arab New Year's Day – they have had 30 days' fasting, during which time they are not allowed to eat, drink or smoke from sunrise to sunset, a severe test, which they endure most cheerfully – though they carry it to extreme lengths and some refuse to have eye drops, as they think it descends to the tummy.

You can imagine what a festival New Year's Day is to them. New clothes – which have to last all the year and sometimes longer – are put on for the first time, the girls wear all their brightest ornaments and the day is celebrated by horse racing, eating and drinking, while the women conduct strange ceremonies, singing and dancing by themselves.

We had arranged to pay a long overdue visit to Tell Jemmeh and at ten o'clock our four camels appeared, with their respective owners and we set off in very good spirits for the nine mile journey.

We soon left the Tell and the cemeteries behind us and went north across the plain. It was a perfect morning, with bright sunshine and a cool breeze, the asphodel is nearly over, but there were masses of small flowers to see, and there were larks who kept us company all the way. As we came to a large group of tents, we could see white horses and camels and festive groups of people. We were passing the tents of the Sheykh of the Tarabins,[27] a man of great possessions, whom we had already met, we dismounted and were met by crowds of Arabs, many of whom were on the work. They had all come to pay their respects to the Sheykh, who keeps open house to all on New Year's Day. We were conducted to the tent – an enormous structure of long strips of woven material, with different patterns and designs all over it. On the walls were gaily coloured saddle bags, and beautiful carpets covered the floor. Perhaps the whole tent was some 100 feet long, though we only saw one half of it.

All the chief men of the district were seated in a square round the central fire, where huge brass ewers of shapes worthy of the Arabian nights stood on the smouldering embers, they rose to greet us and we shook hands all round. The Sheykh himself is dark and keen eyed, his long face is decorated with a drooping black moustache and though he does not conform to the Hollywood standard, he is a man of personality and character. Mr & Mrs S. [Starkey] sat in state on one carpet, and H. [Harding] and I shared the other. Facing us were venerable elders, all with intelligent faces, some were smoking long water pipes and all watched us with amused, friendly interest. Lesser fry stood around about, and coffee and tea was handed round by a Barbary slave. Sweets of rather deadly hue were produced from the saddle bags and placed in front of us, and the Sheykh himself distributed some to his small sons, who were very friendly, and did not seem frightened of their father, but just as dictatorial as English children are.

As an accompaniment to polite conversation, during which we asked if they had news of the war, we heard the sound of galloping hooves, as their young men galloped past the tent, on beautiful Arab horses, or on fast trotting camels. They wheeled and turned with incredible speed and charged forward with cloaks flying and spears in hand – with trepidation we asked if we might photograph the tent, permission was graciously accorded and everyone simply flocked to have their photos taken. I only hope it will come out well.

We tore ourselves away and after impressive farewells we set off again, feeling more biblical in atmosphere than ever. As we went on we met little groups of people who had come to meet us, men and boys from work, all in their new clothes. From a ridge about half way, we could look back and see Tel Fara, and look forward down the plain and see Tel Jemmeh. The former commands far greater distance. Tell Jemmeh is more shut in, and the only long view is out to sea. From here onwards we saw and afterwards passed through waving fields of corn, and with a stretch of imagination, one could recapture the feelings of the children of Israel looking on the promised land –

About one we reached Tel Jemmeh and the skeleton of last year's abode. Piles of pottery still lay in the courtyard where they had been left, and the deserted rooms were carpeted with flowers. We had lunch there, with half the countryside collected outside, and then we made a grand tour of the dig. It is all much longer than the photographs led one to expect – altogether a most impressive excavation, and I thoroughly enjoyed seeing it, as everything seemed so familiar.

It was half past three by the time we had seen it all, and we had to refuse the pressing invitations to have coffee and join in the fantasia, over by the tents. So with real sorrow, we turned away and started home and that's where the trouble began. We were all pretty sore after several hours upon 'ships of the desert', but fired by my success on a camel, I thought I'd make the thing trot. The usual spitting noises did not have much effect, so I tried a stick and the animal obligingly started off at a good steady trot. I was not prepared for the consequences: there was nothing to hold on to and only some precariously balanced bedding under me, so at about the fourth bump, off I came. According to all accounts I landed beautifully and am quite whole and hearty, I've just strained a muscle in my hip, so am taking it easy in bed today. The Dr from Gaza came this morning and confirms the verdict, so you have nothing to worry about and it's an ill wind that blows nobody any good, as you would never have had this long account if the camel hadn't trotted! Mrs S. [Starkey] & Mrs R. [Risdon] have been very kind and are excellent nurses, so I couldn't be in better hands. […]

Had a letter from Lady P. [Petrie] about summer arrangements. Have written to say I will be there for preliminaries and duration of exhib. [exhibition][28] but have not committed myself for the winter yet. She says £3 per month increase, so I made a mistake about the previous figure. […]

[27 March 1928; handwritten: PEF/TUF/DA/115]

C.M.S. Hosp.[ital][29]
Gaza
Palestine
27.3.28

Here am I, for no graver reason than the morning and evening bed-pan. So do not get alarmed that I am in the last stages of decay, or anything. The ladies at camp found this too much for them, so yesterday evening the Dr and Matron came out and brought me here in a car. This morning, chiefly because Dr Sterling is so proud of his apparatus, I was X-rayed to make quite certain that no bones were broken, though any fool, including myself, could be certain that such was not the case. I can stand and no amount of pounding on my hip or leg affects me, the only trouble is that for the moment it is rather painful to walk. What I have is a sprained ligament or however you spell it, and a few days will put me right.

I am in a bright room with 3 windows looking out onto a garden with palm trees and bananas growing and I face the door which opens onto a cool verandah. The Matron, who is pleasant and v. capable and the Staff Nurse look after me, as I am rather a novelty after so many unwashed Arabs. Dr S. is a good man, with many interests, and is well on the careful side like old Roche.

I've been supplied with Arabic grammars so shall do my best to improve a bit while here, for as Starkey says, he can't understand a word of my Arabic, though the men on the work seem to! There will be little scope for it later as work is virtually closed down, and it is the drawing (my pottery! my pottery!) the photography and the packing which remains to be done.

So I think I can revise the date of departure and if I can get a passage hope to leave Haifa on April 20th, arriving in Venice 7 am May 2nd, D.V. [God willing].

Sorry to be so vague and changeable, but as you say it is all part of it! [...]

28th. This did not get posted yesterday, so I just add that I am much less stiff in the hip and can move around without getting any twitches. With all my love

Olga

[31 March 1928; handwritten: PEF/TUF/DA/116]

CMS Hosp.
Gaza
S. Palestine
31.3.28

Dearest Ma,

I have just had a BATH, so am really pure, my hair has been washed into the bargain, and it was cut previously by the barber of Gaza. I have also walked upstairs to the bathroom and had my morning glass of milk with the Matron in her sitting room. So I am really much better and hope to be 'discharged' on Monday. It is probably 'an ill wind' as I am having a thorough rest, which though dull and exasperating is no doubt very good for me.

It was my first bath since the 22nd December, so you can imagine that it was a red letter occasion. I had a visit from one of our diggers yesterday – the boy on the horse in the photo – who came sweeping in after having spent 3 hours trying to make the nurses understand who he wanted to see!

Your very welcome Easter egg has arrived. It intrigued us all for several days at camp, because all registered parcels are heralded by a slip which has to be signed before the parcel is given up, and I couldn't think what it might be! Very many thanks for thinking of it, I manage to dispose of quite a lot in bed.

The banana trees have real bananas growing on them; I sat in their shade nearly all yesterday, quite romantic. [...]

[26–29 April 1928; handwritten: PEF/TUF/DA/117]

S.S. *Aventino*
Lloyd Triestinò

begun at Limassol
Cyprus
26.4.28

My darling Daddy,

I expect you are wondering if I am in the land of the living, or if, at the last moment, I was carried off by a Sheykh, or eaten by a wolf. Strange to say, none of these things have happened so far, and I am on my way to Venice, where perhaps I shall meet Mummy.

I left camp on April 16th by car for Jerusalem. When I got there late in the afternoon I found the town was very full and had some difficulty in persuading the good lady at the English hostel to give me a bed even for one night. Next day I had to move my quarters, and as luck would have it the Museum arranged for me to stay with Mr and Mrs Reynolds who have the big boys' school in Jerusalem.[30] When I arrived and told them my name, they began with the inevitable formula: 'Are you any relation of __ Tufnell?' In this case it was Cousin Laura[31] of Oxford, who is apparently a generous benefactor of the school.

I went round and saw some of the sights that day and in the evening some other English people came to stay and they said: 'are you any relation of Admiral Tufnell?'[32] The result was that I spent the next day with them and saw the Mosque in the morning and in the afternoon we motored to Jericho and I actually bathed in the Dead Sea. It is so funny there, because one can't sink even if one wants to. At the end of it all they wouldn't let me pay a penny for the car, so I had a splendid day quite free!

From Jerusalem I hired a seat in a car going to Haifa, where I arrived on the afternoon of the 20th. I took a seat in a decrepit motorbus up on to Mount Carmel, and saw lovely views from there. The driver whom I sat next to was very friendly and stopped the bus when I wanted to take a photograph.

I joined the boat in the evening and next morning we found ourselves at Beyrouth [Beirut]. I wanted to motor out to see the great temple at Baalbek, but no one seemed to want to go there. At last I found a French couple in the 1st class who seemed to like the idea and we landed and hired a car. We motored for 3½ hours through lovely scenery.

Sometimes we were close to snow in the mountains, and even without the ruins the drive would have been worth while.

We had two breakdowns on the way back, so caught the boat rather by the skin of our teeth.

I hadn't the energy to get off at Tripoli, and anyhow I don't think there was much to see. At Alexandretta I walked round the town, which is more of a village, but it was dusty and hot.

At Mersina the next day, we were on Turkish ground, but they have so much red tape, it did not seem worth trying to land.

Yesterday we got to Cyprus at 5 am and landed at the port of Famagusta. I had arranged to do a trip with the French people again, so we got a car and set off for the chief town Nicosia. The villages were all very clean and pretty, we have really left the Arabs and their ways behind us. We went straight to the Museum at Nicosia and I spent nearly 3 happy hours there. It is beautifully arranged and the Director was very nice and showed us round. […] That evening we reached Limassol on the other side of the island and stayed the night at a hotel. The boat arrived at six and we got on board again and any minute now we shall start for Rhodes.

This is really a cargo boat – the passengers are a side show, so at every port of call we have to wait while sacks of onions, crates of sugar – made in Czecho-Slovakia – or planks of wood are loaded and unloaded.

I am the only English person in the 2nd class and I sit at a table with 10 Germans, all rather sticky and dull. There are some nice Americans – missionaries from India – and the ship's officers – all Italians and amusing to talk to. I am considered to be rather a curiosity travelling alone. Just now I've got a cabin to myself, but I've had some strange creatures there. First there was an American lady, who used scent of a powerful brand and had a small dog, who she had smuggled into the cabin. As soon as I got rid of her at Mersina, 2 amazing Arabian ladies got on. They were mother and daughter and they were like this:

Figure 3.7 Ink sketch by Olga Tufnell of 'amazing Arabian ladies', from letter of 26–9 April 1928. Courtesy of the Palestine Exploration Fund.

They got up early in the morning and sat side by side on the bench in the cabin and watched me dress in amazement. I must have been rather a shock to them. I never discovered all the garments that Mamma wore, but I do know that the daughter wore under a substantial jumper and skirt, a thick velvet bodice and petticoat embroidered with scallops and under that another petticoat and about five other layers underneath and all this in a temperature of about 90° in the shade.

Anyhow by well-organised tactics I won the battle of the porthole and the poor things had to have it open all night.

29.4.28.

Well, we did leave Limassol, and for the first time in my life, I was thoroughly and genuinely sea-sick. Nearly everybody else was too, and one could even hear the waiters feeling bad in the pantry. Probably the heavy sea was due to the earthquake at Corinth, but next morning we found ourselves among the Greek islands, where the sea was like a smooth sheet of glass.

Just before midday we got in sight of Athens. During the morning I found that some nice people called Cuffe[33] were on board and the lady I had stayed with in Jerusalem had told me to make myself known to them, I did, and they said: 'Are you any relation of Carleton Tufnell?'[34] We arranged to see Athens together, they had already been, so they knew the ropes and took me straight to the Acropolis. We spent a peaceful afternoon there on the hill and saw the lovely buildings without any awful guide. In the evening we came back and my total expenses including postcards and tea were 4s/6d!

Now instead of going through the Gulf of Corinth we are going right round the archipelago and our next stop will be Calamata. I'm afraid we shall be three days late in Venice, because of the earthquake.

This is a very pleasant trip. We've seen several lovely places without the trouble of getting there in trains. I forgot to say that we stopped for one hour in Rhodes, where I went ashore with two ladies, one of whom I really already knew, as she was a British School subscriber and I had seen her at the exhibition and had written to her. We even managed to see the Museum, though what there was in it I am very vague about! [...]

[In November 1928 Olga returned to Tell Fara for the second season.]

[16–18 November 1928; handwritten: PEF/TUF/DA/89]

[SS] *Orama*
Toulon.
16.XI.28

This will certainly be a new experience – I'm on nothing more or less than an emigration ship to Australia! There seem to be more children than anything else on board, and there are 168 girls going out on domestic service. So far I am alone in my cabin, which is a blessing, but I don't know what Naples will bring forth.

This morning (17th) we are still sitting at Toulon. I thought we spent an ominously quiet night. We shall be late at Naples and shall only get ½ a day there, but we shall be on time at Port Said. We are waiting for the Xmas mails.

The journey through France was simplicity itself. My travelling companion was typically French of the old school. She was on her way to Nice with her husband, and I heard all the life history of her son Horace who has married an American after travelling abroad to learn languages – Italy and England. The daughter-in-law is not very popular (cigarettes and silk stockings)! We had a cheerful breakfast together and parted later with many regrets. These sort of meetings are good for the Entente Cordiale, I feel. We were very late at Toulon which didn't matter and then I waited about till 2 to send the telegram which I hope will reach you safely. The town seemed a cheerful place, plenty of flowers for sale at street corners and a slight flavour of the east due to many dark-skinned people in Fezes selling carpets! Nobody wanted to see my luggage and I've come right through without any douane. Came on board about 3. The meals are arranged in shifts and are pretty comic at that, there is plenty to eat and as I can be in the air all day, I shall do well.

We never left Toulon till noon yesterday, so are still on our way to Naples. Vesuvius already in sight and lots of amusing little villages to see up the coast. A heavenly day, brilliant sun and as everyone is on deck, we're quite a crowd. I'm enjoying life tremendously and I've settled down to assimilate all the amusing new types and experiences that come my way. […]

[18 November 1928; handwritten: PEF/TUF/DA/119]

Naples
18.XI.28.

Dearest Ma,
Owing to the temporary indisposition of my fountain pen this must be written in pencil. It cannot be more than a blurred impression of colour and clouds of dust with only a dim remembrance of the worthier anticas.[35]

We were in dock by two – one of those rare ones where you go right up and don't have to make bewildering bargains with boatmen. I hadn't made any arrangement with any people on board to join their party so I just went and stood in the excursion office on shore until I heard nice-looking people making arrangements and then I asked if I could join them. We were eleven in two good cars and the show cost me 16/– – it was worth it. I had no idea Naples was so large – there were dilapidated houses with glimpses of picturesque courtyards all the way to Pompeii – a matter of 25 kilometers. We passed two funerals, two dead horses, a wedding complete with blushing bride and a procession to Saint Antonio, to say nothing of those gaily painted carts, cows being milked in the street to order and a bevy of nuns in straw hats like this — <u>Too</u> seductive my dear! As Topsy[36] would say!

Figure 3.8   Sketch by Olga Tufnell of an Italian nun in a straw hat, from letter of 18 November 1928. Courtesy of the Palestine Exploration Fund.

As to Pompeii, it's the area of the place that amazes me. When I think of the no. of baskets required to shift the earth – hard sticky stuff mind you – and the no. of boys to shift the baskets, and the number of men to shift the boys and so on, I'm quite dizzy. Broad paved streets with fountains at the street corners, private houses with painted walls, and tasteful fountains in the best Oliver Hill[37] style, bakeries, wine shops and a theatre all remain. The most elaborate interior that we saw was the public bath. Not a square was missing from the mosaic pavement, and on the walls were raised and coloured friezes and the marble baths looked as inviting today as they did 2000 years ago. If one imagines a good part of Naples in ruins today it would be just about the same, perhaps not so good; we do get excited about mere age.

As it was Sunday, many things were closed, but I've seen enough to realize what a fascinating place Pompeii could be.

We were due to pass Etna at 4 am, so I got the steward to call me, and rose up clad in my warmest garments. All to no avail as I saw no more than last year.

I am still alone in my cabin so am safe for the rest of the journey.

We reach Port Said about 9 am, when I'll post this and send you the promised wire; shall have to wait there till 6 pm for the Kantara train, so I hope Trumper will meet me. If he doesn't there's a man [on] board going to Iraq, who will be travelling on the same train so he will probably look after me.

Wednesday. I am now resting on the Trumpers' spare bed, as they insisted on my spending the day with them. I got here about eleven, having been through the customs quite safely. There is no news so I'll quite sleep as an insurance for tonight, until the family siesta is over about 4.

All my love darling
Yours ever,
<u>Olga</u>

[22 November 1928; handwritten: PEF/TUF/DA/120]

Gaza.
22.11.28

Darling –
I am watching the dawn break after my safe arrival here, at the CMS hospital.

To start from the beginning I sent you a wire from Port Said and while in town with Miss Trumper we met Mr Gardner, who was to travel on the same train. We all went back to the Trumpers and later they saw us into a cab. It was decent of them to look after me all day, it made all the difference having a peaceful one. We travelled 1st as he wanted to and I thought it was worth anything to have a reliable Englishman to be with. Kantara was a simple matter and we had a good cheerful dinner there, followed by coffee just before we left. A 1st class to ourselves meant that we slept solidly until nearing Gaza when I collected my belongings and peered anxiously into the darkness. There were no familiar faces on the platform, but a porter took my things and said there was a car. It was a providential one from Terazi (the man who hires them) already containing 2 Arabs and I found on enquiry that a car had gone to Tell Fara yesterday and had not returned. Apparently there has been very heavy rain and it has been held up.

So I decided to go up to the town in the car and ask the Hospital to take me in. After dropping the others in picturesque and narrow streets we went to the main entrance of the Hospital, only to find it closed, so we found our way to another door and I found two old friends from last year on night duty, so all is well and having had a God-sent cup of tea I'm now writing to you in the hall, I've left a message so that when the car comes they'll know where I am. So all's for the best in the best of all possible worlds and I've enjoyed the journey all through, which has been without the slightest hitch.

I must now face that tantalizing problem of how to go home. There are two routes with attractive points to them.

1) to Crete via Alex. [Alexandria] and then home via Athens and up the Dalmatian coast.

2) To Constanzia via Constantinople and then up the Danube in a steamer meeting you at Brno, what about it? And doing those visits now instead of in August.

Both ways have their disadvantages, what do you think about it?

Weather beastly, but we're consoled by the thought that it's worse in Europe and read lurid accounts of channel steamers aground in Dover harbour and snow on the Riviera [...]

Heard from Ruth Buchanan who repeats her invitation to go to Jerash, but I doubt if I can manage it, as I don't contemplate going to Jerusalem at all this year [...]

[30 November 1928; handwritten: PEF/TUF/DA/121]

c/o P.O.
Khan Yunis.
S. Palestine.
30.XI.28.

Dearest Ma,
We are now going on in full swing and I have my old job in the cemetery for the moment, though I am to go on the Tel later on, and as usual my luck is holding good and we are in the thick of a most complicated area. [...]

The week has been uneventful but this morning Prof. [Petrie] took me onto the Tel to help with the measuring and we had the whole morning together up there. This afternoon was rather a red letter one as I slept for an hour and then washed my hair, which certainly needed it. That tiresome box still hasn't come, though it will probably be here tomorrow, so that not only am I held up with the drawing but all my 'things' for the month are there and I'm managing under difficult circumstances, as Mrs S. [Starkey] is short too! I'd no idea they would be so long.

I don't think it will be such a hefty year from my point of view as last year, as Myers[38] takes the place of Risdon (who of course was on planning for all the first part of the time) and as Prof. does all that now and a vast amount of drawing, he does skulls on the Tel so that I only have Cem. [cemetery] ones to do. That is quite a saving, and we expect some more additions to the party soon.

Apparently Prof. travelled out with Ruth Walters (now Mrs Buchanan) and took a great fancy to her and her husband (who is working at Jerash) I send you her card, which he brought me, please tell Elizabeth as we three once had an amusing discussion about matrimony and so on, and we were a little scepticle [sic] of her views.

I am collecting an Arab costume, as it seems a chance that may never come again and the things are rather attractive, I've got a belt and a necklace, chiefly of cloves, which I wear every day, as it smells rather nice, and is I believe something of a disinfectant. [...]

[Postscript added to Olga's typed version of this letter]

Years later I gathered that clove necklaces were only worn during pregnancy, and my addiction to them caused much amusement to the women [...] I was a source of amusement to the men also for my blatant use of shameful swear words, the meaning of which I was blissfully ignorant.

[5 December 1928; handwritten: PEF/TUF/DA/122]

c/o P.O.
Khan Yunis.
S. Palestine
5.XII.28.

Dearest of Ma's,
Many thanks for sundry letters – also I think there is a reg. [registered] letter waiting at K.Y. [Khan Yunis] which is probably the much-needed instruments. Until today things have gone smoothly enough – and today has been rather a farce all through. We were in for a real sandstorm which increased in fury until part of the roof on the new room blew off and the rest of the morning was spent putting it back, and making all secure against the rain which has now come, thank goodness. Just as the first deluge fell, a bedraggled car made an astounding appearance and Mr Avi-Jonah [Avi-Yonah][39] from Jerusalem descended, complete with

bag and baggage. He is more or less a fixture, though we hope he won't stay long, as a Jehudi[40] is not popular with the men and he has too many friends in Jerusalem for our liking. We don't want him to be too enthusiastic about the finds!

Then we had to get his room ready and so on between the showers and sand and now it is raining in real earnest.

I am the proud possessor of a Bedawy knife; according to the laws of Starkey, anyone striking another on the work is turfed off and the weapon confiscated. One boy made for another this week and I came on the scene to find the offender being held by the scruff of the neck. So I acquired the knife but in the excitement of the moment I forgot about the sheath. No damage was done and since then there have been several pleas for the knife, but it is a rather too nice a trophy to part with!

The enclosed [photo] was taken of me unawares by Miss Crowfoot,[41] it is a typical scene. The other is Prof. and Mr Mortlock, the former in the celebrated cloak (now <u>green</u> with age and showing every sign of historical antiquity). [...]

I had a long letter from Lady P. Tell her of course I will patch Prof's shirt and the flannel has come.

I also heard from Richard Baker; he is probably coming at the end of Jan or beginning of Feb. and will let you know when he comes back. [...]

I can see that I shall have a fairly slack time in the evenings as Prof. does so much drawing, but I shall be able to turn my attention to all sorts of things I had no time for last year. [...]

The Xmas box has come and somehow Xmas has started! The peppermint lumps are especially appreciated in this weather.

[13 December 1928; handwritten: PEF/TUF/DA/123]

c/o P.O.
Khan Yunis.
S. Palestine.
13.XII.28

Dearest Ma, and Daddy,
[...] All continues to be well and you will have confirmation of that as Mrs Benson[42] came yesterday for the night and has promised to write and tell you how I am and her impressions which is rather decent of her, though she is one of those willing letter writers. Lady Agnew was with her and they gave our little Jew – Avi-Jonah – who has been here a

Figure 3.9 Bedouin women and child. Photograph taken during Tell Fara expedition seasons, 1927–9. See letter of 13 December 1928. Olga Tufnell archive, Palestine Exploration Fund. Courtesy of the Palestine Exploration Fund.

week a lift back to Jerusalem. He was a harmless and willing chap, but we are not kind to strangers, I think, and the men hate anyone of the Chosen Race.

Weather is kind again and we've had a pleasant Suk day with an unsuccessful hunt for a bathing place thrown in. I did manage to get some photos of women and girls, not all covered up, which will be good if they come out [e.g. Figure 3.9].

Ploughing is in full swing so the sower is a common sight. [...] There is the usual dearth of news, we can't produce much in our little desert to interest the metropolis. If the King does die,[43] it will be interesting to see how long it is before we hear about it.

[4 January 1929; handwritten; PEF/TUF/DA/124]

c/o P.O.
Khan Yunis
S. Palestine
4.1.29

Dearest Ma,

[...] The second rains still hold off, so we're having fine weather with occasional strong winds.

I've got various odd jobs on hand, but nothing like so much to do as last year. Professor really seems fit and eats nearly everything provided, as well as his favourite custard, though I notice that he is quite game to sample anything new instead. The régime is no different from last year, and I think I also am beginning to put on flesh.

We had a large covey of students conducted by Dr Allbright [Albright],[44] from the American School of Arch[aeology] in Jer[usalem]. They appeared one day in two and threes over the horizon, looking hot and tired, as their car had got stuck some 40 minutes' walk away. The poor things saw all over the Tel and cemetery, were regaled with glasses of lemonade and then trapsed [sic] over the skyline again in search of a belated lunch and their cars.

Did I tell you that the Crowfoots came a second time? With all my love.

Ever yours
Olga

[Note at top of letter]

Enclosed has been duly vetted by Prof. so it is eligible for publication if approved of! Give Lady Petrie my love. I will write again soon – also to Aun. [Auntie].

[10 January 1929; handwritten: PEF/TUF/DA/125]

c/o P.O.
Khan Yunis
S. Palestine
10.1.29

Dearest Ma,

Another week has passed uneventfully. We had one day's rain and since then more has been threatening; today it actually did come down a bit and we were rewarded by a fine rainbow. The crops are coming up everywhere, the first asphodel is out and we shall soon be quite spring like. [...]

Many thanks for various epistles, and (in advance) for the birthday goods which will be most welcome. The peppermints are just finished and the marron glacé box has contained anticas for some weeks past.

We expected Dr Parker[45] to arrive today, but he has not turned up, probably he has done the wise thing and stayed in Gaza till the storm is over; though we've had nothing much here, they've had a real storm there and the sky tonight is lit now and again by tremendous flashes of lightning. [...]

I shall be packing pottery most of tomorrow and must experiment on washing my jumper which needs it and may run. [...] Would you send 5/– worth of Woolworth beads, which it would be rather fun to distribute as presents to the good girls on the work? They should be the showy kind, but if you think they are too offensively gaudy, I was going to say choose some milder kinds but though I shan't enjoy seeing them in wear, the recipient will appreciate them much more if really striking. [...]

[18 January 1929; handwritten: PEF/TUF/DA/126]

P.O.
Khan Yunis
S. Palestine
18.1.29

Dearest Ma,
Your letter of the 9th arrived last night – I don't know what the letter shortage is as I have written regularly, though owing to rain our posts have been delayed in dispatch, as the camel man won't start out if it's too wet.

Last week's excitement was the arrival of strolling musicians from Gaza. They consisted of three ladies and three men and their only instruments were the native drums, the 'derabouka'. It is a small funnel-shaped affair, with skin stretched over the larger end. The small end is tucked under the elbow and tone is varied by beating on the rim. Two of these skilfully played make an effective accompaniment to the wailing songs of the ladies.

I didn't enjoy the evening as much as I should have, as Myers had got a bee in his bonnet that it was going to be a 'risquée' affair, and that I oughtn't to be there. After a lot of discussion I said I would go for a few minutes just to get a general impression and everyone else agreed it was all rot, especially as I'd been invited.

So go I did, though I left early with the unpleasant feeling that I must get away quickly before things got bad, but if one has sat through a musical comedy and performed in any ballroom, one could not see anything so very terrible in the mild contortions of the two good ladies. The elder one, who held her baby in the intervals, was rather meaty, and certainly past her prime. Her dress was dark blue with red woollen embroidery on it and on her head she just wore a kerchief. The western influence was not limited to the style of the dress, though in length it was positively Victorian, as she wore awful black stockings not properly pulled up and shoes with little black bows. The east got its own back, for they both wore silver anklets!

The other dancer was quite young – a slim girl with an elusive detached look on her oval face. Her wispy dark hair was parted in the middle and when she smiled there was a glint of much gold in her teeth and she had a minute ring of it in her nose. Her dress is difficult to describe, you see things like it in renaissance Italian portraits. Cut to fit loosely to the figure, reaching almost to the ground and with long sleeves, it was decorated with bands of pink and yellow braid. In the light of the new moon and one lantern on a pole, with a ring of expectant Bedawy faces forming the background there was something eery [sic] but attractive about the whole scene. The music alone is enough to give that impression – and it is all an entertainment in the real sense of the word, as there were no bored faces round, with the possible exception of the young man above mentioned, who was badly done out of the spicy evening he had imagined and apparently hoped for! To admirers of the Black Bottom[46] this performance would have been a revelation. They vibrate their tummies without moving the head, at an incredible speed, stamp their feet in time to a different r[h]ythm and click their fingers in the air to a third and all the time they are singing in a slow mournful way, throwing the words of the refrain from one to the other.

Dr Parker arrived today, having spent some days in Port Said, as the journey and lumbago had rather done him in. Even now he looks anything but fit, but will probably pick up here in the sun. Just now the weather is perfect; Mr S. [Starkey] has been in bed with some form of chill, but is about again today. […]

I've painted a small Philistine pot in the style of Mrs Risdon, which at the moment looks quite decent, so may do some more. […]

P.S. The last batch of photos was rather a failure – only these two to send out of six.

I've just been transferred to Tel from Cem. [cemetery], rather fierce, but I hope I will take to it.

[27 January 1929; handwritten: PEF/TUF/DA/127]

c/o P.O.
Khan Yunis
S. Palestine
27.1.29

Dearest Ma,

Wonderful to relate your birthday parcel actually arrived on 'the day', which was rather a feat. The contents have already started to disappear and are as good as usual.

I am having a fortnight on the Tel, which is rather a strain but good experience, as there is always some small thing that needs attention, and I don't know anything about walls. Myers who is usually there has been away on a special flint job,[47] which is now over. At the end of the week, I shall take over from him, where he has started trenching for tombs, just S. [south] of the Tel.

Mr Colt arrived yesterday, and I think he will be a success, Prof is pleased with his outlook and so on, and he seems to have been in most countries under the sun.

R.B.B.'s [Richard St Barbe Baker's] letters are arriving forwarded from his Club, so he is evidently on the way. We haven't heard yet when he will actually come on from Jerusalem. I hope it will be before the beginning of Ramadan, when the people are apt to be a bit tired out, in 10 days' time. [...]

[W]e are having fine days now, and the last few nights have been lovely too, very bright moonlight, the full moon rises a brilliant gold, behind the hills, and as she soars into the sky turns more silvery until she is so pale that the stars outshine her in brilliance.

The Sterlings are in England and I'm horrified to hear that their only son aged about 6 is dead. He was the idol of the whole hospital and everyone is in tears, when they talk about it. They've got three daughters, but it's hardly the same thing.

My money has only just seen me through, it was quite a narrow squeak. I don't quite know how I spent £7. Naples was the only extravagance, meals and taxis in Paris, tips, Toulon and my train fare £3.

They say that the wady Ghuzzah [Ghazzeh] is probably flooded so it may be a day or so before we can get across. After all I may be here when Prof. comes, and if the hospital takes compassion on me I shall do well. It is another matron now, the one who was on holiday last year, but she is very nice and I've just had breakfast with her. [...]

[1 February 1929; handwritten: PEF/TUF/DA/128]

c/o P.O.
Khan Yunis.
S. Palestine
1.2.29

Darling Ma,
I am writing again soon to tell you that my depressed mood is over now and things are going on all right, so don't bother. It was very temporary and now that the week is over I see a quiet one ahead of me, and all is well.

Myers goes back to the Tel and I go on to the Trench, which produces nothing at the moment, but which may mean tombs later on. Meanwhile I shall be able to get pottery and so on tidied up at the house and shall be able to help with the film. R.B.B. has written from Jerusalem and we expect him any day.

We are brewing up for another patch of bad weather, yesterday was awful on the Tel and today is not much better, except that we don't have to be in it, and I shall be glad when the rain puts a stop to the whole affair.

Myers is keen on the film and knows a certain amount about the business so he will be a good ally. We have got various ideas on hand, but as Prof. does not take any interest and is not prepared to allot any time to making it, we shall have obstacles to surmount – I do hope successfully, as it is worth doing and the natives are taking to the idea splendidly. […]

[7 February 1929; handwritten: PEF/TUF/DA/129]

c/o P.O.
Khan Yunis
S. Palestine
7.2.29.

Dearest Mà,
(Private) R. [Richard St Barbe Baker] has gone today after 2 hectic days of film taking under horrible conditions, sand, wind and rain followed by a perfectly glorious morning today. Things have gone well, considering the short time we've been able to spend on them and we should have some good 'shots' chiefly suitable for news films. We staged one good scene of boys lifting baskets from a pit and today we were in the midst of a complicated scene of men and boys being taken on to the work, when

Prof. was sighted watching proceedings. He didn't come up and stop us, but went down to the house and when H. [Harding] went down he told him the show was not suitable. Everything was stopped but after some talk R. & I were able to get him round again.

Later in the morning he came up and was filmed and did his part very well. However we've got to go carefully to get a show worth anything and when R. comes back on March 1st, I think Prof will have worked up interest. If Lady P. would write enthusiastically to him about it again, I think it would help. Everyone here is keen on making a success of it.

R. now says in his vague quiet way that he thinks it would be a good thing to fly over various Tels and here [Tell Fara] and take aerial photographs, and as he usually seems to do what he wants, I expect he will turn up one day in an aeroplane.

After a few days in Jerusalem he goes to Transjordania, probably going from place to place on horseback.

The poor chap couldn't have had a worse introduction to the Tel, and he had to sleep in the skullery on the floor in his flea bag, must have been devilish cold.

Haven't heard from you for weeks, but hope to get your parcel and some letters tomorrow. Heard from Mrs Buchanan, Ruth Walters, who wants me to go to Jerash before I leave. Prof is more or less booked for March 29th and I suppose I shall leave early in April. Would like to go to Crete. Will you give Lady P. my love and the news from this letter, the first word [Private] is only put so that you don't read it all aloud straight on end.

Very best love to all
from Olga

[8 February 1929; handwritten: PEF/TUF/DA/130]

c/o P.O.
Khan Yunis
S. Palestine
8.2.29

Dearest Daddy,
[...] So far we don't need a crate of antiquities from Birmingham and we've just had to build a new store room to hold what we've got, but I'll cable you if we run short, and you can send out some brass bowls, beads and anything else bright and showy to make up. Then if we've anything decent I'll just pocket it and bring it back to you!

The filming has been quite fun, but would have been more so if we had had better weather. There are 3 handles to turn on the camera, Baker turns 2 and I sometimes turn the third, and it's quite hectic as you can't rely on the people doing the right thing at the right moment.

He comes back on March 1st when we should be having glorious weather and we want to do some scenes which will be like Bible ones. There are all sorts of possibilities and one day you may wake up in a cinema to see your daughter on the screen, who knows?! [...]

This is a picture of L. [Lankester Harding] at his 1st conference, I expect there will be many more to come and in the end he will look like the gentleman on the left.

Figure 3.10 Ink sketch by Olga Tufnell. From letter of 8 February 1929. Courtesy of the Palestine Exploration Fund.

Tomorrow the men start the great fast of Ramadan; it is a trying time as they don't eat, drink or smoke between sunrise and sunset and then make up for it by eating nearly all night. It means we can only work ½ a day, as they are too tired to do more and this goes on for a month. It's just like our Lent carried to extremes and as Mahamet [Muhammad] never ordered it, it seems altogether rather unnecessary.

Hope to do a few sketches in the afternoon and thought I might try to draw some Bedaway types. [...]

[11 February 1929; handwritten: PEF/TUF/DA/131]

c/o P.O.
Khan Yunis
S. Palestine
11.2.29

Dearest Ma,

[...] All is well in the best of all possible worlds – this may be slightly influenced by the change in climatic conditions as today for the first time for weeks, we've fine sunny weather with a cool breeze. At the moment I'm rather a lady at large, as Colt has been put on the trench, rather against his intentions, so instead of strolling round looking on he has to take an active part in things while I do pottery at the house, v. peaceful, but I don't think I want it to last too long.

This morning Prof. took me off with him to see a flint site a mile or so away, which was an expedition from my point of view, as wicked though it may seem I've never been more than a few yards off the direct route to the Tel since I came here.

Of course the next excitement is to hear from R., as he has promised to send us prints of the still pictures he took, and an account of how the 'movies' came out. [...]

[14 February 1929; handwritten: PEF/TUF/DA/132]

c/o P.O.
Khan Yunis
S. Palestine
14.2.29

Dearest Ma,

[...] We are leading a palatial life, work stops at 1 pm during Ramadan, so as soon as I've got the pottery cleared up to my liking, I'll be able to do some sketching and loaf around a bit, though anyhow I've had a fairly slack time this week. Yesterday morning I helped Prof. with photography for 5 hrs, we got 11 plates done.

Weather distinctly better, Myers has bathed twice in the Shellal pools;[48] however, I expect it would never do for me to do likewise, my reputation being perhaps a bit shaky in local eyes already; on the other hand it would only be another of those actions of the inexplicable English. [...]

[20 February 1929; handwritten: PEF/TUF/DA/133]

c/o P.O.
Khan Yunis.
S. Palestine.
20.2.29

Dearest Ma,

Nothing could have been better than your excellent choice of beads – these have been much admired in many quarters and I think the blue entrances the more sophisticated minds, while the small children like the crystals as much as anything. The customs had treated them rather badly, and broke 2 strings, though they can easily be mended again. The last week has been uneventful but pleasant despite certain vagaries in the weather. I've been down at the house all the time, so in the afternoons I've been painting and after 3 sittings I've produced a watercolour sketch of a small girl, and hope to do some more as time goes on. Am also sketching, was out all this morning and find I'm in quite good form, considering I've not tried to wield a brush since I left Florence – now 7 years ago!

[…] I'm just reading Conrad's *Under Western Eyes* and have just finished Aldous Huxley's *Point Counter Point*. The latter is outspoken but interesting especially after he had got over the fireworks he thought it necessary to indulge in to begin with!

[2 March 1929; handwritten: PEF/TUF/DA/134]

c/o/ P.O.
Khan Yunis.
S. Palestine
2.3.29

Dearest Ma,

[…] The Palestine Post has been kept busy lately, as I had a letter from R. who seemed a <u>little</u> vague about coming down again and since then we've been showering letters and telegrams around. Two of the former today, one saying he was coming on 1st as arranged and the other fixing the 6th as the day for meeting in Gaza. We can't possibly do any day but Friday – market day, so unless everything goes in the melting pot again Friday it will be. He has much forestry business going on.

Weather ideal now, and I lead rather a peaceful existence, helping Prof. in the mornings, painting in the afternoons and accompanying him in a platonic stroll in the evenings, when we talk of this and that.

Dr Parker goes in a day or two. I shall ask him to look you up if poss.; he is a dear old chap, and perhaps he would lunch with you on his way to Bristol. Prof is fixed to leave on 18th, and I am still dallying with various routes and am rather waiting to hear if the Czecho via Danube idea appeals to you.

With very best love,
<u>Olga</u>

[8 March 1929; handwritten: PEF/TUF/DA/135]

Tel Fara.
8.3.29.

I start on this large bit of paper because we've been having a time of it and I shall need it all to unburden my soul, as Topsy might say. I can't remember how far you'd got in the serial, but after various telegrams and so on, we got a message that Baker was coming yesterday morning. When he didn't come, we got anxious, as we had had to cancel our programme to go to Gaza today. Prof. wants a special bit of work finished before he goes and we have to work all out to do it, as we must miss 2 days next week for the Aid [Eid] Festival.[49] Of course the message was wrongly worded, and should have been that he was arriving in Gaza then and was ready to take the picture on Friday. This we did not know until I had trapsed [sic] to Amara Police Post (an hour on a donkey) and managed to speak to him on a 'phone, which in itself is rather a feat. The next arrangement for a wonder actually worked and he has just come, and proposed to leave on Tuesday. This is <u>hopeless</u> as I'd told him in 2 previous letters: we can't make a good job of it, unless he stays at least 10 days. Starks [Starkey] and I talked hard for ½ an hour and he's now staying. You can't expect to take a decent film for exhibition in 4 days which is what he was attempting to do.

There is a scheme that we should go to a deserted Roman city on Monday, which should be rather fun and will no doubt make good pictures.

Woven all around this dilemma has been the arrival at lunchtime of Mrs Crowfoot and 3 young men (we were only expecting 2) and now they've all got to be fed and entertained until tomorrow. Myers and H. [Harding] and Colt are sleeping in the Bedawyn tents, as an experience as well as a necessity to house all the guests.

The Buchanans came last Monday and stayed one night, I enjoyed their visit and had a good gossip with Ruth. They want me to spend a week with them at Jerash, which I must try to fit in. He is tall according to Prof., the image of Trajan – and has a good many grey hairs – though he can't be much over 30 owing to circumstantial evidence. He is leaving the job there as the others are not congenial and is taking a house at Jerusalem, where he intends to learn archaeology thoroughly before taking a post.

Ruth is not keen on the idea as it won't lead anywhere and she wants him to farm in Canada. So how it will all end, I know not. [...]

[19–22 March 1929; handwritten: PEF/TUF/DA/136]

c/o P.O.
Khan Yunis
S. Palestine
19.3.29

Dearest Ma,

Yours, with the eloquent comment on the Danube has just arrived – will let you know when I've heard about my passage.

Prof. has just left with Mayer[50] after a hectic morning on the division,[51] which has again been a very successful one from our point of view, with plenty of good stuff for exhib. purposes.

22.3.29 I have just invested in the sateen necessary to make my 'kibber', that is the coat that is worn over a Bedawy lady's dress. The principal and probably only garments are illustrated herewith:

Figure 3.11 Pencil sketch by Olga Tufnell: 'Bedawy lady' wearing coat (kibber), dress, headdress (wazariat), veil (gonah) and belt. From letter of 19 March 1929. Courtesy of the Palestine Exploration Fund.

The headdress underneath the veil (*gonah*) is the *wazariat*, with coins, shells and beads sewn on in great profusion. A woven belt is worn round the waist and everything is elaborately decorated. I hope my coat may be some use in London for the evenings.

Have had a busy day, doing pottery and finishing a sketch of a girl, have now done 4 Bedawy children, 4 outdoor sketches and 2 paintings of pottery.

PRIVATE

I've ordered 6 bottles (small!) of beer to drink as I think it would be a good fattener, if and when the hot weather comes, much to the amusement of everyone; Mrs S. [Starkey] is even a little shocked, though she swears she isn't! She'll be presenting Mr S. [Starkey] with an infant in July,[52] luckily she has been wonderfully well all the time, never sick at all, but she gets very sleepy. [...]

[Undated letter, probably around 28 March 1929; handwritten: PEF/TUF/DA/137]

c/o P.O.
Khan Yunis
S. Palestine

Dearest,
I'm sailing on the 11th from Haifa on S.S. *Adria*, reaching Trieste on the 17th. [...]

I leave here on the 3rd and go to Jerusalem en route for Jerash. Things are going quickly here and really everything is packed. It's funny to think that I'll be gone in a week.

Very glad about Daddy's windfall, dear old Cousin Louis turned up trumps after all.

Looking forward to seeing you immensely. [...]

[3–4 April 1929; handwritten: PEF/TUF/DA/138.1-2]

German Hospice
Jerusalem.
3.4.29.

Dearest Ma,

I'm off on my wanderings once more, and am now here for 2 days. It was supposed to be a 'quiet place', but woe! is me, the piano is being atrociously practised next door and myriads of trains whistle and hoot, though how they manage it I can't think as there are only 2 a day.

I left Fara regretfully at 9 this morning in a car, stopped at Hebron to see the sights, which were uninspiring. Infidels can only see the outside of the Mosque and the famous glass factory consisted of one furnace where they were making nothing but glass rings, so I was not tempted to buy anything!

On arrival here I did a neat bit of express work. We got in at 1.45 and went straight to the Mus. [Museum] to get the permits. Everyone was out, but I discovered that Mr Lambert lived at the German Hospice, so as I was going there, I caught him just as he was going out. He said the permits were ready but not sent, so he dashed in my car to the Mus. and gave them over to Achmed who I then left at the station, while I did other things in the town. Got to the train just before it went at 3.20, with all the required information.

They will be surprised to see him back so soon.

My next move is to get a car from here to Jerash 60 P.T. [piastres] or rather Amman, where Ruth may meet me.

Then I sail late on the 11th from Haifa, get to Trieste on the 17th, [...] at 3.30 on the 19th [...] shall have to change at Milan, and spend a night in Paris.

Tomorrow I shall go to the Mus. have my hair cut, order my seat in the car and call on the Reynolds.[53] I've also got some shopping to do for Ruth.

Here read supplement

4th [April] [...] I did my call and got away without lunch successfully. Mrs R. seemed pleased to see me and we chatted for a few minutes. After a good substantial meal here I had my hair cut and went to call on Monsieur le Père something something van der Vliet at a monastery. I was shown their miscellaneous collection. But their garden full of flowers was just as well worth seeing. Afterwards I walked back to the Jaffa gate through the Suk, picked up my photos which are rather good and so back here. Then after much talk I had the first bath for 5 months, since the 19th November in fact, and it was good though I started proceedings by pulling a tap when fully dressed which turned the shower bath on all over me.

I've now turned my troubles over to Mr Lambert, as it turns out that one can't send trunk calls by the phone here. I had arranged to ring Ruth up, as she will meet me in Amman. He is nobly going to do the call from a friend's house nearby. [...]

[3 April 1929]

Dearest,

This is written while having a few minutes' peace in the Mus. garden. Everything has gone well and I've done the necessary jobs so far. Arranged for a car tomorrow and this afternoon I'm paying a call on 2 Père Blancs at a monastery! They were going round with Dr Mayer and have an interesting collection at the Pool of Bethsaida [Bethesda].

Just now I'm going to call on the Reynolds with whom I stayed last year, as it is 12, I must go now or else they will think I want lunch.

Notes

1. Petrie 1930, 2. Petrie's identification of Beth-Pelet (Joshua 15:27) was erroneous, and the site has also been linked by other scholars to ancient Sharuhen/Shilhim (Yisraeli 1993, 441).
2. See Olga's postscript in letter of 18 December 1927 (p. 55), pp. 16–17 in Chapter 1, and Chapter 2, notes 22 and 27. See Quirke 2010, 84–5, for a list of the workers from Quft who came to Palestine from Egypt to help train local workmen in archaeological techniques, including the tracing of mudbrick walls (James 1979, 76, Pl. VII). Tufnell records that four workers came to work at Tell Fara from Quft (or Qift; Greek Koptos), 'a village in Egypt which had cornered the market in the supply of diggers for Petrie, and still considers itself paramount in that respect' (Tufnell 1982, 83).
3. For Olga's insights into the organisation of the workers and relationships with the archaeologists at Fara and Ajjul, see Tufnell 1985, 6–7.
4. Petrie 1930, 1.
5. Olga Tufnell interviewed by Jonathan Tubb. Transcript of audiotaped interview, c. 1985.
6. Chapman and Vella 2001; Bennett 1975.
7. Petrie 1930; MacDonald, Starkey and Harding 1932.
8. For an historical overview of the Hyksos see Redford 1992.
9. See note 1 above.
10. Olga's report of the cemetery findings was published in Petrie's report, her publication debut: Tufnell 1930; Petrie 1930, Pl. XXXIXA.2–5. Also see Starkey and Harding 1932 for subsequent publication of the cemetery.
11. Thornton 2015. Also see Stevenson 2019, 35–7.
12. Dr Richard St Barbe Baker, OBE (1889–1982), English forester and environmentalist responsible for initiating worldwide reforestation. As a government forestry official in Kenya he was convinced of the need to plant new trees to maintain the world's ecology, leading to the foundation of the Men of the Trees (1922). The organisation moved to the United Kingdom in 1924 and in 1992 was renamed the International Tree Foundation. Referred to as Richard, R., or R.B.B. in Tufnell's letters.
13. Drower 1985, 373.
14. A number of items of jewellery and textiles once belonging to Olga Tufnell can be found in the British Museum collections.
15. Could refer to either the Mosque of Amr Ibn al As or the Mosque of Ibn Tulun.
16. The Aqsunqur Mosque.
17. See List of Principal Persons, p. xxxi.
18. The layout of the house shows the dig-house rooms from left to right clockwise: Mah. [Mohammed Osman el-Kreti], Mr H. [Harding], two spare rooms, O.T. [Olga Tufnell], store,

Ris. [Risdons], dining room, Starks [Starkeys], and Pottery [pottery/artefact storage]. Water containers are shown in the centre.

19 The sketch shows the location of the house on the southeastern side of the Tell, with a path leading to the highest point labelled '400 ft.' – presumably the path's length. The river is the Wadi Ghuzzeh/Gaza (Nahal Besor), located to the east.

20 See note 27 in Chapter 2.

21 Tribal leader or elder, identity unknown.

22 Arabic, honorific title meaning 'Lady' or 'Madam'.

23 Reference to Ramadan in following week, which would have started 22 February 1928.

24 A corpulent figure depicted in a famous scene showing a seagoing mission to the Land of Punt in the reign of Hatshepsut (fifteenth century BC). Hatshepsut's Temple, Deir el-Bahri, Egypt.

25 Evidently a second turkey named Thomas, after the first eaten at Qau (see undated letter, probably November or December 1927, in Chapter 2).

26 Several of these photographs may have been incorporated into Olga Tufnell's photo album in the Palestine Exploration Fund archives.

27 A Bedouin tribe, also known as Al-Tarabin, the largest tribal group of the Sinai peninsula and Negev region in the nineteenth and twentieth centuries.

28 Exhibit held at UCL, 6–28 July 1928: Antiquities from Beth Pelet/Tell Fara (Palestine). British School of Archaeology in Egypt. Advertised as a free exhibit, with Hilda Petrie in attendance 11 am–1 pm daily. For a summary of summer exhibits in London featuring recently excavated archaeological finds, see Thornton 2015, including Appendix 2.

29 Church Missionary Society, Gaza. Founded 1907, destroyed in the First World War and rebuilt by CMS as Al Ahli Arab Hospital.

30 St George's School, Jerusalem.

31 Wife of Edward Wyndham Tufnell, 1st Bishop of Brisbane.

32 Lionel Grant Tufnell, CMG.

33 Appears to be 'Cuffe' in the original handwritten letter, although later transcribed as 'Luffe' in the typed copy (PEF/DA/TUF/118).

34 Carleton Tufnell, brother of Lionel Grant Tufnell.

35 Antica/antika, meaning an ancient artefact or antiquity.

36 Possibly a family friend or family saying, repeated in letter of 8 March 1929.

37 Fashionable society architect of the day.

38 Oliver H. Myers (1903–66), a member of Petrie's field staff at Tell el-Far'ah (South) (Tufnell 1982, 83). This was his first excavation in Palestine. He had previously participated in Brunton's excavations at Mostageda, Egypt, in the 1927–8 season. In 1929 he worked in Egypt for Alan Gardiner. Between 1930 and 1938 he worked for Sir Robert Mond at Armant. Myers set new standards in the use of statistics in archaeology.

39 Michael Avi-Yonah (1904–74), Israeli archaeologist; Keeper of Records in Department of Antiquities, Palestine, 1931–48; editor of the *Quarterly of the Department of Antiquities of Palestine* 1948–50 and the *Israel Exploration Journal* from 1950; became Professor of Archaeology and History of Art at Hebrew University of Jerusalem and authored numerous works on biblical archaeology.

40 Arabic word meaning 'Jew' or 'Jewish'.

41 Likely Joan Crowfoot, one of three daughters of John W. Crowfoot and Grace Mary (aka Molly) Crowfoot. Also see Chapter 4, letter of 7 March 1932 and several subsequent letters.

42 Friend and travelling companion of Lady Agnew.

43 King George V was gravely ill.

44 William Foxwell Albright (1891–1971), biblical archaeologist, Director of American School of Oriental Research in Jerusalem 1922–9 and 1933–6. The school was renamed the W.F. Albright Institute of Archaeological Research (in his honour) in 1970. He directed excavations in Palestine at Tell el-Ful in 1922 and Tell Beit Mirsim 1926–32, published numerous scholarly and popular works and was editor of the *Bulletin of the American Schools of Oriental Research*, 1930–68. Professor of Semitic Languages, Johns Hopkins University, Baltimore, 1930–58. Also see references to Albright in Chapter 5.

45 Dr G. Parker, a retired medical doctor who had been at Tell Jemmeh and went on to Tell el-'Ajjul.

46 A popular dance in the 1920s.

47 The 'flint job' may refer to an unofficial expedition to one of the sites along the Wadi Ghazzeh, or perhaps to Petrie's initiative to acquire flint tools and other artefacts from those sites

through purchase from local Bedouin, a practice that led to complaints from the Mandate authorities. See Sparks 2013, 149–50.

48 Pools that formed in the summer months at Shellal (Arabic, meaning waterfall) in the Wadi Ghazzeh. They were fed by springs, whereas the rest of the riverbed remained dry. Army engineers in Allenby's campaign in the First World War built a dam across the wadi to hold millions of gallons of water. The overflow formed shallow pools fringed with grass.

49 Eid al-Fitr: religious holiday in the Muslim calendar – the breaking of the fast at the end of the holy month of Ramadan.

50 Leo Aryeh Mayer (1895–1959), Inspector for the Department of Antiquities, Palestine, 1921–9, Director of Archives, 1929–33. Lecturer in Islamic Art and Archaeology at the Hebrew University of Jerusalem, 1929–32, becoming Professor of Near Eastern Art and Archaeology in 1932. Dean of the Faculty of Arts and Rector of the Hebrew University of Jerusalem, 1943–5. The L.A. Mayer Institute for Islamic Art, Jerusalem (opened 1974) is named in his memory.

51 According to the antiquities law, half the finds from an excavation could be kept by the excavator. The other half, including all unique pieces, were to go to the Palestine Archaeological Museum.

52 John Starkey, born 1929.

53 The Reynolds of St George's School, mentioned in letter of 26–29 April 1928.

References

Bennett, Crystal M. 1975. 'Harris Dunscombe Colt (1901–1973)', *Levant* 7: iii–v.

Chapman, Rupert L. and Nicholas C. Vella. 2001. 'Harris Dunscombe Colt in Malta', *Palestine Exploration Quarterly* 133: 50–5.

Drower, Margaret S. 1985. *Flinders Petrie: A Life in Archaeology*. London: Victor Gollancz.

James, Frances W. 1979. 'Petrie in the Wadi Ghazzeh and at Gaza: Harris Colt's Candid Camera', *Palestine Exploration Quarterly* 111: 75–7.

MacDonald, Eann, James L. Starkey and Gerald L. Harding. 1932. *Beth-Pelet II: Prehistoric Fara*. London: British School of Archaeology in Egypt.

Petrie, W.M.F. 1930. *Beth-Pelet I*. London: British School of Archaeology in Egypt.

Quirke, Stephen. 2010. *Hidden Hands: Egyptian Workforces in Petrie Excavation Archives, 1880–1924*. London: Duckworth.

Redford, Donald B. 1992. *Egypt, Canaan, and Israel in Ancient Times*. Princeton, NJ: Princeton University Press.

Sparks, Rachael T. 2013. 'Flinders Petrie through Word and Deed: Re-evaluating Petrie's Field Techniques and their Impact on Object Recovery in British Mandate Palestine', *Palestine Exploration Quarterly* 145: 143–59.

Starkey, James L. and Gerald L. Harding. 1932. *Beth-Pelet II: Beth-Pelet Cemetery*. London: British School of Archaeology in Egypt.

Stevenson, Alice. 2019. *Scattered Finds: Archaeology, Egyptology and Museums*. London: UCL Press.

Thornton, Amara. 2015. 'Exhibition Season: Annual Archaeological Exhibitions in London, 1880s–1930s', *Bulletin of the History of Archaeology* 25(1), p.Art. 2. DOI: http://doi.org/10.5334/bha.252.

Tufnell, Olga. 1930. 'Burials in Cemeteries 100 and 200'. In *Beth-Pelet I*, by W.M.F. Petrie, 11–13. London: British School of Archaeology in Egypt.

Tufnell, Olga. 1982. 'Reminiscences of a Petrie Pup', *Palestine Exploration Quarterly* 114: 81–6.

Tufnell, Olga. 1985. 'Reminiscences of Excavations at Lachish: An Address Delivered by Olga Tufnell at Lachish on July 6, 1983', *Tel Aviv* 12: 3–8.

Yisraeli, Yael, 1993. 'Far'ah, Tell el- (South)'. In *The New Encyclopedia of Archaeological Excavations in the Holy Land*, edited by Ephraim Stern, 441–4. Jerusalem: Israel Exploration Society.

4
Cyprus, 1929–30

Olga had decided to have a break from the excavations at Tell Fara after she had found the previous two seasons very tiring.[1] It is also worth noting the occurrence of riots in Palestine in the summer of 1929, which may have influenced her decision. For a change of scene, she offered her skills in drawing and painting pottery to the Swedish-Cyprus Expedition. Einar Gjerstad initiated the Swedish-Cyprus Expedition in 1927 after his preliminary investigations in 1923 revealed much work to be done in the field of Cypriot archaeology. Gjerstad's aim was to establish a chronology by means of scientific investigation, and in so doing he was involved in the excavation of no fewer than 25 sites covering a huge chronological range. There was a particular focus on excavations at Lapithos, Nitovikla, Ayia Irini and Enkomi.[2] Cyprus was already an important arena for British archaeologists during the 'long nineteenth century', a prelude to this scientific revolution in archaeological excavation and international collaboration.[3] One of the British archaeologists active in Cyprus in the 1920s and 1930s was Joan du Plat Taylor. Like Olga, Taylor was connected to the Institute of Archaeology in London, and is mentioned a number of times in the letters as they travelled and spent time together.

Olga's Christmas present that year from her Uncle Bertie[4] was the first stage of the journey to Cyprus, including a short stay in Paris. Also in the travelling party were her cousin, known as 'Uncle' Arthur,[5] and his wife Daisy ('Auntie D.' in the letters). From Paris the train took them to Monte Carlo where they joined a Canadian Pacific liner, the SS *Empress of Australia*, on part of her round-the-world cruise. After Athens Uncle Arthur and Auntie Daisy went their own way, leaving Olga on her own. She enjoyed herself exploring the Acropolis and the National Museum and spent Christmas with a Greek family. From Athens, she sailed on to Cyprus.

Cyprus at that time was still a British Crown Colony – and basking, superficially at least, in the colonial lifestyle of the day. Olga, who stayed in the centrally located Palace Hotel, Nicosia, had the necessary introduction to Government House, which ensured her a social round of tea parties, gymkhanas, dances and expeditions of all sorts; she bought a pony ('Woolly') and learned the art of tent-pegging. She lost no time in introducing herself to the Cyprus Museum, Nicosia, apparently to start drawing and painting objects for the Swedish-Cyprus Expedition[6] and to visit sites with Gjerstad. Olga indulged her passion for seeing life among the people first hand and was especially interested in women's dress and local customs. She was fascinated to watch them (always with an archaeologist's eye) engaged in crafts, such as weaving at Lefkoniko and pottery making at Kornos.[7]

Sir Ronald Storrs,[8] the governor (former civil governor of Jerusalem), was good to her and offered the use of his library; it was unfortunate, to say the least, that in 1931 his house containing his library and art collection was destroyed by fire owing to the actions of anti-colonialist insurgents[9] – a foretaste of the struggle for independence from British rule in subsequent decades. Olga's relationship with officialdom was somewhat faltering, as indicated in the letter about her dinner invitation to Government House, but her letters of introduction to Storrs, and her meeting his wife, Lady Storrs, as well as Rupert Gunnis (Storrs' private secretary, who worked in the Cyprus Museum), opened doors that may not have been afforded to others.

Working in the Cyprus Museum was an excellent opportunity for Olga to become more familiar with Cypriot pottery, especially given her later work at Tell ed-Duweir (Lachish), which included many Cypriot imports. Olga was also engaged in giving occasional tours of the museum to visiting tourists. Such visits proved beneficial in raising funds for excavations on Cyprus, including through sales of 'duplicate' antiquities, an entirely unacceptable activity today, but practised at a number of museums in the past. The letters give a few insights into the role of Rupert Gunnis at the museum and his seeking out of antiquities on the island, prior to him becoming Inspector of Antiquities.

The Cyprus Museum is a hub for archaeology on the island, and at that time was managed by a committee led by the British high commissioner, including the archbishop, the mufti and the cadi (a Sharia court judge) who acted as vice-presidents, alongside elected members. This was the situation in the years prior to the establishment of the Department of Antiquities of Cyprus in 1935 and greater enforcement of archaeological regulations.[10] The time of Olga's visit was a period in which archaeological heritage management was still in the hands of a British-led administration made up of a small number of individuals.

Travel and tourism are a salient part of Olga's account, and her travel to Cyprus via the French Riviera and Athens indicates a shift to more upscale destinations and modes of transport compared with her letters to date. Presumably this was feasible due to her uncle's generosity. On Cyprus, in addition to trips to villages to view pottery making, Olga was able to travel by private car and pony trek with friends, visit many coastal spots and get up into the mountains, as well as visit archaeological and historical places, including Morphou, Leondari-Vouno and Bellapais Monastery. Olga presents an account of meeting the family of Mehmet, a Sudanese man, and his Cypriot wife, at a betrothal ceremony for two of their daughters, which provides insights into ethnic diversity and Muslim marriage practices on the island.[11]

The initial group of letters in this chapter are handwritten. Once established in Nicosia, Olga appears to have had access to a typewriter. The transcriptions are taken from what are likely to be typed originals.

Letters of December 1929–April 1930

[13 December 1929; handwritten: PEF/TUF/DA/139]

Le Grand Hotel Paris, 12, Boulevard des Capucines, Place de l'Opera.

Le Dec. 13 1929.

Dearest Ma,
Yesterday morning was fine and warm and we wandering [sic] in the streets and shop-gazed and were able to eat a goodish lunch at the Printemps with Irène, a friend of Olivia. Naturally Uncle B. [Bertie] was at the works. Rain afterwards and so to the Louvre – not the shop – where straight as an arrow from the bow I made my way to the Egyptian gallery. Find I remembered it quite well from last time.

The evening programme was decided when Uncle B. came in about 7.30. We dined at Prunier's, exclusively French and the Scott's[12] of Paris! They had oysters – I, shrimps, followed by 'petite marmite' and lobster. Then we hurried, but comfortably, in a taxi to the Theatre Michel where saw 'L'Escalier de Service' again exclusively French and I think we were the only foreigners there.

The theatre was small, dirty with hard, almost unpacked stalls and there were no trimmings in the way of orchestra. The French seem happy without American luxury and come for the entertainment, all as it should be, and they get what they want.

The show was definitely amusing and I suppose the most risqué I've seen in my young life! They didn't care what they said, but they said it well, so that one couldn't help laughing.

Then bed and another morning today round the shops. Things are expensive; I see no point in smuggling stockings in, they are more expensive and not worth the money, so that I paid too much for 2 measly woollen pairs.

Uncle B. called for us at 12.30 as we were to lunch with the Bénards at their house and were duly transported there in their car. The house is almost next door to the factory and is much ornamented interiorly with palms in pots.

Madame is fat and genial and Mons.[ieur] is thoroughly pleasant but evidently much worried by his strike. The food was all that could be desired – the ménage was homely and unpretentious and I enjoyed my glimpse into French family life.

More Louvre this afternoon when Auntie D. [Daisy] and I waded through many rooms to find the pictures we wanted to see.

Now I'm all booted and spurred for the next lap southwards to Marseilles and on – leaving here at 9.30. Also I rather tremble for my bill – this hotel is the one over the Café de la Paix near the Opera, central and chic – wow! I've enjoyed my sojourn in the gay city and look forward to getting south, where – according to the *Daily Mail* – they are having the finest weather for this time of year. Look after yourself darling.

With all possible love
Olga

[Saturday 14 December 1929; handwritten: PEF/TUF/DA/140]

Hotel Windsor
Monte-Carlo

Saturday 14th
(so I'm told)

Dearest Ma,
Stage 2 safely accomplished. We said goodbye to Uncle B. about 7.30, having drunk the healths of the various expeditions. His noble Xmas present to me was the Paris trip, so I had no need to fear the bill. It was a splendid one.

We eat at the station surrounded by our 'bagages', and found ourselves installed in the train with an Englishwoman, quiet and docile and rather ill, and a Frenchman. Both amenable with regard to windows. Couchettes consist of a place to lie flat on and a pillow, which is quite enough for a train.

No events of importance till Monaco, where my saddle caused the douane considerable anguish. First they said they wouldn't open it, then they decided to, which resulted in much trouble for them because there was no screwdriver. It was quite heating and so disappointing for the tiresome customs man when it really was a saddle and not a machine gun to pot at the Prince.

Hotel here thoroughly English. We have adjoining rooms and have already done a turn in the town.

The shops here far more enticing than Paris. Many pretty things everywhere. I succumbed to a box of preserved violets and rose leaves etc. which looked prettier than anything to be had in town. I thought just what the Dr ordered for Cousin Bertha[13] – it can be from you too if you like.

The town is straight from a musical comedy – palms, faultless grass and gay borders. Lights everywhere high and low and quite a good selection of chorus girls I imagine. Taken in the right spirit it is attractive.

We shall to bed early tonight, tomorrow we lunch in Nice with Mr Slingsby and shall do something in the evening if we feel inclined.

Much love to you all, look after yourself
Best love from us both
<u>Olga</u>

[undated, immediately following Saturday 14 December 1929]

Hotel Windsor
Monte-Carlo

Supplément.

Dearest Ma,
Owing to the unfortunate fact that I put a French stamp on your letter instead of a Monacan, my last epistle could not be sent from here and has been unavoidably delayed.

However here it is and a bit more. Glorious sun <u>all day</u>, our rooms lead right onto the garden and there I spent the early hours till it was time to catch the eleven bus for Nice. We drove along the Little Corniche through all the picture postcard views one knows so well. No flowers to speak of yet except in the unbelievably tidy flower beds. The towns lead one into the other and we soon found ourselves in Nice. The Slingsbys (Ms and 2 charming children) have an airy flat, 8 Rue Palermo, Nice and would take one female paying guest. She is French and the children much more so than English, cooking good and pleasant surroundings, so you needn't fear to recommend it.

Soon after lunch we found another charabanc to take us back via Grande Corniche, much higher in the hills. The vehicle was a more primitive affair, and we stopped to pick up real inhabitants – in fact we were the only foreigners to attempt it. At La Turbie, thanks to Auntie D. who'd done it before, we got out, saw the Roman tower due to Augustus and walked down the Roman road to our hotel. It took us an hour in the fading light, though a full moon shed a bright glow on land and sea. Through the olive groves we saw the many lights below us of the coast but we couldn't devote all our seeing to these delights for the going was bad over genuine Roman cobbles and down flights of rough stone steps. We came down just on top of the hotel, so that we felt like two pebbles which had been carelessly dislodged near the old tower and had kept rolling until prevented by the bulk of our hotel.

We came in to find bridge still going on – I don't think it ever stops here.

Auntie D. says she is not writing while I am sending all the news, but she joins me in messages of 'luv' and goodwill etc.

We expect the boat in tomorrow about 10, so hope to have a flutter in the Casino in the evening.

Hope this missive will reach you without further mishap, special messages to Lady Petrie and Dédé.

Yours ever
<u>Olga</u>

[18 December 1929; handwritten: PEF/TUF/DA/141]

Canadian Pacific Round-the-World Cruise, SS *Empress of Australia*.

Dec. 18th 1929.

Dearest M.
Yesterday was rather an unexpected and successful day. I rang fruitlessly for my breakfast in the morning and was still dressing when Uncle Arthur

burst into the room and said we must be ready in 10 minutes for a day's drive. We were ready and packed in 20 minutes, bill paid and all.

Our host was Count Kinsky;[14] the name sounded familiar and about an hour later I remembered why – the next door neighbours of Dobrenska. I've not divulged the fact to him yet, he is rabidly anti-Czech and as there are many he may not be the Posteyn one, but I shall work round to it!

The day was perfect with a faint haze which means later heat; our two cars were open and we were bound for a hill-top eyrie called Gourdon. Along the Grande Corniche through Nice; then inland towards the Gorge de Loup on a ribbony road, which edges the steep and arid hills. Only olive and some pine trees grow among the gray rocks, small villages dominated by their church spires perch on convenient hills, and here and there a small stream drops surprisingly over 300 ft of cliff.

Le Gorge de Loup is a large cascade which falls into a water-worn hollow, good of its kind. Lunch in a sophisticated restaurant, which has the wit to make itself look rural, and here we were in sight of Gourdon, still seemingly inaccessible 3 or was it 6000 ft above the sea.

Gourdon is the kingdom of an Englishwoman – a Mrs Norris, I think; she is old and satisfied to live in her perfect castle high above the world.

Even here she cannot get complete peace for the Ct [Count] sent in his card and the seven of us invaded her garden. It is all clipped box and cyprusses [cypresses] on stone-edged terraces, looking far out over the hills. A fountain adds to the coolness of the unrelieved green and masses of white doves disperse any suggestion of gloom.

Inside the rooms are floored with black marble or in the hall, red stone, the dining room and all the others too are 'in keeping' as everyone said very loudly, there were pots of pink cyclamen on old oak tables and massive fire-irons in the stone-mantled hearths.

A place to end one's days in gracefully. On through Grasse and then down to the sea, where we had tea at the Carlton Hotel, Cannes. Another musical comedy place with a pink sugar sunset against the dark silhouettes of palm trees.

Back to Monte at no mean pace along the Petite Corniche, after a hectic interval at the Galeries Lafayette at Nice, where I bought a bathing dress.

Dinner on board hastily, for the others were going to the Casino. I abandoned the idea as I'd had a long day on top of the usual nuisance. I shall, at any rate, be spry for Athens.

I've a good cabin on D deck, but it was slightly damp this morning about 6.30, the sea came in and I woke up to find my porthole spinning round like a threepenny bit. However we cleared up the mess and no harm done. Auntie D. taking it quietly this morning.

Later.
She got up for lunch, we've spent the whole day out. Plans for Naples tomorrow nebulous, but will post this early and write again later. I am headed for Herculaneum whatever the others do.

Love to all,
Olga

[21–22 December 1929; handwritten: PEF/TUF/DA/143]

Canadian Pacific – SS *Empress of Australia*.
Dec. 21.
1929

Dearest Ma and Daddy,
Tomorrow I get off this ship and find myself at the mercy of the Athenians. The journey has been very pleasant and warm, and I am just beginning to enjoy deck tennis and so on. On the other hand I am jolly glad that I'm not going on all the way.

Dec. 22.
Am writing from the Hotel d'Angleterre and have your letters of 11th and 15th, but will go on from where I left off.

Our expedition to Pompeii on the 1st day was disastrous – I think I told you that we were all taken there in a special train and that the gates were shut and no amount of telephoning to Naples could get them open again! So after a wait of 2 hrs we went back to the ship, and had to sally forth again the next morning, but the cruise took care to do us well in a special car, so that we were able to see Herculaneum as well.

You had my impressions of Pompeii last year and I've nothing special to add to them. Herculaneum is far more fascinating as the work is still going on and they are doing it very carefully.

Here they work in hard lava and use pneumatic drills like they do on the roads in England. The wooden roofing beams, though charred, can be seen in the scarp and they are preserved and cased in glass, so that one can still walk up the wooden staircases to the upper floors and see the wooden beds and cupboards with all the contents in position inside.

The houses are all half-timbered with an overhanging 1st story; there is in most cases a small courtyard with a well and you can picture the whole thing if you imagine an old English Tudor cottage. In some cases four stories are preserved and latticed windows still remain. Uncle Arthur was thrilled and is becoming a keen archaeologist and has borrowed *Egypt and Israel*[15] to read.

In the afternoon Auntie D. and I wandered in the town and tried to buy a piece of coral for ol' Giles. At one shop near the port they wanted to charge L 250 [lira] for a small piece. She walked out saying in Italian 'Do you take me for an imbecile?' Later at another place we were offered a better piece for L 40 and on our way back to the ship the original man swooped on us from his lair and we ultimately bought the piece we had first seen for the rather different sum of L 25. The man said (to propitiate us) that he was sorry he had asked such a large sum but he thought we were English or American!

The next two days on board were pleasant and warm, except for one small interval near the Straights [sic] of Messina, which was well worth it.

We were watching the dark and ominous clouds to the S.W. as we glided on a calm sea through the Straights. On shore Reggio was lighting its battery of twinkling lights and Scylla and Charabdis [Charybdis] seemed mere legends. Then the clouds were torn with flashes of forked lightning, though no thunder came our way. It was then that we saw a strange turbulence on the water, a greyish patch which rose up and became like those gossamer sea anemones with their moving tentacles. It became larger and nearer and a grey funnel rose from it to meet another grey wisp from the sky. The ends joined, they became one and dissolved suddenly in a whirl of spray like a pack of cards. We had seen a water-spout and a good one, so that the Straights had lived up to their reputation for strange wonders.

[23 December 1929; handwritten: PEF/TUF/DA/144]

Grand Hotel d'Angleterre
C. Tchomos Directeur – Propriétaire
Athenes, le 23rd Dec. 1929

Dearest Mà

Two letters of 16th and 18th to hand – very many thanks for them. Am established on 4th floor here in a room 210 drachma a day – half pension – about 10/6 with a good view of the Acropolis thrown in.

As I told you the aunt and uncle cut short their sightseeing trip and went back to the ship about 3 yesterday. It was too bad that everyone got so soaked in the morning – all bad staff work, I fear. Of course as soon as they left the weather cleared up and the evening was brilliantly sunny.

I went to tea with the Petrochino family and walked there according to the map all by myself. They are just about the sort of people for me – very keen on everything and speak perfect English. Admiral Panas who lives next door was there – and who should walk in but Mr Payne[16] of the B.S. [British School at Athens] so plans for nearly my whole stay are settled already.

Their house is large – well, and what is more, sparsely furnished except in the matter of books. Many English publications – *Times* – *Ill. Lond.* [*Illustrated London*] *News* etc. and French ones as well. She reminds slightly of Mrs Bruce – the same efficiency and boundless good nature, he adds to these virtues a great love of the arts. They have a family and friends who are constantly popping in and out and ringing up and people turn up to meals just as they like.

This morning at ten Mr P. called for me and we spent a morning in the Mus[eum]. As Museums go it is small, so that there is some chance of seeing things properly. Statuary, pottery and the Mycenaean things are the three specialities. Brought up on the statues of Egypt, I find much to admire and deplore in Greek work. The earliest of all obviously owe much to Egyptian influence, but to my mind their finest things are those of the second period, when their own instincts were being followed and before they had acquired that facility of expression which is usually considered their best period.

There is a lovely funerary relief of a warrior – according to legend the one who brought the news of the victory at Marathon and then fell dead.[17] There are some fine heads in the round, but on the whole I prefer their reliefs among the earlier ones, there is such feeling of line. Perhaps my choice of a chef d'oeuvre is a damaged statue of a disk thrower – perhaps – crouching ready to spring.

Mycenaean things full of interest – both for themselves and for their Egyptian connections. But these I must see again.

I had lunch – and a very good one too – with the P's, Mr Sloman who has a school at Spezia was there – a nice mild Oxfordy sort of man and in the middle of the meal a fascinating Greek turned up and managed to get through the courses he had missed while getting through much talk as well. When I say fascinating, he is certainly not an Adonis, looking rather like this:

Figure 4.1 Ink sketch by Olga Tufnell. Greek professor encountered in Athens, from letter of 23 December 1929. Courtesy of the Palestine Exploration Fund.

a very animated he-goat, too sweet, with a booming voice though small and a very learned Professor to boot, though this last fact is not obtrusive. He knew all about F.P. [Flinders Petrie].

After the meal, Mrs P. and I went out and I found myself wrapping up parcels for a children's Xmas party in a crèche. Quite amusing to see all the same philanthropic work and the same bickerings going on so far away. Tea with Mrs P. in a quiet tea shop and now letters – dinner and bed. When you get back to QP [Queensbury Place, London] you will find in my MS Drawer in Office, 3rd on right, my famous synopses, which I forgot to bring, also if you can find me a large pair of wooden calipers like this I should be much obliged. Enclosed is the warrant.

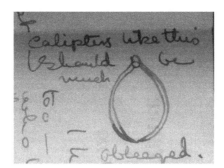

Figure 4.2 Ink sketch by Olga Tufnell. Wooden caliper for pottery illustration. From letter of 23 December 1929. Courtesy of the Palestine Exploration Fund.

All my love dearest to you and Daddy.
Ever yours
Olga

[Working notes and records; undated, composed in Cyprus; typed:
PEF/TUF/DA/2754]

Olgaedeker's Short Guide to Athens

First published
Dec. 1929.

Informations

Currency:	very dirty 373 drachmas – £1. 18 ½ " – 1/–
Arrival:	If by steamer to Piraeus or Phaleron. The latter mud nothing, but mud if wet, Piraeus easy, both entail taxi to Athens 5kms. Costing at least 60 drs. [drachmas].
Hodels:[18]	Luxe – Petit Palais – prices fabulous 1st. class – Hotel Grande Bretagne – prices preposterous £1 a night and no eat. Gay.
X	Family – Hodel D'Angleterre – prices possible, position central, Place Concordia. 1 sing. bdrm 210 drs. a day, ½ pension, e.g. dinner or lunch and breakfast. bth. Service gd especially in the matter of shutting windows. Food decent. They 'spik of de Eenglish'.
Sightseeing:	The visitor arriving at 'the purple-crowned city' of Athens, should make an early visit to the summit of Mt Lycabetos. He can reach it on his feet from near the Royal Palace (that was) and will ascend many steps that wind up the side through olive groves. He will be well rewarded when he reaches the view-point under the shadow of the small church. He will perceive a beacon, placed there on the occasion of a recent peace conference in the hope that it would inspire the delegates. Unfortunately it did not, and remains as an object of derision to Athenians.

Spread below a magnificent panoramic view of the city is obtained, and the visitor should not fail to identify such outstanding features as the Acropolis, which should not be confused with the American Library.

[in pencil]   X recommended

Restaurants: Informations on this point leave something to be desired. There are English Tea Rooms on the same side as Hotel d'Angleterre on Place Concordia, patronised chiefly by Greeks. They say light lunches there are good.

Other establishments not personally inspected by the author are: Pantheon.

Other hotels not personally inspected are: Hermes, Alexandre le Grand, Mykenae and Apollon. All v. cheap.

Remarks: British School at Athens, at foot of Mt Lycabetos, has a hostel, where, if rooms are vacant, you can be housed 6/– a night, no meals. I told the Director Mr Payne that you were perhaps coming, and he will be on the look out, he knows some friends of W.G.s.

Taxis: The visitor should never feel virtuous when abstaining from a taxi, as a means of locomotion, as they are extremely cheap. The meter starts at 7 drs. and the cars are luxuriously fitted and indistinguishable from private vehicles.

Important
Intending visitors to Cyprus.

Should come if they can. £7 second class Lloyd Triestino from Piraeus. 3 days trip. Accommodation here primitive but possible, and everyone very willing and cheerful. A hearty welcome will be extended to Mr and Mrs C. at the Palace Hotel, Nicosia, which has the honour and privilige [sic] of housing the author of these Hints.

[24–25 December 1929; handwritten: PEF/TUF/DA/145]

Grand Hotel D'Angleterre
C. Tchomos Directeur-Propriétaire
Athenes, le 24 décembre 1929
and Xmas Eve, by Jove!

Dearest Family,

I expect you will all be together at this festive season and hope you will not have returned to your respective occupations by the time this reaches you.

I've spent a very pleasant day. I found a note here last night from Mr Payne, saying would I lunch instead of going there at 10.30, and offering to take me to the country afterwards. This I couldn't do as I was booked to go with the Panas. Owing to the new arrangement I had the morning to myself and explored the main streets, the cathedral, new but pleasantly Byzantine inside, and the old tiny[?] Byzantine churches which remain, much below street level, like rather precious carved boxes. One near the Cathedral was empty, but the other contained among other things a genial priest, who thought I had come for my Xmas present of a new pair of boots or so many yds [yards] of calico. When he discovered his mistake, he detailed a young girl who spoke a minute quantity of French to show me round, but I was not much wiser when she had finished her explanations. However we all smiled a lot and I put something in the poor box so all was well.

Then after consulting the map I walked straight to the B.S. and had a very nice tête-à-tête lunch with Mr Payne in his barrack of a house. There are two, one for him and one for his students and they must cost a pretty penny to maintain. We talked shop solidly and he knows lots of people that I do. I go there tomorrow morning to see some rather exciting books and hope to send some notes to F.P. about the Fara tombs, which will however probably be sending coals to Newcastle. One can but try.

Soon after two, I went to the Panas' and we went off in their car to Daphnae, stopping at the old cem. [cemetery] on the way. Many new houses are going up on the outskirts to accommodate the million refugees from Asia Minor and the Turks. When you realise that the pop. of the whole country is only 6–7 million, it is possible to see what a strain such an influx is. When they came they were literally without food or clothes, and in England we have hardly heard of it and know nothing of the consequences.[19]

Daphnae is a Byzantine church and monastery now deserted in a picturesque hollow of the pine-clad hills. Two tall cyprusses [cypresses] mount guard on each side of the church door and inside are mosaics of the usual subjects, much damaged by white wash and the Turks.

Then shopping in the town and a rather Xmasy tea at their house. They have a nice son about 14 and Mrs Panas is a tall dark good-looking woman. Then back to dinner here and now bed.

With best love to all
from
Olga

Xmas Day

As there was no post out today I kept this letter back to add the doings of the day which has been very good, despite bad weather. First thing I sallied forth and invested in two large bunches of flowers for my two hostesses, white roses for Mrs Petrocochino and stocks and anemones for Mrs Panas. When these were duly delivered I went to the B.S. and spent the morning looking at books and trying to trace the whereabouts of some things. All rather full of possibilities.

Then a Xmas lunch complete with turkey and plum pudding, both very good though the turkey's legs stuck straight up in the air! Then we tried to conquer the usual after dinner feeling by solving English x word [crossword] puzzles, the son is amazingly good at them and the whole family's English is more than ordinarily good. Then we decided as late as 4.30 to brave the elements and climb Mt Licabetos [Lycabetos] which we did and were well rewarded. Great banks of clouds had been sweeping from the north and crowning Mt Hymettus all day long, but as we reached the top of Licabetos where a small church is the clouds to the south-west broke and the hills of the Peloponesus were turned to gold by the setting sun. The Acropolis stood out black against this colour, but the houses to the north of us were touched by the belated sunlight. Wet and shining roads stretched north to Marathon 45 kms away and we could see the island of Aegina and many smaller ones in the now calm sea beyond Piraeus. When we came back we had deserved our tea and now bath, dinner and bed as usual. The meal here does not begin till 8.30 and the majority don't come down till an hour later.

Again, au revoir and much love
Olga

[28 December 1929; handwritten: PEF/TUF/DA/146]

SS *Celio*.
Dec. 28. 1929.

Dearest Ma,

I sent you a hurried p.c. [postcard] to say I had left Athens and now I'll add some details of my last day there.

On the 26th I went with Admiral P. [Panas] and son to Acropolis in the morning. Weather perfect, with a good north wind blowing, which is just right for Athens. I don't suppose I have anything to add to my first enthusiastic impressions 2 years ago. Those honey-coloured inspirations remain the same – nothing to match them in the world. A scheme is on foot to pull down the old Turkish houses to the N of the Acropolis and excavate under them, but in a way it seems a pity. Then lunch at the hotel and later in the afternoon we drove out to the smart suburb to tea, in a teashop kept by a family of 13, 8 girls and 5 boys. I'm sure people just go there to see them, it is the fashionable thing to do.

Dinner at nine at the Petrocochino's. An amusing meal and plenty of talk. Panas walked home with me and that was the last I saw of them. In the morning I met Mr Payne at the Museum at 10 and we went round solidly till one. He is Director over a much older man and must be brilliant. He is fair, very lanky and may suffer slightly from an inferiority complex. His wife comes out next month, and I can go and stay at the School hostel on my way back, which would be pleasanter than a hotel.

He lunched with me and we talked shop and scandal of a mild sort, as he knows all the same sort of old birds. Exchanged a few legends; he is an Evans [Sir Arthur][20] protégé.

When he went at two, I finished packing, paid my bill, got through the avenue of outstretched hands and drove to Piraeus with the hotel interpreter. It was as well that I had him, as various portions of luggage had to be collected from strange places, and the whole process occupied nearly 3 hrs. The boat was late in, but [I] was aboard about 6.

Have a Cypriot lady in my cabin, which is otherwise all right. Have been on deck all day, there are few people in First Class, but include a rather disagreeable-looking English couple, bound for Cyprus – wonder if I shall come across them!

Have arrived at Nicosia after my usual good luck and adventures. Found a Mr and Mrs Grant at Limassol on landing. He has come here to take charge of the Turkish School. We shared a car to Nicosia and am staying for the present at the Palace Hotel, only a few doors from the

George. The latter is full and swear they never had my letter which I take with a pinch of salt. They are very willing and pleasant here and lunch was quite decent. The rooms are rather barracks and bare and will need quite a lot doing to them to make them habitable. The Grants are a cheery couple who seem very pleased with life. I have a large balcony with some large cypress trees included in the view. I don't know about prices, but they seem quite enough for what one gets.

[31 December 1929; typed original: PEF/TUF/DA/147]

Palace Hotel,
Nicosia
Cyprus.
Dec. 31st.

Dearest Ma,

[…] I told you that the Grants seeing me look rather lonely in the customs, took me in their car (I having bargained for a seat for 6/– with the driver previously). So that they paid less for their car and I had the pleasure of their company. The drive to Nicosia takes about 3 hrs and is through barren hills, which wind into the distance and end in a blue, high range, where Kyrenia lies, on the horizon. […]

They were inclined to be haughty at the George, and anyhow had no rooms at the moment, so I came on here, and have made an arrangement with the owner for 8/– a day, which is none too cheap, as the accommodation is fairly primitive. They are building two bathrooms. My room faces north, but I shall have another which gets the morning sun soon. Anyhow they seem very willing here and anxious to please, which cannot be said of the George. […]

I had a bit of a stroll in the town by myself yesterday afternoon and this morning, as he was out on business, we went there again. It is full of possibilities and there is any amount to be learnt of primitive arts and crafts. There are little booths, where everything is made on the premises, brass founders, bakeries, turners, carpet makers, carpenters of all kinds, a silversmiths and many others, which I have not identified yet. All too fascinating and I hope to take a series of photographs of all the different types and processes.

After lunch I wandered round to the Museum (only a few doors off) and saw Mr Markides.[21] He is very much worse than when I saw him two yrs ago, and finds great difficulty in talking now. It is another form of

Figure 4.3 Unidentified street, Cyprus. Written on back: 'Baskets and brooms for sale. In the foreground an itinerant pastry-cook.' Olga Tufnell archive, Palestine Exploration Fund. Courtesy of the Palestine Exploration Fund.

that awful paralysis. Then I saw Mr Gunnis,[22] who was arranging things in a case.

As usual, that strange place, the world, has proved to be very small. He knew Gilbert[23] very well and sat next to him in the same form. Like Roger, all those school days are now very vague to him, since the war.

He seems pretty mad about archaeology and we went off in his car to see a cemetery site, as he thought the tombs there might be the sort I am looking out for. His man found a good cylinder in the rubbish, and I came away with an interesting set of sherds. I shall make a type collection for anyone who wants it in London. The tombs were all dug out and robbed about sixty years ago. I was deposited in the hotel, and he told the manager I was to [be] specially looked after and given a good room, or he would loose [sic] the patronage of Govt. Ho [Government House].

The net result is that I can have the run of the Mus., have any pots out I like to draw, make a Corpus, which they will arrange to publish, dig anywhere I like (tell it not in Gath, and anyhow I should not avail myself of this the first year).

I shall get some experience se[e]ing what the Swedes do and learn my pottery thoroughly, while drawing. There is a very nice courtyard inside the building, and I shall hope to set up shop there in the air.

So far, the weather has been perfect, today just lovely, and the people here seem to think that for the present it will continue.

Anyhow I feel that the new year is going to start off well, and that I shall be able to get some good work done under pleasant conditions. I am just getting a bath arranged, in my room, a tin communal affair – and a can of water.

I am posting my letters of introduction, with the exception of the Storrs one; he is away for a bit. Think I shall have plenty to do without much social life, though there is plenty on the island. It is of the tea-party, bridge cum dance-at-the-club variety. Shall look forward to getting a mail on Thursday, though this must be posted before the letters come in. Much love and all good wishes to everyone.

<u>Olga</u>

[5 January 1930; typed original: PEF/TUF/DA/149]

Palace Hotel,
Nicosia,
Cyprus.
Jan. 5th., 1930.

Dearest Ma,
[…] Things have gone very well for me here. They are most kind in the Museum and I shall be able to get more books than I expected. The next person I must see is the Swedish man, he seems to be the real expert here, and I think he may suggest a more useful job than the Corpus, which seems to be done here with good photographs. Anyhow we will see. To turn to more mundane matters, there is a good and amusing hairdresser in the town, and apparently such strange things as sufficiently respectable night-clubs exist – who would have thought it. So far I have spent most afternoons at the Mus. Yesterday morning, by appointment, I went and did my song and dance at Govt. Ho., which simply consisted in writing in the book, and sucking bulls eyes with Gunnis in his office afterwards. He is rather a mixture of Roger Hinks and Oliver Myers, has a good library of books on Cyprus, and seems very energetic in connection with the preservation of anticas in the town.

In the afternoon, we did some sightseeing in the town, under difficulties, the rain he rained and has been coming down all night, and I think I hear it starting again now. St Sofia, the mosque that is, and the Lusignan cathedral that was, is a fine building in the French style. We put on shoes and shuffled through the mosque onto the bright carpets, all oriented towards Mecca. The Grand Mufti[24] was reading the Koran to a select assembly of the elect. He is small and withered, with a soft white beard, which was lit up by the light of the window behind him. His listeners could not resist turning round to look at the interlopers, so that we saw that after all they were not carved images.

The little Greek church is crowded with early icons and is a friendly place compared with the Mosque. The two priests were evidently friends of Gunnis, in fact, he seems to know everyone in the town, from merchant to beggar. He makes a practice of it, and he certainly has not got the superior Eton manner. [...]

[7 January 1930; handwritten: PEF/TUF/DA/150]

Palace Hotel
Nicosia
Cyprus
Jan. 7. 1930.

Darling Daddy,
Just now I am sitting out in the sun and we've had several days of good blue-sky weather with three or four real bad ones in between. As long as they are nicely sandwiched it will be very pleasant. You can pick your own oranges and tangerines off the trees here, and narcissi are being sold in the streets.

Everyone is kind and pleasant and I have actually had some callers. I am negotiating about a pony, but so far nothing is settled. The Museum people are very helpful and the assistant there gave me my first Greek lesson last night. It is <u>horribly</u> difficult and it's awful tackling yet another alphabet. [B]ut somehow it seems silly to be here some months and not know a word.

The people in the hotel are nearly all Civil Servants and family, this is not the 'chick' [chic] place, the 'George Hotel' a few doors off has more white paint on the outside and a fatter proprietor. Otherwise I don't think there is much to choose between them. The food here is good, the other night we had partridge (homegrown) for dinner, I was wondering if they have any pheasants; if so perhaps you would like to come and buy and shoot here! […]

I suppose the birds are now in residence and require their table de hote dinner served to them daily, hope they will do you proud this spring and reward you with plenty of eggs. […]

[11 January 1930; typed original: PEF/TUF/DA/151]

Palace Hotel,
Nicosia,
Cyprus.
Jan.11.1930.

Dearest Ma,
[…] I've been having a very pleasant time, since Monday the weather has been ideal, but today there are signs of a change. Have been out all day, even when working in the Mus., where I have my table in the courtyard. Mr Gjerstad[25] met me there last Tuesday, by appointment, and pointed out some pots, which it would be good to do in colour, so I am going to try my hand at them. Funnily enough, Sir Ronald [Storrs] at tea today suggested the same thing, as being a good job, so if I am successful, I shall have official support in publication. Don't talk about it to everyone, as I may not bring it off.

Then I had my first Greek lesson, which is very difficult, and I don't expect I shall ever get very far, I want to know enough to talk to maids, and cab drivers, who are the only people in this place who don't know English.

I was given an introduction by the Agricultural Dept. head, who lives in the hotel and is a nice solid Scotsman, with a nice solid wife, to the Vetinary [Veterinary] Surgeon here, who would be most likely to know of a pony. I called and he said he would let me know. In a day or two I had a message to say he had heard of something, and then he invited me to lunch to see the stud farm at Athalassa. Name of Roe, car a Hillman, Irish from Tipperary and with a love of horses and animals in general which is more than in keeping with the tradition of his race. […]

As usual in a bachelor establishment everything was very well arranged and comfortable, with good food at a moment's notice, and a wonderful log fire such as I have not seen since I left home. In the afternoon he took me to a village some 10 miles away, where he had business. There I had my first taste of Cypriote hospitality. Luckily he was a good prompter and talks the language well. We visited a farm, where the living apartments consisted of one room. Very clean and contained two large beds at opposite ends of the room, standing against the clean whitewashed wall. There was besides a cupboard and some chairs; we occupied two each, the extra one being for our feet. The hostess put on her best dress in the background and we were brought the regulation refreshments, which were kept in the cupboard. On a tray there were four glasses of water, with a cake such as you see at Gunter's[26] perched on top. In a saucer were four luscious preserved figs running with juice as well as a plate of turkish delight. According to instructions, I speared the fig on the fork, succeeded in getting it whole into my mouth, and then took a sip of water to wash it down. This was the unpleasant part, as it had a grey milky look, but I was assured that it was harmless.

The women were making lace – here it is done on a flat cushion with a needle and cotton, rather like endless buttonhole stitch; it goes very quickly and they sell to tourists at good prices. They were just the same unsophisticated folk as the Bedawy [Bedouin], and made us welcome without a trace of shyness or self-consciousness. On the way back, we climbed to the top of a hill to see the castle of L------------- [(L)"EONTARI VOUNO" added in pencil; Leondari-Vouno], the name I must get later, built some 1000 years BC.[27] The sun was just setting and a chill wind sent us down sooner than I liked. Four or five stone-cut cisterns were new to me, and one of them is roofed over and still in use.

As Mr Roe had to go to Farmagusta [Famagusta], where the possible pony lived, he arranged to take me the very next day, while the weather lasted. It did and we drove there by way of Larnaca (some 52 miles) under a very blue sky. But when we reached the coast the sea was bluer, almost unbelievably so, when one remembers with a shock that we are still in the middle of Jan.

Farmagusta [sic] is surrounded with a forest of windmills, the modern kind, like Cousin Lionel's at the bungalow. They draw water for the gardens and orange groves that spring up round the town, from a distance all there is to see are these spectral mills and the skeletons of the many mediaeval churches, which once adorned the town. After lunch at the English club, we went to an orange grove – the first close-up I've had of oranges and lemons and tangerines, growing by the thousand. I can't give you an idea of the colour or the quantity, it is awful to think that this year 'there is no demand' and much of the fruit may be wasted, when it would do so much good in the slums of the world. Prices range between 16/– and £2 per 1000, and the Palestine growers are so strong that the Cypriote people can't get their stuff shipped.

Various jobs were done after lunch and suddenly we arrived at the police station, and to my amazement, soon after I found I had bought a pony for the sum of nine pounds. It seems the best thing to do, if I am going to ride more than 15 days a month, and I shall be able to sell him when I leave at a very small loss. Food, stabling and groom to bring him to and from hotel will be £2:5:0 [£2 5s.] a month. Hiring is 3/– for the regulation two hours, so a long trip would always be more expensive.

Woolly, as I shall call him, is twelve and has been in the police force some years, he ambles rather than trots and has a good mouth, he is very amiable and I'm sure we shall get on well. He arrives on the 15th, my kit has come from Palestine, so all is well.

The walls of Farmagusta [sic – Famagusta], which go right down to the sea, enclose a few deserted churches, part of the modern town, and

Figure 4.4 Olga on horseback, Cyprus. Olga Tufnell archive, Palestine Exploration Fund. Courtesy of the Palestine Exploration Fund.

no less a thing than a golf-course, due to the ingenuity of the English inhabitants. [...]

This morning, as I had played truant for 2 days, finished the job I've been doing for Mr Payne at the Mus. During the afternoon, a note comes from Gunnis 'Lady Storrs would be so pleased etc.' for tea today, so I duly repaired thither at the appointed hour, rather unhappily clutching my right-hand glove which had split. I was shown into a long room, with many windows and chintz-covered furniture; all the new books about. Gunnis came and talked, followed almost at once by Lady Storrs. The usual passport worked at once, and all I had to do was recite the movements, ailments and illnesses of the following, whom she knew [Olga lists various relations ...]. Then it all had to [be] repeated when Sir Ronald came in, plus Petrie family, and traditional legends to the fore as usual.

She is nice, her unpopularity may be due to shyness, she has a touch of Lady Tudor about her. She was charming to me, thinks I ought not to stay at the Palace, and will look out for a really suitable family for me, I said it depended on the family. He is beefy and has small eyes, am not very attracted, but must give him his due, he offered me the run of his library and I can have all the books I want, came back with two, and can change them when I like for more. That is really decent. Was brought back here and now to bed, feeling that I've had a good week, and that everyone is being very friendly and kind. Major Baker (not Richard [St Barbe Baker]!) called here and at the Mus. yesterday to ask me to join in the mounted police sports, tent-pegging etc. Have you heard anything so comic? Though I have made no secret all along that I am potatoeish on a horse and that I wanted something docile to ride, perhaps I shall soon be performing in the local Rodeo, who knows?

A quiet Sunday, drawing in the morning and reading of my borrowed books, *Elephants and Flowers* by a Constance Sitwell, pleasant though slightly precious snatches of India. The other is the *Cradle of God*,[28] which you saw reviewed. So far it is a spirited resume of Bible history, largely composed of suitable quotations strung together aptly. The more I think about it, the less necessary a book on the contemplated lines seem; have not written to Harris [Colt] yet, but feel that a sketch of nomad life and their attitude to the outside world would be more to the point and less hackneyed.

Went to the football match of the year this afternoon – all Cyprus versus the Turkish Lycee, of course Mr Grant had to put in an appearance so I went too. They played a good clean game, altogether very sporting, it was the audience which had not got the spirit of the game, there was hardly any shouting or applause, which is to me far more thrilling than the actual play. [...]

Wednesday: Three quiet sunny days, have painted one pot at the Mus. and finished the drawings for Mr. Payne. Now today the pony has arrived from Farmagusta [sic] and after being groomed down at the Vet's is going to his stable in the town. He looked a little tired, so I shall have a short ride tomorrow.

I have changed my room at the hotel for a better one looking on to the same verandah, the other was dark and rather near the sanitary arrangements, such as they are. There is a nook where I can sleep out, and shall start the first warm night. [...] Contemplate buying a few coloured cloths, native ware to enliven my room, they would always come in useful at home.

Later: my room looks quite cheerful now, with red and yellow cloths and my shawl on the bed. [...]

Much love from
Olga [signed in pencil]

[22 January 1930; typed original: PEF/TUF/DA/152]

Palace Hotel,
Nicosia.
Cyprus.
Jan. 22. 1930.

Dearest Ma,
Many thanks for yours of the 4th and for enclosures. Before I forget it, would you send me some visiting cards, just a few. [...] The callipers are just what I wanted and have already been put to good use. [...]

There is little exciting news this week. I have been riding daily in the mornings and am getting on well, yesterday the pony had quite recovered from his journey and was skit[t]ish, luckily he was quiet the first few days and now I feel more capable of tackling him. We go out into the country and I am gradually learning my way about. I had tea with the Du Platt [Plat] Taylor[29] Ma and Pa at the George on Sunday to meet a Miss McLaughlin who rides and we are to go out together on Wed. I fancy she is rather hot stuff and trains racers. If it had been fine today I should have gone to the local Rodeo which everyone attends and learns tentpegging and so on, [...] but it had been put off owing to rain. I think this is the first solid bad day we've had.

On Saturday I went to Athalassa again with Mr Roe and after lunch we did a five-mile walk and saw the farm. They seem very keen on good stock, cows, pigs, horses and donkeys. All the work is done by prisoners on probation, mostly boys of 16–18, and they live in a good airy building and have the best garden I have seen out here. Sweet peas and carnations growing out of doors in January, yet none of the Europeans seem to trouble to grow them. […]

Apparently the great social function here is the SALE. There is always a general post of houses going on, and everyone attends each sale where the accumulated rubbish of fifteen or twenty years fetches tremendous prices. The cult of the old is raging, and empty sardine tins fetch a shilling each. […]

Wed.

Enjoyed my ride with Miss McLaughlin who is a nice girl, and has not been riding so long after all. She came off once, but may be my turn tomorrow! […]

[26 January 1930; typed original: PEF/TUF/DA/153]

Palace Hotel,
Nicosia,
Cyprus.
Jan. 26.

Dearest Ma,
[…] Another motor trip yesterday to Kyrenia. Miss McL. [McLaughlin] and I were just coming back from our usual ride, when we were met at the crossroads by Mr Roe, who had already tried to collect me from the Palace. He said 'I've got to be in Kyrenia in half an hour, come as you are, or not at all', so we leapt off our horses and drove off at a steady fifty. The foothills before the northern range, are bare eerie hills, which have been folded in some far-off cataclysm, so that the strata are vertical, and between each ridge of rock the peasants plough and hope for a meagre crop. As we got up the pass, we came to olive trees, with grass growing and the first anemones in bloom. […]

Kyrenia might be anywhere in Italy or even Cornwall; the harbour is tiny and surrounded by straight grey houses; the castle built in the same period as the Farmagusta [sic] one, is almost in the sea, a sleepy, peaceful place. While waiting for Mr Roe we picked anemones and crocuses, both growing on the rocks and almost watered by sea-spray.

Lunch in the Hotel, which is the best in the island accordi[ng] to report. Then on to the Bel Paese [Bellapais] monastery,[30] one of those fine ruins in perfect surroundings of trees and grass and streams, which would be so much [more] appealing if they were peopled with monks or nuns. As it is, the great refectory, with an immense view along the coast, houses nothing more human than a few bats, the oranges that grow in the cloisters are eaten by the gatekeepers' children and the great marble washing trough has run dry. So much wasted on a few tourists and picnic parties, who can think of no better way of spending their time than by scribbling on the walls.

Home across the same pass where we stopped to pick anemones. On our way we attempted to call on Mr Campbell, and took the car up a long and muddy track which cost him £300 to build. His bungalow had that deserted air and when someone came we heard that he was in Limassol, presumably with the Boyles, who are having a law case with the Buchanans, so I shall be between the Devil and the deep sea, when I stay with the latter.

Saturday I was called for to go somewhere near Limassol before I had finished my breakfast, so that as I had several things to do, I stayed at home and went for a good ride. In fact I have ridden every day except one since I've had Woolly.

Sunday was my birthday and what should I get but a characteristic wire from Tit [Tuffy],[31] as follows 'Many happy returns. Cannot afford more. Writing. Tuffy.' […]

Today, Tuesday, has been most eventful and amusing. Was at the Mus. from 10 to 1, changed afterwards and was ready when Woolly arrived all spick and span for the Rodeo. Arrived there with Miss McL. to see masses of police charging about all over the place and waving spears and swords and polo sticks. Made us two feel rather small and nervous. However we trotted round and I did the bending, that is riding round and in between sticks. Then Mr Roe after some magnificent charging on his own horse, insisted on seeing what Woolly could do in the tent-pegging line. It was sweet to see the fat little thing galloping like a charger, and Mr Roe could almost pick the peg up in the hand. Later we had a lesson on a bit of waste ground, and we both learnt some useful things, it's surprising how much one can do wrong! Major Baker is rather a strange card, after walking round the town all the week in riding breeches and almost clanking spurs (I won't swear to the spurs) and talking horses all the time, on the Rodeo day when he has his chance, he appears in mufti.

Some worthy and eminently county people from Scotland arrived yesterday, a mother and two daughters called Murray-Stuart. They will be a useful accession to me. [...] Both the girls ride, and are buying horses, and from their hearty look, I'm sure they are very expert, they ride bareback in Scotland all the year round and so on. [...]

All my love, dearest, and to Uncle Bertie, you do send these on to Daddy don't you, they are meant for him too. [...]

[4 February 1930; handwritten: PEF/TUF/DA/154]

Palace Hotel
Nicosia
Cyprus.
Feb. 4

Darling –

[...] Lunch at the Col. Sec's [Colonial Secretary's] last Wed. went off all right. They have a charming house with decent garden and a large room for dancing. In the evening I dined with Miss Lyall and Dr Gosden at the Chief Justice's house where they are p.gs [paying guests]. V. charmingly furnished – in fact nearly all the houses I've seen have been. That was my only evening out since I've been here – which is good.

Friday uneventful, on Sat. morning had an appointment with Gjerstad at the Mus. to look at my things. I know now what sort of work he wants and think I shall be able to do it. He asked me then if I would like to go with him to Vouni[32] on Monday and needless to say I accepted with alacrity.

On Sunday it was arranged that the Grants and I should lunch at Athalassa; we were fetched before one and spent a cheery afternoon there. It is the Richmond Park of Nicosia where the élite drive round on Sundays in their cars and Dr Roe's house stands aloof on a small hill, but gets the benefit of the trees, chiefly wattle and pine, the former will be golden next month and the crops round there are emerald green and beyond one can see the purple ranges of Kyrenia and Troodos as a perfect background. The bungalow is white and low and bougainvillaea and poinsettia grow there. [...]

The red-letter day this week was of course Monday. At 8.30 am I was booted and spurred and met Mr G. [Gjerstad] outside the Swedish house, five doors from the Hotel. We started at once and had gone some way before I realised that we were in a cavalcade of 3 cars containing many of the celebrities of the town. Mr Daw, director of Agriculture,

Mr Ussher who I told you about he and his wife are in the next room in the hotel, Mr Jones manager of the Ottoman Bank, a Mr Turnbull, Mr Markides, Curator of the Mus., various hangers-on and satellites and bringing up the rear Mr Gjerstad and myself. Vouni is some 90 miles away on a hill overlooking the seat at Morphou Bay. We crossed the plain – squares of newly-ploughed rich red earth alternated with squares of jade or emerald green where the earlier crops were coming on. We passed through muddy villages and saw in front of us the sea. [...]

At Morphou we stopped for a few minutes. It is where they ship copper ore to the world and oranges. There are ramshackle tin huts and a factory chimney or two, it is dirty, the children are dirty and there is that squalid atmosphere of trade. We left it behind us and came to Soli. Under the cornfields are houses and a market place, a palace and a temple and down by the sea there are clear traces of a harbour. Above is a theatre, the only ancient one found in the island and this Mr G. excavated in 1927. It has no special peculiarities; like so many of its kind its position is the most striking thing about it. It is stripped of its marble and stone, as recently as 1916 the Public Wks Dept had much carried away to build a new bridge. Then up through a fertile valley on a winding road towards Vouni. We left the cars a mile or so away and walked up the steep part. Below us was the sea, with promontories and rocks for all the world like the Cornish coast.

The Palace came as a surprise when we reached the top, as it sloped down slightly towards the sea. Little more than a ground plan is left now of what was once a magnificent pleasure palace of 500 yrs BC. The lower courses were of stone, the upper courses were of mudbrick and have perished. One can trace courtyards and colonnades, there are 2 large cisterns and there was a system of central heating by steam. Then the view – to the right the great curve of Morphou Bay – to the left a jagged coastline and inland green hills and valleys topped by the snow-capped peaks of Troodos.

Some of the party were only mildly interested and left soon, but Mr Markides, Mr Ussher and self stayed while Mr G. talked to his foreman and then we ate our welcome lunch. Reluctantly we trailed back to the cars and started home. On our way we passed through Lefka, one of the richest districts in the island, where abundant water produces the best fruit in the island. At 5.30 we were back here again, and I had thoroughly enjoyed my day and learnt much from my host about Cyprus and its peculiarities. [...]

On Friday there is a show here in aid of some charity arranged by the English. Various sketches, songs and dances. The Grants are roped in to do one, lasting about 5 minutes and I am saying 6 lines as secretary Shall do it comic in contrast to the leading lady with a plentiful supply of teeth and fatuous smile. Afterwards I go down to Limassol to stay with the Buchanans for a few days. While I'm away I'm hiring out Woolly to Mrs Murray-Stuart so he won't be eating his head off in his stable. […]

[Undated; probably 9–12 February 1930; handwritten: PEF/TUF/DA/155]

Palace Hotel
Nicosia
Cyprus.

Dearest –
[…] I fear me it is no good harping on the Du Platt [Plat] Taylors' house, as it is still a ploughed field and the foundations have yet to be laid. It has taken them 6 months to buy the land and despite optimistic promises to the contrary, I expect it will take at least as long again to build the house. They go there every day and they hope for the best. The daughter [Joan] arrives tomorrow from England. However, I think I'm pretty well off here and it is nice to be independent. This is certainly cheaper than the George and the people are much more obliging.

The Grants leave tomorrow for their new house, which they will make very attractive. They've asked me to spend my last week in Cyprus with them, whenever that is, which is sweet of them. I intended to go to Limassol tonight with the Buchanans, but have been frustrated for the following amusing reason. Altogether I got rather tied in knots. Last Wed. had a printed card the size of a house asking me to dinner at Govt. Ho. on Monday (tomorrow) when I saw Gunnis the next day I said casually that I was sorry I should not be able to come. 'Oh! but he said you more or less <u>must</u> it is really a command!' Then I was faced with telling the Buchanans whom I had not even met so that I couldn't go on the appointed day. However they were quite understanding, though she is perhaps a bit difficult.

The show on both days went well, the Thurs. performance was to all the school children and I got 2 good laughs owing to my appearance alone; I had just six terse lines to say. The Friday audience was thin and sticky and quite English, the Greeks did not patronise the performance, largely, I suppose for political reasons.

As usual the performers enjoyed themselves heartily. All through I was oozing tact to Buchanans and Gunnis alternately but next day my stock slumped with the latter.

Had been to lunch at Athalassa and afterwards we motored out to Kythrea to see the horses who have been sent for 3 wks to eat the succulent green grass that grows there. All the time my formal acceptance was sitting undelivered in my bag. Terse note awaiting me in the evening at the hotel. Was I coming or not? from Gunnis. Note of explanation from me via messenger post haste. So now I hope things are smooth and the way paved for tomorrow. Have ironed yellow dress, probably one and only occasion of wearing same.

Today Sunday thoroughly enjoyed my ride alone on Woolly who is a perfect pony. I unwisely lent him to Mrs Murray-Stuart who is thoroughly 'horsy' so I thought to be trusted in that line. She took him out from 10 to 1.30 and he came in done to the world and soaked. He has quite recovered and now that I've had him clipped he looks too smart for words, but personally I don't think him so sweet.

After lunch Mr Roe came in and six of us crowded into the Hil[l]man and went to Athalassa. All the resources of the farm were displayed and we went round the prison, which is rather like the Dunmow workhouse, in as much as it looks a nice place to end one's days in. A cheery tea and home in time for dinner.

<u>Private</u> Today the Grants moved in to their house and after seeing Woolly clipped at his stable I went to give her a hand with curtains and so on. Joan Du Platt [Plat] Taylor arrived today and at 2.30, we foregathered and rode out to the site of their house. She is all steeped in M.A.M. [Margaret Alice Murray][33] and is feeling a little superior at the moment. She was also recommended to do a Corpus and I shall leave her to it, though I think anything she or I could do would be feeble compared to Gjerstad's Corpus which will be due shortly. He is <u>the</u> authority and expert here and I felt as soon as I saw his material for the Corpus that he had better be left to it. […]

There are plenty of comedy effects in the hotel. Imagine my horror this evening when I came in to find my room bare – not a single one of my things in it. I went into the Grants room and found it a chaos of my things – the principle was good but the execution of the move bad. I went downstairs and asked the reason of the upheaval. The poor manager was astounded and distressed to the last degree. It was Mrs Murray-Stuart who had asked to be moved and not me at all. So now I have the upper hand with the management and shall move into the best room in the house as soon as it is free, sun all the morning and a large balcony to myself. […]

12th Hope you enjoy the account of the dinner, I didn't enjoy the eating of it. Yesterday lunched at Athalassa to tell Mr Roe about my escapade; he had heard several versions during the morning and came round to dig me out and hear the story straight from the horse's mouth. Then came back and changed in time to mount poor shaven Woolly and go to the Rodeo. There I was made to gallop round and am being initiated into tent pegging, have not got to the sword yet. […]

I can't think what Lady Petrie means about my not wanting her to write, what a very strange idea and why? I do badly want the 2 bks I asked her for, Bethpelet I get free and Gerar[34] I may have to pay for. If she won't send it without the money perhaps you could settle it for me.

Very much love dearest to you all
Olga

[Undated, referring to 10 February 1930; handwritten: PEF/TUF/ DA/2743]

A. Lamentable History.
How
Little Olga All But Dined At
Government House.

One day when little Olga was eating her rice pudding in her palace, a nice smart policeman brought her a beautiful invitation to dinner. It was all printed on a card like a tea tray and there were King George's arms in gold as a heading. Olga like a good little girl knew one must always go to the first invitation received so she said she couldn't go to the dinner-party as she had been asked to spend some days at the sea.

But the man who wrote the invitations said 'Oh! you have got to come, or else THEY will be very cross and they may never ask you out again.' So the obedient girl told the kind friends who had asked her to the sea all about it and they said 'Go to the party by all means and don't eat too many sweets.' So then Olga accepted the invitation in writing and put it in her bag and there it stayed till the same man wrote and said 'Are you or are you not coming to dinner,' So then she said 'Of course I am and thank you very much for asking me.' So Olga ironed her dress and darned her stockings and brushed her hair for the party and ordered a motor car to take her there. Then the silly maids moved all her things from her bedroom and put them in another one in piles on the bed and she couldn't find any of her clothes. However she got dressed in time and went downstairs to wait for the car. It didn't come and she said 'Where is the car?' and they said 'Oh! the car has gone to Kyrenia!' and she said 'Then how am I going to get to Govt. Ho. in 10 minutes?' So then a boy on a bicycle was sent to get a carriage but he was gone a long time. So Olga ran down the road with the manager to the crossroads. It was very dark and there was no car or carriage to be seen and they tore their hair together.

Suddenly a big car with flashing headlights came along and Olga through [sic] herself in front of it and waved her arms so the car stopped and she said 'Are you going along that road?' and then they said 'No but where do you want to go?' and so Olga told them all about it and they said jump in and we will send you there with our chauffeur. So the chauffeur came out of their house and drove very fast towards Government Ho. running into a carriage on the way but nobody seemed to mind and he went straight on and at last passed the sentries and arrived. Olga thanked the man and gave him 3/– and dashed in to find lots of men in red and gold standing about. They said 'it's ten minutes past eight' and one of them took her through many terrible empty silent rooms to a large door and from behind the door came an angry murmur. She felt like the Christian who is being thrown to the lions, it was opened. She had to go through into an immense room full of people covered in medals. Getting smaller and smaller she had to walk the whole length of the room and sit down next to the ADC [aide-de-camp] at the foot of the table. Soup was finished, they shoved some fish in front of her and for 2 courses she hardly knew what she was eating. After the champagne had circulated she felt better and began to sit up and take notice, and enjoy her food. After dinner she was put on a sofa and had to tell her hostess all about it, then on another sofa she told the Colonial Secretary all about it, [and] by the time she got to another sofa with the Governor she had got quite good at telling people all about it and quite amused him, so that he said how primitive Cyprus was and he hoped to see me again. Then the A.D.C. amused himself by playing a game of general post with everyone. So that no one ever said three consecutive sentences to the same person and when the clock struck 10 o'clock up gets the Governor and his wife, and they shook hands all round and marched out of the room, leaving the guests mildly astonished and wondering what to do next. So everyone went home but there was a supplementary party as a consolation at the Col. Sec's house which was fun for little Olga, she danced round and enjoyed herself and was asked to go there again the next night.

In the morning at breakfast everyone had heard all about it in fact the poor child got quite notorious and everyone has started asking her out to things and she wrote a polite letter thanking the people who lent their car, so it wasn't so bad after all and it's an ill wind that blows nobody any good BUT —————— The last person who was late at Govt. Ho. was told he could wait in the sitting room and could have some coffee later but little Olga thinks that was only said to show her what a naughty girl she had been.

The End

[13 February 1930; handwritten: PEF/TUF/DA/156]

Limassol.
13–2:30

Dearest Ma,

This is just a line to tell you of yesterday's adventures as there is an odd mail going out today. Well, it was a wet and dreary day when we left Athalassa after lunch and it cost us many a pang to sally forth. As we crossed the plain and came to the hills we felt more resigned and could imagine that we were motoring in Scotland. Moor broken by streams, solitary trees and a background of dark hills capped by moving clouds. After crossing the pass, the sun showed in fitful gleams; we were well ahead of our time and stopped for coffee at the half-way house. Mr Roe suddenly remembered (or I accuse him of inventing!) a church in a village a mile from the road where there is a piece of the True Cross, probably the most genuine of the lot. It was, or so we thought, a case of walking. We stopped at an inn and started off when the landlord called us back and said we could go on a good road in the car. We thanked him enthusiastically and set out according to his directions, the road looked good, we crossed a bridge and started up hill and found ourselves skidding in an appalling quagmire! There was a deep ditch on each side of the road and despite every effort we landed comfortably in one of them. We reviewed the situation, collected stones and managed to move the car a bit. But the Hillman is heavy and the mud was deep. At last we enlisted the sympathy of some peasants who promised to send help from that miserable village which had lured us from the straight and narrow way. It started to rain and the dusk was falling and the Elinor Glynish[35] situation was quite humorous as we cowered under the bridge to keep dry; an hour passed and help came. An enthusiastic set of fellows tugged, pulled and pushed, and at last the car was extricated. Largesse was bestowed, we did the last

20 miles quite peacefully and arrived like drowned rats, or rather Roe did about 7.30. Our religious fervour had cost us 2 hrs and nearly £1, which has cured us of any desire to see relics of the past!

The B.'s have a nice house here, which they are about to part with and are on their way thankfully to England. The wind he blow and the sea is just the other side of the road.

Much love to all
Yours ever
<u>Olga</u>

Figure 4.5 Kolossi Castle, Limassol (medieval/Crusader period). Written on back: 'Kolossi, near Limassol, where Richard Coeur de Lion spent his honeymoon.' Olga Tufnell archive, Palestine Exploration Fund. Courtesy of the Palestine Exploration Fund.

[23 February 1930; handwritten: PEF/TUF/DA/157]

Palace Hotel
Nicosia
Cyprus.
Feb. 23. 1930.

Dearest Mà,

[...] Mr Ussher called yesterday evening, bringing with him the chief Forest Officer, didn't get his name, but Richard [St Barbe Baker] said I should meet him. I mentioned the latter and both men knew him and smiled! The C.F.O. [Chief Forest Officer] says he can give me a permit at any time to stay in the forest huts, so if J. Du Platt [Joan du Plat] Taylor and I go expeditions we can have somewhere to lay our heads.

The chronicle of events up to date: Last Thursday, as per schedule, Mr Mountain called for me about 10 a.m and we motored to Nicosia, without a hitch. He is a nice man, mad about stamps and has had an adventurous life in Africa. [...]

It seemed quite homelike to be welcomed back at the Palace (I had done a little encouragement in the tip line before leaving). Went up and saw the Grants at tea time and on my return found letters from you, H.P. [Hilda Petrie], F.P. [Flinders Petrie], Elyne etc.

Friday, finished 4th pot in the Mus. so you need not imagine that I am overworking! Have now embarked on a terrific bowl, simply covered in decoration, shall probably go mad before it is finished. Rodeo in the afternoon, uneventful, and no Mr Roe to impart instruction. Played my first game of bridge in the evening and lost heavily. [...]

[On Sunday] 300 [American] tourists from the *Homeric* and some 20 of us to sell them all we could in the sale room of the Museum. Force of habit was altogether too strong for me, I found myself conducting about 120 round and doing all the usual patter in my exhibition room voice! But the great thing was to get them quickly to the sale. Oh! gosh oh! gee. I'd rather do a week of exhib. than an hour of undiluted Americans. They won't take anything with a break in it, and the flat bowls to be used as ashtrays went best, altogether we made £75.10.0 in 1½ hrs so the Mus. will be able to afford some excavating.[36]

In the afternoon rode to Govt. Ho. to put my name in the book, rather belatedly after the dinner.

Deluge of rain this afternoon, pony and I only got slightly wet, but the whole ground was flooded. [...] Tomorrow's orgy of excavating is off I fear, we should only get covered in mud.

Wed: Well we did go grubbing round a bit and had an amusing morning. I was invited to tea at the Markides. He is the Mus. Curator and is very ill poor man with some type of paralysis which makes him yawn continually. So he is not exactly the thing to make a tea party go. Mrs M. is tremendous in girth and only speaks French and there is a daughter who is her mother in miniature. A nice girl but she plays the piano. About the most painful performance you could imagine, execution good but just like a barrel organ.

People fired sentences at each other across a rose infested carpet and it was all rather sticky, but it is always amusing to see a Greek household, though this is rather an Anglicised one. [...]

[3 March 1930; handwritten: PEF/TUF/DA/158]

Palace Hotel
Nicosia
Cyprus.
March 3. 1930

Darling Daddy,
Very many thanks for your birthday letter and kind contribution, very gratefully received. Things are going pretty well here and I find my days are full and mildly amusing. Am getting on slowly with my painting at the Museum, but is quite tricky work. Shall be really sorry to part with my sweet pony Woolly when I go; he goes like the wind but is quiet and has now got used to motor cars and such like impediments. On Tuesdays and Fridays there are Police Sports which we irreverently call the 'Rodeo' but as only 2 or 3 can really ride it is not a very apt description. Am trying to tent peg now which consists of going all out at a peg stuck in the ground brandishing a naked sword! but you will be glad to hear that I still use a walking-stick, when it comes to the sword I shall surely stick it in to me! Next Sat. there is going to be a mounted paper chase at Athalassa, it will be amusing to see how long I shall stay on.

I want to concoct an article on sport in Cyprus for Mr Day; there is quite a lot to be said and then there is the racing season beginning now. Cyprus exports stock and imports racing animals from England. Now everything on 4 legs that can race is being put in training and the Spring Meeting ought to be rather amusing. They say it is nice out here until the end of April so I may stay till then that is to say if you will be able to brass up any more chink. Have spent roughly £25 on board and lodging, £9 for pony and extra for its food and groom, but I hope to get at least £15 for it when I go.

How are the little birds and will they do their duty in the egg-laying line? When will you want me to pack eggs? Am thinking of coming home on a Prince boat – here. Alex. Manchester for £12, but it takes a month and one is liable to be the only passenger!

Much love darling and good luck
Ever your loving, <u>Olga</u>

[3 March 1930; handwritten: PEF/TUF/DA/159]

Palace Hotel
Nicosia
Cyprus.
March 3. 1930.

Dearest Cousin Lionel,

I'm so sorry to hear you have not been so well just lately and do hope that the winter in England is nearly over now and that you will soon have some sun to cheer you up. Wish you could be here, we have plenty of fine days and it is hardly ever too cold to sit out. This is a very different life for me; it seems so funny to have no definite hours to conform to, and now that I'm used to it, I find no difficulty in filling them. I work mildly at the Mus. in the morning and ride my small pony every afternoon. He really is a great joy and I never thought I should get keen on riding, but I enjoy it all and am joining in a mounted paper chase next Saturday.

People are very friendly and kind and I get plenty of excursions and motor drives and an occasional outing in the evening. Miss Taylor, who is the girl I knew out here before coming, and I want to arrange some trips on horseback into the hills. There are various lovely places to be seen and as she talks Greek we should have little difficulty in getting about.

Bathing at Kyrenia will soon be in full swing; I went there some weeks ago and called on Mr Campbell, but he was away at Limassol. His house is most fascinating. After you cross the pass from Nicosia to Kyrenia you drop down through a fertile valley to the sea. His bungalow is perched on a hill overlooking the road, though to get there, you have to follow a drive for some miles to circumvent the ravine. His garden is right down in a hollow and I believe he has a most ingenious additional water supply from the rain water from the roof. [...]

Last week we had the *Homeric* in with 300 American tourists, that meant a lot of money to the island and next Sat. another 400 are expected, but I don't know what ship they are coming on. They land at Larnaca and are brought here in cars which takes about an hour. Then they rush round the Museum, see the bazaar and get back to the ship in time for dinner.

I suppose I shall soon have to start thinking about the return journey – I do wish there were a few magic carpets about now and that one could dispense with train journeys.

Probably in 2 months' time I shall be walking in to tea with you! […]

[4 March 1930; handwritten: PEF/TUF/DA/160]

Palace Hotel
Nicosia
Cyprus.
March 4. 1930.

Dearest Mà.

[…] This week has been a pretty quiet one. Last Sunday there was a paper chase at Athalassa, but as it came on an 'unfortunate' day for me I did not do any running and was taken there and back peaceably by Mr Wayne who cannot be energetic as he has just had typhoid. About 50 people turned up to tea and about 20 (nearly all girls!) ran. Afterwards we all went to the top of Leondari Vouno to see the sun set and so home. Yesterday I rode in the Rodeo and had the usual morning at the Mus. The bowl I'm doing now is turning out rather well. Hope I can keep it up. […]

The Murray Stuarts leave tomorrow – rather sad for me as they are v. cheerful company and replaced the Grants. Hope something new and amusing will come off tomorrow's boat, otherwise I shall be the only female in the hotel. We had an amusing dinner 2 nights ago followed by consequences and other absurd games. […]

[10 March 1930; handwritten: PEF/TUF/DA/161]

Palace Hotel
Nicosia
Cyprus.

March. 10. 1930.

Dearest Ma,

[…] Can't think of any special events on Thurs and Friday. They were I think peaceful days at the Mus with the afternoon ride. On Sat. morning another 350 tourists came and had to be fleeced for the benefit of archaeology – I had the luck to pick a decent couple from Massachusetts who bought £6 worth. Two large jars were destined for standard lamp bases, rather an ingenious device. 'They will look nice on the library table, dear!' They were disposed of by 12.30 and in the afternoon I was supposed to be picknicking [sic] with the Taylors; it rained at the crucial moment and the girl and I got soaked on our ponies, so the show deteriorated into a sticky tea at the George.

Sunday was quite amusing. Football in the morning – Nicosia v. Skiriotso, all the mining people came in full force and the game is interesting to watch when one knows most of the people. Then there was a men's tennis tournament in the afternoon at the Club and that also I attended with Molly Hepburn in the search for 'copy' for my *Field* article. There was nothing to distinguish it from any provincial gathering for the same purpose. Then we went for a drive in Mr O'Reilly's car along the Troodos road and ended up here with cocktails, all very cheerful and facetious. […]

I hour oushed round last Friday – 7th – to see if I could find a wireless to listen in to you. It would have been thrilling to hear your voice so far away, but could not get in touch with anyone. […]

Will you ask Lady Petrie to send me another copy of *Egypt and Israel* as I have sold mine. I have 5/6 for it, which will hand over on my return. If she likes to send 'A.E.' [*Ancient Egypt*] too, I might be able to do something about it, either at Mus. or Gjerstads, but should want all three (or is it two) copies out to date. […]

Wed. […] To Mr Jeffery's small Mus. of XII–XVth cent. architectural detail. He is Director of Ancient Monuments and is usually referred to as the 'Ancient Monument' himself. He much resembles Budge both in fruity odour and the variety of food and drink that can be traced on his coat front. Long winded but interesting if he keeps to the point. […]

[Undated, possibly 16 March 1930; handwritten: PEF/TUF/DA/162]

Palace Hotel
Nicosia
Cyprus.

Dearest Ma,

[...] Was up bright and early today Sunday, to attend the betrothal ceremony of Mehmet's two daughters. He is the pony's groom and a well-built highly intelligent Sudanese. The invitation had been given the day before and Mrs Christian said she would come with me. Mehmet attired in lovely blue cloth trousers edged with black braid and blue woollen stockings to match embroidered with red birds climbing on trees called for us, nominally at nine, but it was really nearer ten, in a gharry.[37]

We decided we could not pay for it without offending him and shall have to give a present instead. We drove to a house in the middle of the town near the P.O. [Post Office] and went up steep and narrow stairs to the first floor where we shook hands with innumerable ladies including M's [Mehmet's] mother and wife. The former a delightful Sudanese with the humorous eyes and vivacious ways of her kind, the latter a most remarkably attractive person. Short, fair and freckled with an engaging plumpness and a placid intelligent manner – a Cypriote. Hilda Trevelyan in *What Every Woman Knows*.[38] Mehmet is the father of six, the two brides (both of rather uncertain age), another small girl, very European, and three boys. The room we were shown into was full of females, fat, thin, young and old, seated in rows. At the end was a raised dais, on which were 2 chairs. These were flanked by four large decorated candles and on a table in front were 2 cakes iced and decorated and 2 small looking-glasses and a bunch of violets. On each side of the platform were huge vases of artificial flowers of the most striking colours in yellow pots.

After we had sat some time and received the smiles of the assembly and had been thoroughly eyed and commented upon, we had coffee and cakes and as the latter were hard and substantial we had to resort to the usual deception to dispose of them. Luckily further offers of food were interrupted by the appearance of the brides to be. The dark one, Aysha, in an orange silk dress, the fair one Zarifa (I think) in pale mauve. Both wore white veils and elaborate crowns; their faces had been painted and their hair curled with geometrical severity. They took their seats without speaking a word and sat like statues. The brother-in-law was the only man present and he was a concession to us and acted as interpreter – he is a P.O. official. Nice man and there we sat for an hour or more and were at last much relieved to see some people behind us take their departure, when we felt able to do the same. We left after much handshaking and compliments all round, the brides still sitting on their chairs, the cakes still uneaten, but it was going on all day like that, and nothing more was going to happen. It may be several years before the weddings take place, and much as I wanted to I couldn't ask how much the girls were worth, though this would have been an open topic of conversation in Palestine! [...]

Wed. evening. We are planning an expedition, which, if it comes off, should be very pleasant. The idea at present is that Joan Taylor, Mollie Hepburn and I should send our ponies out to Lefka, motor there, spend a day or two with Mr O'Reilly and then ride on up through the hills to Kikko [Kykko]. Spend the night and then on to Stavrous,[39] where there is a forest hut. From there to Polis, where there are tombs and Mr Gjerstad is working. Leave the ponies and motor to Papho[s], which is a dull journey to ride, and after a day or so return to Polis and ride home by another route through the forests. Perhaps spending 12 days en route. Sounds ambitious, doesn't it? [...]

[25 March 1930; handwritten: PEF/TUF/DA/163]

Palace Hotel
Nicosia
March. 25th 1930.

Dearest Ma,
Another week has gone and if I can get the passage I expect to leave here on April 25th – a month from today. Apparently it is difficult to get anything at that time, so shall come on whatever line I can.

Last Friday had tea and played ping-pong at the Henniker-Heatons and met one of the Air Force crowd, who is staying at the Palace and had arrived from Egypt via Pal. [Palestine] the previous day. Everything on four wheels was to be seen on the Morphou Road, where the aeroplanes were to land some 4 miles outside the town. It was like Epsom Downs, with all classes and creeds on trek. Thousands walked or went on donkeys and there were improvised charabancs from any old truck and a few kitchen chairs. A few minutes before three the Gov. [Governor] arrived and at the appointed hour the 2 planes like mosquitoes came in sight, soon they were circling round and had landed – the first planes to arrive on the island – except for a few in the war. The big bugs went to see over the machines and I went with Dr Millard, who had brought me and some others in his tin lizzie.[40] Funnily enough I was allowed through the barrier, though he was not, as the sargeant [sic] in charge was a friend of mine, though I didn't stay when I found they couldn't get in.

Ever since there has been a continuous stream of sightseers – the island has never experienced such a thrill.

Sat. uneventful, went for a ride with a girl who gave me jim-jams because she couldn't control her horse which kept running away – and I imagined myself picking up the pieces, though luckily we got home without mishap.

On Sunday morning – Mollie Hepburn – the prettiest girl here, I think, Kenneth Jacobs and I started off to spend the day with young Reilly at Lefka. He is Asst. Conservator of Forests and Commissioner for the district. We covered the 34 miles in under 2 hours, despite the roads, and found him ready to start for the sea. We had a bathe, very pleasant and warm, followed by a substantial picnic, and we all did justice to cold roast chicken and potatoes. Then back to Lefka and the football ground where the villagers for miles around had assembled to see the Turkish School play the mines. The game was good and the boys won. [...]

Tuesday had tea with the Bakers and was summoned to dine at Govt. Ho. and 'made a fourth'. An Oxfordy young man just arrived was to go too and we shared a car and arrived on the doorstep just as all the lights went out. So we groped about with candles from the dining room table and I thought it an excellent 1st act, for it was Greek Independence Day and they fully expected trouble. The next thing should have been an assault with pistol shots and the faithful Rupert defending the life of his master with his own.

Just as my hopes ran high the lights went on again and we went in to dinner. Sat next to Sir R. [Ronald Storrs] and on my right had Major Benton Fletcher, whose work I know well from his connection with the Petries.[41] So we had plenty to talk about as he was full of messages to them. [...] Then I did play a late game of bridge made worse by the thought that dawned on me just as we were beginning that I had come without a penny – result loss 4/6 plus 2/6 car, total cost of doubtful entertainment 7s/0d. Luckily Capt. Gunnis drove us back.

Finished my 12th pot today and did I tell you that the Mus. has offered to buy them, so I have one purchaser at any rate and I'm not sure the Swedes won't be bidding too. Think I should ask about £25 for the lot, what to [do] you think? Woolly is going at £15 + saddle so that I should be about £50 to the good when I leave – if I do some more painting. [...]

[1 April 1930; handwritten: PEF/TUF/DA/164]

Palace Hotel
Nicosia.
Cyprus.
April 1. 1930.

Dearest Ma and Daddy,

[...] Last Thurs. dined at the Colonial Secs. met the other woman I hadn't seen before and we had the usual after dinner programme of dancing and ping-pong. Spent most of Friday at the Mus. where sundry tidyings and clearings out of old muck is taking place. Quite like old days in the Edwards.[42] Have finished the large jar I was tackling rather successfully. [...]

Reappearance of Mr Roe, who has been in Egypt, has been a scare of foot and mouth disease here but a fortnight's work has he hopes averted the catastrophe. Went to Lefkoniko, where I was let loose in the village to pass the time while he did a job, as best I could. Found myself invited into every house along the road and regaled with jam in spoonfuls and pieces of bread, specially made for Easter. The rooms I saw were very clean, large white beds and in one elaborate chamber the walls were hung with coloured plates, à la Czech, and flat coloured rush baskets. There was a fine carved chest and some good bits of embroidery.

Figure 4.6 Girl with loom, Lefkoniko, Cyprus. Written on back: 'Lefkoniko. My hostess at her loom. She sits on the floor and has a hole dug for her feet and the loom weights.' See letter of 1 April 1930. Olga Tufnell archive, Palestine Exploration Fund. Courtesy of the Palestine Exploration Fund.

Each house had its loom and everyone was keen for me to photograph. Spoke more Greek than I've done before and saw some of the prettiest girls I've seen in the island. So it was a successful outing and a jolly good way of seeing things. Wed. evening. Unexpected invitation to a dance of all things, so it rather curtails the letter writing. Quite looking forward to it after 4 mths, makes me feel quite young and skittish, hope I can keep it up. Have booked passage Ap. 24. Marseille Ap. 30, home about May 1.

[6 April, probably 1930; handwritten: PEF/TUF/DA/165]

Palace Hotel
Nicosia
Ap. 6.

Dearest Ma,
Wed. night was a small dance at the George. Reilly, Jacobs and self went, from here, all togged up, me in my yellow, as I thought there would be no chance to wear it again. About 8 couples, but was rather damped for me by Mrs du Platt [Plat] Taylor who sat and knitted in the only sitting-out place with her eagle eye on all, so that one's feeble witticisms, if any, sounded too footling by the time they had passed her censorship. Left at twelve, when everything was over and to bed feeling less inclined for the gay night life of Nicosia. [...]

It is amazing how one's misdeeds find one out. A fierce lady arrived last week and accosted me at dinner by name. She turned out to be one of the audience at the Bournemouth lecture and she is given to saying the most terrific things in a loud voice at mealtimes, dark mumblings about goddesses, all most embarrassing so that I have to keep my eyes glued to my book. Of course it is all over Nicosia and she is quite dotty.

Tues. [April 8] 2 car loads went to Cerno [Kornos] today, where they still make handmade pottery. The forms of which there are only a few differ but little from the ancient ones. Our arrival was a tremendous event in the village and we were all thoroughly American leaping round with cameras. Will send the results next week and meanwhile enclose a few snaps taken by others on the 1st Troodos trip.

Am having a tea party today on my balcony, I have the whole of it so can do what I like, just been buying the cakes, hope I've got enough, expecting 6 young ladies. Rode for 2¼ hrs this morning with Joan Taylor and can keep going quite decently all the time.

My ticket for the 24th has come, so shall be on the move then – at Marseilles on the 30th and with you I suppose on May 1st or 2nd. [...]

Figure 4.7 Potter at Kornos making a vessel by hand. Kiln in background. See letter of 15 April 1930. Prior publication: du Plat Taylor and Tufnell 1930, fig. 4. Olga Tufnell archive, Palestine Exploration Fund. Courtesy of the Palestine Exploration Fund.

[15 April 1930 and later; handwritten: PEF/TUF/DA/166]

Palace Hotel
Nicosia
Cyprus.
Ap. 15. 1930.

Dearest Ma,
This will, I suppose (D.V. [God willing]) be the last letter I shall write to you from here, as I shall be coming by the next mail and would arrive with, or before any letters. So that is really good!

Last Wed. had my tea party which went off well, that night there was a Masonic dinner here, and I got quite a lot of amusement out of the various noises that proceeded from below though when these were prolonged into the early hours, it was less comic.

Thurs. morning who should appear in the Mus. but the Woolleys[43] travelling incog. [incognito] apparently, so that they are wisely evading all the questions and 'Have you had a good season?' remarks. Gunnis was showing them round, so did not speak.

The place is swarming with archaeologists and celebrities. The Sitwells[44] were here some time in full force and also Breasted junior,[45] and who should turn up last week but Dr G.F. Rogers of Cambridge.[46] Lady Petrie will know him, he is an old stager at the Exhib.. He is very jovial and about 6 ft 6" and has a niece with him to match. Had tea with them at the George and have been down town with them. Can't remember anything about Friday but suppose it was uneventful. It was a day of anticipation of the social event of the season. Saturday was the Police Sports [...] attended by Governor and all, he looking rather artistic in check trousers and an immense black hat. All the élite were disposed in covered stands and we were well fed. The events were quite amusing to watch and well organised. When one knows many of the competitors it makes it fun. Then was introduced to the Dennis[es] who took me with them back to stay with Mr Campbell.

I've told you something before I think about the eyrie he lives in on top of a hill overlooking the sea on the Kyrenia pass. It is a fascinating position, and inside it is comfortably arranged and well thought out in the most approved Dondaesque [?] fashion. Views from all windows unspeakably fine and from mine I could see the sunrise without stirring from my bed!

He is very keen about trees and so I worked round to the Men of the Trees[47] hoping he would join, only to find that he is already a member! He has planted hundreds and has a scientific vegetable garden and must be almost self-supporting. [...]

On Monday morning the Dennis[es ... and] Mrs Christian [...] got a car and we drove to Lapithos. [...] I wanted to see the pottery making. Here they work on the wheel and not by hand as at Korno[s] but it was difficult to find much going on and it was not their day for glazing.

Thoroughly worked up by then, we went on to Lambousa, where there is a fine old monastery, built right on the sea-coast. Now it is a farmyard and the church in the centre is bedraggled and dirty, though there are some good icons left among the rubbish. All [a]round are tombs which have been plundered and the place is strewn with potsherds. There is a strange rock which has been hollowed out and used as a burial place or chapel which I must find out about. Lunched at Kyrenia with Mrs C. and then took a 2/– seat in a car back to Nicosia and landed straight at the Moat in order to attend the Turkish Sports – the same idea as the previous Sat. [...]

Tues. Opening of the Legislative Council today. Secured a strategic position with the Taylors and saw the show such as it was in comfort. [...] There was a Zapti guard of honour and my friends of the Rodeo ground formed a mounted escort with pennons flying to the Guv. [Governor] who was all togged up in cocked hat and silver braid. I looked at Gunnis similarly attired (but without the silver) for some time without recognising him. Rode later and called on Gjerstad, asking him to come and vet my things.

There is a strange sort of German-Swiss edition of Baron Munchausen here – tells tall stories and will buy anything from Raphael's undiscovered pictures to alligators. Has asked me to go to Kyrenia tomorrow, but it depends on Gjerstad.

Well so long and looking forward to seeing you all soon.

Notes

1 Olga Tufnell interviewed by Jonathan Tubb. Transcript of audiotaped interview, c. 1985.
2 Winbladh 1997; Göransson 2012.
3 Kiely and Ulbrich 2012.
4 Gilbert Davidson, Olga's mother's brother.
5 Arthur Wyndham Tufnell, son of Edward Wyndham Tufnell.
6 There is no published reference to Olga Tufnell's contributions in the Cyprus Expedition volumes.
7 Referred to as 'Korno' or 'Cerno' in the letters. Observations of potters in the village of Kornos led to a short article (du Plat Taylor and Tufnell 1930). An ethnographic study of the Kornos potters was carried out in later decades (London 2000).
8 Sir Ronald Henry Amherst Storrs (1881–1955), military governor of Jerusalem 1917–20, civil governor of Jerusalem and Judea 1920–6, governor of Cyprus 1926–32.
9 Storrs 1937, 508–9.
10 'Historical Background', Department of Antiquities website, Republic of Cyprus, http://www.mcw.gov.cy/mcw/da/da.nsf/DMLhistory_en/DMLhistory_en?OpenDocument, last accessed 26 July 2020.
11 See letter of 16 March 1930; also see Asmussen 2010 for further information on marriage customs and dowries.
12 One of London's oldest restaurants. Famed for its fish and seafood.
13 Bertha Penrose, with whom Olga stayed in Florence in 1921.
14 Probably Ulrich, titular Prince of Wchinitz and Tettau (1893–1938), of the House of Kinsky, formerly Austro-Hungarian nobility.
15 Petrie 1911.
16 Humfry Payne (1902–36), classical archaeologist, worked at the Department of Antiquities, Ashmolean Museum, Oxford, 1926–8. Director of the British School at Athens, 1929–36. Excavated at Knossos and Perachora.
17 Pheidippides.
18 Either intended as a humorous misspelling of Hotel, or a typographical error.
19 The Lausanne Agreement of 1923 sanctioned an exchange of population according to religion between Greece and Turkey, resulting in an influx of refugees.

20 Sir Arthur Evans (1851–1941), principal excavator of Knossos, Crete, and authority on Minoan civilisation.

21 Menelaos Markides (1878–1942), the first curator of the Cyprus Museum (1912–31). Studied Classical archaeology at University of Oxford and excavated at sites in Cyprus, including Lapithos.

22 Rupert Forbes Gunnis (1899–1965), collector, amateur historian and scholar of British sculpture, best known for *Dictionary of British Sculptors 1660–1851*, published in 1953. Inspector of Antiquities for the Cyprus Museum in 1932–5, and published *Historic Cyprus: A Guide to its Towns and Villages, Monasteries and Castles* (1936). He was private secretary to the governor of Cyprus, Sir Ronald Storrs, 1926–32.

23 Gilbert Tufnell, Olga's elder brother, died 1918. Was at school (Eton) with Rupert Gunnis.

24 A mufti is an Islamic scholar who interprets or expounds Islamic law. The office of the Mufti of Cyprus, the spiritual leader of the Turkish Cypriots, was abolished by the British governor of Cyprus in 1929 (Pericleous 2009, 140).

25 Einar Gjerstad (1897–1988), Swedish historian and classical archaeologist, leader of the Swedish-Cyprus Expedition, 1927–31, Research Professor, University of Lund, 1957–72.

26 London tea-room and restaurant.

27 Also known as Vouno Leontari or Liontarovounos (Leontari Hill), in the modern borough of Aglangia in Cyprus.

28 Llewelyn Powys, *The Cradle of God*. London: Jonathan Cape, 1929.

29 Joan Mabel Frederica du Plat Taylor (1906–83). Moved to Cyprus in 1926, serving as volunteer in the Cyprus Museum and subsequently Acting Inspector of Antiquities, Cyprus, excavating at Neolithic Khirokitia from the mid-1930s. Co-published a report on the classification of pottery in the Cyprus Museum with Veronica Seton-Williams (1939). Librarian, Institute of Archaeology, University of London, 1945–70. She conducted archaeological fieldwork in Turkey and Syria at Coba Hüyük with John Waechter and Veronica Seton-Williams and also excavated at the Phoenician site of Motya (Sicily) and conducted maritime archaeology at Cape Gelidonya (Turkey).

30 Bella Paise or Bellapais, a Premonstratensian abbey.

31 All male and some female members of the Tufnell family could be affectionately referred to as 'Tuffy'.

32 A late Iron Age/Persian-period palace site on the northern coast.

33 Joan du Plat Taylor had been a student of Margaret Murray in London.

34 Petrie 1928; Petrie 1930.

35 Elinor Glyn (1864–1943), English author best known for writing romantic fiction.

36 Rupert Gunnis played an active role in the acquisition of antiquities as well as their sale in the Cyprus Museum to visitors. See Symonds 1987 for a description of his activities.

37 A horse-drawn open carriage with hood.

38 George Bernard Shaw's play illustrating the growing emancipation of women, seen by Olga when living in London.

39 Known today as Stavros tis Psokas.

40 Model T Ford car.

41 Major Fletcher worked with Petrie in Egypt in 1910.

42 The Edwards Library at UCL, attached to the Petrie Museum of Egyptology.

43 Sir C. Leonard Woolley (1880–1960) and his wife Katharine Woolley. C.L. Woolley was a British archaeologist, Assistant Keeper, Ashmolean Museum, Oxford, 1905, excavating Carchemish (with T.E. Lawrence as assistant) 1912–14. An authority on ancient Mesopotamia, excavator of Ur 1922–36, Tell Atchana 1937–9, 1946–9.

44 Edith Sitwell (1887–1964), and brothers Osbert (1892–1969) and Sacheverell (1897–1988), together formed a well-known literary circle. It appears that only the brothers were present during this visit.

45 Charles Breasted (1897–1980), son and biographer of James Henry Breasted (1865–1935), 'father of American Egyptology' and Director of the Oriental Institute, University of Chicago, 1919–35. Charles Breasted served as his father's assistant for many years and often visited Egypt and Palestine on Oriental Institute business.

46 G.F. Rogers went on to become Professor of Social Anthropology, University of Cambridge, 1937–50.

47 Organisation founded by Richard St Barbe Baker; see Chapter 3, note 13.

References

Asmussen, Jan. 2010. 'Intermarriages and Interethnic Lovestories in Cyprus', *Halkbilimi* 25: 81–8.

Göransson, Kristian. 2012. 'The Swedish Cyprus Expedition: The Cyprus Collections in Stockholm and the Swedish Excavations after the SCE', *Cahiers du Centre d'Études Chypriotes* 42: 399–421.

Kiely, Thomas and Anja Ulbrich. 2012. 'Britain and the Archaeology of Cyprus I: The Long 19th Century', *Cahiers du Centre d'Études Chypriotes* 42: 305–56.

London, Gloria. 2000. 'Continuity and Change in Cypriot Pottery Production', *Near Eastern Archaeology* 63(2): 102–10.

Pericleous, Chrystomos. 2009. *Cyprus Referendum: A Divided Island and the Challenge of the Annan Plan*. London: I.B. Tauris.

Petrie, W.M.F. 1911. *Egypt and Israel*. London: Society for Promoting Christian Knowledge.

Petrie, W.M.F. 1928. *Gerar*. London: British School of Archaeology in Egypt.

Petrie, W.M.F. 1930. *Beth-Pelet I*. London: British School of Archaeology in Egypt.

du Plat Taylor, Joan and Olga Tufnell. 1930. 'A Pottery Industry in Cyprus', *Ancient Egypt*, 119–22.

Storrs, Sir Ronald. 1937. *Orientations*. London: Nicholson & Watson.

Symonds, David. 1987. 'Rupert Gunnis (1899–1965)', *Cahiers du Centre d'Études Chypriotes* 7: 3–10.

Winbladh, Marie-Louise. 1997. *An Archaeological Adventure in Cyprus: The Swedish Cyprus Expedition 1927–1931*. Stockholm: Medelhavsmuseet.

5
Tell el-'Ajjul, 1930–2

In October 1930 Olga returned to the Petrie expedition in Palestine after
her sojourn in Cyprus and summer at home. The security situation in
Palestine was somewhat different from earlier years. Riots in Hebron
and elsewhere in the summer of 1929 following the 'Wailing Wall'
incident in Jerusalem led to a trebling of the British police force in
Palestine.[1] Three newcomers joined Petrie's expedition team that year –
Ralph Richmond Brown, who was to become photographer, J.G. Vernon
and Norman Scott. Petrie's objective that year was to examine the
previously unexcavated site of Tell el-'Ajjul (brought to his attention
by Starkey),[2] a huge area of some 33 acres, 4 miles southwest of the
modern town of Gaza (Figure 5.1). This large mound, largely consisting
of various levels of ancient mudbrick architecture, is now located within
the Gaza strip. It was of great importance in the Middle Bronze Age
(2000–1550 BC), and considered by Petrie to be the site of ancient Gaza.
He called it the 'City of the Shepherd Kings', after the 'Hyksos' rulers, who
at the time were thought to be nomadic invaders and subsequently
rulers of Lower Egypt. This was a continuation of Petrie's interest in the
Hyksos echoed in his earlier expedition to Tell Fara (see Chapter 3).

At the time Olga Tufnell was writing, areas to the south of Gaza
received little rainfall, and were home to many Arab Bedouin who
traditionally follow a pastoralist or semi-nomadic way of life. The
process of sedentarisation, taking place gradually from Ottoman times,
intensified through the creation of villages during the Mandate period.
There was a complex relationship between the Naqab (Negev) Bedouin
tribes of the region and the British colonial administration, ranging
from peaceful cooperation to armed resistance.[3] The workers employed
by Petrie at this time were mainly Arab Bedouin, in addition to fellahin
(farmer villagers), who often worked under the supervision of Egyptian
Qufti (see pp. 59–61).

Tell Ajjul SE corner.

Figure 5.1 'Tell Ajjul SE Corner', undated. Olga Tufnell archive, Palestine Exploration Fund. Courtesy of the Palestine Exploration Fund.

Malaria was rife at Ajjul (as Tell el-'Ajjul was known colloquially) that autumn, the outbreak being so serious that Petrie appealed to the Department of Public Health for assistance. He lent his own workmen to the Department to dig canals (Figure 5.2), hoping that the expense would be worthwhile. Before Petrie's arrival, prisoners from Gaza's jail were commandeered to fill in the pools.[4] This example of archaeological workforces being occasionally employed on engineering projects reflects the intersection between archaeology and public health, and the role that foreign expeditions played in assisting authorities, local communities and workforces. Petrie was keen to highlight the benefits to workers and the conversion of the area back into a 'Promised Land' in his fundraising campaigns.[5] At the same time, the anti-malaria initiative was to benefit the foreign archaeologists working there and visitors to the site. Prof. and Lady Petrie decided to stay at Fara in the old camp or in Gaza until winter rains could fill the wadis at Ajjul and sweep away the mosquitoes. Meanwhile Starkey, Harding and Olga formed a skeleton staff at Ajjul, enjoying their peaceful situation until they were rejoined by the Petries and the rest of the expedition early in 1931.

Figure 5.2 Canal cut to help relieve Wadi Ghazzeh from malaria. Hilda Petrie/Ajjul archive, Album 2-12. © UCL Institute of Archaeology.

The Ajjul camp was built in the Petrie tradition of a courtyard surrounded by huts on three sides with a wall and gate on the fourth. Olga continued with her work, digging on the Tell, drawing and recording in the pottery shed, and assisting Dr Sperrin-Johnson, a retired professor of biology, with the daily clinic. In her letter of 3 January 1932, Olga reports seeing around 100 patients a week, highlighting the unofficial public welfare role of the expedition and its offer of public health to workers and other local people. It is worth noting the acute health challenges faced by the Bedouin population, among others in Palestine – especially malaria, tuberculosis and trachoma. Major gaps in healthcare in Palestine were beginning to be filled by the creation of new hospitals and employment of doctors and nurses, augmented by Christian missionaries and charities.[6] During the British Mandate, where access to state hospitals was difficult, Christian charities often supported Arab communities, whereas Jewish healthcare organisations emerged to serve many Jewish communities.[7] It should also be acknowledged that traditional healing practices that had developed over generations in Palestine were beginning to be impacted and displaced by modern, colonial medicine. Yet given the challenges faced by the Mandate authorities to provide basic health services to the region, especially in less densely populated rural areas, Tufnell and Sperrin-Johnson appear to have filled an important gap.

There is little mention in these letters of the day-to-day finds during excavations, although Olga's drafts of newspaper articles give a sense of the site and its history as it was understood at the time. She participated in only the first two excavation seasons, published by Petrie in *Ancient Gaza* volumes I and II.[8] Petrie was gratified in the first season to find the great fortifications encircling the site and equid burials in tombs which he believed confirmed his dating of the site to the 'Hyksos' period of the Middle Bronze Age, chariots and horses being associated features.[9] Olga was personally involved in excavating some of these equid burials (Figure 5.3). The second season provided rich rewards for the excavators, with a series of superimposed 'palaces' on the mound dated to the Middle Bronze and early Late Bronze Ages. Hoards of jewellery were found underneath building floors, including the famous 'cenotaph' deposit in the 1931–2 season, which featured gold armlets, earrings and toggle-pins.[10] Interestingly, this is not alluded to in any of Olga's letters home.

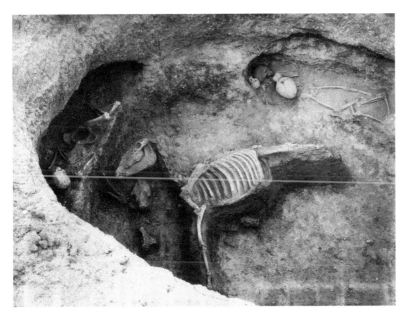

Figure 5.3 Excavated tomb containing equid and human burials (ascribed to 'Hyksos'), Tell el 'Ajjul, 1931. See letter of 13 March, probably 1932. © UCL Institute of Archaeology.

These seasons at Ajjul marked the beginning of the disintegration of the expedition team, with tensions demonstrated within the letters. The 'Taylorian', the rooms that Harris Dunscombe Colt Jr. built as an addition to the camp, became a divisive factor.[11] The younger members gathered there after work to relax and even dance to a portable gramophone: activities that Petrie, with his rigorous attitude to work, deplored. Drumming was also a popular evening pastime among the younger team members. Colt was beginning to irritate Petrie with his casual approach to the work, and even more so with the acquisition of a puppy, which annoyed both Petries with its undisciplined habits. Both Starkey and Harding were becoming impatient with Flinders Petrie's leadership. At the same time, Lady Petrie's idiosyncrasies were becoming hard to bear (e.g. see Olga's letter of 28 February 1931). Olga admitted later that conflict with Lady Petrie was the main reason why Starkey and his colleagues left the expedition.[12]

Petrie's theories and methods were also being challenged by a younger generation. It became obvious that the site was proving more difficult than Petrie had at first realised because of its size and complexity. Stratigraphic recording was as yet an early science, and although Petrie had been revolutionary in its application at Tell el-Hesi nearly 40 years earlier, he found Ajjul, with its numerous collapsed buildings and floor levels, an overwhelming project.[13] His insistence on basing his chronology on outdated Egyptian models was also causing his conclusions to be wide of the mark. Criticism was levelled at Petrie by Albright and others, referred to by Olga as the 'anti-Profs' (letter of 13 March 1932).

Petrie's work continued at Ajjul until 1934 with new team members. Renewed excavations were undertaken by Ernest Mackay and Margaret Murray in 1938.[14] The site of Tell el-'Ajjul, and those associated with its excavations, continue to be mentioned in subsequent letters from Olga over the next several years (see subsequent chapters).

In addition to archaeology, there are important insights into travel and social life in the letters. From 1929, there was an airport located outside Gaza managed by Imperial Airways. They began weekly flights to India from Croydon (London), with principal stops at Genoa, Rome, Baghdad and Basra, arriving at Karachi within seven days.[15] The Ajjul team, who did not travel by plane as it was too expensive, may well have benefited from access to more rapid communications afforded by airmail. There are also references to parties at the airport camp, providing an alternative entertainment venue for expedition team members.

Olga and her colleagues would travel to a few locations, but none particularly far afield. Hebron, Beit Jibrin, Ashdod, Arad, Khalassa and Tall Rafah were among the archaeological and historic sites visited, with Gaza being a more regular fixture for shopping, visits to the doctor, social visits and Arabic lessons. In addition, there is much written about taking long walks and bathing in the sea, which was just twenty minutes on foot from their camp, as well as references to nature and birdlife in this area. Olga and fellow team members took part in many religious festivities and events, as well as music and dancing. There were also experiments with making films, using the 'Ciné' camera referred to in a few letters.[16]

Letters of October 1930–April 1932

[Saturday 18, probably October 1930; handwritten: PEF/DA/TUF/167]

SS *Lotus*
Saturday 18th

Dearest Ma and Daddy,
The journey across France was not at all too bad and though there were six of us in the carriage, I managed to sleep most of the time with my feet on the seat opposite. We were all English, 2 men and 1 wife (Baghdad) Iraq Railways, the two archaeologists Winkworth and Railton for Ur and self.

Breakfast at Avignon was welcome and the transit from train to boat was easy as usual. The *Lotus* might be worse but it is her last year in service, so one cannot expect much. The food not bad and the company mixed. I sit between a Belgian lady and an Egyptian gent. who has to correct my Arabic exercises every day.

I succumbed yesterday soon after lunch, it was raining, windy and cold, so that there seemed nothing better to do. Today things are getting tropical and I foresee that I shall be wearing summer things in Alex. [Alexandria]. We stay there 2 days, which I did not quite realise, but I suppose I can fill them by going to the Museum. [...]

As you can imagine there is no news, except that we get to Jaffa at 9am on Wednesday. [...] Shall post this as soon as I arrive but don't know if it will make any difference.

Much love to you both
Ever your loving
Olga

[22 October 1930; handwritten: PEF/DA/TUF/168]

[The letterhead on the stationery is from the Cyprus Palace Hotel of Nicosia. Olga crossed it out and wrote at the top of the letter: 'No! No! I haven't got here by mistake.']

Tel Ajjul.
22.10.30

Dearest Mà,

Here I am and found yr letter awaiting me. Spent the 2 days at Alex. quite satisfactorily. Saw the sights with an Englishwoman who knew the place during the war. The Mus. [Museum] is dull, being entirely Graeco-Ro. [Graeco-Roman]. The Zoo is really well kept and has a specially pleasant elephant. Left Alex. yesterday midday and got to Jaffa this morn at 10. Mr Railton had asked me to lunch on shore, so we descended together and got through the customs and I chartered a car door to door £2. Had my last civilised meal at the Palatin Hotel (and it was a good one), having bought fruit and so on in the town to take along. The road was more than usually bad and I bounced about from Jaffa to Askelon [Ashkelon], and through Ashdod (too biblical my dear, as Topsy would say) reached Gaza most thankfully at 3.30. There I picked up Terazi to show us the way and we found ourselves at camp by 4. All seems very pleasant, though still unfinished and it has been a real pleasure to see everyone again. Building goes on and there are about 20 men employed on it. The Tel is just behind the house, and from this side it seems quite small and unimposing though apparently it is very large. The sea is 20 mins. walk away and H. [Harding] has bathed daily as it is v. hot. Luckily there is a reef which forms a bathing pool so there is no danger if one keeps inside it. We have mosquitoe [sic] nets as they are still about so shall buy one locally to replace temporary camp one which I shall use tonight.

Thurs. Slept well but have to go to Gaza today to see the Dr – usual quarantine tiresomeness.

It is all most civilised, the train runs along just in front of the house and we can sit in the shadow of the fig trees. They are ripe by the way, and I've eaten at least a score already.

We had a bit of a dehayah [*dahiyah* – dance] last night – it was lovely to hear them singing again and to see them sitting round the fence.

Well, darling – very best love to all,
Ever yours
Olga

[27 October 1930; handwritten: PEF/DA/TUF/169]

c/o P.O.
Gaza.
27.10.30.

Dearest Mà,

It has been perfect here so far, only a thought as to what is to come to cast a shadow on the proceedings. The house is still being built and I am in a room temporarily. It has been quite like old times and we have laughed more than I've ever done since Qau. Starks [Starkey] has been in great form. The baby [John Starkey] is very well, though I think it may not always be easy for him. He can't very well be left alone as there is nowhere to leave him, so that he may get rather autocratic with his entourage always in attendance [Figure 5.4].

A visitor to the camp is a sweet heron who was clubbed on the head by a boy. He installed himself in my room and has refused meat and drink ever since he came though I bought beetles for him at great expense!

Figure 5.4 John Starkey (son of J.L. and M.R. Starkey) with nannies 'Arlia' and 'Jermum' at Tell el-'Ajjul, November 1930. See letter of 27 October 1930. Starkey family collection. Courtesy of Wendy Slaninka.

H. and I bathed 2 days ago and since then daily after sunset. It is a mile down the wadi to the sea but well worth it when one gets there; the sea is hot, definitely so and now that the moon waxes stronger it is as light as day. Not a soul for miles of course, though this evening there was a large escort of boys who sang cheerfully as we came home and who swim like fishes in the sea. It is only our moral support which would induce them to behave so lightheartedly after dark.

We are so civilised here that a train passes our door daily, but we still haven't got used to it. There are one or two houses and gardens about.

Woe is me! Just when I contemplated being able to eat as many figs as I liked, we heard in Gaza that the Wadi Ghuzzeh ones produce fever, so have reluctantly foresworn them. Have made myself a most successful mosquitoe [sic] net, which is in use nightly, though the mosquitoes are not the malarial kind.

The arrangements are very palatial especially Colt's 2 rooms and we are actually having 2 aunts [huts?] to be erected near the house, as you have to walk miles in order to find a possible place. What will Prof. [Petrie] say?!!

I distinguished myself this evening by losing my clothes after I'd undressed and bathed. I couldn't find the dam[n]ed things and had nearly to entertain the idea of walking home in my bathing suit. Luckily when all the suite had looked for them some time I came across them most thankfully.

We are expecting the Miss Gardners[17] any day; they come for 3 wks or so before joining Miss C.T. [Caton Thompson][18] in Egypt.

Already we feel that we've been here for ever and English existence seems a dream. [...]

[1 November 1930; handwritten: PEF/DA/TUF/170]

c/o P.O.
Gaza,
S. Palestine.
1.11.30

Dearest Daddy,
You would like this place – so different from Tel Fara, where we were before. There is a dried-up river-bed behind the house, which ends only a mile away in the sea. Instead of the usual waste of sand, there are reeds and rushes, tamarisks and fig trees, gourds and tomatoes, all watered by

fresh water pools, which are the home of innumerable duck and also, alas! of mosquitoes. The latter pest should be over in a fortnight when the first rains come.

The valley is a sportsmens' [sic] paradise; besides duck, there are geese, quails, sand-grouse (or is it grice!), snipe, teal, plover and partridges. Gaza's sportsmen come out in cars or on donkeys and stand vividly silhouetted in the dusk against the skyline – occasionally – very occasionally – we hear a shot, but never have we seen the bag and no one has offered to give or sell us any game. When I see a dead bird, I will wire.

The fish are more exciting, as you can actually see them gambolling about in the waves and several times a week, a man (undoubtedly the Old man of the sea), arrives and sells us, after much bargaining, part of his catch. Good but small and not so difficult to bone as most small fishes.

I found a tremendous snake-skin the other day, at least 1¼ yd long, but in trying to turn it – a most exasperating job – the dam[n]ed thing broke and is no more. I am told that we hear jackals at night, but so ignorant am I, that I haven't succeeded in distinguishing them from dogs. C[h]ameleons and lizards abound and there have been many scorpions about – unpleasant customers!

All this sounds very wild and then I have to spoil it by saying that we are in sight of the railway and that there are at least two white-washed 2 storied buildings included in the view from the house.

The party is still the Old Firm, the Starkeys, Harding and Self and today we began digging, which has not been possible before as we have only just got our permit. [...]

[14 November, probably 1930; handwritten: PEF/DA/TUF/171]

Tel Ajjul.
Nov. 14.

Darling Mà,
Gosh! oh gosh, it has just dawned on me that it is Nov. 14, you know one hasn't the slightest idea of dates or time out here and nobody's watch goes, and all this vagueness is most demoralising. I am so sorry, but I hope better late than never – many happy returns of the day darling.

Well, we were sitting quietly eating our lunch on market day, when the unwelcome sound of a car was heard and who should emerge but Prof., Lady P. [Petrie], Scott and Vernon[19] quite unannounced, fresh from Jerusalem. Lady P. and Starks together prevailed on Prof. to go back to Gaza for the night and until next week to avoid risk, but I understand they had a hard struggle for it. Lady P. was looking none too well, rather doubled up and has (I hear) had some of the usual b. [bilious] attacks on the way. They seemed pleased with their rooms and did the entire tour of the tel. [...]

H. has a fine Ciné Kodak so you may look forward to seeing some funny pictures when we come back. At four daily I sally forth with various bottles and dose the whole work. He took me doing it the other day, in fact every incident of the day will get done in time.

Starks' London box arrived today after a slight accident and damage. This time virtue has not been rewarded because my old rubber boots, which were inside, have been torn to shreds and I can't wear them. So I might have had those nice ones we saw after all!

There has been much talk and trouble about land and landlords and poor S. [Starkey] has had his hands full and has spent much time in Gaza being diplomatic. We hope today will have seen things settled.

We have 2 very fine lavatories, politely referred to as the 'aeroplanes', why I no longer remember. They are necessary here, as the country is very open and the one small wady behind the tel quite inadequate.

We have yet to hear what the powers that be have to say about them.

Touch wood my hospital is empty at the moment, but I suppose that with malaria it may be full again at any time. The risk of new cases now is slight as we have had some rain and the wind is much stronger, all told some 20% of the people here have gone down with it, so we know for another year that it is no good starting so early. A pity as the weather till now has been heavenly and we have been a very happy party. All rather dreading the new elements about to descend on us, Scott is known all over the work as Humpty Dumpty – Starks nickname for him – and I fear many think it quite a sound surname and they are likely to come out with it at any time.

Went to the village today to pay the ladies a visit. Saw a bride, all painted up and very pretty; she is not allowed to leave her tent, but seemed very cheerful with all.

The Ps [Petries] and Co. are stuck in Gaza according to the Dr till the wadi clears, can't help feeling sorry for them, but they are in a comfortable home with Miss Evans, and I hear that Lady P. is in bed, but Miss Evans says she is too maddening as she won't eat what the Dr tells her! So it is just as well that she should not be here.

We expect Miss Gardner back from her trip in the Wadi tomorrow DV [God willing]. So every day has its excitement and 'dousha' (noise), in fact I mean to keep a chart, some days it is very high.

If you want to know what we have been talking and thinking about, read Genesis, the bits where Abraham and later Isaac dig wells in the Wadi Ghuzzeh and dispute with Abimelech. One of the wells we are disputing about is at least 3000 yrs old – who knows? it may be the same. Can you please send me my bible after all, there is no camp one and Mr S's [Starkey's] is not so full of notes as mine. […]

[21 November, probably 1930; handwritten: PEF/DA/TUF/172]

Tell el Ajjul.
Nov. 21.

Dearest Mà,
[…] We have had various descents on us from the Gaza party, culminating in one yesterday, when it was decided to move the main body of the camp to Tell Fara, if even for a month.

Poor Starks was carted to hospital yesterday with a bad attack of malaria, he has been down 4 days but we want him to convalesce quietly without the worry of things happening around him, which he can't attend to. Harding goes today to Fara accompanied by Scott to roof the old house and get it in order and yrs truly will be conducting excavations at Tell Ajjul for a week all on her own, Mrs S and the baby to keep me company.

Lady P. came out with the lorry this morning and is I suppose 'putting things in order'. Have only a few slight cases in hand now and as the work really runs itself and we have cut down temporarily by half all should be well. […]

The whole party except the S's, H. and I to go to Fara next Wed., so really things are turning out better that [sic] we could possibly expect. Lady P. very anxious that I should go there for a change of air, oh! gosh oh gee! […]

[30 November, probably 1930; handwritten: PEF/DA/TUF/173]

Private

Tell Ajjul.
Nov. 30.

Dearest Mà,
Starks is out of hospital I'm glad to say and we are all well, touch wood! Day before yesterday a bad blow fell – a letter from P. [Prof. Petrie?] now

settled at Tell Fara to say that either H. or I were to come out next Suk [market] day with 'a few weeks baggage' – presumably because they will need someone as interpreter! Already we get rumours of strange doings and they have collected all the bad hats to work for them. I don't think it will fall to me to go as H. would be far more suitable to cope with things. Lady P. [Petrie] wanted me to go over for a 'rest cure' but somehow the idea did not appeal! It will make 7 in camp there and only S. and I here – it is amusing that they can't manage without us, for they refused all offers of help at first!

You should have seen them on the day they came out from Gaza. F.P. [Flinders Petrie], Mrs B. [Benson] and the driver in the cab of the lorry and H.P., Brown [Ralph Richmond Brown], Mahamed [el-Kreti?] and 2 boys perched on the luggage in the truck. They must have been shaken to bits. They asked me to go over then, but I said – 'How could I when I was the only one on the work.' My reign I'm glad to say passed off very smoothly and Starks had no fault to find. It was an interesting experience to have no one to refer to about anything for 5 days.

It is sad about Sidholme in one way – it must be a lugubrious job clearing everything up, but it must be a tremendous weight off Uncle Bertie's mind.[20] Give them all my love. We bathed on Nov. 30th. Doesn't it seem marvellous and though it is cold at night now the days are perfect. The mosquitoes must be nearly dead.

Last Suk day I cleaned out my room only to find that a large rat had made a nest in my nice Witney blankets.[21] Luckily the family had not arrived and after a thrilling chase all over my room and Harding's the blighter was ultimately caught by the carpenter among the medicine bottles in the 'hospital'. One blanket completely ruined, but the poor dear had made herself so comfortable.

The Cinés [film] have come out beautifully – S. and H. have invented a magic lantern out of a biscuit box – too professional – to show the pictures. They enlarge to a foot across and show up well – what we want is a projector.

Dec. 1. The Petrie box arrived this evening, so my leather coat and other necessaries will be available.

When writing to Lady P. you might remark that you are glad to hear from me that fresh food is so easy to get again this year. Apparently at T. F. [Tell Fara] they do little but open tins – here I have avoided all tinned food so far!

Much love darling to everyone
Ever yours
Olga

Have sent an account of T.A. [Tell 'Ajjul] to Mortlock – hope it may appear in D.T. [*Daily Telegraph*]. […]

[Olga's undated draft for article intended for the *Daily Telegraph* published in or around March 1931; typed document with multiple handwritten edits (incorporated): PEF/DA/TUF/3206]

Excavations at Tell el Ajjul, S. Palestine.

Sand-covered mounds in South Palestine has a thrill for excavators, for they are nearly always the deserted site of an ancient town.

One of these mounds, or 'Tells', is now being worked by Sir Flinders Petrie and his assistants of the British School of Archaeology in Egypt at Tell el Ajjul, south of Gaza. The pottery sherds found on the surface show that the town was contemporary with Abraham. It is some 28 acres in extent, more than three times the size of Tell Fara or Tell Jemmeh, where the School has dug in previous seasons.

The town was protected by a great earth bank, which dropped down into a deep trench and the whole formed a rectangular enclosure, which invaders would find an effective barrier. Bronze arrowheads and clay pellets, to be shot from slings such as David used against Goliath, give evidence of raids and skirmishes, and large stones found at the bottom of the trench conjure up lurid thoughts of mangled enemies.

A discovery which promises to be unique in the history of Palestinian archaeology, shows that though Tell Ajjul was a flourishing port only a mile from the sea, it was not always a peaceful town. The excavators have already traced some 40 ft of an underground passage, large enough for a man to walk through. It may have been a secret entrance way to the well-fortified city. Probably it was cut underneath the sloping causeway which was the recognised means of entry, and it leads in an easterly direction away from the mound.

Where does the tunnel begin within the walls and where will it end? Work is necessarily slow and tantalizing, for only one man can wield his pick in the restricted space and the filling of the tunnel is hard dry mud.

The men who planned and executed this ambitious scheme, and the great trench, must have been very competent workmen and they had the energy needed for the tasks, which is so sadly lacking among modern Arabs.

The deep wells near the town gateway are a further monument to their skill. Some are stone lined, others have spiral staircases, and the water-level is some 50 feet below the surface. It is a link with the past to watch the modern Beduwy [Bedouin] women, balancing large water jars on their veiled heads, as they come to draw water from wells which have not been used since Abraham's day.

There is no doubt that Tell el Ajjul – Hill of the Calves – was a flourishing centre of trade two thousand years before Christ. Ships anchored at the mouth of the Wadi Ghuzzeh, and exchanged their wares for spices and slaves from the East. Delicate polished weights imply that goldsmiths worked here and fashioned the earrings and beads which are sometimes found.

What catastrophe overtook the city and its inhabitants soon afterwards? It is a problem for the expedition to solve.

A thousand years before Solomon reigned, the town had lost its importance and in the Roman period the mound must have looked much as it does today – a sand-covered waste – while down on the green edges of the valley bed well-to-do Romans from Gaza built their summer villas near the sea.

The armies of Asia and Europe since the beginning of history have passed close to Tell Ajjul. They have left their mark, if it be only an Assyrian seal or an Egyptian amulet. Silver coins of the Crusaders are a reminder of the English-speaking peoples' first link with the Holy Land, and regimental badges, broken gramophone records and bully beef tins are all that remain of Allenby's push in the Great War, with the exception of rows of white gravestones in the Cemetery nearby.

Slowly the history of this deserted town is being wrested from the sand; on the mound itself brick walls are discovered daily, which must be planned and photographed [Figure 5.5]. Planning and photography are as much an essential part of the work as the direction of the 400 workmen.

Each pot is drawn to scale and numbered so that it can take its place in the series which will provide chronological evidence at the end of the season. Sir Flinders Petrie was the first archaeologist to recognise the importance of pottery as dating material, and every sherd is examined by him personally.

It is the Professor's fifty-first season in the field; his energy knows no bounds. He is up before sunrise, he draws all the objects found on the work – and they run into many hundreds – he plans all the buildings and he surveys the site [Figure 5.6]. At the end of the day he is ready to discuss the finds with his assistants, and he looks forward to the next morning, which will produce fresh problems for his attention and new hopes for a successful season, which he so richly deserves.

Figure 5.5 Bronze Age street at Tell el-'Ajjul. Hilda Petrie/Ajjul archive, Ajjul Album 2-1. © UCL Institute of Archaeology.

Figure 5.6 Petrie at Tell el-'Ajjul, 1933. Petrie Museum Archives, PMAN 1746. Courtesy of the Petrie Museum of Egyptian Archaeology, UCL.

[10 December 1930; handwritten: PEF/DA/TUF/174]

T. Ajjul.
Gaza
Dec. 10.

Darling Mà,
[…] Very many thanks for y[ou]r letters and the Fortnum's[22] box which arrived 2 days ago and seems most tempting – I know it will be sampled long before Xmas comes. […]

We expect the Colts here any day. They have gone to Jerusalem and S. went in to Gaza to meet and travel as far as Lud [Lod] to talk over news. He had to catch a 4.30 [illegible] and we have had an awful storm in the night. Thank goodness it has brought the water down the wadi – the mosquitoes are dead! Long live Professor and I suppose they will all come over here and I shan't be altogether sorry as S. and I have as much as we can do. Mr Royds,[23] the extra no., has arrived I hear; it will be interesting to see if the bright pictures of him are well founded. Anyhow he speaks Arabic.

I went into the Bazaar at Gaza last Suk day which Lady P. opened. She spoke v. well, quite short and useful but she wore her riding breeches under a white and mauve crepe dress and they showed, besides giving her a bulky look behind! After the show we came out together and she and H. went on to Fara. There was little to buy at the bazaar, all I could find to invest in were some toys for John and some toffee. But we feel we must do everything we can for the hosp. [hospital] because they have been so decent to us. I gather that H.P. [Hilda Petrie] in Gaza was not a roaring success but the O.M. [presumably 'Old Man', i.e. Petrie] has been charmingly tactful all round.

My coat arrived with a large tear in it from a nail in the box from Maples. F.P. was much annoyed and has written them a stiff one. […] Could you send me one of those mend-a-tear outfits – bits of rubber in a tin box – to repair the damage? Herewith a drawing of my fairy foot – shod and unshod; we saw the boots at Harrods I think, they had straps at the top to keep water out.

Well darling, I suppose Xmas will not be a very gay affair for you […] and Sidholme is sold. […] So cheer up and look forward to 1931 which should be full of new impressions. […]

[19 December, probably 1930; handwritten: PEF/DA/TUF/175]

Dec. 19. Tell Ajjul.

Dearest Mà,

Gosh we are living through some times! The Ps [Petries] arrived on Wed. and a few hours later the Colts got here in their super lorry. The revolution began right away that night, with wine being put on the dinner table and we had a cheery meal, with F.P. as witty as any.

Next morning I was called by him at the devil's dancing hour and was out before sunrise and spent a busy day on the work – probably my last one, as Vernon and Scott came today and H. and Brown complete the 13 on Sunday. We have had to put up separate little tables to accommodate the crowd.

Today, Suk day, has been spent in batting round, but horror of horrors the younger generation played the gramophone <u>all</u> the morning in the courtyard and they are evidently intending to keep up the standard they are used to – 'cocktails and laughter and what comes after – nobody knows' as the song puts it. All of which promises a good time with the exception of H.P. who is the same as ever and more so. Here she will get regular meals, the only thing that may save us. [...]

[23 December 1930; handwritten: PEF/ DA/TUF/176]

Tell Ajjul.
Dec. 23.

Darling Daddy,

[...] Now that everyone is installed here, we are having a time. The first few days were awful but now things seem to be settled and there is not so much batting about. Anyhow Mummy is having a quiet winter, relieved from certain trials and tribulations. Here they have to be laughed at, for at such close quarters life would not be worth living if we took things seriously. [...]

One of the men out here now has a gun, so we should be able to secure some ducks and things to eat, if he is a slightly better shot than the natives.

What with one damned thing after another it is now New Year's Eve and still your letter has not gone. [...]

We have been most gay and have been to 2 parties, one on Boxing Night at the Kuesevich's[24] house in Gaza and one at the Imperial Airways camp outside the town. The first was half Arab though we danced (one of the ladies asked her husband's permission each time she took the floor); we had an immense meal and kept going till midnight. Then last night's show was arranged on the spur of the moment. The camp where the India Air[25] planes land is very well run. Electric light, baths and nice bedrooms, it should be good when you consider that the flight to Baghdad cost £25 for 6 hrs.

My stock is rather low, I quite expect to be sent home for general insubordination. Have had to oppose H.P. in various matters and once I got quite angry with her – not without cause, believe me!

Dr Parker has now arrived, so that my medical services will be suspended, so I shall have an easy time. [...]

[25 January 1931; handwritten: PEF/ DA/TUF /177]

Tell el Ajjul,
Gaza.
S. Palestine.
Jan. 25.

Dearest Mà,
[...] We are very gay and giddy here nowaday[s] thanks to Terry [Teresa] Colt and have riotous evenings in the Taylorian which is now complete and hung with Arab tenting lent by Mr Reading of Gaza which originally belonged to the Emir Abdulla.[26] We are now contemplating a film on the Cine Kodak to show the scenery hereabouts with a plot of deepest melodrama running through. I am to double the parts of witch and vamp, Terry heroine, H. hero, Colt villain and so on.

It is now Ramadan so there is some chance of the wild scheme materialising, though doubtless it will entail the heartfelt disapproval of the powers. We stop work at one now for the day, so have the afternoons to play about in. The last few days have been divine and such a relief after some days of incessant wind and sand. Yesterday we walked to the sea and back and Brown had the temerity to bathe.

Have now finished the two articles for USA and send you rough drafts just to amuse you [see below for example]. It is the dickens writing the same thing 3 times over.[27]

I am getting quite expert on the drum and know about six different beats. The film when (or rather if) we show it in London will have a drum accompaniment with 'motifs' for the principal players and a theme song running throughout in the best American manner.

At the moment I am concentrating on the storeroom and have not been near the cem. [cemetery] for a week, so comparatively I am a lady at large and never have breakfast before 7.30. Even then except for the Professorial party and Mr Royds, I am usually the first down except for the early shift. [...]

Poor Scott is in hospital with dysentery, he has had no luck all the season, otherwise – touch wood – everyone is well. We really did do a bit of roof holding the other night, when the wires snapped in Scott's room and the roof blew away. Then another night Lady P. held hers on 'all night' but no one was as impressed as they were meant to be, and Harding was called in to put it on in the early hours. [...]

[Olga's draft article, possibly one of two referred to for newspapers in the United States c. March 1931: PEF/DA/TUF/3207]

A Deserted City

Walls have ears, and if only they could repeat their knowledge, excavation would be an easy job. For three thousand years the walls of a deserted city in South Palestine, near Gaza, have been muffled with sand – the last human sounds they heard may well have been the shouts of camel drivers leaving the city in the days of Isaac. Then silence reigned, except for the cries of birds in the marshes below the town, and gradually the sand crept up from the sea, only a mile away, shutting out all other impressions.

Thirty centuries have passed. Now the walls re-echo again to the shouts of Arab children carrying baskets of sand on their heads. Men fill the baskets and each day the willing workers reveal more of an ancient stronghold now known as Tell el 'Ajjul – Hill of the Calves.

The Golden Calf? Perhaps the memory of some temple dedicated to Isis or Ashtoreth, cow goddesses of wide appeal, may have lingered into Arab days, and now that Sir Flinders Petrie's expedition is digging the site, there may be concrete proof of it. Anyhow a tradition persists that a statue of a calf was found on the mound in recent times.

The only visible traces today of a once flourishing sea-port are the great earth banks which enclose it. They form a square, and depressions on three sides indicate where the entrances may have been. Ships from Syria, Cyprus and Egypt anchored at the mouth of the Wadi Ghuzzeh. Merchants from the East came bringing their wares, incense, spices and slaves to exchange them for goods from abroad, alabaster from Egypt, copper from Cyprus and wool from the North.

The site is strewn with painted sherds of Cypriote and Syrian make, there are fragments of alabaster of finest quality, and surest test of all, there are many weights of different sizes, some so minute that they can only have been used by goldsmiths, testifying to a flourishing trade.

Suddenly, about two thousand years before Christ, this prosperity came to an end, fine ware is absent, and soon the town had dwindled into obscurity, never to be occupied again.

What was the reason for the change?

Speculation is fascinating but useless. It is possible that the mouth of the river became too much silted up, or that the development of the land route to Egypt made Gaza a better stopping-place, or that malaria had become such a severe problem in the district that it was necessary to abandon the town in favour of Gaza, further from the unhealthy marshes of the estuary. Facts which the archaeologist gleans from bricks and pottery sherds and broken bones may still provide the answer.

Meanwhile work proceeds, and a deep trench has been found which supplemented the defence provided by the earth bank. The earth from the trench was piled up to form the bank, which gives a slope of some eighty feet to be negotiated by would-be invaders. Arrowheads of bronze and hard clay pellets, to be discharged from slings like David used, show that the defences were not purely ornamental. When raids were likely these defences could be heavily manned, and it is not pleasant to think of great stones hurled down the slope, leaving destruction in their wake.

In peace-time, veiled women came out through the gates, carrying large water jars to the wells. There were stone-lined wells, and others with spiral staircases leading down to them; when cleared today by Arab boys, neck deep in water, they recover the broken sherds dropped there by some laughing Rebecca of long ago. For it is in part of this valley that 'Isaac's servants digged and found a well of springing water'.

If it were not for the aeroplanes which pass over on the route to India, and the Palestine–Egypt railroad, which is in sight, it would be easy to imagine oneself alive in the days of the Patriarchs, and [while] each day adds to our knowledge of the past, it seems more certain that in the south country at any rate, time has stood still.

The skyscrapers of our modern civilisation, with their towering walls, belong to a different order from that of the present-day Arab hovel. Here however 3000 years have passed and yet the camel-drivers of Isaac's time would see much to remind them of their old home town.

[4 February 1931; handwritten: PEF/DA/TUF/178]

Tell Ajjul
Gaza.
Feb. 4.

Dearest Mà,

Many thanks for yr Brno [Czechoslovakia] letter and 2 p.cs [postcards]. The former was duly shown to H.P. who is well but very nearly unbearable. Bat, bat, bat all day about nothing mostly, so that it is quite likely that the rest of the camp will be already installed in the lunatic asylum when she arrives. I did not know she could be so generally unfair, it demoralises us all and no one cares a hang about anything.

Colt has been ill for 10 days with a species of flu, so has Vernon and Scott has just come back from a fortnight in hospital with dysentery, however their dropping out has not made any real difference! It is a case of 'too many cooks' here and nobody feels any responsibility, because they are given to understand that everything they do is wrong.

Miss Matthews from Jerusalem, Miss Grimes and Mr Reynolds, with whom I stayed when last in Jerusalem, are here for the night, putting up 3 extra has been quite an effort, but 2 slept in the Taylorian and Mr R. in the antica storeroom and we sat down 15 in the evening to dinner.

Went to tea with the Cafferata[s][28] on Ali Montar [Tell Ali Muntar] last Sunday. He is Head of Police in Gaza and has a new wife. They live in [a] tent until their house is ready and it all seems ideal in fine weather. During the rains, well – they think differently. She lived two years in Cyprus before her marriage and knows all the people I do, so we had a good downright gossip.

The effect of our repression in the camp circle is that everyone goes quite mad when away from it and that we are much more gay and giddy than ever before and when we go out we are positively rowdy. Tomorrow we are going to Askelon now Migdol in the truck, which should be a gay excursion.

I fear me I did not write last week, so you never heard about our party at the Readings. It was a wet night and we went in in the truck, the Ps having gone first to dinner. We skidded all the way to Gaza, I don't believe we went straight once and found all the 'elite' of Gaza assembled when we ultimately arrived. Mr R. [Reading] is land commission[29] and has the best house in the town. A real house of the Arabian nights. A wooden door gives access to a garden of shady trees – surely there is a fountain somewhere not far off. Something even more massive among portals admits to a paved courtyard of vast proportions open to the sky. On each side wooden staircases lead to the upper storey and everywhere there is a fine disregard of the weather – everything is open to wind and rain. When we arrived the rain had stopped and the moon lighted up the scene during fitful appearances. The rooms are all vaulted and one at least had a deep recess – where once a Turkish pacha [pasha] sat to receive his guests.

We danced, ate and made merry in the usual way and Prof. and Lady P. looked on through a cloud of smoke. When we got ready to go at about one o'clock we heard the drums beating at the mosque next door – an impressive persistent drumming all the more effective at that hour and we saw the minaret lighted for the feast with coloured lamps.

H., Brown and self are getting quite snappy with the drums ourselves. You should see us sitting on the Tell at sundown among the red anemones with the pipes and the drums, making wild primitive – very primitive – sounds on them as the sun sets into the sea.

I am now on the cem. again and have my own gang, which is more satisfactory than trying to run a show with someone else. [...]

[14 February, probably 1931; handwritten: PEF/DA/TUF/180]

Tell Ajjul
Gaza.
S. Palestine
Feb. 14.

My darling Daddy,
[...] We are leading our usual hectic existence but manage to be extremely gay in between whiles. Now that we have a large room (built by the generosity of a friend of the Colts) where we can make as much noise as we like and let off steam generally, well we just do! We sing, dance to the gramaphone [sic] and have ballets just as in the old days of long ago. Every now and again a FACE appears at the window and goes away when looked at and so we are hurriedly making curtains to shut out the sinister sight. H.P. is well up to form and has thought of several new stunts – we are now wondering when they are going, but they talk of April 15th which is terribly late. [...]

There is a wild scheme afoot that the Colts, Harding, Brown and self should go to Petra in Transjordania when the season's over in the Ford truck. It would be great fun and then I should go on to Cairo to stay with the Clevelands for a week or so. If it comes off we should leave here about April 10th, and I should get home early in May.

Last market day we went in the truck to Askelon north of Gaza which was a great town in the days of the Philistines and was used and fortified again by the Crusaders. It is a lovely place by the sea, strewn with columns, statues and carvings of the Roman period. Half of it has fallen into the sea and it is amazing to see columns and walls half sticking out of the water. We had a very cheerful day and came home in the dark singing loudly. We are most unarchaeological this year, all due to Mrs Colt who is so lively and amusing that even Prof. thaws when her Ladyship is not looking.

We shall soon have got through Ramad[a]n which is rather a trying time. The men fast all day, they don't even drink or smoke and then they gorge at night. Net result they upset their tummies and tempers and can't do a proper day's work, so we knock off at one o'clock and end up by three days' holiday at the end of the month. Shall hope to do some expeditions then. [...]

[19 February, probably 1931; handwritten: PEF/DA/TUF/181]

Tell Ajjul
Gaza
S. P. [South Palestine]
Feb. 19.

Darling Mà,
[...] I think the trouble may be that I am in the firm's bad books; a certain extent (only HP's, mind you) and very likely she doesn't want to have to say pleasant things about me which she doesn't mean. And yr explanation may have something to do with it as well. However there is nothing to worry about, she is her usual difficult self only more so. As for the chin, it has not been any too good, though I use the [surgical] spirit, my only comfort is that Mrs Colt always has them [spots] too, and it is no small one!

The Aid [Eid] is early and Starks and H. have gone with the Colts to Jerusalem, Beisan [Beth Shan] and Megiddo for a spree. Was not asked. Brown and Vernon have gone to the Dead Sea walking from Beersheba. So we are a small party here. Walked to Deir Belah [Deir el-Balah] on Tuesday with Dr and Mr Royds – a matter of 11 miles there and back, so felt quite proud of myself. Saw the wailing at the tombs and met many friends. Yesterday I was asked to spend the day with the Readings. They fetched me and we went for a drive in the afternoon. He is one of those unostentatious little men who is responsible for anything good in the British Empire. Has 8 children. Today the Cafferatas are coming to fetch me for a picnic tea and supper, so I'm not doing so badly and have got some arrears made up.

A letter has been posted to Messrs Cook by F.P. so we are all very hopeful at hearing a definite date for departure ere long. So far there are only rumours.

Have really been very flourishing, touch wood, all the season, and have not been feeling nearly so tired as yr before last. Most evenings we do ballets of the Wellsian kind[30] and we must be feeling pretty energetic for them. [...]

[28 February, probably 1931; handwritten: PEF/DA/TUF/182]

Tell Ajjul.
Gaza
Feb. 28

Dearest Mà,
[...] The holidays are over, I spent a day with the Cafferatas who took me to Faluja, an out of the way village off the beaten track. He was there on duty and we waited about surrounded by a mob of small children calling out 'Yehudi' and throwing mud when they thought it safe! I found the others back from their wanderings when I got home; they had a saga of adventures to recite, most of them connected with mud and breakdown, so it was just as well I stayed at home.

The week has been uneventful. Slightly wet, had half a day off yesterday because of rain and I have been busy waxing skulls, not much good my writing to you with this hard pencil. The sun today has been lovely and I lay out all the afternoon reading Lorna Rea's book *Rachel Moon*, v. well written. I allow myself one a week out of those supplied by Hatchards[31] to the Colts, so am probably more up to date than you are with the laggardly Mudies.[32]

The situation here is going from bad to worse – for not only have we one unbalanced mind to deal with but two! Colt goes off the rails now and again, has awful fits of depression followed by periods of gay irresponsibility when he cares not what he says! He and H.P. have great scenes followed by hours of punctilious politeness; it might be funny if it was not for poor Prof. who is worn out with it all and the perpetual nagging. She is as bad as ever about meals now, is always 'too busy' for food and has now started a quite new stunt of standing at the dinner table. The weekly pay and roll call absorbs her whole time, she does nothing else, and the queries are endless.

Have had several weeks now without any attention focussed on me and so far have managed to keep out of all the rows. Suppose she has given me up as hopeless, just do my various jobs as well as I can and speak to her as little as possible. Any conversation leads to grumbles about members of the camp and that is not much fun. It is all so maddening and unnecessary but communications with Messrs Cook are proceeding and we hope to hear definite news when they are going soon. Then I suppose your trials will begin, but hope you have enjoyed your winter. [...]

[12–13 March, probably 1931; handwritten: PEF/DA/TUF/183]

Tell Ajjul
Gaza.
12th March.

Dearest Mà,
[...] We have spent a moderately quiet week, except for rather an exciting attempt at murder; much gore was shed between the combatants and they are both in hospital prior to an extended visit to prison.

There is no news at present as to the date of departure but putting 2 and 2 together we have come to the conclusion that our troubles may be over about Ap. 6. Don't know when I shall leave but am all for this Petra trip if it takes place. Have written an article for the *Field*[33] which will be illustrated by specially taken photos. Hope to send you a copy in my next. Has passed the powers that be so all is well.

The days are warmer now and we shall soon be able to bathe daily once more. My last swim was on Sun. 28th and don't think that was so bad. Tomorrow we shall probably excursionize to Tell Rafah, H.P. wants to come as usual, but everyone feels they want their day of rest, so I don't know if she will get asked. [...]

Friday 13th – Despite ominous date we have had a most amusing day. Terry, H. and B. [Brown] and I bathed this morning and it was divine. Lay on the sand for ages afterwards and played games. Then this afternoon the P's were invited to Tell Raffa [Rafah], just on the Egyptian border and seven of us went there and back without mishap. The Tell is outwardly all Roman, everyone was pleased and polite, we watched the sunset over the sea and got home before eight. Most successful outing and should clear the air!

No photos come yet.

[24 March, probably 1931; handwritten: PEF/DA/TUF/184]

Tell Ajjul
Gaza
March 24.

Dearest Mà,

[…] I send you these photos – H's one of me is not for publication – I felt like cutting his throat for not telling me about the whisp – but everyone says it is characteristic and must admit they're right.

Keep these two of Migdal [Migdol] carefully for me, they are Brown's photos of the mosque and <u>suq</u> there and required some ingenuity to get. I stood ostentatiously with my camera pointing in the opposite direction and collected the inevitable crowd while he did the real one in peace.

The Ps leave on the 17th, the Colts intend going on the 12th taking Brown, H. and me, everything is v. touchy so I don't know if we shall get to Petra after all. Have heard from the Clevelands who tell me to come anytime so shall probably be in Cairo by 25th and shall have Brown for the journey which is good.

Am concentrating on the storeroom now in preparation for the division. Eruptions in all quarters are now frequent, the atmosphere is distinctly heavy and everyone is talked at and not <u>to,</u> if only they were not so roundabout in their methods things would be better. […]

[The Tell el-'Ajjul 1930/1931 season ended. Olga returned for the 1931/1932 season.]

[14–16 November 1931; handwritten: PEF/DA/TUF/185]

On board SS *Hobson's Bay*.
Aberdeen and Commonwealth Line [part of letterhead]
Nov. 14. 1931.
Finished Nov. 16.

Darling Daddy,

This is to wish you many happy returns of the day and I think this letter should get to you by then as a mail goes back from Malta. We get there on Tuesday and have now passed Cape St Vincent and are due near Gibraltar in about 10 hrs. We don't stop there so shan't see any sights.

There's no doubt that this is the most comfortable trip I've done, a 2 berth cabin of ample dimensions to myself on B Deck and an obliging steward. The food is amusing and we are apt to find tripe on the menu, and I am still plucking up courage to try some.

The passengers are a mixed lot, as you can imagine. [...] We play tennis and cards and there is a good panatrope gramophone. Tonight there is a cinema show so I think they do one proud for the price.

The first day out was pretty rough, but I survived and the fishes waited in vain for nourishment. We've not seen any exciting birds or fishes so far though they say there ought to be some porpoises later on. [...]

Am really having a good trip, divine weather – Malta for 4 hrs tomorrow. [...]

[1 December 1931; handwritten: PEF/DA/TUF/186]

Tell Ajjul.
Gaza
Palestine.
Dec. 1st . 1931.

Dearest Mà,

Two letters of yours dated 21st and 24th came today and I hope by now you have had some of mine. On second thoughts – don't use P.O. 20 unless you have something very urgent or private.

Last Sat. morning some 80 men started work on the Tell and Cem. Officially I have not started yet as I am doing oddments about the house and expect to get going in the new palatial storeroom soon. I have however had 2 days on the work and we got a small grave straight away. Things are really shaping well as regards the new rooms – I moved in yesterday to mine – whitewashed by my own fair hand – new spring mattress belonging to the firm, cement floor, wooden door made like a stable one to come and my old blue curtains from last year up again, all rather too short for their new windows. Your photo is above my bed and L's [Louis or Lionel] opposite to it. The veg. garden is under the window and radishes and spinach have already made an appearance. Lady P. [Petrie] has had her floor cemented too!!!!! She is very busy picking up things in the courtyard all day. Ba[34] has taken her out driving in the Ford and she is apparently very good at the wheel. The students have a deep-laid scheme to present her with an Austin 7 'with esteem and affection' which would ensure a peaceful season.

Had a charming letter from Miss M. [Murray] about the gown,[35] the M.P. [Hilda Petrie] much intrigued as to why she had written – also one from Cousin Joan enclosing £ 2.2.6 as an Xmas present, it is sweet of her.

So sorry about Mr Paton, he was quite a young man.

My cow I want would cost £30–40 so I doubt if we shall have her, though the powers that be have been quite amenable. [...]

Much love to you all
from Olga

[10 December 1931; handwritten: PEF/DA/TUF/187]

T. Ajjul
Gaza
Palestine.
Dec. 10. 1931.

Darling Daddy,

I believe you are honouring No. 14 with your presence at Christmas, so write there to wish you a good time and a specially happy New Year.

I have been getting on well so far and the trials and tribulations have not been hard to bear, as we all get together and 'larf' about them.

The sparrows are playing havoc with our garden in which we have planted many seeds which came up after 3 days! A garden is fun when things happen so quickly. We have put in 2 banana trees and hope to sit under its shady leaves before the end of the season.

I got here too late to see the birds migrating this year, in fact there has been nothing exciting in the way of wildlife except the cow which I saw in the pantomime, which Mummy will tell you about!

We have just begun to find things and I am pleasantly busy but not too hecticly [sic] so. [...]

The Imperial Airways machines no longer come to Gaza on their way to Baghdad, but have deserted us for Tiberias, so that we feel quite quiet without the daily hum of aeroplanes.[36]

The party is settling down and the Warren Hastings[37] are a very charming couple, even though they both were at the same co-education school! [...]

[10 December 1931; handwritten: PEF/DA/TUF/188]

Tell Ajjul
Gaza.
Dec. 10. 1931. Palestine

Dearest Mà,

[…] All continues well here and don't worry about bandits – a man who spoke Arabic was held up with many others on the Jericho road, and they wanted his boots as well as his watch. So he said 'Ya habibi' (oh! my dear) you really can't take my watch and my boots, which do you prefer?' So they chose the boots!

We went to an amazing show 2 nights ago. The men from Khan Yunis invited us to a play, which turned out to be nothing more nor less than our pantomime, complete with Pantaloon, Columbine, policeman and cow. It was however the frankest thing ever seen on any stage, Mrs H. [Harding's mother] and I were a little overwhelmed when the cow was milked at the end of Act II and there was a real splashing sound just under our noses. We left just before the Grand Finale, the bedroom scene as we thought it might be even more blush-making. However these minor details apart, it was a marvellous performance, full of real humour, character and skits of doctors, us and the world at large, not to mention themselves. Apparently the show takes place before a real wedding but this was specially staged for our benefit. The cow was in the true pantomime tradition, two men covered with black arbiyahs,[38] while the foremost had twisted red horns, and it was a very lively animal. I was able to say in answer to enquiries of my opinion that I had never seen anything to equal it in England! […]

The Hastings are a great success and have joined the rebels. Dr Sperrin Johnson[39] has strange mannerisms, pants and snores as I know to my cost but will be a distinct asset.

Col. Clarke[40] is a typical English sahib but I don't think this is quite the life for him. Miss Bentwich[41] is a well-meaning woman and you know what that means.

Dinner bell has just gone, so I must too if I don't want to sit next to H.P. Later – Things going pretty well, she had her first b [bilious] attack today but is better this evening.

Poor Starks is in hospital with an attack, but he has not been feeling very grand all the season.

I do the medecines [sic] as usual, with Dr J. to refer to in cases of difficulty and am really learning something from him. Also I do the storeroom with Miss B. [Bentwich] and Mrs H. to assist and go out for waxing and drawing in the field, so there is greater variety than if I sat on the same little patch all day. […]

[28 December 1931; handwritten: PEF/DA/TUF/189]

Tell Ajjul.
Gaza.
Dec. 28 1931.

Dearest Mà,
Your Xmas letter, Daddy's and Tuffy's telegram all duly arrived for which many thanks.

Christmas Day, being Friday, was a holiday but we spent it quietly enough and as is usual ate heartily – on Xmas Eve two parties of carol singers came from Gaza, the second lot arrived at 12.45 in a lorry some 20 strong, chiefly police who had dined well but not wisely. Lady P. came out in her pyjamas and told them to go away, so the Xmas spirit was not very noticeable.

On Boxing Night seven of us went to the Annual dinner at the Kueseviches – a strange mixture of east and west in their vast vaulted hall. We were all frozen with cold and only managed to warm up when dancing began. About 12.30 we went on to Reading's mediaeval mansion, where it was a bit warmer and eventually we got home v. cheerfully about 2.

There is a cold epidemic on in both senses of the word. A virulent variety has assailed us all in turn – mine is better now, and we have been breaking the ice on the water in the mornings, though it is gloriously sunny later on, so no one can say we don't have seasonable weather.

The Cemetery is pretty busy and we have a goodish share of exhibitional wares already. [...]

[3 January 1932; handwritten: PEF/DA/TUF/190]

Tell Ajjul.
Gaza.
Jan. 3. 1932.

Dearest Mà,
[...] All continues well here, the first b. [bilious] attack it is full force today, so we have a little peace, nobody is as sympathetic as they should be!

We have now arranged to have Arabic lessons in Gaza once a week with a Sheykh, H., Ba and I, so shall go in on Thursday evenings in the truck. H. is also negotiating the purchase of a piano which will make our evenings even more hectic than they are already. Prof. calls the Taylorian 'Coney Hatch'[42] no 'Coney Island'! and even as I write we are all congregated listening to the gramophone. Sheila Hastings is a great asset and real fun and not so noisy about it as our dear Terry. Colt is expected tomorrow as ever is, having sent for the truck on Saturday – The days pass busily enough, we have more than enough to do in the storeroom and I suppose I see well over 100 patients a week and pass on the puzzles to the Dr who is really teaching me a lot. [...]

[8 January 1932; handwritten: PEF/DA/TUF/191]

Tell Ajjul –
Gaza.
Jan. 8. 1932.

Dearest Mà,
Two letters of yours came close together, one addressed to Lady P. had a good old gaff as an address, my dear, you put P.O. Box <u>20</u> which is H.'s private box, we gave her the letter and she was much puzzled by your mistake. Her's – 24.

She has been in bed for nearly a week, with undiagnosed complaint, Dr has been splendid, thermometer and stethoscope every four hours. I asked him if her temp was normal, he said 'Oh! quite, but I'll keep her in bed as long as possible.' Said I 'Dr you <u>are</u> an asset.' He said 'No, I'm not, I'm a philanthropist.'

As for the spots, I'm glad to say that apart from a few flea bites I am spotless and have been since my arrival, strange to say. Surely it shows that the place agrees with me. [...]

Colt arrived complete with mongrel puppy, aged 15 mths who had been doomed to death owing to his preference for shoes and carpets. He has already eaten Prof's sponge and behaved in an unseemly manner outside Lady P's door and the atmosphere is positively electric. Both Prof. and H.P. are going to Jerusalem tomorrow to stay at Govt. Ho. I gather though have not been informed of course. So while the cat's away – we are having a party tomorrow night, all the folk from Gaza, rather overwhelming but has to be faced, as we went there at Xmas. They will be 3 marvellous days. [...]

Planted the nasturtiums today all along the wall outside my door where they get plenty of sunlight – the lupins, stocks and mignonettes that Ba planted are all coming up slowly but well. We are eating radishes out of the garden and the spinach and lettuce and turnips are all well on.

Ramadan starts tomorrow with its half days, no work after one pm, so we may do some expeditions. [...]

[14 February 1932; handwritten: PEF/DA/TUF/192]

Tell Ajjul
Gaza.
Feb. 14. 1932.

Dearest Mà,

[...] Last Thursday night we went in for our first Arabic lesson from Sheykh Ahseyr[?] abu Shareik[?]. He lives in a perfectly good mosque in the midst of [a] garden of palms; we were led through a courtyard to a vaulted hall with a marble floor. In the centre was a large sunk tank with a carved marble fountain head at one end. We sat on a dais and were plied with tea and coffee alternately while we learned the rudiments of writing. The old boy was as pleased as punch because he was going to Haifa to sing for His Master's Voice, so in due time you will be able to hear him chant from the Koran.

The following day Starks, Harris, W. Hastings and I went off in the car eastwards to Beersheba. We spent some time at Tell es Saba [Tell es-Seba/ Tel Sheva], the old and original Beersheba, marching round for pottery and then pushed on to Tell Melk where we lunched by the side of a Roman well. Then on to Khorbet es Kasifa; we drove up onto a deserted stony hill and stopped. At once dozens of people rose up out of the ground at us and we realised we were in the middle of a troglodyte village. The houses were all caves, some with fine stone doorways. There was a good shop also in a cave where we found a beautiful old Arab coffee grinder which Colt bought.

As I write an expert coffee grinder is here doing the traditional r[h]ythmical grinding, rather attractive. At Kasifa there are early Christian churches in almost perfect condition, stone granaries and wells galore set in a country of rounded hills green with grass just now. People bring their flocks from Gaza and the sea coast thereof to feed and grow fat.

Just at sunset we reached our real objective, Tell Arad, where the King of Arad turned back the Israelites when they tried to get north during their wanderings. It is a commanding green mound with traces of Greek building on top, [and] the hills of Moab were clear and purple in the evening light. A shepherd whose flocks were feeding on the slopes offered me a lamb which I refused reluctantly. We turned home and said goodbye to our nice guide who had come with us from Kasifa. At Tell Melk we had an amusing tea in the police outpost occupied by one policeman whom we had known at Fara.

The car brought us home about 9.30 having overcome all obstacles – bogs, ruins, stones, ditches and ploughed fields. It is marvellous what Harris and Starks can make her do. [...]

The piano is expected tomorrow; we wonder what the P's will say at the new sign of decadence in camp. The worm turned last week and I told Prof., who let himself in for it by taking her part against me, exactly what I and everyone thought of Lady P. in camp and her methods. He could only be sympathetic and went so far as to say he had his troubles too, which he certainly has.

[24 February 1932; handwritten: PEF/DA/TUF/193]

T. Ajjul.
Gaza.
Feb. 24th 1932

Dearest Mà,
[...] We went a full carload to Tell Hesy,[43] where Prof. worked in umpteen 2. The road was vague and stony though we got there moderately early in the afternoon and were able to wander round and pick up early bits of pottery – found wild periwinkles growing and started homeward about 5 rather hungry as we had eaten nearly everything for lunch. Then of course in our cross-country obstacle run, we stuck in a sandy wadi and had to put in some good hard work with picks and putting stones under the wheels to go out again.

Eventually we did and proceeded further only to run out of petrol, which was an unstatesmanlike thing to do! However it was bright moonlight and Starks, Harris and Sheila started to walk on to get to the main road and hail a car. We others rummaged in the food box and found some sausages, lit the Primus with the last remaining match and cooked sausages on a biscuit lid and drank hot tea. Then Warren, Ba and I felt chilly and walked on, expecting to meet the relieving car at any minute. So we walked and we walked until we found ourselves at the war cemetery at Gaza[44] – had walked from the other side of Beit Hanūn [Beit Hanoun], a matter of 5 or 6 miles.

There we did meet the others coming with a fresh supply of petrol, but still fresh and absorbed in conversation we walked on beyond Gaza and were picked up about 10.30 and transported to camp, where we ate heartily. It then transpired that Starks and the others had walked almost as far as we had, when a car caught them up, which they hailed. The occupants told them to get in and all three squeezed in somehow, only to find a corpse as a fellow passenger. So they all drove on quite cheerfully to the native cemetery, where the car pulled up in a crowd of mourners and wailers – all howling their best – one can't imagine that sort of thing happening anywhere else.

The week was busy but uneventful. I told you, I think, that Col. Clarke went in to hospital with some sort of gastric 'flu' contracted in Jerusalem. Lo and behold 2 days later, H.P. had a temp of 102° and we promptly and thankfully bundled her in too, with sighs of relief. Our joy was short lived as she was back in 2 days, since when she has however been pianissimo and in her room a lot, only emerging v. early before anyone is about and again in the evenings.

Yesterday we set off again to go to Hebron – we pottered a good bit on the way and saw 2 tells, one very early and intact. From Beit Jibrin one goes through a deep valley, with cyclamen growing among boulders and many small firs planted by the parental [Mandate] government. As usual we reached our destination about dusk and paid the inevitable visit to the tomb of Abraham and Sarah, for the benefit of the Arab boys we had with us, who were wild with excitement at their first visit of Khalyl [Hebron] – one of the four places of pilgrimage.

We called on the Millers – a magistrate, who, at 35, is retiring on pension and is therefore selling up his goods and chattels. [...] We didn't get away till 8.15 and took the Beersheba road. Harris drove magnificently over a tricky road and we got home after midnight – and felt quite devilish up so late! Had soup and sherry and went to bed, only to dream that we were coming home again and that Terry and Harris [Colt] would talk outside the Professorial bedroom with the usual result.

It might be worth your while to invest [in] a good scale map of S. Palestine, to follow our various adventures into the blue on Suk days and I would always find it useful.

H. has been asked to go to Cairo to attend a conference about pottery and to edit a corpus, which will be a lifetime sort of job, but with no screw [wages] to it I fear – anyhow a good feather in his cap. [...]

The piano is now installed and provides much amusement, we are often pretty gay in the evenings. Terry and her sister are tremendous assets, and the noise at meals should be heard in Gaza. [...]

[7 March 1932; handwritten: PEF/DA/TUF/194]

Tell Ajjul
Gaza
March 7.   Palestine

Dearest Mà,

For once I spent a quiet Suk day last week with Kitty[45] on the seashore. We took food and a book which turned out to be well worth reading; *Apartments to Let* by Norah Hoult, a bit depressing but very true to life. [...]

The week has been full of alarums and excursions and the atmosphere has been somewhat strained. Things culminated night before last in a mass meeting organised by Col. Clarke, who has completely veered round to the rebels, when all grievances were voiced. In so many words the demands were reasonable enough, and they were passed unanimously, though I'm pretty sure nothing will come of them. HP made as many objections as she could.

People are being sacked day by day and the money will not permit many more days' work. Just now we have the Crowfoots[46] staying for a night, also a Prof. from N.Y. Univ. [New York University] sat down 18 to dinner tonight, so we have a house full.

Last week I went into Gaza and invested in 5 yds of stuff total value 4s/9d and Kitty very kindly made me a dress and bloomers, which you will see pictured in a photo Ba took which I hope to send soon, (though the bloomers are not in evidence!)

[13 March, probably 1932; handwritten: PEF/DA/TUF/195]

Tell Ajjul
Gaza
March 13.

Dearest Mà,

[...] Herewith my long-deferred effort in the *New York Herald*,[47] from 'Arabs discover wall' to 'at end of each season' is undiluted me and I am the only one mentioned in the beginning, so Colt is very pleased that even the Petries are not worthy of notice! Also a quite decent batch of photos.

The Crowfoots stayed for a night last week and a Prof. Kraemar[48] of N.Y. came for a night and stayed 4 days. He was most unprofessorial and a keen dancer and Terry and Kitty gave him so good a time that he could hardly tear himself away. On his last day, being Friday, we went to Beit Jibrin and Tell Duweir, which is considered to be Lachish by Albright and the anti-Profs.[49] A fine sight with stone buildings simply bursting from the ground. We also saw the early Xtian [Christian] mosaics at Jibrin, which are quite the best I've seen, very pleasant birds and animals in natural positions, really thoughtfully designed. A roof has been built over them so they are safely housed under lock and key.

At Jibrin we hoped to ring up Hebron to secure a car for Kraemer to take him to Jerusalem but as the police station only had wireless and we were not official we were rather stuck and had to do 28 kilo[metre]s more to Hebron. We left there about 25 to eight and reached home tired but cheerful near midnight.

The Guys[50] have been staying, from Megiddo, and Mr Way, the Colts' friend, is here again. Last night the bright young things went to the Cafferata's for dinner, taking their own supplies. He is Police Officer in Gaza, and was the one who made the now famous stand at Hebron during the riots,[51] where he stopped trouble by his firm action.

He and his wife live on Ali Montar [Tell Ali Muntar], in a little house with a wonderful view. We spent the usual ribald sort of evening and staggered home in the lorry about 12 which is a late night indeed!

More domestic troubles here, it is endless. There was a meeting some days ago at which various resolutions were passed which Prof. agreed to, but when it came to the point of signing the minutes he refused. It is all comically pathetic. Col. Clarke, who was an active rebel leader, left yesterday, so we have lost useful support – not that I feel any real changes will be made by resolutions at meetings. H.P. has much quietened down in the last month and is positively polite to me, so the various outbursts have served their purpose.

[23 March 1932; handwritten: PEF/DA/TUF/196]

Tell Ajjul
Gaza
March 23. 1932

Dearest Mà,

I have let the post day slip, but hope this will not get to you too late as the Hastings will take it straight to England. They leave today, as the powers that be have posted a notice to say that voluntary workers are no longer needed. A telegram of protest was sent and signed by all concerning H.P. to the Committee. So we have burnt our boats, they cannot ignore it and we expect to get the sack.

Last week we went via Asluq to Khalassa [Al-Khalasa], way down south. A country of sand dunes interspersed with scrubby little bushes called 'hatab' which is sold all over the south as firewood. The ruins of

Khalassa were Roman and disappointing as all the best building material and some tessellated floors have been cleared to Gaza and elsewhere.

We were home by 6.30 in time for Ba's birthday party duly celebrated by cake, cocktails and candles.

Am busy now doing the division lists, on the method advocated by me at beginning of the season and completely turned down by Prof. If he hadn't done so all would be finished now so I am not in the best of tempers.

Last night, in honour of the departing ones, Kitty, H. and I turned out 3 ballets complete with costume – Jungle Echoes, The Inconstant Nymph and the Palestine Waggle. The last is a title provided by Prof. [illegible, crossed out] the chart he is making of decorations – it simply screamed to be translated into dance.

We performed on the last year's work at the south end of the Tell, lighting by Allah and very efficient the moon was too, with a perfect background of sea and glistening pools in the valley below.

Today the car goes to Askelon but I shall take a peaceful day here. […] I expect I shall be back about May 1st roughly speaking, which will be earlier than last year.

[7 April 1932; handwritten: PEF/DA/TUF/197]

Tell Ajjul
Gaza.
April 7. 1932.

Dearest Daddy,

Work is now at a standstill as we are waiting to hear when the Museum officials come down to take our best spoils. We have had a hectic fortnight preparing the lists for them and now it is pleasant to have nothing definite to do but bathe and laze.

The weather has been ideal for harvesting – the first harvest I have seen, every other year the crop has not been worth taking in. The landlords descend on the field with a host of satellites early in the morning with all their cattle. A row of men work along the field just pulling up the corn by its roots [Figure 5.7]. You'd be surprised how quickly they do it. The workers are paid by results, with a certain amount guaranteed and many came right up from Egypt for the harvest, just like the hop-picking season at home. Cattle and camels are turned loose to glean and then they carry huge loads to the threshing floors. So much activity is surprising in this part of the world.

Handwritten caption on image: *Harvesting at Tell Ajjul, March–April. Abd el Marti on Right.*

Figure 5.7 'Harvesting at Tell Ajjul, March–April, Abd el Marti on right'. See letter of 7 April 1932. Olga Tufnell archive, Palestine Exploration Fund. Courtesy of the Palestine Exploration Fund.

Last week we went for a very pleasant trip eastwards to Arad, where the children of Israel were turned back by the King of Arad when they first tried to get north out of the wilderness. Nothing remains but a high green mound, but we were lucky enough to see gazelles there, wild of course and many strange birds and flowers, quite new to us.

Our own wady Ghazzeh is full of wild life, quails, and water birds galore and H. even saw a pelican. Yesterday we went to the sea to bathe and while we were there, two minute sailing boats came into view. We imagined them to be the ordinary fishing smack, but were surprised to see when they came closer that their occupants were wearing yachting caps and were certainly European. When they saw us they came ashore and lifted their frail collapsible boats out of the water. As they were flying the German flag I accosted them in German and asked if they had come from Gaza. 'No' they said 'we have come from Germany' and I incredulous asked where they had come from <u>now</u>. From Munich in Germany they persisted and so it proved to be. They had come down the Danube and through the Baltic [sic, Black Sea] to Constantinople and then along the coast of Asia Minor and down the coast of Syria and Palestine. They were on their way to Port Said, and intended to sail down the Red Sea to Deir es Salaam in order to try and find work in Tangyianika [sic, Tanganyika]. They had been 6 months on the way and carried tent, Primus stove, repair outfits and everything with them in their canvas-covered boats which they could lift in one hand. They were brothers called Wolfe and had both been in the War. [...]

[11 April 1932; handwritten: PEF/DA/TUF/198]

Tell Ajjul.
Gaza.
Ap. 11. 1932.

Dearest Mà,
[...] We are enjoying a period of forced inactivity – the lists have gone and the packing can't be started till the division is over. It is very pleasant; have done one sketch so far and put in a ten or twelve mile walk yesterday with H. We went in to Gaza to buy some things and took donkeys from there down to the sea. Clutching two Beladi loaves [flatbread], tin of sardines and 2 bottles of lemonade we careered down to the beach where we dismissed the donkeys and walked home along the sea in easy stages.

Terry and Kitty have gone and Colt has taken them to Jaffa. He himself leaves next week but I fear the Ps will not be off till the 23rd. [...]

Last Suk day we went north to Ashdod – a bumpy journey; the girls are well known for their good looks and none of our connoisseurs were disappointed. Tea on the beach at Askelon, with the new moon just rising, was only marred by ourselves; now the car has gone for good and we must rely on our own legs for transport! [...]

[19 April 1932; typed original: PEF/DA/TUF/199]

Tell Ajjul
Gaza
April 19th, 1932

Dearest Ma,
I am so sorry to have misled you about dates, but the end of the digging is one thing and the end of division and packing quite another matter. In fact this year things have been terribly held up, as the Museum people had another division or two to do before ours, and we have been waiting here kicking our heels for over a fortnight. It has even delayed the P.s, who intended to leave on the 20th, and now cannot go till the 23rd, as the

division is now scheduled for the 21st and 22nd so they intend to make a thorough job of it.

It was a relief to hear from Mr Colt that Richmond [E.T. Richmond] told him that this is the first year that we have sent up an adequate list. I went completely against the Professorial suggestions and H. and I prepared a colossal compendium of information, so evidently it is just the sort of thing that appeals to their official minds. It took us over a fortnight to do!

You can imagine that we are having a pleasant time, bathing has become pretty regular, and we look for flint sites and forage round a bit every day. Everyone has gone now but the P.s, Starks, H. and Ba and O'Brien (T.P.). Ba has just been to Cairo to visit friends and now leaves on the 20th, as he has a long standing engagement with Miss Murray, that she would coach him privately if he got home by May 1st. O'Brien has just returned from a trip east to Ain Gedde [En Gedi] and the Dead Sea. He went with one camel and two men, dressed as a Bedawy, but even then it was none too safe a proceeding as famished bands of starving people from Transjordan are crossing the frontier and shooting and pillaging as they go.

Fired by Dr Sperrin Johnson's example, who has written a light operette, H. and I thought we would see what we could do. The result so far is encouraging, he has done all the music and I have contributed most of the lyrics, of a perfectly idiotic affair called the 'Golden Calf'. We suggest performing it at 14 during the summer – what do you say?

Last Thursday I spent the day in Gaza with the Readings. They have been asking me all the season, but I have never been able to go. He is Land Settlement Officer and has a vast experience of the East and is full of amazing stories. L. [Louis] may like to know that he is fully convinced that the next menace to the B.E. [British Empire] will be from Russia via Palestine and Egypt. The Russians have built an enormous aerodrome only five hundred miles from Jerusalem on their frontiers, which can serve no other purpose than as a base for operations in this direction. There is nothing to stop them getting clean through to Egypt and controlling the Canal. [...]

Saturday was Khurban Bayram, a great festival for the Moslems.[52] It corresponds amazingly closely to the Jewish Passover. Of course everyone is arrayed in their best and we started out about eight to visit the tents. At Hubbe's[53] tent we had stewed kid and bread, handed to us a bit at a time, all the choicest morsels. The children all had crosses of blood on their foreheads and even the dog was protected in this way from the evil eye. It is curious what a significance is attached to the cross down here. In Egypt it is completely taboo among Mahomedans, but here, not only is it used on this occasion but it is a favourite motif in embroidery and design.

At Abdulla's[54] tent, we had a burnt offering. He was busily stirring a huge black pot when we arrived full of savoury stew. Soon he removed the pot, and took out a black mass from the embers of the fire. This he dissected carefully, he cut it in half and then in quarters and it proved to be the heart of the goat, which had been 'burnt with fire'. By that time I was feeling pretty sick since my last meal, so had to refuse the tempting morsel, but Starks had some and said it was very good.

Then we mounted donkeys and set off to visit Sheykh Freyr at his tent some three miles off. We were seen coming from a distance and his men set out to meet us. He is a nice lad, who has been taught English, but has not lost a pleasing simplicity of manner. He still goes barefoot and spends all his time down here, instead of among the young bloods of Jerusalem or Beyrouth [Beirut]. The Sheykh's eldest son came galloping up on a white horse and thus accompanied we arrived at the tent, which is on a hill surrounded by fig trees. A glorious spot for his summer quarters with wide views in every direction. Sheykh Freyr met us at the door of the tent and everyone seated round him rose. We sat down, made conversation, drank tea and so on, my clove necklace[55] was freely commented on, and I told them how much it was admired in England and they were delighted. Then Ali[56] suggested that we should go over and [see] the dancing and the horses at the festival some half hour away; as we left the tent we saw the sheep being killed that we were to eat presently.

It is refreshing to see how little satisfies these people in the way of amusement. Perhaps there were thirty greybeards and a horde of children to watch a dozen horsemen, who galloped madly up and down in front of us. The sight is good. Flying cloaks, waving swords and shouts of valour made up the accompaniment, and in a group by themselves the women, shrouded in cloaks, two or three under each, kept up an unending chant. I was made to join in with them, much to the general satisfaction. After some time, we wended our way back to the tent and went to call on the ladies of the establishment.

Some of them have visited me at various times for medicine; it was one of the previous ladies who asked me if I couldn't give her something to produce a child. I noticed that she was not there anymore! The women were really charming, quite the best looking lot I have ever seen, which is only to be expected, I suppose, because the old boy just changes them, if they get at all passé. About one I went back to the men's side for the meal, plates and forks were provided for our benefit, but the others had their lumps of meat dished out to them on flat flabby loaves of bread.

The mail goes now, so must stop without more ado.

To be continued

Love Olga

Notes

1   Knight 2011.
2   Drower 1985, 383.
3   Nasasra 2017.
4   Petrie 1931, 1; Henry 1985, 2; Olga Tufnell interviewed by Jonathan Tubb, transcript of audiotaped interview, c. 1985.
5   Sparks 2013, 5, fig. 5.
6   Abu Rabia 2005.
7   Davidovitch and Greenberg 2007.
8   Petrie 1931, 1932. Petrie directed two further seasons of excavations at Ajjul (total of four seasons 1930–4). Olga left at the end of the 1931–2 season, subsequently joining Starkey, Harding, the Colts and Richmond Brown to excavate at Tell ed-Duweir. For a more complete overview of the Ajjul excavations see Tufnell 1993.
9   Petrie 1931, 4; plate VIII. Later discoveries at Tell ed-Daba in Egypt suggest they were sacrificed donkeys rather than horses.
10 Drower 1985, 390.
11 James 1979; Drower 1985, 387–8. The 'Taylorian' was a recreational building in the camp, named after the carpenter who built it at Colt's expense. It may also be a tongue-in-cheek reference to the University of Oxford's Taylor Institute Library, known as the 'Taylorian'.
12 Ussishkin 2014, 33.
13 Drower 1985, 388–90.
14 Petrie 1933, 1934; Petrie, Mackay and Murray 1952. Also see Stewart 1974.
15 Pugh 2008, 314.
16 Parts of these films are within the Gerald Lankester Harding archive at UCL and have been digitised as part of the Filming Antiquity project: https://www.filmingantiquity.com/.
17 Eleanor W. Gardner, Research Fellow of Lady Margaret Hall, Oxford, and her brother, Captain Gardner. They had come to join Gertrude Caton Thompson in the Fayum. Also see note relating to letter of 28 February 1935; PEF/DA/TUF/248.
18 Dr Gertrude Caton Thompson (1888–1985), pioneering British prehistorian in Egypt and East Africa. Worked with Petrie 1921–6 on archaeological and geological surveys in the Fayum, at Abydos, Qau and Badari. She also worked in Zimbabwe and in the Hadhramaut (Yemen) with Freya Stark. Fellow of the British Academy 1944, honorary doctorate, University of Cambridge, 1954. Also see reference to Caton Thompson in letters of 1935 and 1937.
19 J.G. Vernon and Norman Scott.
20 Sidholme was the name of Olga's grandmother's house. It was left to Olga's brother Gilbert on her death. It was sold in 1930.
21 Witney is a town in the Cotswolds, England, where prosperity was based on the wool trade and the manufacture of blankets in particular, for which the town became famous.
22 Fortnum & Mason – long-established and fashionable grocer in Piccadilly, well known for sending goods abroad.
23 G.F. Royds, a new team member.
24 A Jewish family long resident in Palestine.
25 In 1929 Imperial Airways began weekly flights to India from Croydon, stopping at Genoa, Rome, Baghdad and Basra, arriving at Karachi in seven days. The fare was £130 and only 15–18 passengers could be carried, as most space was taken up by mail which was more profitable (Pugh 2008, 314).
26 Abdullah bin al-Hussein (Abdullah I), ruler of Transjordan.

27 A version of the *Daily Telegraph* article. Published versions appeared in newspapers around the world in February and March 1931.

28 Captain Raymond Oswald Cafferata (1897–1966), married to Peggy Ford Dunn, with two children. At the time of Olga's letter, he was British superintendent of the Palestine police for the Gaza district. While serving as an Assistant Superintendent he was awarded with the King's Police Medal for Gallantry for his actions in the 1929 Hebron Massacre. A former 'Black and Tan' of the Royal Irish Constabulary. See Cahill 2009, 64–5.

29 Reading is referred to as 'Land Settlement Officer' in letter of 19 April 1932 below.

30 As mentioned in Chapter 1, H.G. Wells rented a house, Easton Glebe, near Easton, home of Daisy, Countess of Warwick, where Olga spent two years sharing a governess with her daughter.

31 Hatchards in Piccadilly, London's oldest bookseller.

32 Mudie's was a lending library established in 1842. By 1862 it was the Circulating Library, located in New Oxford Street, London.

33 *The Field*, the country and field sports magazine.

34 'Ba' was Ralph Richmond Brown's nickname.

35 Margaret Murray had been awarded an honorary doctorate by UCL; her students had clubbed together to buy her a gown.

36 See note 25 above.

37 Referred to as either Warren Hastings or the Hastings. E.F. Warren Hastings and his wife Alice later joined the Tell ed-Duweir Expedition, 1936–8.

38 Arabic, arbiyah or abaya: long flowing outer garment worn by Muslim women.

39 Dr John Charles Sperrin-Johnson. A Professor of Biology from the University of Auckland, New Zealand. He assisted the camp clinic as a volunteer. He was also interested in measuring skulls (Drower 1985, 387).

40 A retired colonel with an interest in military fortifications.

41 Muriel Bentwich, sister of Norman Bentwich, Attorney-General, Palestine. Noted as a gifted musician (Drower 1985, 387).

42 A Victorian lunatic asylum.

43 Tell el-Hesi, site of Petrie's first excavation in Palestine in 1890. It was considered by him to be biblical Lachish because of a nearby placename, Um Lakis (Petrie 1928, 2). J.L. Starkey's subsequent excavations at Tell ed-Duweir showed that his site was in fact Lachish (see Chapters 6 and 7). Petrie's work at Tell el-Hesi was significant as being the first systematic archaeological excavation in the Near East, recording pottery and other finds relative to their stratigraphic position. Also see Hardin, Rollston and Blakely 2012 for a summary of Tell el-Hesi and its identification.

44 Commonwealth War Cemetery in Gaza City, completed in 1920 for Commonwealth servicemen killed in battles for Gaza in 1917. Also used in the Second World War and since 1948 for peacekeepers.

45 Kitty Strickland, Teresa Colt's sister. Both were nieces of Lord Strickland.

46 John Winter Crowfoot (1873–1959), Director of the British School of Archaeology 1926–35, excavated Jerash 1928–30, Samaria Sebaste and Ophel (Jerusalem) 1931–5. Chairman of the Palestine Exploration Fund, 1945–50. Honorary doctorate from Oxford University, 1958. Married to Grace Mary (aka Molly) Crowfoot (1877–1957), who helped run the excavations at Samaria and was a specialist on ancient textiles. It is not clear if any of the three Crowfoot daughters were present.

47 'Progress of Science and Industry; Uncovering a 4,000-Year-Old Seaport; Relics Disclose History of the Ancient Hyksos', *New York Herald Tribune*, Sunday 21 February 1932, p. 3. Professor Ralph Van Deman Magoffin, Department of Classics, New York University, is listed as the article's author, with acknowledgement that the text is 'based on information supplied by Olga Tufnell, a field executive of the British School of Archaeology at Tell Ajjul'. The article featured photographs entitled 'Where Archaeologists Unearthed Old Civilization in Palestine' showing workmen removing earth from Tell el-Ajjul, excavations of the 'oldest horse yet found in the Near East', and women collecting water from a 3,000-year-old well. The section contributed by Olga Tufnell makes up approximately half of the article and varies only slightly from the two alternative versions of the text presented in this chapter.

48 Casper John Kraemer Jr. (1895–1958), Classics professor at New York University.

49 Albright and colleagues who disagreed with Petrie's identification of Tell el-Hesi as the site of biblical Lachish, in addition to other interpretations, and his general approach to archaeology.

50 Philip Langstaffe Ord Guy (1885–1952), field archaeologist and administrator, Chief Inspector of Antiquities, Palestine, 1922–7; Field Director of Megiddo Expedition for the Oriental Institute of the University of Chicago, 1927–35; Director of the British School of Archaeology in Jerusalem, 1935–9; Director of Surveys and Excavations, Israel Department of Antiquities and Museums, 1948–52. Married to Yemima (née Ben Yehuda), with daughter Ruth from her previous marriage.

51 The riots in August 1929 at Hebron followed disputes between Arabs and Jews over the Western Wall, Jerusalem. This marked a period of rioting culminating in massacres of Jews, especially in Hebron and Safad (Sherman 1997, 78–9).

52 Also known as Aid al-Adha, Feast of the Sacrifice.

53 Perhaps one of the members of the expedition workforce.

54 Perhaps one of the members of the expedition workforce.

55 See letter dated 30 November 1928.

56 Perhaps Salman Ali, pictured in Figure 6.12. Probably a member of the expedition workforce.

References

Abu Rabia, Aref. 2005. 'Bedouin Health Services in Mandated Palestine', *Middle Eastern Studies* 41(3): 421–9.

Cahill, Richard A. 2009. '"Going Beserk": "Black and Tans" in Palestine', *Jewish Quarterly* 38: 59–68.

Davidovitch, Nadav and Zalman Greenberg. 2007. 'Public Health, Culture, and Colonial Medicine: Smallpox and Variation in Palestine during the British Mandate', *Public Health Reports* 122(3): 398–406.

Drower, Margaret S. 1985. *Flinders Petrie: A Life in Archaeology*. London: Victor Gollancz.

Hardin, James W., Christopher A. Rollston and Jeffrey A. Blakely. 2012. 'Biblical Geography in Southwestern Judah', *Near Eastern Archaeology* 75(1): 20–35.

Henry, Ros. 1985. 'Olga Tufnell: A Biography'. In *Palestine in the Bronze and Iron Ages: Papers in Honour of Olga Tufnell*, edited by Jonathan N. Tubb, 1–5. London: Institute of Archaeology.

James, Frances W. 1979. 'Petrie in the Wadi Ghazzeh and at Gaza: Harris Colt's Candid Camera', *Palestine Exploration Quarterly* 111: 75–7.

Knight, John. 2011. 'Securing Zion? Policing in British Palestine, 1917–39', *European Review of History* 18(4): 523–43.

Nasasra, Mansour. 2017. *The Naqab Bedouins: A Century of Politics and Resistance*. New York: Columbia University Press.

Petrie, W.M.F. 1928. *Gerar*. London: British School of Archaeology in Egypt.

Petrie, W.M.F. 1931. *Ancient Gaza I*. London: British School of Archaeology in Egypt.

Petrie, W.M.F. 1932. *Ancient Gaza II*. London: British School of Archaeology in Egypt.

Petrie, W.M.F. 1933. *Ancient Gaza III*. London: British School of Archaeology in Egypt.

Petrie, W.M.F. 1934. *Ancient Gaza IV*. London: British School of Archaeology in Egypt.

Petrie, W.M.F., Ernest J.H. Mackay and Margaret A. Murray. 1952. *City of Shepherd Kings* and *Ancient Gaza V*. London: British School of Archaeology in Egypt.

Pugh, Martin. 2008. *We Danced All Night: A Social History of Britain between the Wars*. London: Bodley Head.

Sherman, A.J. 1997. *Mandate Days: British Lives in Palestine, 1918–1948*. New York: Thames and Hudson.

Sparks, Rachael. 2013. 'Publicising Petrie: Financing Fieldwork in British Mandate Palestine (1926–1938)', *Present Pasts* 5: 1–15.

Stewart, James R. 1974. *Tell el 'Ajjūl: The Middle Bronze Age Remains*. Studies in Mediterranean Archaeology 38. Göteborg: P. Åström.

Tufnell, Olga. 1993. 'Ajjul, Tell el-'. In *The New Encyclopedia of Archaeological Excavations in the Holy Land*, edited by Ephraim Stern, 49–53. Jerusalem: Israel Exploration Society.

Ussishkin, David. 2014. *Biblical Lachish: A Tale of Construction, Destruction, Excavation and Restoration*. Jerusalem: Israel Exploration Society.

6
Tell ed-Duweir (Lachish): The first season, 1932–3

At the end of the 1931–2 season at Tell el-'Ajjul, Starkey told Petrie that he wanted to leave, as he felt he was ready to lead an expedition on his own. Harding and Richmond Brown supported him. Olga was torn – she regretted leaving Petrie, to whom she owed so much, but her support for her expedition colleagues was greater. Olga also had the opportunity of excavating an impressive new site. Funding was essential for the project, especially in its first year, and Starkey had been promised financial support by Sir Charles Marston, Sir Robert Mond and Sir Henry Wellcome, all previous supporters of Petrie's expeditions in Egypt and all of whom were interested in locating a biblical site. Olga was commissioned to write up all that was known about two possible sites: Tell ed-Duweir, thought to be the site of biblical Lachish, and the much smaller site of Tell esh-Sheikh el-'Areini, then thought to be ancient Gath, one of the cities of the Philistines. Sir Henry Wellcome, the principal contributor, favoured Tell ed-Duweir.[1]

Colt, who had also been at Tell Fara and Tell el-'Ajjul, but whose relationship with Petrie had deteriorated, also wished to be associated with the new project, promising financial assistance as a co-director. New recruits arrived, including Charles Inge and W.B. Kennedy Shaw, a surveyor. Thus in October 1932 the joint British and American Wellcome-Colt Archaeological Research Expedition began work at Tell ed-Duweir under Starkey's direction. Starkey realised immediately that a long-term programme of excavation would be necessary. His aims were (at their broadest level) to seek the extent to which foreign influences had imposed themselves on pre-Hellenistic Palestinian culture, especially through questions surrounding the origins of the 'Sea Peoples' and the earliest contacts between Egypt and Mesopotamia.[2]

Tell ed-Duweir is enormous (Figure 6.1), standing at around 40 metres above the surrounding valley and covering 18 acres at its

Figure 6.1   East side of Tell ed-Duweir with the expedition camp on left side (opposite southwest corner of the mound). The Wadi Ghafr passes in front of the mound. Wellcome-Marston Expedition Archive, Department of the Middle East, British Museum. © UCL Institute of Archaeology, courtesy of the Wellcome Trust and the British Museum.

summit. It is located alongside the Wadi Ghafr, which can overflow during the winter rains (Figure 6.2). The site was strategically important in the history of the kingdom of Judah as a site halfway along an east–west route from Ashkelon to Hebron, eventually leading to Jerusalem. In contrast to mounds they had worked on previously at Tell Fara and Tell el-'Ajjul, where buildings were made from mudbrick, at Tell ed-Duweir stone was the more common building material.

Over a year before excavations started, Starkey was already making connections between the carved panels from Sennacherib's palace at Nineveh, Iraq, displayed at the British Museum, which depicted the Assyrian assault on the city of Lachish, and photographs of Tell ed-Duweir. These are early indications that Starkey hoped to prove William Foxwell Albright and John Garstang correct in their suggestions (based on non-biblical written sources) that ancient Lachish was Tell ed-Duweir, rather than Tell el-Hesi as Petrie had asserted.[3] This quest to identify Tell ed-Duweir with Lachish and to solve a riddle of biblical archaeology was not fulfilled until the discovery in 1935 of the 'Lachish Letters'. The evidence, however, was still inconclusive at this time (see Chapter 8).

The neighbouring Arab village of Qubeibeh (Al Qubaybah)[4] is mentioned in the letters (this and subsequent chapters), although it is not clear how often Olga and the expedition team members visited.

Figure 6.2   Olga standing in the Wadi Ghafr, 4 February 1935. Camp buildings and the imposing Tell ed-Duweir in background. Wellcome-Marston Expedition Archive, Department of the Middle East, British Museum. © UCL Institute of Archaeology, courtesy of the Wellcome Trust and the British Museum.

The letters and the names of people within them provide a link to the history of this village of several hundred people, especially as many members of the expedition workforce came from there. The village included a mosque, two schools, several shops and more than 140 houses. The population of Qubeibeh was largely made up of fellahin (farmers), and the surrounding land was used primarily to grow cereals.

Olga's letter of 6 February, probably 1933, may refer to disputes and tensions between the expedition and local landowners over the use of agricultural land on and around the Tell, including the location of the expedition camp.[5] Clearly one of the most important elements of a successful expedition was the keeping of good relations with the local community, and Olga's letters allude to a largely peaceful coexistence that included visits to the homes of mukhtars (village heads) and villagers, invitations to dinner and attendance at festivals and events, as well as help with medical needs. A photograph apparently of a young bride, from the time of the first season, appears to have been taken by Olga Tufnell in the village, and is important from the perspective of Palestinian costume (Figure 6.3).[6]

Figure 6.3 Young woman in traditional dress. Photograph labelled 'Dubkah'. Olga Tufnell archive. Courtesy of the Palestine Exploration Fund.

The camp was again organised on the Petrie model (Figure 6.4): first a dig-house had to be constructed, with long, low mud and stone buildings around a courtyard, with wooden roofs covered in tarred felt, a few bell tents alongside and a couple of sheds. One possible difference was that Petrie never allowed a 'native' to enter the courtyards of his camps,[7] whereas the Tell ed-Duweir camp was presumably more accessible to local people. There was only one truck, used for transporting

Figure 6.4a Expedition camp. Photo taken from the southwest corner of Tell ed-Duweir, 1938. Wellcome-Marston Expedition Archive, Department of the Middle East, British Museum. © UCL Institute of Archaeology, courtesy of the Wellcome Trust and the British Museum.

Figure 6.4b Annotated image of Figure 6.4a, based in part on personal recollections of John Starkey (pers. comm., 30 September 2010), who lived on site as a child.

A: Starkey quarters (two doors); B: Dispensary (location may have changed later); C: Olga's room; D: Harding's room; E: Dining room; F: Courtyard; G: Colt's house and garage (later becoming camp workshop?); H: Toilets; I: Other expedition quarters; J: Garages; K: Wall and gate; L: Area of ancient cemetery (excavated by time of photograph); M: Pottery store?/ further expedition quarters; N: Drawing office with full-height window.

Figure 6.5 Hubdeh and Ayesha in the camp laundry, Tell ed-Duweir. Wellcome-Marston Expedition Archive, Department of the Middle East, British Museum. © UCL Institute of Archaeology, courtesy of the Wellcome Trust and the British Museum.

supplies from Gaza and initially clearing heaps of dumped soil. In charge of all the equipment was 'a wonderful man called Mr Pummell. He was very much liked and didn't know a word of Arabic.'[8] Hubdeh and Ayesha (family names unknown) were among those employed to help with domestic needs in the camp (Figure 6.5). A few other insights into dig life at Tell ed-Duweir can be found in Veronica Seton-Williams's memoirs.[9] She mentions the 'chief assistant' to the expedition, Diab Basham, who only had one arm – apparently the other had been bitten off by an angry camel when he was a small boy.[10]

A wide range of expedition members (staff and volunteer visitors) were involved between 1932 and 1938, and a list of them and the seasons they served in can be found in the final Lachish volume.[11] As with all excavations of the time, however, most of the work was done by gangs of workmen (Figure 6.6), diggers who filled the baskets, and children who carried them. Two Egyptian Quftis were employed as foremen, who worked alongside other skilled local diggers from Petrie's former expeditions.[12] Women and children were also involved in the excavations, and sieved for finds. Workmen were paid two shillings a day, children one

Figure 6.6 Group photograph of workers at Tell ed-Duweir, undated. Photo album labelled with the following names: standing, left to right, 'Hamid M./Ibrihim M./Abd el-Karim Salameh/Salman Aly/Tewfiq Saleh/Mustafa M.'; front row, left to right: 'Mahamed el-Bata/Ahmed Mdalay [?]'. Olga Tufnell archive, Palestine Exploration Fund. Courtesy of the Palestine Exploration Fund.

shilling.[13] W.F. Albright, also excavating at the time, gave further advice on assembling a staff.[14] In addition to the usual surveyors, draughtsmen and so on, he advocated employing someone with a talent for wrestling who would be useful in amusing the local mukhtar and keeping him friendly, while a modest repertory of songs at hand would keep the younger members happy. He disapproved of mixed camps on grounds of expense and possible scandal. Here at Tell ed-Duweir, however, there were plenty of excursions and village entertainments to provide a distraction from work, and to reinforce relationships between the local community and the foreign archaeologists.

At first Olga was accommodated in a tent while her room (Figure 6.7) was being built. She later cultivated flowerbeds outside her corner room which 'evoked the brief but brilliant illusion of an English garden'.[15] A short distance away Colt built a stone house for himself, but by Olga's

Figure 6.7 Olga's room at Tell ed-Duweir. The photograph on the fireplace on the right is of Olga's mother. The one on the left could be her brother Louis or cousin Lionel, but has not been identified. By the bedside are books including *Ophthalmic Science and Practice*, the Holy Bible and Hutchinson's *Holiday Omnibus*. See letter of 26 December 1932. Wellcome-Marston Expedition Archive, Department of the Middle East, British Museum. © UCL Institute of Archaeology, courtesy of the Wellcome Trust and the British Museum.

account he was rarely in it. Olga continued being as useful as ever, sorting and drawing pottery in the pottery shed (Figure 6.8),[16] typing catalogues and records, taking her share of digging and dispensing first aid and medicines to the camp, the workmen and their families in the nearby villages.[17] The clinic she established at Tell ed-Duweir was perhaps one of the most important yet understated of Olga's contributions to the expedition and the local community, and an extension of the public health efforts already undertaken in earlier projects. Letters to Dr Strathearn of the Ophthalmic Hospital in Jerusalem (e.g. 9 February 1933) and training in Jerusalem indicate the extent of Olga's commitment to treating local inhabitants, numbering between '30 and 40 people a day', many of whom were eye cases. Although Olga does not go into specifics about the range of cases, she appears to have become familiar with treating

Figure 6.8 G.L. Harding and Olga Tufnell in pottery shed at Tell ed-Duweir. Wellcome-Marston Expedition Archive, Department of the Middle East, British Museum. © UCL Institute of Archaeology, courtesy of the Wellcome Trust and the British Museum.

eye infections such as conjunctivitis and trachoma with eye drops and ointments. Given the numbers, news of the clinic must have spread far and wide beyond the confines of Qubeibeh.[18] This highlights one of the key areas of positive relations with local Arab inhabitants that continued throughout the expedition. Her unofficial role as nurse and eye doctor must have afforded her and colleagues great respect – a factor that has often gone unrecognised.

The first season at Tell ed-Duweir produced pleasing results. As recounted in Starkey's lecture to members of the Palestine Exploration Fund in summer 1933, the expedition uncovered a Persian-period 'governor's residence' (Level I, late 5th–4th centuries BC), and traced the Judaean city's defences including the western revetment (Figure 6.9),[19] which Olga had a hand in excavating, the southwest bastion, the gate system and roadway, and part of the podium of the Judaean palace-fort

Figure 6.9 Partially exposed section of the western double wall of Str. IV–III. Published in Tufnell 1953, pl. 12.1; Starkey 1933: pl. VII: 'Looking north along western revetment ... four uppermost courses exposed, showing panelling. Upper city wall against skyline (top right).' See letter of 15 January 1933. Wellcome-Marston Expedition Archive, Department of the Middle East, British Museum. © UCL Institute of Archaeology, courtesy of the Wellcome Trust and the British Museum.

(Levels IV–III, *c*. 900–700 BC).[20] These early finds already enabled the architect H.H. McWilliams to envisage reconstructions of the Iron Age city that proved so important to an interested public and sponsors alike. They also examined areas on the northwest lower slopes and southeast of the mound, which had begun to yield tantalising finds of the Late Bronze Age (1550–1200 BC).

A note on excavation methods employed at Tell ed-Duweir is important, as little is mentioned in the letters or the final publications in terms of methodology.[21] Excavations were conducted largely using an open plan approach intended to expose architectural features and outlines. There was a general focus on exposing significant architectural remains level by level, recording them, and removing their remains in order to reach the next stratum. Records were made of the relative depth of material encountered in each level, rather than recording stratigraphic units. The excavation methods do not appear to have been vastly different from those used by Petrie, although there was a better overall standard of control and documentation. Given the large workforce and a lack of sifting, important material may have been lost to the spoil heaps. The desire for a rail and chute system indicates the high expectation of the pace and scale of excavation. Explosives were also in use to help remove large boulders and, in some cases, the roofs of collapsed tombs.[22] As with Megiddo, a well-funded 'big dig' in Palestine being conducted by the University of Chicago,[23] there were also ample resources and use of technology and engineering techniques. Yet stratigraphic control and attention to detail were a lower priority for both expeditions. This contrasts with approaches employed contemporaneously at Tabun Cave and Samaria by other British archaeologists, showing that a more finely graded stratigraphic method could indeed be achieved at Palestinian sites.[24]

Although the expedition was based in a fairly isolated location in the Judaean foothills, the team generally had relatively quick access to Jerusalem by road. A number of sites and villages were visited during this period, as mentioned in the letters, including 'Makerah', Arak al Manshiyah, Zakariyah and Tell es-Safi. There are few mentions of Hebron, which was 24 kilometres southeast of Qubeibeh.

Olga reports staying at the Fast Hotel or Beaumont House in Jerusalem during her visits there. The letters include some information about the academic lecture circuit, including at the newly built YMCA building. Lectures mentioned include those by Dorothy Garrod, the British prehistorian; John Iliffe, the Keeper of the Palestine Archaeological Museum; and John Crowfoot, excavator of Samaria. The lectures were important social events for meeting old fixtures and newcomers alike and were often accompanied by drinks, dinner and sometimes dancing at the King David Hotel opposite, another new venue in Jerusalem and an important place for networking and letting off steam.

Travel and social gatherings continue to be an important theme in the letters. Olga's outward stopover in Malta combined high-profile networking with archaeology. The visit to the home of the Prime Minister of Malta, Lord Strickland, through H.D. Colt's wife Terry and her sister Kitty, brought Olga into contact with the British elite of the crown colony. She was able to visit the prehistoric temple complex of Tarxien, a relatively recent and significant archaeological discovery.

Letters of November 1932–March 1933

[29 November 1932; handwritten: PEF/DA/TUF/200]

On board SS *Hobson's Bay*, Aberdeen & Commonwealth Line

Nov. 29.

Dearest Mà,

We have just left Malta after a most hectic and amusing day. Kitty came off to the boat to meet me, which was really sweet of her. It was very tiresome to get off it again as the red tape and regulations were strict and tiresome and all the time lunch was awaiting us at Villa Bologna. She had the Strickland car waiting for us at the Customs and we motored straight to the Villa, to find the lunch-party waiting with that horrible hungry expression, all except Mabel[25] herself who gave me a very warm welcome. Ld. [Lord] Strickland[26] was not there. The villa is a perfect palace, built 1745 under Italian influence, lovely orange groves, trees laden with fruit, and the largest aviary I have ever seen, full of gay parrots and peacocks and fan-tailed pigeons.

The lunch was some meal, after food for a week on 'Hobson's Bay'. Directly afterwards, laden with a huge bunch of roses and a basket of fruit (by the way we had pomegranates for lunch from the garden!) we went in the car to the Hypogeum, 'the greatest neolithic monument in the world'. Down a flight of green and slippery steps into a labyrinth of passages and shrines carved by flint out of the limestone rock. Traces of red spiral decoration remain on some ceilings and an oracle hole bears witness to the use of the whole as a temple, perhaps 4000 years ago, some enthusiasts would make it much earlier. From there to Tarxien, the Neo. [Neolithic] temple above ground, which you know so well from lantern slides. Smoothly worked blocks have perfectly regular spirals cut on them in relief, unwieldy morsels of 'fat ladies' lie about and the whole place is on a minute scale with tiny doorways which might have been made for Miss Murray, no wonder she loves it![27]

Then of course I had to see the Sports club, with its tennis courts and ball boys, its racecourse and polo ground all so utterly English. By then it was nearly four, and as the boat sailed at 4.30 we hurried down to the customs house and I embarked in a boat with my bouquet and here I am again [...]

Have had a warm invitation to stay in Malta on my way back. Harris and Terry [Colt] arrived in town on 22nd so I just missed them – if you could get in touch with them through Sir Charles [Marston][28] perhaps they would bring out my shoes – they usually have so much luggage that a little more makes no difference to them – it doesn't much matter as I did pack the old green horrors after all.

Saw the loveliest slip of a new moon this evening, which will I hope bring good luck to the expedition.

Dec. 1st. We get in tomorrow morning about 9, when I hope I shall find Cmdr Trumper to meet me. The last few days have been very pleasant and sunny and I have played deck tennis and gossiped quite a lot, with a good deal of sleep thrown in. [...]

My next news will be from camp, which should be a hefty consignment; it is getting very exciting to see what has or has not happened.

Very much love darling to you and Daddy and Tit and good wishes to all the lodgers.

Ever yours
Olga

[3 December 1932; handwritten: PEF/DA/TUF/201]

Tell Duweir
Dec. 3. 1932

Dearest Mà,
Where had we got to? I landed at Port Said having said an affectionate farewell to the Howards, and found my way after the inevitable wait at the Customs to the Trumper's house. He was on the Canal but his wife and daughter were home and busy packing and selling up before leaving Port Said for good. He retires this year and they settle in England after 25 yrs abroad.

Rang up Mrs Selous who was in bed with a cold, but I braved the consequences and went to see her at the Consulate, which she has already made into a charming home with lovely things from Basra. She must be v. well off and her boy of 4 reminds me of Carlie.

About 7 we went to the station and met Commander Trumper, who stayed talking until my train left. He said he was immensely interested in the 'INV.' (from now onwards for short) and that he hears quite a lot about Russia from the ships' captains who go through the Canal. The export of sugar from Odessa to <u>India</u> where it is sold at ridiculous prices is a case in point. I asked him to write something down and he may do so when he has time next year.

Trained to Kantara, at 8 crossed the Canal and had my usual good meal at the Restaurant there to the accompaniment of a small boy juggling and doing tricks very dexterously. No news at Kantara awaiting me, so the Station master phoned down the line to make sure a car should meet me at Gaza. What is more it actually did. When the driver heard I was going to Duweir we knocked up Terazi the owner of the car to get more petrol. Old Fahmi came out in his nightshirt and we all proceeded to his shop in the main street where we drank hot milk and ate biscuits before starting off. Motored from 5 to 6.20 with the dawn ahead of us all the way. I was a shock to them when I arrived, as I found the letter I had written still with Terazi after 6 days. Now I am installed in a Beladi [local] tent all worked in blue and red and yellow with intriguing quotations from the Koran all round, which I can't read in the least. The house is being built facing E. just under the brow of the hill, nearly all solid stone, I am to have a v. good corner room with 2 windows which still only lacks a roof.

The views from my window are glorious and the air is extremely dry, so it should be healthy. Water unpleasant but wholesome. Wind strong, my tent aches and groans but there has been glorious sun all day. Slept solidly after lunch and then took some hurried photos, so as to have something to send you in a few days.

Starks [Starkey], H. [Harding] and Ba [Ralph Richmond Brown] have gone off to visit Ajjul; apparently Prof. [Petrie] has written saying S. has taken his measuring rod and his washerway[?];[29] do you remember the fuss there was when S. wanted to start one? Now it is all the other way round! Shall probably go to Hebron for a few days soon to make some contacts there and visit Dr Strathearn[30] whom I knew in Cyprus, as he has offered me some special instruction in eye work. [...]

Colt is sending a man from America to do the accounts, so I can set my mind at rest.

[10 December 1932; handwritten: PEF/DA/TUF/202]

~~Pension~~ Beaumont House
Jerusalem.
Dec. 10.

Dearest Mà,

Since I last wrote many things have happened. I spent 2 days at Duweir under canvass [sic], looking round and meeting old friends. Within 15 minutes of my arrival there were some would-be patients, so I had to attempt to justify my reputation!

On Tuesday Ba and I came to Jerusalem, he had to get the car overhauled and I was up for this course at St John's Ophthalmic Hospital,[31] run by the Order of course. I go every morning at 8 and watch the Drs in the Outpatients Dept. They are all most helpful and anxious to instruct me in the mysteries. Every type congregates there from shackled prisoners to heads of Govt Departments, so there is a good slice of human nature to be seen.

In the afternoons we have been sightseeing and walking the walls; yesterday we spent an instructive hour at the German community seeing the models of the Temple area through the ages, most instructive when reading Josephus. The car was out of action till today when we went up to the Mt of Olives, where I had never been before, and saw the magnificent view over the town to the W. and over the Dead Sea and the Jordan to the E. fine enough at any time, but what must it be like at dawn or sunset.

Have been at the Fast Hotel in the middle of the town till today, when I moved here to be with the Crowfoots, who suggested it when they were at Duweir last week. I have a very nice room here with balcony full of geraniums for half the price of the Fast, i.e. 8/– a day, though of course I am not paying, this being on the head of the firm. I expect to go back to camp on Tuesday, unless the rains come on, when I should have to stay here indefinitely, which the Lord forbid.

The postal arrangements are going to be a bit precarious; post to come once a week from Hebron via the police. If it rains there will be nothing at all, so don't be surprised if news is rare and scanty. I have heard nothing from you so far. I expect you got the telegram with the address which Starks sent.

Paid a formal call on [E.T.] Richmond in his den the other day who was very pleasant and asked how we all were and whether we were 'happy' now – I said we were!

There has been some trouble about goods and chattels with the P's [Petries], all things which are private property and were according to Prof. 'wrongfully taken' from the camp. So Starks, H. and Ba went there and explained matters, though I don't think the interview was too cordial. […]

[Undated; handwritten document: PEF/DA/TUF/2755]

[This rhyme was found among the letters. It appears to be from Tell el-'Ajjul and refers in a light-hearted way to Olga's various activities in her camp clinic. It is transcribed here, and given the title 'Ten Little Arab Girls'.][32]

Ten little Arab girls sitting in a line,
One went to hospital and then there were nine,

Nine little Arab girls eating off one plate,
One ate far too much and then there were eight.

Eight little Arab girls staring up to heaven,
One had her hair washed and then there were seven.

Seven little Arab girls had pills put in a mix,
One had quinine as well and then there were six.

Six little Arab girls, thank God they're still alive,
One ate the thermometer and then there were five.

Five little Arab girls, as I've mentioned once before,
One cried 'O buttoni' [?] and then there were four.

Four little Arab girls calling out for tea,
One spilt the whole lot and then there were three.

Three little Arab girls with nothing much to do,
One [illegible] and then there were two.

Two little Arab girls, sitting in the sun,
One went home to Ma, and then there was one.

One little Arab girl, Olga said 'What fun'.
She tore up the temp. chart and then there were none.

No little Arab girls, what a dismal plaint,
Olga went clean off her head, so now she's a saint.

[13 December 1932; handwritten: PEF/DA/TUF/203]

As from c/o P.O.
Hebron.
Palestine.
Dec. 13. 1932.

Darling Daddy,
This is to wish you happy Christmas and a good New Year with plenty of
pheasant orders and may tobacco shares go up.

Dr Smallwood[33] will be tickled to death to hear that I have been
doing a course on eye treatment and diagnosis with Dr Strathearn of
Order of St John in Jerusalem's Ophthalmic Hospital. Have been there
5 days so far and have seen 20 different diseases and learnt to treat
the commonest slightly more scientifically than I have done up till now.
They have all been very decent and I shall go again when I have some
more free time.

I am staying in this pension (Beaumont House) with Mr and
Mrs Crowfoot. His great aunt was Elizabeth Tufnell, a daughter of a
parson at Ensdon[?]. He knows Joan and Charles Tufnell too and is in
fact a connection by marriage. He says that I am ridiculously like his great
aunt, and yet we must be poles apart!

Leave here tomorrow and dig in for good at the Camp. We are
all very optimistic and Starks feels as confident as ever that great finds
await us on the Tell. Anyhow we shall soon see. [...]

I shall be able to do something about your cataract – I don't think!
– when I get back, anyhow I shall be able to tell you which sort you've got.
They've made some wonderful jobs of many cases here of it.

[21 December 1932; typed copy; PEF/DA/TUF/205]

Wellcome Historical Museum Expedition
and Colt Archaeological Expedition
c/o P.O. Hebron, Palestine.

Dec. 21st, 1932

Dear Dr Strathearn,
Enclosed please find 'Tufnell's Treatise on the Eye', which will, I expect,
prove more amusing than instructive; if you could find time to correct

the glaring errors, it would be a great help to me, and it would give the patients a better chance of recovery from my ministrations.

Enclosed is a cheque[34] for the funds of the Hospital, half from me and half from the Expedition, with very many thanks for all the trouble you and Drs Hamilton and Manson have taken over me.

with all good wishes to them and to Miss Paton-Jones,
yours sincerely

[26 December 1932; handwritten: PEF/DA/TUF/206]

Tell Duweir.
c/o P.O.
Gaza.
Dec. 26. 1932.

Dearest Mà,

Dear, dear, I haven't written since I was in Jaffa on the 14th, the days have been full of small jobs and posts are rare things here. I expect there is a whole bundle of Xmas letters waiting at Hebron, but I haven't seen a sign of them; in fact I really advise your sending letters to Gaza, at any rate the truck does go there once a week, but Hebron seems to be completely off the map.

I hope your Christmas went off well and that Daddy and Loulou[35] were in good form. We had the traditional dinner here including an excellent turkey, otherwise no special festivities and we worked by general consent during the day.

I am settled in my room which is if anything too large for me, stone and mud walls, cement floor and wooden roof covered by tarred felt, lovely view over the hills from one window and shall be very comfortable [see Figure 6.7].

The first few days after I came back from Jerusalem were unusually windy and house and all were nearly blown away, now the weather is clear and fine and I sit in the sun all the morning watching a few men who are digging out the town wall. The site is really magnificent and the ramp is intact, all round I believe, we have exposed over 20 ft in 5 days – 20 x 20 in fact and it makes an imposing section all of the time of Rehoboam[36] – earlier periods are also well represented and we have got an eye on what we take to be Joshua's wall in brick.[37]

The party is a pleasant one at present – both Donald Brown the American and C.H. Inge are good additions and so is Mr Shaw[38] who does the surveying. Harris [Colt] arrived day before yesterday and went away again the next day in his flashy red, black and silver Lasalle car;[39] we all anticipate a certain amount of trouble as he still persists in thinking that he is the leader of the expedition, however I am determined to keep out of it and enjoy myself, in my own way, regardless. Col. Clarke[40] and Mr Way, both hangers on, come shortly and so does Terry in about a month.

Can you please send me the new Douglas Byng book of 'collected poems' which I saw announced in the *Times Lit. Sup.* either Bodley Head or Jonathan Cape I think, as I know the camp would love it – they quote snatches daily but never get all the words. [...]

[4 January 1933; handwritten: PEF/DA/TUF/207]

Tell Duweir
c/o P.O.
Gaza.
Jan. 4. 1933.

Dearest Mà,

Private – to be edited
We are well into the New Year without our having noticed it much, the only celebration was a drink or two and the trick of getting a banana into a whisky bottle was performed with some success!

Harris [Colt] has spent most of his time in Jerusalem so far but is having a 7-roomed mansion built for him here. I doubt if he will inhabit it much as the King David's Hotel Jerusalem can prove very attractive. He still insists on his position and things are at a deadlock for the moment – very possibly he may not come in at all, which would be all to the good and we have ample financial support in England. However, I am remaining as neutral as possible.

The work is going well, the fortifications are magnificent and in marvellous preservation, the 20 ft stone revetment is intact all round the mound and if it could all be cleared it would be more impressive than Jerusalem. We are more and more convinced that this is Lachish, a unique feature is the recessing of the walls which can be seen in the reliefs themselves.[41] Apparently these walls date from Rehoboam, but we need not fear any lack of early stuff and already we have a roomful of pottery. Ramadan is on now and we work till 1pm, that gives us an afternoon to do odd jobs in and to get straight. Things can only move slowly as we have only one carpenter.

The air is really good here, though Duweir is no higher than Beersheba, I feel very fit and well and sleep like a top, the bottle we bought at Harrods has never been opened and what is more was a needless purchase, and I think I am putting on a bit of fat. [...]

I send a few more photos and wish I had more varied news to give you. We are well into the usual routine now so there is not much to say. [...]

[15 January 1933; handwritten: PEF/DA/TUF/209]

Tell Duweir.
c/o P.O.
Gaza.
Jan. 15. 1933.

Dearest Mà,
[...] I am enjoying my job on the wall which progresses rapidly as so much is to be seen without digging at all. Shall have traced the whole of the W. face in a few days from now [Figure 6.9].

I see a good few patients daily and had an attendance of 37 yesterday which is just a bit above average.

Weather perfect from our point of view but it spells disaster for the landowners, as their crops will be ruined.

You will be glad to hear that I have been quite spotless all the time out here – what can it be that makes the difference?

Harris comes and goes on daily visits about twice a week to see how his palace of 7 rooms is getting on, he is a good postman so shall take this opportunity of writing a hurried line. [...]

Ramadan is on now, which gives us a nice quiet afternoon and soon we shall be thinking of the 3 days holiday at the end of it. We are really more out of the world here only 25 miles from Jerusalem than ever we were at Ajjul and now that the truck is undergoing extensive repairs we are dependent on camels for transport except when Harris is here. The Museum people are down today with him and are seeing the sites.

[Note at top of letter] Please thank Anna for her Xmas card.

[25 January 1933; typed original: PEF/DA/TUF/210]

Tell Duweir,
c/o Post Office,
Hebron.
Jan. 25th, 1933

Dearest Ma,

[…] Harris brought the shoes but he had the devil of a time with them. I thought Terry would bring them. At the customs they asked him the usual question and he said 'No', whereon they immediately rummaged and produced the shoes, so they asked who they belonged to and he said he was bringing them out for his wife, they asked where she was and he said in Malta, so the story sounded rather thin and he had to pay 5/–! […]

Heard from Daddy for my birthday and hope he will get the oranges safely which were duly sent off next day. Sorry that he has flu and do hope he is better by now.

The fast of Ramadan is over and the holiday is on [Figures 6.10, 6.11]. I am spending it here getting to know the people a bit better, and I had no desire to go to Jerusalem full of holiday-making effendis. [42] Have hired a horse in the village and rode 3½ hours this morning with Salman Ali, [43] who is that cheerful-looking chap on the shaggy pony of the photograph in my album [possibly as in Figure 6.12], so now I feel as stiff as a poker but very well and fit. Shall ride again tomorrow which will be agony, I expect. We went to a Tell about an hour away and met various people on the way, you may find the Tell marked on the map, something like Makerah perhaps [see Map 5].

I have had my room mudded by special process and a fireplace of the local village pattern is being put in, it looks just like a beehive but is not sufficiently advanced yet for me to try it, these mud erections take days to build. Meanwhile I am hugger mugging in another room, while the walls dry out, which will I hope be by tomorrow, when I will get really settled in at last. […]

We expect Terry and Mr Way at the end of the week, which will change the atmosphere as the latter is by no means popular and the former a bit dynamic for camp life. Harris is so seldom here that we don't notice him at all and the rest are all thoroughly congenial. We have started our Arabic conversaziones again and the burst of Arabic that I am indulging in now should go far to get me out of my rut.

Am reading *Yesterday and Today in Sinai* by Major Jarvis, which you might like to get from the library as it is a vivid picture of the Arabs as we

Figure 6.10 'Ramadan Festival'. Procession of men and boys in the village of Qubeibeh. Undated. Olga Tufnell archive. Courtesy of the Palestine Exploration Fund.

know them and quite humorously written. Have also got Bruce Lockhart's latest, with indefinite vistas of new novels from Hatchards, which is a good reason for the presence of the Colts. [...]

Very much love to you all
from
Olga

Aid 1933

Figure 6.11 'Aid 1933' (28 January–3 February 1933), presumably at Tell ed-Duweir. See letter of 25 January 1933. Olga Tufnell archive. Courtesy of the Palestine Exploration Fund.

[6 February, probably 1933; handwritten: PEF/DA/TUF/211]

Tell Duweir
c/o P.O.
Gaza.
Feb. 6

Dearest Mà,
[....] We had five fine days and now we have had four v. wet ones which have precluded all work. However there is lots to do in the house and I have taken the opportunity to do some house decoration and my room, now complete with Bedawy [Bedouin] fire place and some scarlet paint against the mud walls really looks rather pleasant.

Terry [Colt] and Mr Way came down yesterday – a great feat both for the car and the driver as everyone had agreed that the roads were impassable. Anyhow all this weather means that the crops will be good and the people 'mabsut' (pleased). Brownie (the American) and I are having Arabic lessons with Gerald [Harding] almost daily which is excellent practice. [...]

The night before a deputation had suggested I should go and watch the procession start for the local shrine Sheykh Ali, on your map I expect, and would I be there by eight. So I got up early and walked over to the village having given the staff leave to go to the Mosque. When I got to the village I was invited into the house of one Rashid, who was the first villager to be nice to us and brought us water all through the disputes with landowners at the beginning. He has a really charming wife and 2 small girls who are regular cards and imps of mischief. I was shown into their room – see photo[44] – all spick and span and decorated by her with multi-coloured designs. You can see the remains of my very good breakfast of eggs, bread, honey and tea in the foreground.

We sat and talked a long time and she showed me all her clothes and possessions and still the procession did not start.

The two Muktars came and invited me to their houses and I graciously consented to visit Musl (the good one) next and soon I was taken there. He has a marvellous stone house unlike the others which are of mud and stone but when you get inside the usual crowds of animals and poultry wander freely round. He has an upper chamber where guests are received and there I ate a solitary stately meal of chicken and rice and coffee, after which I saw all the ladies of the village, all wearing their party clothes for the festival. The Muktar's wife had on a lovely shawl and since then I have acquired for 15/– an even better one which I use as a bedspread. Soon afterwards the procession did start and we all traipsed out to see it when a shower fell and everyone took refuge in the nearest house. I sat in the one and only shop for sometime and then the procession went on in the direction of the cemetery, me in front with the camera, hurriedly taking photos. By then they had abandoned all idea of going to the local Sheykh, partly owing to the weather and partly because I was a bit of a novelty. When the cem. [cemetery] was reached a Zikr[45] started – one of those barbarous pre-Moslem rites, which they still practise though they are well aware that they are a bit unorthodox. They form a circle and bow up and down chanting 'Allah' 'Allah' while the local derwishes [dervishes] revolve wildly in the centre until they go off into a trance during which they munch cactus leaves, thrust nails through their cheeks, sit on swords and do other unnecessary but to them praiseworthy things.

By the time this state of holiness had been reached, my films had given out so I have no pictures, which would otherwise have been unique for this part of the world, as the Zikr is usually conducted at night.

I made my adieux and got back to camp to find it was 2pm so the festivities had taken time.

Tomorrow night I believe we are all going to a dinner party in the village which promises to be rather fun. [...]

Very best love and many thanks for the book which is much appreciated, the Col. sent it down via Terry together with the waterless hot water bottle which was his 'Xmas card' to me! [...]

[9 February 1933; typed copy: PEF/DA/TUF/212]

Wellcome Historical Museum Expedition,
Tell Duweir,
c/o Post Office,
Hebron.

February 9th

Dear Dr Strathearn,

Very many thanks for your very helpful corrections and additions to my notes. I am now seeing between 30 and 40 people a day here, and a large proportion of them are eye cases, funnily enough one of the Kubeibe [Qubeibeh] men actually saw me when I was at the hospital in my white coat, so my prestige is slightly higher than it should be! I try to impress on them the importance of going up to you and offer them notes to take up when they go. There seem to be many bad cases in the village with heavy discharge, chiefly among the children.

I am not clear if it [is] safe to use the same treatment for trachoma in children (Cu. Zinc drops and Vas. Flav.) between the ages of 2 and 7, so have been relying on boracic until I had more definite ideas on the subject. I have seen some cases with very red lower and upper lids but with little swelling, is this conjunctivitis or something else? Is Protargol a safe treatment for small children?

Hoping to see you down here when the weather is more settled and with renewed thanks,

Yours sincerely

[17 February, probably 1933; handwritten: PEF/DA/TUF/213]

c/o P.O.
Gaza
Palestine
Feb. 17.

Dearest Mà,

Very many thanks for the *Criterion*[46] – the price is indeed a swiz and an iniquity.

Last week we all went to a dinner party in the village with an old boy known as Hajji Ibrahim;[47] his house was most picturesque, 2 large rooms with vaulted mud ceilings with lanterns hanging from them. All the rugs and cushions of the entire village were spread on the floor and through innumerable little windows and lookout holes there were bits of sky studded with stars. Though we were very late in arriving owing to an emergency call to a patient in the village, we waited quite hungrily for a long time before food appeared. The procession when it did appear was prodigious – plates and plates of rice, chicken and sauces of various kinds to supplement it and piles of bread looking rather like well-worn shammy [chamois] leather. We fell to quite cheerfully but were defeated in the long run by the copious supplies which were then passed on to the worthies of the village all grouped in the outer room and the courtyard beyond who made short work of the remainder in a silence only relieved by the sound as of waves washing on a sandy shore.

We did not stay late and walked home by the light of a full moon.

Last Tuesday I attended a very different function, Harris and Terry, Shaw and Ba and I went up to Jerusalem in the Lasalle, leaving here at 5.45 we got to Jerusalem at 7.45 over roads which were slimy with mud, jolly good going in fact. After cocktails in the bar of the King David Hotel we had a hurried dinner and repaired to the new YMCA building to hear Miss Garrod[48] on the prehistory of Palestine – same old lecture delivered in the same competent way without a trace of inspiration. The hall was packed and we stood the whole time. Fortified by more drinks we left J. [Jerusalem] about 10.15 and were back in camp by 12.30. Her lecture is only the 1st of a course, Guy next week and Crowfoot after that and we are going up for all weather permitting, which makes a pleasant break in the routine. Weather glorious and all going smoothly now. [...]

[23 February 1933; handwritten: PEF/DA/TUF/214]

Tell Duweir
c/o P.O.
Gaza.
Feb. 23. 1933

Dearest Mà,
[...] Nothing of note has happened this last week except that Père Vincent[49] came down for the day with 3 other White Fathers (he is

considered to be the greatest living expert on Pal. [Palestinian] Archaeology). Starks was in J. [Jerusalem] so Gerald and I showed them round in a piebald mixture of French and English. They were most enthusiastic and say that part of our revetment is Middle Bronze[50] as we had rather suspected but not dared to hope for. [...]

Tomorrow some of us are going to Tell Safi and Zakarya [Zakariya] and I hope to get copy for my article for *Illus. Lond. News* [the *Illustrated London News*]. [...]

[4 March, probably1933; handwritten: PEF/DA/TUF/215]

Tell Duweir
Mar. 4.

Dearest Mà,
[...] All going on well and we have just reached water in a Bronze Age well 157 ft deep, 18 ft of water so the village is justly elated.

Last week we had a good trip to Arak el Menshiyeh [Arak al Manshiyah], Safi and Zakariyah in a car from Jerusalem tied together with string. The driver, who might have been Harry Tate[51] himself, carried on with the utmost unconcern, prising open the door with his knife when it was handy and climbing in through the window when it wasn't. Tell Safi is a fine site, Blanchegarde of the Crusaders, but Zakariyah is disappointing, but it was sunset and cold when we got there.

Last Tuesday, Terry, Harris, Ba and I went to Jerusalem for Crowfoot's lecture and then on to dance at the King David. Unfortunately they had nearly all eaten something with [sic] had disagreed the day before, so we were not all so lively as usual. But I did enjoy a marvellous bath and changing into evening things and having 2 sophisticated meals. Got home about 4 am that morning having left at 5 pm, but I felt spry enough the next day having had a fair share of 'phiz'. [...]

[10 March, probably 1933; handwritten: PEF/DA/TUF/216]

Tell Duweir.
c/o P.O.
Gaza.
March. 10.

Dearest Tuffy,[52]
Herewith an article which I hope you will like for the *Investigator*.[53] H.H. McWilliams[54] is a very clever young architect who is now here doing

reconstructional drawings of the Tell. As he says in his account of a month's stay in Russia, he went with every confidence in the new Utopia and he is anxious to warn other architects who may be led astray by glowing accounts and promises that it is no good going to Russia to get employment even if it be unremunerative. I don't know if you pay for articles, but if so a cheque sent here will not be scorned. We have not titled it so you can do your damnedest there.

Sir Charles Marston is coming here shortly, so I shall take down your photograph before he comes, as he and wife are having my room as it is by way of being the most comfortable. Shall be interested to see whether he mentions you! […]

Things are going well here, we have found a lot in the time and are enjoying things immensely, today being our Sunday we are all going to bathe at Askalon [Ashkelon]. […]

[15 March, probably 1933; handwritten: PEF/DA/TUF/217]

Tell Duweir
c/o P.O.
Gaza.
March. 15.

Dearest Mà,

After a perfect day last Friday at Askelon, bathing in a positively warm sea and basking in the sun afterwards, it turned nasty the following morning and has been blowing off and on ever since.

The week has been rather momentous as Sir Charles [Marston] has arrived in the country, accompanied by his wife, 2 daughters [Marjorie and Melissa] and a private chaplain who says grace for him. Last Monday he sent for Starks to Jerusalem and he was with him for 3 days culminating yesterday when they came down here and spent the day.

Their visit was a great success and they seemed pleased and impressed with all they saw and Sir Ch. [Charles] said we were not to worry about funds as they would be forthcoming. Then who should be in Jerusalem at the same time but Bobbie [Sir Robert Mond][55] complete with harēm and we are expecting them down here today but it is rather foul, so I hope they won't come. Needless to say we do not expect Lady M [Marston]. When I was in J. last Tuesday night I ran right into them in the King David Hotel, and shook Robert firmly by the hand, but as usual he had not an inkling as to who I was. […]

After dinner [...] to a lecture at the YMCA which was not good, too long and technical altogether for the audience. It was Iliff[e][56] speaking whom you heard at Selfridge's 2 yrs ago, he seemed very nervous, speaking for the 1st time in the new hall of the building which is very large and quite good.

The Colts have spent £200 on their house and now it looks as if they may not be here next winter as C. is determined not to keep to the original arrangement in London. He evidently means to lead something and I believe he is toying with the idea of a Roman site further North and I wish him joy of it. All this 'entre nous' as nothing has been said yet, but one cannot help saying or at least thinking 'I told you so' as it was obvious from the first that the partnership could not be successful when both sides were working for such different aims – our aims you know and his is merely social recognition and an 'entrée' to what he considers the best circles in London. The work itself has practically no interest for him.

We hear that Lady P. goes home at the end of the month and that Prof. is staying in Jerusalem for 6 wks, when we hope to get him down here for a few days to see the site. Ann [the Petries' daughter] goes a week after or before Lady P. so you will have the latter on your hands fairly soon now and she will get a good innings before I appear. Apparently there will be no exhibition this year and the objects such as they are will be staying in Palestine. As Prof. has retired I suppose they no longer have the use of the College [UCL] and the BS[AE] will have to move.[57]

We have now started work on the Palace, and Palace it must surely be or at any rate Chief Government Building for we have found about 40 jar handles, from wine and oil jars marked with a seal 'For the king' followed by such names as Hebron, Socoh and Ziph which were I suppose taxing centres. This is all of a period before 586 BC, when the town was destroyed by Nebuchadnezzar, as we believe.[58] The plastered[?] floor levels are all intact and we find great storage jars standing on them.

The whole town makes a brave show now that we have traced one line of defences all round and have found the entrance way and the threshold of the city gate. [...]

[24 March, probably 1933; handwritten: PEF/DA/TUF/218]

Tell Duweir
c/o P.O.
Gaza.
March 24.

Figure 6.12 Boy on a horse. Starkey family collection. Perhaps the boy mentioned in letter of 31 March 1928, or Salman Ali mentioned in letter of 25 January 1933. Starkey family collection. Courtesy of Wendy Slaninka.

Dearest Mà,

Last week was full and interesting – Sir Charles came down on Thursday with Lady M. and their tame chaplain and the following day who should turn up but Bobby himself. The day Sir C. came I had a bad tummy – the first and I hope only one this year – so was not my brightest and went off to bed about tea time, but they were thrilled with all they saw. Bobbie was of course more intelligent to take round and we spent a very pleasant day showing him the sights. He was very pleased because he had just visited the Haram in Khalyl [Hebron][59] and been shown all round. It is death for Jews to go there, did you know he [Mond] had been baptised and ate 2 helpings of ham for lunch with great relish. He was full of his telescope which is housed at Sidmouth, and he remember[ed] Grandpa[60] and actually knew his name, he got mine right <u>once</u> but was rather apt to call me Mrs Colt and Mrs Starkey at intervals!

On Tuesday I went up for the lecture as usual and as we got up a bit earlier, I had my hair done, as I had arranged to stay the night to do various jobs in the morning. After the lecture we found Ba at the King David, where he was staying with his Ma who was on her way to Egypt. She was ill all the time in Jerusalem, which was sad for Ba, though he never intended to bring her down to camp. If you were in Palestine wild horses would not keep you away, I know, and why don't you come out next season, my room is so large and comfortable, you could easily spend a week or two, the only drawback being the outside lavvy and very much outside at that!

We saw Sir R. [Mond] at the hotel who took us over and introduced us to the family circle. He was full of praise for the dig and said if he had done so much work in the time and with our resources he would indeed be pleased, in all of which Sir C. agreed with him. We hear Garstang[61] and other digs green with jealousy.

Had a lovely bath at the Fast Hotel and went at 8.30 next morning to the hospital and saw eye cases and culled information. Joan Crowfoot was also there and I went back to lunch with her at Beaumont Ho. [House] and then they motored me home, which was very decent. They start work at Samaria next week. [...]

As to coming home, I suppose it will be about the usual time end of April and beginning of May. Terry and Ba are motoring home through Asia Minor and Constant. [Constantinople] but I do not expect to be in on that as they will be starting early and it takes more than a month to do. [...]

Notes

1 Henry 1985, 3. See Melman 2020, Chapter 4, for a detailed overview of the site of Tell ed-Duweir and the British-led expedition. Also, according to Olga Tufnell, Sir Henry Wellcome favoured Tell ed-Duweir in part because of the challenging scale of the project to excavate stone-built settlements, and the requirement for a greater scale of funding (Olga Tufnell interviewed by Jonathan Tubb, transcript of audiotaped interview, c. 1985).

2 Tufnell 1953, 32. Ironically, neither of these two questions was much elucidated by the six seasons of excavations at Tell ed-Duweir.

3 Albright 1929, 3, n.2; Garstang 1931, 172–3; Starkey 1933, 198; letter from P.L.O. Guy to Ovendon, 27 January 1938, Palestine Exploration Fund/BSAJ archive.

4 See Abu-Sitta 2010, 36; map 471. Also referred to as Qubeibeh Ibn Awad.

5 Garfinkel 2016, 88–9.

6 Also see Weir 1989 for more on Palestinian costume, and especially pp. 159–60 for this image with caption: 'Bride dressed for her "going out ceremony", Qubeibeh ibn 'Awad, southern plain, 1932–1933'.

7 Olga Tufnell interviewed by Jonathan Tubb. Transcript of audiotaped interview, c. 1985.

8 Olga Tufnell interviewed by Jonathan Tubb. Transcript of audiotaped interview, c. 1985.

9 Seton-Williams 2011, 74–9.

10 Seton-Williams 2011, 77 describes Diab as 'chief assistant'. Elsewhere he was described as a site guard.

11 Tufnell 1958, 9.

12 Ussishkin 2014, 38.

13 Tufnell 1953, 33.

14 Albright 1949, 1–22.

15 Tufnell 1953, 2; cited in Melman 2020, 146.

16 Most of the drawings of objects and pottery published in the Lachish volumes were done in the field by Olga Tufnell and Lankester Harding, as noted in Tufnell, Inge and Harding 1940, 12; Tufnell 1953, 10.

17 Tufnell 1950.

18 The Field Report for 1936–7 includes mention of patients coming from as far as Beer-Sheba (25 miles away), cited in Melman 2020, 146.

19 The published figure caption states 'Looking north along western revetment … four uppermost courses exposed, showing panelling. Upper city wall against skyline (top right).'

20 Starkey 1933.

21 For an overview of excavation methods employed at Tell ed-Duweir, see Ussishkin 2014, 38–48, and Zammit 2016, 222–7.

22 Seton-Williams 2011, 77.

23 See Cline 2020 for an overview of the Megiddo expedition and its members.

24 Edwards 2013.

25 Kitty Strickland, Lord Strickland's daughter and sister of Teresa Colt, who had visited Tell el-'Ajjul earlier that year.

26 Lord Gerald Strickland (1861–1940), Prime Minister of Malta, 1927–32.

27 Margaret Murray excavated the megalithic site of Borg in-Nadur in Malta in the 1920s.

28 For biographical note see List of Principal Persons, p. xxx.

29 May be the item referred to as a clothes basket in letter of 12 April 1933.

30 Dr John Strathearn (Lt Col., CBE, later Sir John), consultant ophthalmic surgeon to the Department of Health, Palestine.

31 The first St John Ophthalmic Hospital (now known as the St John of Jerusalem Eye Hospital) was built in 1882 in Jerusalem. It was resited in 1960 in East Jerusalem, with the intention of giving ophthalmic care to two million Palestinians and providing outreach clinics in what are now the Occupied Palestinian Territories. The original hospital building is now the Mount Zion Hotel.

32 An adaptation of a US song and nursery rhyme from the nineteenth century, 'Ten Little Indians'.

33 The well-loved doctor in Olga's village, Little Waltham.

34 The amount donated was £5 according to a receipt provided by Ophthalmic Hospital Jerusalem (PEF/DA/TUF/204).

35 Nickname for Louis, Olga's younger brother.

36 Tufnell 1953, 53–5.

37 Tufnell 1953, 52.

38 Donald Brown, Charles Inge and W.B.K. (Kennedy) Shaw were all new members of the expedition. Kennedy Shaw is also referred to by Olga as the architect in the first season, later followed by Holbrook V. Bonney (Tufnell 1985, 8). W.B. Kennedy Shaw (1901–79), botanist and surveyor in Palestine and Libya, subsequently worked for the Palestine Department of Antiquities and served in the Second World War as an intelligence officer as part of the Long Range Desert Group Special Forces against Rommel's Afrika Korps. He was later married to Eleanor Dyott (see Chapter 8). For biographical entry for Charles Inge, see List of Principal Persons, p. xxx.

39 The LaSalle automobile was manufactured in the United States as a cheaper version of the Cadillac.

40 For earlier appearance of Col. Clarke see letter of 10 December 1931.

41 Assyrian reliefs in the British Museum showing Sennacherib's assault on the city of Lachish in 701 BC.

42 'Effendi' was an Ottoman Turkish title of nobility or officialdom, roughly equivalent to 'Sir' in English.

43 Salman Ali, also known as Salman Aly, one of Olga's workers at Tell ed-Duweir (see Figure 6.6).

44 Possibly a photo in the Olga Tufnell archive at the Palestine Exploration Fund.

45 Also known in Arabic as *Dhikr*, a devotional prayer of remembrance in Islam. The variation cited here reflects Sufi traditions.

46 Literary magazine, founded 1922.

47 Hajji Ibrahim of Qubeibeh.

48 Dorothy Garrod (1892–1968), pioneering prehistorian and excavator of Palaeolithic and Epipalaeolithic (Natufian) sites in Palestine within the Carmel Range, working closely with Dorothea Bate (Bar-Yosef and Callander 2004). Disney Professor of Archaeology at University of Cambridge 1939–52 (first woman professor at Cambridge), served in the Women's Auxiliary Air Force 1942–5, worked in Lebanon 1958–63.

49 Louis-Hugues Vincent, 'Père Vincent' (1872–1960), Dominican Father and Professor of Archaeology at the École Biblique, Jerusalem, 1895–1960.

50 It is not immediately clear whether the comment refers to the 'outer revetment wall' of Level IV–III, the construction of which is still conventionally assigned to Rehoboam's reign (928–911 BC) (Ussishkin 1993, 905–6), or the extant part of a Middle Bronze Age glacis at the northwest corner of the mound. As Olga refers to the 20 ft stone revetment in her letter of 4 January 1933, it is assumed that she was referring to what was considered to be the Iron Age revetment. The debate regarding the dating of the outer revetment wall continues. Recent excavations by the Hebrew University of Jerusalem suggest this outer revetment should be reassigned to the Middle Bronze Age (Garfinkel 2019).

51 Harry Tate was a Scottish music-hall comedian whose most famous sketch was 'Motoring'.

52 All male and some female members of the Tufnell family could be affectionately referred to as 'Tuffy'. Also see letter of 10 January 1930. The letter is likely to be to a close family member. The reference to the photograph could indicate it was to her brother Louis or cousin Lionel (see letter of 1 December 1931).

53 An article written by H.H. McWilliams, subsequently published in *The Investigator*.

54 Herbert Hastings McWilliams (1907–95), known as 'Mac'. South African architect, artist, author, naval officer and yachtsman. In 1929 he gained a diploma from the Architectural Association, London. Travelled widely in the early 1930s, including to Egypt as part of the Oriental Institute of the University of Chicago expedition to Sakkara (1932), and to Palestine as architect to the Tell ed-Duweir expedition (1932–3). Published account of car journey from Palestine to London in *The Diabolical* (1934). Practised architecture from 1935 in South Africa. Joined the Royal Navy in 1940, surviving sinking of HMS *Hecla* in 1942 (McWilliams 2013). Continued in architecture after the war. Represented South Africa in yachting in the 1948 Olympics. His naval paintings and drawings can be found in the Imperial War Museum, London, the Ditsong Museum of Military History, Johannesburg, and the Nelson Mandela Metropolitan Art Museum, Cape Town.

55 Sir Robert Mond (1867–1938), chemist and industrialist, interested in archaeology, and sponsor of the Tell ed-Duweir Expedition. Son of Ludwig Mond, the founder of Brunner Mond chemical firm, which amalgamated with ICI in 1926. Worked on the Thebes necropolis, Egypt, with Alan Gardiner. Major benefactor of the British School of Archaeology in Jerusalem. A friend of Olga's family through A.F. Lindemann, her grandmother's second husband (see note 60 below). Treasurer of the Palestine Exploration Fund, 1930–8.

56 John H. Iliffe (1902–60), Keeper of the Palestine Archaeological Museum, Jerusalem, 1931–48. Director of Museums, Liverpool, 1948–59.

57 According to Drower 1985, 392, Petrie was to retire from UCL in the summer of 1933. The future storage of collections from Petrie's Palestinian excavations on behalf of the British School of Archaeology in Egypt was of great importance to him during the last years of his tenure as Edwards Professor of Egyptology at UCL, but space at that time eluded him. Petrie eventually (in 1935) 'gave' the collections to the fledgling Institute of Archaeology, which was to become part of UCL in 1986, where they are displayed and stored as the Petrie Palestinian Collection (Ucko 1998, 356–7; Ucko, Sparks and Laidlaw 2007).

58 These stamped jar handles are more commonly known as *lmlk* stamps (Lamelek – meaning [belonging] 'to the king'). There is now a common view among scholars that Level III was destroyed by Sennacherib's army in 701 BC. This date, however, was subject to prolonged controversy and debate. Many scholars (including Albright, K.M. Kenyon and G.E. Wright) accepted Starkey's view that the Level III destruction should be attributed to a Babylonian campaign in 591 BC or slightly earlier (hence the reference to Nebuchadnezzar in this letter). Tufnell (1953, 342–4) and Diringer (1953) attributed most 'royal' jar handles to Level III,

considered to have been destroyed in Sennacherib's Assyrian campaign of 701 BC. It was not until the Tel Aviv University's renewed excavations at Lachish in the 1970s that this view became more firmly established (Ussishkin 1993, 907; Rainey 1975). The presence of these stamped jar handles in Level III of Tell ed-Duweir provides an important chronological horizon for the distribution of early (eighth-century) and late (seventh-century) types in the kingdom of Judah. It is unusual that the discovery of these jars was not published until the preliminary report two years later (Starkey 1936).

59 Haram al-Ibrahimi, Al-Khalil (Hebron), also known as the Cave of the Patriarchs/Machpelah or the Sanctuary of Abraham. Tensions in Hebron were very high (as today), given its intense religious significance for Muslims and Jews. Dozens of Jews were killed by Arabs in the Hebron Massacre of 1929, which followed rumours that Jews planned to seize the Temple Mount/ Haram ash-Sharif in Jerusalem. Also see Chapter 5, notes 1 and 51.

60 Olga's step-grandfather A.F. Lindemann was a scientist and amateur astronomer. He had built an observatory in his garden at Sidholme, for which Sir Robert Mond had donated a telescope. This was later presented in 1927 to the Norman Lockyer Observatory at Exeter University, then a centre of astronomical excellence (Birkenhead 1961, 27). When this ceased to function the telescope was given to the Sidmouth Astronomical Society.

61 John Garstang (1876–1956), Professor of Archaeology, University of Liverpool, 1907–41. Founding director of Department of Antiquities, Palestine, and the British School of Archaeology in Jerusalem. He drafted the antiquities laws of Palestine (1920–6) and excavated Tell es-Sultan, Jericho (1930–6), funded by Sir Charles Marston. He was the founding director of the British School of Archaeology, Ankara (1947).

References

Abu-Sitta, Salman H. 2010. *Atlas of Palestine: 1917–1966*. London: Palestine Land Society.

Albright, William F. 1929. 'The American Excavations at Tell Beit Mirsim', *Zeitschrift für die Alttestamentliche Wissenschaft* 47: 1–17.

Albright, William F. 1949. *The Archaeology of Palestine*. Harmondsworth: Pelican.

Bar-Yosef, Ofer and Jane Callander. 2004. 'Dorothy Annie Elizabeth Garrod (1892–1968)'. In *Breaking Ground: Pioneering Women Archaeologists*, edited by Getzel M. Cohen and Martha Sharp Joukowsky, 380–424. Ann Arbor, MI: University of Michigan Press.

Birkenhead, Earl of [Frederick W.F. Smith]. 1961. *The Prof in Two Worlds: The Official Life of Professor F.A. Lindemann, Viscount Cherwell*. London: Collins.

Cline, Eric H. 2020. *Digging Up Armageddon: The Search for the Lost City of Solomon*. Princeton, NJ: Princeton University Press.

Diringer, David. 1953. 'Early Hebrew Inscriptions'. In *Lachish III: The Iron Age*, by Olga Tufnell, 331–59. London: Oxford University Press.

Drower, Margaret S. 1985. *Flinders Petrie: A Life in Archaeology*, London: Victor Gollancz.

Edwards, Phillip C. 2013. 'Redemption in the Land of Archaeological Sin: Great Excavators in the Middle East during the 1920s', *Buried History: Journal of the Australian Institute of Archaeology* 49: 23–36.

Garfinkel, Yosef. 2016. 'The Murder of James Leslie Starkey near Lachish', *Palestine Exploration Quarterly* 148: 84–109.

Garfinkel, Yosef. 2019. 'Innovations Concerning the Fortifications of Canaanite and Judean Lachish', *New Studies in the Archaeology of Jerusalem and its Region* 13: 273–300 (Hebrew).

Garstang, John. 1931. *The Foundations of Bible History: Joshua, Judges*. New York: Richard R. Smith.

Henry, Ros. 1985. 'Olga Tufnell – A Biography'. In *Palestine in the Bronze and Iron Ages: Papers in Honour of Olga Tufnell*, edited by Jonathan N. Tubb, 1–5. London: Institute of Archaeology.

McWilliams, Herbert Hastings. 1934. *The Diabolical: An Account of the Adventures of Five People who Set Out in a Converted Ford Lorry to Make a Journey from Palestine to England across Asia Minor and the Balkans*. London: Duckworth.

McWilliams, Herbert Hastings. 2013. *War at Sea: Letters Home, 1941–1945*. St Albans: Holywell House.

Melman, Billie. 2020. *Empires of Antiquities: Modernity and the Rediscovery of the Ancient Near East, 1914–1950*. Oxford: Oxford University Press.

Rainey, Anson F. 1975. 'The Fate of Lachish during the Campaigns of Sennacherib and Nebuchadrezzar'. In *Investigations at Lachish: The Sanctuary and the Residency (Lachish V)*, edited by Yohanan Aharoni, 47–60. Tel Aviv: Institute of Archaeology, Tel Aviv University.

Seton-Williams, M.V. 2011 [originally published 1988]. *The Road to El-Aguzein*. London and New York: Routledge.

Starkey, James L. 1933. 'A Lecture Delivered at the Rooms of the Palestine Exploration Fund, on June 22nd, 1933', *Palestine Exploration Quarterly* 65: 190–9.

Starkey, James L. 1936. 'Excavations at Tell el Duweir, 1935–6. Wellcome Archaeological Research Expedition to the Near East (Lecture)', *Palestine Exploration Quarterly* 68: 178–89.

Tufnell, Olga. 1950. 'The Excavations at Tell ed-Duweir, Palestine, Directed by the Late J.L. Starkey 1932–38', *Palestine Exploration Quarterly* 82: 65–80.

Tufnell, Olga. 1953. *Lachish III: The Iron Age*. London: Oxford University Press.

Tufnell, Olga. 1958. *Lachish IV: The Bronze Age*. London: Oxford University Press.

Tufnell, Olga. 1985. 'Reminiscences of Excavations at Lachish: An Address Delivered by Olga Tufnell at Lachish on July 6, 1983', *Tel Aviv* 12: 3–8.

Tufnell, Olga, Charles H. Inge and Gerald L. Harding. 1940. *Lachish II: The Fosse Temple*. London: Oxford University Press.

Ucko, Peter J. 1998. 'The Biography of a Collection: The Sir Flinders Petrie Palestinian Collection and the Role of University Museums', *Museum Management and Curatorship* 17(4): 351–99.

Ucko, Peter J., Rachael T. Sparks and Stuart Laidlaw. 2007. *A Future for the Past: Petrie's Palestinian Collection. Essays and Exhibition Catalogue*. Walnut Creek, CA: Left Coast Press.

Ussishkin, David. 1993. 'Lachish'. In *New Encyclopedia of Archaeological Excavations in the Holy Land*, edited by Ephraim Stern, 897–911. Jerusalem: Israel Exploration Society.

Ussishkin, David. 2014. *Biblical Lachish: A Tale of Construction, Destruction, Excavation and Restoration*. Jerusalem: Israel Exploration Society.

Weir, Shelagh. 1989. *Palestinian Costume*. London: British Museum Publications.

Zammit, Abigail. 2016. *The Lachish Letters: A Reappraisal of the Ostraca Discovered in 1935 and 1938 at Tell ed-Duweir*. Unpublished D.Phil. dissertation, University of Oxford.

7
The journey home overland, 1933

At the end of the first season at Tell ed-Duweir, Olga was thrilled by an invitation from Teresa Strickland Colt to join her party travelling home overland by car. She asked for parental approval (which was forthcoming), but no doubt would have been determined to go anyway. Herbert Hastings McWilliams (Mac), the expedition's architect, was the driver on this seven-week journey. He published an illustrated account of the journey the following year in a book entitled *The Diabolical*.[1]

Teresa (Terry), the instigator of the plan, was an exotic character whose presence considerably enlivened the camp. McWilliams describes her as 'wearing the most astonishing garments, with red boots, and a straw hat as big as an umbrella, looking like an animated Mrs Noah, yet who, when she chose, could appear in the smartest costume, just as if she had stepped out of a drawing in *Vogue*'.[2] She had planned an itinerary through Syria via Damascus and Aleppo, turning west to Antioch and then home through Turkey, Romania, Hungary, Austria and Germany.

It became obvious that the Colts' LaSalle car was not suitable for such a journey on rudimentary roads and where spare parts would be unobtainable. After much discussion it was agreed that a modification of the expedition truck – a Ford station wagon – would be a far more suitable option, and would remain useful in subsequent seasons (Figure 7.1). The problem, then, was to find a coachbuilder who could undertake the necessary changes. After much difficulty a man was found who had once built an ambulance and was confident he could do the work, at Teresa's expense.

It was decided that a new body had to be fitted onto the chassis consisting of 'simply a box, with a sort of cage behind, two metres long, so that a person could stretch out and sleep in it … the cage part was roofed and had wire windows and canvas screens, the rest of the structure was

Figure 7.1 Print of McWilliams's drawing of the 'Diabolical Strength'. See letter of 12 April 1933. Olga Tufnell archive, Palestine Exploration Fund. Courtesy of the Palestine Exploration Fund.

made of wood'.[3] In the end it would resemble nothing so much as a 'travelling cage for animals'.[4] As there were also three men in the party, McWilliams, Richmond Brown ('Ba') and Capt. Ponder ('Pongo', a friend of Teresa), a tent had to be made for them to sleep in, leaving Olga and Teresa to sleep in the adapted car. When the party were invited to inspect the finished work, they were horrified to find the words 'The Diabolical Strength' painted on the bonnet. The signwriter and engineer had together attempted a literal translation (with the aid of a dictionary) of the expedition's Arabic nickname for the vehicle – *el affrit el Kader*. It was decided that the name was entirely suitable (due to its great fortitude and hidden strength) and must stay.

The expedition set off from Jerusalem on 8 May. Olga and Richmond Brown left the party at Budapest and continued by train via Vienna, Cologne and the Hook of Holland, reaching London on 11 June. The entries in this chapter provide an abbreviated version of McWilliams's account as far as Budapest, adding a few further details and Olga's own observations and impressions. Modern and alternative place names, if known and where they differ from those mentioned in the letters, are added in square brackets. The archival record of the journey, now in the Palestine Exploration Fund, consists only of the typed documents. These may date from shortly after the completion of the journey and were typed up by Olga from a handwritten diary.[5]

The photographs from this journey, including those taken by Olga and others, provide a glimpse of some sites and monuments that have been impacted by conflict, disturbance and neglect in recent years, especially in Syria. The photographs therefore provide an important dated record of cultural heritage sites and monuments encountered by those travelling through the region.

The fashion for such overland journeys by motor car from Palestine to Europe was to become more widespread. For example, Olga's archaeological contemporaries Kathleen Kenyon and the Crowfoot sisters (Diana and Joan), who had been working at the archaeological site of Samaria, made a similar journey overland by motor car in 1935, although notably without a male driver.[6]

Olga was able to obtain visas easily for Syria and Turkey in Jerusalem, and then for southeast European countries in Istanbul. Encounters with police, soldiers and customs officials are mentioned a number of times in the letters, ranging from a near arrest at Baalbek on suspicion of illicit digging, to being stopped multiple times in Syria and Turkey at checkpoints and customs. The only restriction of entry encountered was to the archaeological site of Carchemish, which is bisected by the Turkish–Syrian border.

Archaeologists have continued to drive expedition vehicles between the United Kingdom and the Middle East, albeit on better roads. Since the onset of civil war in Syria in 2011, however, such journeys have become impossible. Modern political boundaries and entry restrictions between countries in the Levant, for example between Syria, Lebanon and Israel, sadly make overland contacts and movements between these places today much more limited than they were in Olga's time.

As with other typed originals, handwritten corrections are incorporated into the transcribed text.

Letters of April–June 1933

[7 April 1933; handwritten: PEF/DA/TUF/220]

Tell Duweir.
c/o P.O.
Gaza.
April 7.

Dearest Mà,
Many thanks for your letters of 24th and 27th – at last I can answer your query about dates and rather excitingly too – Terry [Colt] is having the

truck re-built, engine done over and complete new body, suitable for camping in, 2 sleep inside and 3 in a tent and I have been invited to go too from Jerusalem to London! The party will consist of her, Ba [Richmond Brown], McWilliams and self and we hope a fifth as Ba and I may have to get off at Constant. [Constantinople] to be back in time for things in London. It seems too good an opportunity to miss – a wonderful chance to see Asia Minor and get some idea if the Amazon trip is at all possible.[7] As to dates we hope to leave here about May 5th and expect to take 3 wks to get to Constant. There I may take train with Ba if we are at all late or if we have time in hand shall go on at least to Budapest. As to cost Terry has guaranteed that it shall not cost us more than £40 apiece, and as we expect to camp out most of the way it may even be less. So you may expect me sometime during the 1st week in June if all goes well, and can get in touch with me after the 5th c/o Cooks Constantinople and Sofia and Budapest if you want me back urgently. I enclose a rough list of the places on our way and we have not yet worked out the ancient sites we can include.

Let me know what you think of all this and if I have the parental approval which I am pretty sure of as you are both sympathetic to any such adventure. The rather comic agreement I wrote out to safeguard her and us and make it quite clear that I am travelling privately and not as a member of the Colt Archaeological Expedition!

The truck will be fitted with proper seats in front and the whole of the back is to be wired in to take luggage and 2 sleeping berths for us two. Mac [McWilliams] and Ba are both excellent drivers and mechanics and we are taking stores and cooking apparatus to be independent of doubtful local accommodation. So I think the plan is feasible and practical and should work out all right. I do feel one must snatch these chances while one can. Write soon and tell me what you think.

[Enclosure, Memorandum of Understanding; carbon copy from original: PEF/DA/TUF/219]

I am joining Mrs H. Dunscombe Colt's party travelling by car via Asia Minor and Constantinople to England. I do not hold her responsible for delays that may occur en route, while it may be necessary for me to leave the party and complete the journey by train if time presses.

I am paying my share of the petrol and living expenses for as long as I am with the party on condition that the other members do the same, and do not hold Mrs Colt responsible for any damage to me or my property on the journey, while she does not hold me responsible for any damage to her or her property. It is understood that I am travelling privately and am not connected with any expedition and wish no mention of my name in the press and guarantee not to use Mrs Colt's name or the party's experiences for publicity.

[12 April 1933; handwritten: PEF/DA/TUF/221]

Hotel Fast, Jerusalem [letterhead]
April 12. 1933

Dearest Mà,
I am up in Jerusalem for the night to deliver the division lists to the Museum and get my passport visaed for Turkey and Syria at least; if Bulgaria and all the other numerous strange countries cannot be had here we may have to get them in Stamboul [Istanbul].

Incidentally I have had my hair washed so feel tidy and shall at any rate feel clean when I have had a bath in the beautiful tiled bathroom that is awaiting me. Terry is up too so we are on the spree together.

I enclose a print of Mac's drawing of the truck [see Figure 7.1] as it will be when re-conditioned with sprung seats like a car to seat 5 in front and a wire cage behind to take luggage which we can lock and will provide sleeping accommodation for Terry and me.

Feel more settled now that the list is gone, expect the division next Wed. 19th which will leave us till end of the month to pack up.

The Colts went down to Ajjul the other day to return the famous clothes basket, they saw Prof [Petrie] and Mrs B. [Benson] but Ann and Lady P. [Petrie] had gone to Tiberias. They thought Prof. very well though he has had a bad leg and been in hospital with it. Rumour goes that a certain lady left him there and did not wait to see what the X ray revealed but went on motor tour to Tiberias!

This morning went to R.C. [Roman Catholic] Mass at Abbey Church of the Dormition in Mt Zion, v. long plainchant with procession to follow. Afterwards Mrs Richmond, Director of Ants. [Antiquities] wife, also RC and newly converted at that, came back here to breakfast with us, so have made her acquaintance more adequately and have an invitation to go there when I like.

Am now waiting for Terry to come in for lunch, where the hell she has gone to I can't imagine, it now being 1.45, but shops have a great lure for her. We go back after lunch and I expect this is my last excursion before leaving for good.

You will have had my letter about Bobby [Sir Robert Mond] by now, he can't be quite a pauper yet as he has made us a very generous gift – <u>entre nous entirely!</u>

[Note at top of letter] Can you possibly get and send VAN [sic – von] DER OSTEN *Explorations in Asia Minor*.[8] Can you get it here by May 7. <u>If not don't bother.</u> It is in 3 small grey vols, not big tomes. I know it is no good asking a bookseller, you are our only chance.

[3 May 1933; handwritten: PEF/DA/TUF/222]

Tell Duweir
c/o P.O.
Gaza.
May 3.

My darling Mà,
It was really wonderful of you to get the Van [sic] der Osten's here in time – <u>very</u> clever Mà, and most grateful thanks – I think they will be an excellent guidebook for all the things we ought to see, though whether we shall is quite another matter.

We are now expecting to leave Jerusalem on Monday morning. I shall go to J. on Sat. and stay on Sunday doing odd jobs. Shall try and see Prof. Ba saw him and called at Beaumont Ho[use]. He was v. pleased to see him and show him all the results of the work.

Capt. Ponder has arrived from Malta, known as Pongo. He is very military and 'oh ah! um!' but I think he may improve on acquaintance – The latest is that he met a man in the street in J. [Jerusalem] who saw his regimental tie and said what ho! come and have a drink, so they did at the Fast [Hotel] and when Terry [Colt] joined them she thought they were bosom friends and asked him to join the trip! The sort of thing she does, but we know quite a lot about him as he has been to camp and is a rich young man called Fergusson who has been dabbling in archaeology at Jericho – but rather got Garstang's goat because he never turned up on the work. Anyhow as he is following in his own car (a Riley) it may be jolly useful to have an odd car in hand in case of emergency.

Starks leaves here on Friday and goes straight home and will be there in a week. I will ask him to ring you up and give you the latest news.

We have nearly packed everything now and I have only got my clothes to do. One suitcase is going in the boxes, the other (Rev.)[9] I take with me.

This will be my last letter from camp, personally I have enjoyed the season having stuck to my intention of keeping well out of all strife and I have nothing to grumble at.

Have been sleeping out here for the last week or so, under my net, which by the way I am taking with me, being fully aware of the dangers of the Anatolian plain. I am sewing it on to my flea bag (lent by Shaw) so should be safe enough.

Shall hope to send you p.c.s [postcards] all along the route and will hear from you I hope at Damascus and Stamboul [Istanbul] – c/o Cook.

[8 May–10 June 1933; typed originals: PEF/DA/TUF/223]

[Cover note, typed by Olga Tufnell, undated]:

O.T.'s letters home, May 8 to June 9
Budapest, where Ba and I took the train to London, arriving there June 11 1933, via Buda–Vienna–Koln–Hook of Holland.

for further details of this trip see H.H. McWilliam's <u>The Diabolical</u> Duckworth, 1934
Also Pongo's [Capt. Ponder's] account, author and title to be added.

<u>THROUGH TURKEY WITH TERRY</u>
We're off! We left Jerusalem about 11 am yesterday (May 8th) in the brand new diabolical one and made good going all the way, reaching here as the sun went down.

<u>Tabcha. Sea of Galilee [Tabgha]</u>
We passed Samaria again and Shechem, now Nablus, and crossed the great hill shoulder which divides the hill country from the plain of Esdraelon. Everywhere the wheat harvest was beginning – great expanses of corn shimmering like waves in the sun and wind, little patchwork pieces had been cut and all along the way one saw the most modern machinery working side by side with sickles such as Naomi used.

Nazareth, with its barrack-like religious building only made bearable by fine groups of cypresses against the skyline, did not check our progress and soon afterwards the character of the country changed and we were in the basalt area. The horns of Hattim [Hattin] where the Crusaders were defeated by Saladin was on the left and in the distance 800 feet below sea [level] the lake of Galilee shone palely blue. The usual hair pin bends brought us to Tiberias, white in the distance and rather grubby close to and then we skirted the lake to Tabcha [Tabgha], a convent surrounded by trees which is really quite a sophisticated hospice. Bourjainvillia [Bougainvillea] in unbelievable profusion, cypresses – a full moon and the lake made a complete Hollywood setting. Reluctantly to bed about 10 and the next morning we took the road again by 9, climbing straight from 800 feet below sea level to 2000 feet above it with the snow-streaked head of Hermon always before us.

May 10. We could have spared ourselves the usual trepidations about customs for the English ones were only beaten for cheery good-heartedness by the French–Syrian douane 2 kms further on. Not a thing did they open or tax and I am meeting the douane official in Damascus next year. The customs are at Rospina [Rosh Pinna] on the Jordan, not far from the point where the placid waters of the Huleh lake contract and become a turbulent noisy stream which falls in the Sea of Galilee and emerges again as the Jordan. As we had to wait sometime we sat on a rickety bridge and watched the water flow and explored the banks, finding wild raspberry canes and lupins. From Rospina we climbed up onto the barren plain which is so surprisingly the frame for Damascus. Hermon formed a barrier to our left and on the right we could see the softer browner contours of the Gebel [Jebel] Druze. Red-roofed bungalows gave place to basalt stone houses we had seen near Tiberias and subtle differences made us aware we were no longer in Palestine. About 3 pm close to a conical mountain we had seen before us for some time a dark green patch emerged and as we approached winding canals flowed peacefully, twisting and writhing like a dark green snake between its banks.

Rather unbelievably our first association with Damascus proved to be apple tart, for as we came nearer to the fields and orchards we smelt a pungent pleasant smell, and when we stopped to trace the cause of it, we found a small tree with narrow silver leaves with little bell like flowers which reminded us of cloves, but I have still to learn if they really were or not.

We are putting up at the Omayyad Hotel, quite the most sophisticated here, we got in about 4 pm and after a hurried wash went out to see the Mosque before it closed.

Outside the usual huddle of shops and street vendors crying their wares, inside perfect peace and restfulness. The cool greyness of the stone is set off by jewel-like splashes from the closely spread carpets.

Outside in the large courtyard are lovely green and gold mosaics of the time of Justinian, showing Damascus in its heyday.[10]

(Of all the religious buildings we saw later on our wanderings, nothing can compare with this.)

Ba, Mac and I went to see the Azim [Azem] palace [Figure 7.2], a house which is preserved in its original state. First a rose-filled courtyard, approached through a narrow arched door, then a series of rooms opening from it all decorated in the best Arab style. One green and pink room was reminiscent of modern decorators but where they just miss the others succeed. Three long windows on two sides of the room, with three alcoves on each of the other two sides; the panelling all a mellow green and the recessed part of the alcoves a salmon pink. The panels in the green woodwork all picked out in the faintest of little designs, like Victorian nosegays.

There were baths, which had had fine glaze[d] tiles, and at least half a dozen reception rooms none of which pleased me quite so much as the green and pink room. Back to the hotel through the Suks [markets], which as usual had more glamour than reality among their wares, and after a European meal, Ba and I went up in a carriage to look out

Figure 7.2 Courtyard of the Azem Palace, Damascus, Syria. See letter of 10 May 1933. Olga Tufnell archive, Palestine Exploration Fund. Courtesy of the Palestine Exploration Fund.

over the town by moonlight. It was one of those dilapidated vehicles, held together with string and urged forward only by the encouraging noises of the driver. The ringing clop-clop of the nag's hooves on the metalled road was the only other sound in the Damascus suburbs, and in the silver light our shadows loomed preposterously against the shuttered houses.

May 11. Travelled on through the valley of the Abana river, one of the two strange rivers of Damascus who lavish their all on the gardens of the city and so lose their strength to reach the sea. The French have planted the slender Lombardy poplar where water abounds and we found them shimmering and whispering in the breeze beside the stream and sat under their shade at lunch time in a coppice where the undergrowth consisting of wild rose and homely bramble wrought havoc with one's stockings.

By then we had come down into the plain of Baalbek, facing the Lebanon, still streaked with snow in the crevices, looking just like a gigantic poster hoarding in an unintelligible language.

At Baalbek soon after 3; while Terry and Pongo went to look at the Temple [Figure 7.3], Mac, Ba and I searched for a camping site. After exploring vainly near the town we took the car up the hill and ensconced ourselves above the springs Ras el Ain, where we hoped to be out of the reach of small boys. However we were soon surrounded and dinner was cooked under their supervision, in a strained atmosphere, as some members of the party did not feel they had been sufficiently consulted about the choice of a site. Bitter imprecations suggested that trouble was brewing.

Ba, Mac and I had reserved the evening to see the Temple by moonlight. We sat by the gate, waiting to be let in for some time and amused ourselves by terrifying passers by with a free use of Dujardin's Luminous Spectacles.[11]

The French have 60 men reconstructing there, putting stone in place and digging down through the rubbish; they have made things much clearer since I was there last.

My guide book days, when I used to write you long descriptions of each court and pedestal, are (thank goodness, you will say) over, so I will content myself by saying that we picked Zatar Miriamiya[12] in the first court and its sweet fragrance followed us round as we flood lit the architectural details with our torches. The climb up the hill about 10.30 was an effort, but our first night out was a perfect one and I was perfectly

Figure 7.3 Ruins of the Temple of Jupiter, Baalbek (Heliopolis), Lebanon. See letter of 11 May 1933. Olga Tufnell archive, Palestine Exploration Fund. Courtesy of the Palestine Exploration Fund.

happy lying on the floor of the car with my head duly bristling with curling pins poking out of the back end for all to see.

May 12. Of course we had to cope with sightseers at break of day, but only the youngest and hardiest would face the climb so our patience did not wear too thin. After breakfast, not to mention consequent washing up, we struck the first camp and went down to the spring to fill our water bottles.

The water bubbles up through a green haze of watercress but is as pure and refreshing as anything we have had. On the road to Homs we met Mr M.A. [Fergusson] and thereby hangs a tale.

We had stopped for a moment to put down the hood or something, when a car came dashing past and drew up across the road in front of us. Soldiers and officials poured out and surrounded the car and their leader, an effendi in tarbush, demanded angrily by what right we had been excavating at Baalbek. We said we had done nothing of the sort and tried to prove it by the virgin condition of our spade and pick. Their evidence was what they had seen, great holes dug at dead of night, and as additional proof they produced a sinister little plan marked with a cross which was actually a message left at the hotel for Fergie who was to meet us there to tell him where to come and not the position of buried treasure as our friends hopefully imagined.

However it took us a good two hours to convince them of our innocence: the fatal word 'Hafariyat' [excavations] takes a lot of getting over and we expended much food in making the peace. At Libwe we saw the chief source of the Orontes, emerging from bare stony ground, and straight[a]way turning a desert into a garden. The road onwards was bad and we felt it the more as a gale blew continuously and dust devils attended us on our way. We were glad to see Homs about 4, but only caught a glimpse of the mound and revetment which so impressed Prof.

In the villages we now saw a complete change. Instead of the flat-roofed gray mud houses, we were now passing white plastered beehives built of mud brick [Figure 7.4], huddling closely together each behind its own protective wall, just as one sees in the Sennacherib reliefs at Nineveh.

Rastan [Al-Rastan] was a typical village of this kind, but as we turned to skirt it, leaving the houses to our right, we almost fell into the valley of the Orontes. Here again desert and sown meet, the left bank of the road was dusty wilderness, the right bank sloping down to the now powerful stream was planted with vines, almonds, apricots and onions. The wind still blew; we drew up and watched the enormous water wheel 'hama' going round, humming persistently like a bee in search of flowers and we decided then and there that the valley was the camp for us.

A little road ran low close to the river and above it on the slopes of the valley we saw a little red-roofed house surrounded by poplars. With

Figure 7.4 Beehive houses, probably at Al-Rastan, Syria. See letter of 12 May 1933. Olga Tufnell archive, Palestine Exploration Fund. Courtesy of the Palestine Exploration Fund.

our eyes fixed firmly to the side valley below the house, we negotiated a bad road and drew up into the selected spot. Ba and I were sent to interview the landlord to whom house and land belonged. Even before we reached the gate men came running towards us with roses and our host came out to meet us and gave us hearty permission to camp, though of course his courtesy required that we should be offered his house and all that therein is. He was Bekyr Berazi, Faharya being the name of his estate; he was the owner of the huge waterwheel we had seen and many a fair acre at Rastan and Hama.

Cross-eyed and prosperous he looked, but he welcomed us pleasantly and led us into his cool living room with a marvellous view as all the furniture. His garden, watered from a large tank, was full of flowers, mostly pink and yellow roses, rather the sort that the Persian merchant had to bring home for his youngest daughter.

Later, after Ba had narrowly escaped smoking a nargyle [nargileh – water pipe], he [Bekyr] came down to see our camp, highly amused. He had tea with us and came back again for dinner which we cooked under his nose in the tent. At last to bed to the sound of crickets and grasshoppers in the light of an old moon.

May 13. This morning we awoke at 4.30 to find interested spectators around despite the fact that Bekyr had appointed a guard to keep them away. We dressed under some difficulty, then I took myself down to the river and washed clothes for everyone on a stone.

We left our host full of courteous wishes for our return, and after a solid day's motoring, broken by a few minutes at Hama, where we watched those great wheels revolving [Figure 7.5] and people coming and going through the shallow waters of the Orontes and an hour for lunch, we finally reached Aleppo.

Figure 7.5 Carpenters repairing waterwheel at Hama, Syria. See letter of 13 May 1933. Olga Tufnell archive, Palestine Exploration Fund. Courtesy of the Palestine Exploration Fund.

Vague fragments of the witches' curse in Macbeth, something to do with the rump-fed runyon [ronyon] 'Her husband's to Aleppo gone, master o' the Tiger; but in a sieve I'll thither sail,'[13] float round me here.

The town is a maze of narrow streets as we found to our cost, when we nearly got wedged between stone walls, lured on by an urchin who assured us that the road was perfect. The citadel is a magnificent affair built on the old Tell, with glimpses of earlier walls protruding all around. Hope to see it inside and out before we leave (Alas, I never did).[14] The Museum is good, or at least has good things in a bad building. Especially the ivories from Arslan Tash, and Max von Oppenheim's reliefs from Tell Khallaf [Tell Halaf]. Hope to go there again tomorrow (also unfulfilled)[15] and also to Carchemish, which also means the Euphrates.

May 14. Hotel Baron, Aleppo. Two nights spent here; we have had such a disappointing day. We wanted so much to see Carchemish, and as the car wanted a few alterations, we hired one to go there 65 miles. It was thoroughly windy and the ground was no more interesting than a flat pancake, perhaps I was prejudiced as I felt abominably sick. The driver said it took 2½ hours to get there but of course it was well over three. When we did arrive, at Jerablus the French officer and his assistant were both away, and it was their job to conduct us over the frontier. Though we had our passports duly visaed, prayers and entreaties with the Turkish officials were of no avail (I now wonder whether something more solid would have had a better effect)[16] and we had to content ourselves by looking at the mound across the railway embankment which is the frontier. Damned red tape. We saw the Euphrates which was perhaps a slight consolation, though the wide turbulent and muddy torrent between flat sandy banks was not worth three hours each way of horrible discomfort. Bought large and ornamental boxes of chocolate in Jerablus and oranges, felt better on the way home, and everyone was most virtuously cheerful.

May 16. Alexandretta. I am sitting on the beach here after breakfast. We camped just below Baylan on the pass last night, 684 m above the sea and awoke to see the salt lake, Ak Deniz, below us with the Kurd Dagh [mountains] behind. All night we had the sound of running water percolating through our dreams, as there was a little stream within two feet of the car which was perfect for washing up our dinner. We left there about eight and have just finished an excellent meal of eggs, rolls, and coffee in the local restaurant on the quayside.

Yesterday was one of the most successful days of the trip. We left Aleppo about eleven and soon found ourselves among the hills driving along an excellent road, straight as a die, which had all the marks of

Figure 7.6 On the Roman Road near Antioch. Written on back: 'Summit of Baylan Pass over Anti Taurus, about 680 m over sea level. Looking S. Preserved stretch of Roman road with new road on left. Good surface, well graded all the way to Alexandretta.' See letter of 16 May 1933. Olga Tufnell archive, Palestine Exploration Fund. Courtesy of the Palestine Exploration Fund.

being Roman [Figure 7.6]. The plains were full of crops and as we topped a pass we found a stretch of Roman road all paved with great square blocks. We then realised that under the smooth surface of the modern road, the old paving blocks remained which is after all the best way of preserving them. We had lunch at Bab el Howa [Hawa], where a Roman arch still spanned the road and there were remains of a police post or roadhouse.

As we approached Antioch the land became a perfect paradise of growing things and running streams, with the grey crags rising on our left. When we were close to the town, we saw the scanty remains of the walls and citadel which had defied the Crusaders; small sections climbed the almost perpendicular hill and gave one some idea of the impregnability of the place, until treachery opened the gates of the city to Bohumund [Bohemund]. Antioch became the centre of one of the four divisions of the Crusader power and many knights stayed there rather than go on to the bleak plains of Syria and Palestine. We saw our last sight of the Orontes; we had followed it from its sources at Libwe, camped at its edge near Rastan, seen it working the great water wheel at Hama and left it at Antioch, where it meanders in snake-like twists and turns on its way to the sea at Latakia.

From Antioch we made a detour to see the falls at Daphnae. They were really very like many we have seen in the Ardennes and at certain points the water rushed through stone mills which were grinding corn. It was surprising to find trippers there in plenty and the attendant crowd of small boys to help them over stones. The place was liberally besprinkled with silver paper, empty cartons and cigarette ends, we might have been at Branksome Chine [a beach in Dorset].

We left about 5 and skirted the hills until we climbed up by a thrilling series of hairpin bends. Then we found our ideal camping place, cooked our dinner and so to bed.

May 16 continued. While I was writing the above, a policeman tapped me on the shoulder and took me off in a friendly way to the police station, where I had to give Daddy's full name and yours and so on and so on. The others were all roped in by degrees and I am sure that all the rest of our time will be mostly spent in police stations. When we had finished at Alexandretta, we did the douane and then crossed No Man's Land until we came to the Turkish customs, where the star and crescent on a red flag was flapping in the breeze.

A soldier who spoke nothing but Turkish stopped us summarily and we were taken to the station some minutes away and waited a bit until the big man was fetched from the village. They get a car once a month at Payas [Yakacık], so when we unpacked our lunch and ate it among chickens, children and the washing on the line, we caused quite a sensation. However everyone was very nice and friendly, and it only took two hours to get through and they charged us nothing.

At Dourtyol [Dörtyol] they were tediously long, though pleasant and polite, and they regaled us with tea to while away the time. When we did go they gave us a guide, a nice boy like an El Greco peasant. Some way outside the town we came to a bridge – not that it deserved the name as it consisted of a few planks balanced on 6 rotten-looking logs. We all got out and felt busy testing the ford and jumping up and down hopefully on the logs. Then another car full of turks in caps came along and they encouraged us on with nods and becks and wreathed smiles, so we all held our breath while the truck went safely over.

That was only the first of many similar bridges to say nothing of marshes and other obstacles, but in due time we pitched in to the plain of Issus [Cilicia Pedias/Çukurova Plain] within sight of a most enchanting Rackham[17] castle called Toprak Kaleh [Toprakkale]. It was here that Fergie's car stuck in the river and that we hauled it out in record time, with one eye on the village all the time, for we feared the inevitable policeman, who would keep us there if he found us for hours while he mumbled over our passports.

May 17. Up at five this morning, about a record for us and so worth mentioning. Moved on at eight and came to the river of the Pyramus [Ceyhan] River. Crossed the bridge and came to the town of Missis [Misis]. On the side of the road a promising Tell lured me up on the scarp, where masses of Roman and late Arab sherds lay, the latter the remains of Ibrahim Pasha's occupation. There should be earlier stuff too, as witnessed by a fine obsidian flake. My prowl was cut short by the inevitable policeman and we moved on quickly to avoid an hour of passport [control.]

Storks abound here and we see flocks of them daily. One has decided to stay and build a nest on the top of the mosque. Through a dull plain, only enlivened by small tells at intervals, which of course I could not stop and see, so they were worse than useless. At one bridge we came across an eagle transporting her young, two very fluffy babies, which she left squawking on the bridge while she hovered anxiously near, until we had taken a movie and gone on.

Adana on the Sarus [Seyhan] River was a largish town boasting a theatre to say nothing of a police station where we spent the regulation time. The river flows under an erratic bridge composed of all sorts of arches, the foundations date from Justinian and the general effect is distinctly pleasing.

Everywhere the people are charming; they never crowd round and clamour for baksheysh[18] as the Arabs do. They look frightful villains in their cloth caps from Birmingham but the women provide a touch of colour with gay handkerchiefs and coatees[19] over their baggy trousers like the men.

From Adana, we followed a straight road towards Tarsus, but turned off just before to go north into the Taurus [mountains], a blue range with two jagged openings, one of which had to be the Cilician gates. It grew dark and we pitched camp soon after six near a tiny village on the edge of a dry water course, where a stone bridge provided a good bathroom.

May 18. Next morning saw us climbing up to the Cilician gates through a gorge full of flowering shrubs and emerald green plane trees with towering crags behind, wreathed in wisps of cloud. At Mazar Olik [Mezarlık], a tiny shop spotlessly clean was built by the side of a spring gushing from the hill.

The only other house in sight was a potter's home next door; he sat outside fashioning his pots from very red clay, slightly mixed with lime particles, on a wheel. His kiln outside was open at the top, his forms did not show any marked ancient survivals that I knew, all were flat bottomed.

All this road was paradise for scenery and after the lurid accounts of the surface that was not too bad either. Towering cliffs hemmed us into a valley full of shrubs and flowers, but as we approached the gates, it clouded over and even as we passed between the two grey masses of the gates themselves, the rain came down sheetlike and [we] struggled with hoods and mac[k]intoshes which kept us dry but restricted our view for the rest of the day.

Bozanti [Pozantı] seemed a typical Swiss village with emerald trees, a clean station and a straggling street of white houses. Mac bought a chipmunk whom he hopes to tame.

We followed the gorge through heavy showers to Ulu Kushla [Ulukışla], a station on the Taurus railroad, which we had kept alongside all the way. I found wild asparagus growing and most exciting flowers.

Ulu Kushla in the rain looked dreary enough, but a probably bug-ridden hotel seemed preferable to pitching camp in the storm, so after coping with Turkish officials at the station, we found the local lawyer who spoke English and he took us to the smartest khan of the place.

We found an empty room on the first floor with queer beds and queerer bedding, but we had everything cleared out, put up our own beds and camped there. It was here where the famous ultimatum was delivered by one of the party, whose feelings had been outraged and sore ever since the night at Baalbek.[20] Since no one showed panic at the momentous decision, things simmered down and continued more serenely afterwards. We slept well that night, well fortified by Keatings.[21]

May 19. Had my shoes cleaned by urchin on hotel balcony, very rickety, and then we took the road again in sunny weather and travelled across a pass 6000 feet (hope I've got it right) up on to the Anatolian plain, which is itself about 4000 feet up. Air like wine, lovely villages and streams surrounded by many hedges, planes and poplars. Bor [Bulgar Maden] was even more picturesque than usual and had extensive Hittite remains, which of course we did not see. Nigde [Niğde] further on had a Seljuk citadel perched on the Tell. Ba and I, holding our noses, investigated the rubbish but only saw mediaeval sherds. We bought boots just like those the gods wear in the sculptures, which were used for various purposes later on in the journey.

From Nigde, we followed a flat plain towards Kaisariyah [Kayseri] and about 5 came to a cleft in the rocks where two jagged cliffs faced each other – Kush Kaleh [Kuş Kale] and Chifte Kaleh [Çifte Kale]. We passed through and came upon a magnificent sight. The snow peak of Ardjias

Dagh [Argaeus/Mount Erciyes], 16.000 [sic] feet,[22] rising sheer from misty marshes of the plain below; the ledge where we stood before winding down to the plain again seemed an ideal place to camp and it had an additional attraction for me as I knew there was a site of sorts at Kush Kaleh just behind. Rock tombs, dwellings, cup marks and ruts worn in the soft volcanic rock made it a happy hunting ground, but the daily chores of camp life when there are six cramp much wandering.

We did spend the morning there and Ba and I found Early Bronze age sherds and obsidian flakes and some later Iron Age pottery. The police came as usual out of the blue and we felt we had better move on, so slid down into the plain only to stop again for police formalities at Develi Kara Hissar [Karahisar-I Develü], where a hill behind looking like a humped camel inspires the name.[23]

Injesi [İncesu] seemed attractive, built in a hollow with a fine Seljuk khan, but we had to push on to encircle the mountain and reach Kaisariyah [Kayseri, Figure 7.7] before dark. Had our first puncture just outside, but soon changed the tyre and drove up in state just in front of a military band. The first Oteli [hotel] was rather queer, but now we are settled at the Istamboul Oteli, which is remarkable for cleanliness, though the drains stink. Ba was recovering from a touch of fever, and Fergie was just

Figure 7.7 Entry to Kayseri (Kaiseriah), Turkey, looking southwest. Mountains of Arjius Dağ (Argaeus) beyond. Referred to in letter of 19 May 1933. Olga Tufnell archive, Palestine Exploration Fund. Courtesy of the Palestine Exploration Fund.

going down with a bout of an obscure form of dysentery which he is liable to, so this seemed a haven of rest.

Dinner at a restaurant where they played their one European tune ad lib for our benefit. By that time Terry's bright eyes and red dress had produced an interpreter in the form of a steam roller mechanic, who spoke English, as he came from Cyprus. We all had dinner ordered by him, consisting of white soup, grilled chops, and coffee all of which reminded me of some meals we had in C-S. [Czechoslovakia] together.

Thankfully and cheerfully to bed though not before eleven.

<u>May 21st.</u> Hoped to start again today, but Fergie was bad in the night, so we are staying an extra day while he is in hospital; if he is not better [we will] push on tomorrow.

In the end it was arranged to leave Fergie at Kaisariyah for three days and that he would come on by train and put his car on too, so we moved off about three after all and rejoined the road to Ankara.

We motored through a gorge which led eventually to a bridge over the Kisil Irmak (Halys River) [River Kızılırmak] which rises in the Ak Dagh [Akdağ] and curves south, embracing in its territory the most fertile part of the Anatolian plain. Great banks of clouds were moving across the sky like so many brigades forming for battle, the Erdjias Dagh [Arjius Dağ] was blotted out and grey smears on the clouds showed that rain was falling near the town. We got caught but not badly near a village, where we stopped for water and then pushed on to find a dryish camping ground which we got in the plain. Flat and uninteresting for view (we are rather spoilt in that respect), but dry and comfortable enough.

May 22. On again across the plain, greyer today and losing most of its charm from the lack of towering clouds, the sky was the fleecy uniform grey of England, and it was not until we slid down from the plain to cross the valley of the grown Halys River again that we saw a menacing block of clouds in front of us. A lovely bridge spans the river at Chesme Koupri [Coupri], one of those arched wonders which seem to have but one course of stone at the highest point. The water forces its way between two natural grey buttresses near the bridge with a purposeful murmur. I found yellow jasmine and yellow roses growing in the crannies of the rock and wild larkspur in the fields.

From Chesme our troubles began, for the storm which we had seen in front had wrought havoc with the road. We slid sideways through bogs, we careered giddily up slimy slopes with a sheer drop on one side, we rushed marshy holes to the destruction of the bottles inside.

For the first time we were seeing Turkish roads as they really are. However Mac drove very confidently through everything; in the dark we strained our eyes looking hopefully for the lights of Ankara, the more pessimistic ones thought we were on the wrong road as the way seemed interminable, but the lights of Ankara, when they did appear, cheered us all up. As an arrow from the bow we made for the best hotel (Ankara Palace), terribly modern and quite ruinous, but undeniably pleasant to a bumped and shaken crowd.

May 23. Finished this in bed waiting for a BATH, it has rained here solidly for a week, so how we shall get away again I can't imagine.

I had expected a travesty of European life here, just a cheap imitation to laugh at but somehow it is nothing of the sort, and at every turn one is impressed with the feeling that a practical sensible scheme is being carried out by efficient hardworking people who have their heart in the business, from the man whom we saw emptying the Gazi's[24] Sea of Marmora on his model farm [see below, p. 256] to the general manager of this hotel.

Like the new quarters in Prague, there are still large areas to be cleared of rubbish, stones and shanties, but parks and gardens are being laid out on a vast scale and one has every confidence that in a few years' time every dirty corner will have been swept and garnished by the indefatigable Gazi. Whether this will be a moral as well as a material change remains to be seen.

The old town is largely confined to the great pinnacle of granite which is crowned by the citadel. Seljuk walls surround it, the most indescribable hotch potch of building I have ever seen, the walls have been run up of any available material, Greek inscriptions, Roman and Byzantine sarcophagi, bits of columns sticking out at queer angles; the wonder is that the whole thing stands at all. In and out among these ruins are little Turkish houses, discreet and modest, white or pink walls, lattices, overhung stories, heavy iron knockers and from any point on the citadel, one can look out over the new town and see the latest ideas in architecture springing from green fields and avenues.

The people look villainous, but I can't blame them if they are forced to go about in stinking caps from Birmingham when they might be picturesquely and more practically attired. It is difficult for the Gazi or anyone else to sift the corn from the chaff of western civilisation and it is pathetic to see their attempts to educate the flapper[25] in film worship by producing a film magazine like the *Filmgoer*.

As for the Gazi himself, his statue on horseback or on foot adorns every square of importance and dominates every viewpoint. Each shop has an enormous enlargement, tinted or plain, and his name is on everyone's lips. I had my hair done by a rather full-blown fairy who knows the great man himself; we have seen his house Chayanke, a white truncated villa in modern styles on the slopes of the hill overlooking the town and have actually caught a glimpse of the Gazi himself, riding aloof in a closed car between clusters of sentries back to his house.

Somehow the new counts more than the old here, and instead of telling you more about walls and pottery, I must tell you about the model farm which Mustafa [Atatürk] has built on a hill outside the town.

Laid out in straight lines with straight tar-mac roads approaching it, the place had something of a Roman air; it is the recreation of a mastermind and nothing has stood in the way of the fulfilment of a fancy. The public are allowed right up to the house, and can if so minded peer in, as we shamelessly did, to this small white house where he spends the summer (furniture inside appalling and hardly in keeping with the austere modern lines of the exterior).

They can have tea in the flag-decked garden beside the concrete Sea of Marmora, which somebody, joking, suggested he should build and which he took seriously and had it made straightway. Rows and rows of acacia trees have been planted and down below are chicken farms and cattle sheds in best modern style.

May 24. We fully expected to leave Angora [Ankara] and were packed with luggage in the hall, when we heard from all sides that it was impossible to attempt the road to Eski-Shehir [Eskişehir] with the roads in their present state; it was madness they said, so like good children we took their advice and stayed on. The great craze in Ankara seems to be the cult of lambs as pets, wearing coloured ribbons and following their masters and mistresses like dogs.

May 25. We found a Capt. Storey-Cooper in the hotel, who had motored in his Dodge car from Bangalore in India, 7000 miles, so we joined up with him to share a guide as far as Eski-Shehir. Rattled merrily along for many miles over flat cultivated plain and pasture. Passed Sivri-Hissar [Sivrihisar], with delightful mosques and odd gables and half-timbered houses. Ran into black clouds and caught the end of a terrific storm which proved our undoing not much further on near a lonely farm on a marsh.

After overcoming many obstacles, we stuck in a ditch, we rocked her, we pushed but we sunk further and further in. Farm hands brought oxen and they pulled with no success, so we resigned ourselves to a night in the mud. The men dug her out with spades all night, while I provided coffee for the poor dears. About two am Terry and I curled up in S[t]orey-Cooper's car and woke up two hours later to take a ciné [film] of the car coming out, togged [tugged] by sleepy oxen [possibly Figure 7.8].

Figure 7.8 The Diabolical pulled from the mud by oxen. See letter of either 25 May 1933 or 2 June 1933. Olga Tufnell archive, Palestine Exploration Fund. Courtesy of the Palestine Exploration Fund.

Covered in mud [Figure 7.9], we packed the luggage in again, and took the road more warily. Still slimy and muddy, we had breakfast at Eski-Shehir, and an excellent meal it seemed with unlimited omelette and coffee served by an attentive hotel proprietor. We made Boyzuk [Bilecik] soon after lunch and camped below it in the valley by the side of a large stream. Scraped some mud off and slept thankfully and late until next morning.

May 26. Good thunderstorm put us on the road again rather hurriedly. Very lovely country all the way, perfect villages and amazing views with Mount Olympus (the third of them) hidden in clouds. Inegol [İnegöl] we found pleasant, like an English cathedral town on a Sunday; great plane trees growing round the mosque and birds singing. Everyone polite and not a bit officious or tiresome, due to no tourists.

Brussa [Bursa], not far from the sea, is a large prosperous place with many mosques. Boys were selling cherries on twigs, wound on with raffia. Vegetation absolutely lush. Poppies in fields under olive trees.

Reached Mudanya in time to see the sun go down into the glassy sea. Tried to find a good camping place on the slopes outside the town, but could not find enough flat ground and had to pitch on a waste patch near houses on the edge of the sea.

May 27. We are on the boat for Constantinople [Istanbul], after a comic morning trying to bathe and dress in the middle of what proved to be the Turkish Army's parade ground. Soldiers all round us presented

Figure 7.9 Stuck in the mud between Sivrihisar and Eskişehir, Turkey. Left to right: Teresa Colt, Ralph Richmond Brown, Olga Tufnell. See letter of 25 May 1933. Olga Tufnell archive, Palestine Exploration Fund. Courtesy of the Palestine Exploration Fund.

arms, attacked, crawled on their bellies and marched and ran, while we struggled into knickers and clothes with our skin stickily salt.

Two company commanders eventually came while we were having breakfast and most politely asked us to move on which was no wonder, as we were rather a distraction for the troops in our bathing gear.

Certain amount of bother getting the car on board the ferry [Figure 7.10], but now we are settled supine in chairs awaiting our first sight of the Golden Horn.

Figure 7.10 Loading the Diabolical onto a ferry, probably Istanbul. Letter of 27 May 1933. Olga Tufnell archive, Palestine Exploration Fund. Courtesy of the Palestine Exploration Fund.

White houses took shape on the horizon, first a mere mass of buildings, then domes and minarets, then a light-house sentinel for the Golden Horn. A string of swallows flew low across the sea from Europe to Asia with a counter stream flying in the opposite direction. (I have since heard that they are the lost souls of the Sultans' wives, but why they should be considered responsible for the fantasies of their masters I can't imagine – anyhow I thought they hadn't got souls.)[26]

The Golden Horn was sparkling and gay, and as we drew alongside, the same motley collection of shipping as in the India docks; there was nothing but the silhouette of Saint Sophia and Suleyman the Magnificent to assure us that we were not in the Pool [of London].

Frightful fuss getting the car unloaded in which Ba and I did not join, as we were sent ahead to book the rooms and collect letters from Cooks. Incidentally we had a cream cake tea as well. Nothing more to record that day. Rooms at 4 Turkish pounds each, with pension [board], better than the eight charged at Ankara.

May 28. Feeling fresh and strong, we tacklled [sic] the Hittite Museum first and saw much instructive stuff.

Afternoon devoted to [Hagia] Sofia, terribly disappointing at first sight, but I'm sure it would grow on one; before I came away it was making its spell felt. Sombre at first sight with appalling carpet from Maples by the yard, on the marble floor, it compares badly with the sunny coolness of the Damascus mosque. Then one reminds oneself that Sofia is only masquerading as a mosque; in imagination one tears down the awful green painted texts on the walls, rolls up the imitation prayer rugs and cleans the paint off the walls and dome. Even under the paint one can clearly see the shadows of mosaic crosses throughout and outside above the west door no effort has been made to remove a row of crosses, though each one inside the building has been disarmed or covered in a tell-tale layer of paint.

Without her Moslem disguise, Hagia Sofia becomes the finest building of Christendom; pillars from [the temple of] Diana of the Ephesians topped by lovely capitals, above mosaic with many crosses and unguessed at other designs now hidden from sight.

Somehow it was unexpected to find a double row of chestnuts in flower outside; everywhere one feels the West prevails, and when the East was dominant here it was a bit of a cuckoo in the nest.

The Blue Mosque built about 1500 AD is only a few yards from Hagia Sofia. It has the advantage of a higher position and a wonderful view from its barred windows of the Sea of Marmora.

It has the advantage of colour, blue and white tiles set off by great splashes of red carpets with discreet patches of green at the holy points. Sultan Ahmed Gomaa is built as a mosque by Moslems and carries its six garlanded minarets proudly enough, which can hardly be said of her more venerable neighbour who suffers her four minarets rather shamefacedly.

The Mosque of _____ [left blank – must refer to Little Hagia Sophia] built by Constantine or his successor about 100 years before Sofia and the earliest religious building still in use here, was thinly disguised and made no bones about its Greek inscription above the pillars.

May 29. Attacked the big Museum ground floor, a wilderness of Greek statuary, relieved by the perfect sarcophagus of the Satrap from Sidon and the very lovely one called 'of Alexander', the latter with pastel traces of the original colouring.

Upstairs pottery from Palestine exciting enough if only it were better arranged with good labels.

Yeri Batun Serail is the name of the underground cistern [Basilica Cistern], the larges[t] of many near Hagia Sofia. We walked down a few slimy steps and found ourselves looking at a forest of columns, their bases reflected in the clear water. The columns were a hotch potch collection with different capitals to each which made them more amusing.

The Palace took us the afternoon, walking through little gardens shaded by cypresses and planes into cool tile-covered rooms with queer angles and passages. Would that it had all been like that, for in many of the chief rooms Maples had had their fling and the Tottenham Court Road was more noticeable than the glamour of the East.

Wonderful collection of arms and china, the costumes of the Sultans carried one straight to the Arabian nights, but the so-called Tresor was tawdry enough with the exception of the XVIth century emerald and gold throne with a perfectly embroidered cushion on it.

Somehow it is difficult to realise that fifteen years ago Abdul Hamid sat smoking in these chambers and that in the carefully secluded hareem [harem] his wives intrigued and chattered surrounded by eunuchs who are now the only living reminder of these days.

May 30. Shopping in the morning, everyone so helpful and friendly. Prof. had advised us to see the column in the palace garden to 'the Victory over the Goths' put up by Claudius, plain and un-pretentious, it commemorates the saving of the Mediterranean world from destruction.

Went to the church with mosaics at Chora, should say mosque, but the words still stick when it is so obviously a church built on the same plan as St Mark's, with very lovely mosaics in blue and gold. One specially good over the door of the Death of the Virgin.

The Golden Gate may not be literally so, but it is quite sufficiently lovely to deserve the title. It is the only place where one can see Greek domestic architecture standing. Two square towers, which originally had red tiled roofs, flank the doorway which led once into the city. The whole thing is built of blocks of marble with a plain beading round the top. Dark cypresses set off the yellow glow of the stone.

Publicity has engulfed us here and we have crowds round the car; all of which is rather unnecessary when this is the clearing house for round the world motorists. Several parties here now, including two women motoring alone from Antwerp to Singapore which really is a bit of a feat.

May 31. Left Stamboul about eleven and rather lost our way so doing, ultimately landed up at the Police Post which marks the entrance to the military zone, where the usual formalities took place. Going through we saw a few cows and a flock of sheep on a treeless plain, but the small flowers were lovely all the way. All signs of military ones were lacking.

Camped near a stream beyond Chorlu and are now on our way to Adrianople.

June I. Our worst day. Kept sticking in chocolate-coloured mud, and when we really thought we were through, a hailstorm came and wrecked our chances for the rest of the day, beating in our faces and reducing the roads to complete morass. Just stopped where we were and camped on the road.

Two policemen sent out to guard us, Mustafa and Stefan, who stayed with us until we were in bed, thoroughly interested in the proceedings and then went off to the village to sleep. The sergeant came in the middle of the night and woke us up shouting for them, to see if they were on the alert. Mustafa and Stefan looked rather crestfallen next day.

June 2. Moved on with a cortege of six bulls who pulled the car some way until it got hopelessly bogged in a river bed. Ba and I had walked on to the village, so did not assist in the digging proceedings. Were cheered to get into Lulu Borgas [Lüleburgaz] (oh! auspicious name) where the roads changed abruptly for the good and we sped along and were very surprised to reach Adrianople (Ederne) soon after four, as we little expected to do so.

Saw 3 mosques hurriedly, one very good and all most attractive from the outside. The town is well placed, with many minarets and domes rising from the trees which were as welcome a sight after the treeless plain we had followed from Stamboul as those were at Damascus. The Maritza flows on the left of the town and is the boundary for Greece and Turkey and Bulgaria. Am now sitting in the car during the last round of the frontier game getting into Bulgaria.

The Passport Officer here is quite a fair artist and we spent more time examining his pictures than he spent over our blameless passports. He spoke German and was as pleasant as all the officials are. Camped near the road surrounded by cornfields which provided inadequate cover for morning strolls, as the road was more frequented than usual. Saw men wearing kalpaks[27] and the tight black breeches and high boots which you know so well. Women wearing bright red aprons and gay scarves, all most refreshing after the drab trappings discarded by Whitechapel Road, which we had seen in Turkey.

June 3. A good day's run following the Maritza, towards the evening we were following the road when we saw a gay collection of boys and girls all wearing Sunday clothes. Thinking it was a wedding party we stopped to take photos and then discovered that they were coming away from a fair, we heard the sound of fiddles and drums and felt we must go [Figures 7.11 and 7.12]. The covered wagons with gay striped hoods had been formed up in a square, the fourth side occupied by a small white

Figure 7.11 Women and children in wagon, Bulgaria. Written on back: 'Cart of holiday makers at yearly feast of Tataro, June 3 in Bulgaria near Stare Zagore'. See letter of 3 June 1933. Olga Tufnell archive, Palestine Exploration Fund. Courtesy of the Palestine Exploration Fund.

Figure 7.12 Dancing men at festival, Bulgaria. Written on back: 'Dancing the dubka near Stare Zagore, Bulgaria'. See letter of 3 June 1933. Olga Tufnell archive, Palestine Exploration Fund. Courtesy of the Palestine Exploration Fund.

and blue shrine covering a holy well; there were booths selling paper windmills and hecticly [sic] coloured sweets and each wagon in the square was a separate arbour for the older folks, who sat surrounding a huge spread of meat and vegetables and rice, looking rather as if they were at Lords', while the boys and girls were dancing something resembling the 'dubka',[28] instead of playing cricket, round a band consisting of several fiddles, pipes and drums.

Girls wore long skirts, with fetching scraps of pale mauve crochet with sequins sewn on hanging below. Embroidered aprons and blouses and ribbons of course and everyone wore flowers in their hair, roses or syringa. There were hardly any ugly ducklings in European clothes among the men and none at all among the girls.

We were told it was the Feast of Tataro, a yearly affair, evidently centred round the Holy Spring. We were lucky to see it so unexpectedly. On to Stare Zagore and beyond where we camped in a quarry.

June 4. The village simpleton caused us some amusement in the morning by stealing our eggs which he deposited in a bush like a broody hen; we retrieved them from their hiding place a few yards away and placated the poor lad with bread, honey and cigarettes.

We motored north through cornfields and fruit orchards until we came to grassy park land like any corner of the park at Easton.[29] Beyond we could see blue hills which were the Balkan mountains which we had to cross. At the foot of the pass was a gold dome church, one of the first signs that we had left the Moslem world. Climbed steeply a perfect road full of excursionists on Sunday outings, sides precipitous and view glorious. At the top a black pall of cloud met us and marred our first sight of the country north, it rained and the roads were unbelievably slimy as we started down the other side, but I discovered wild strawberry plants which brought memories of the Ardennes. After some hours we reached Turnovo, the old capital of Bulgaria, swarming with soldiers. We saw a regiment come by, marching badly, smelling filthy, all young and raw, but singing some national marching song divinely in parts. Dined sumptuously at the best restaurant on a terrace overlooking the river's hairpin bend, and the tiled tiered roofs spread out below, for the sum of 1/– a head, inclusive of wine. We pushed on for the frontier soon after eight.

Rain and slime all the way to Rustuck (Rusa) [Rustchuk (Ruse)] on the Danube – our first sight of the river was uninspiring, the farther bank invisible in the gloom, just a stretch of dull water bordered by cabbages.

Omelettes and bread in an all-night restaurant, ordered in a pantomime language, and thankfully to bed.

June 5. Up early to make arrangements and to ship the car. All formalities promptly and simply carried out, for 2:10:0 [£2 10s 0d] we had a barge and tug of our very own to take us over to the Rumanian side, where we were by midday. The river is no bluer by daylight, but it is impressive as a water way, when one sees tugs and barges of all nations on the water, including the *Mary Jane* from London.

Giurgiu was en fete; we had lunch to the strains of the 'Blue Danube', played on one of these devestating [sic] mechanical organs. On our way we saw groups of boys dressed in national costume with ribbons round their hats, garlic tucked in their belts, bells fastened round their knees and spurs on their heels, doing the good old ritual dance, with a fearsome devil wearing a hairy mask, dancing round to the strains of a cembalo[30] and fiddles.

A straight acacia-lined road to Bucharest, which we reached about 4. Found it a large town with fine buildings, broad streets, thronged with expensive limousines and a general air of luxurious prosperity. No slums visible either coming or going, only neat whitewashed houses on the outskirts, decorated with painted blue birds and trees, the peasants nearly all wear lovely embroidered costumes.

Splendide Hotel (138 lei for bed) took us in. Overcome by proximity of civilisation had my hair washed in an amusing place for men and women full of lovely young girls.

Not knowing where to dine, we consulted our taxi driver, who took us to Roata Lumii, a small restaurant, evidently in vogue, where we had an excellent meal for 10/– a head including wine. Tzigane orchestra. Home full and merry, about one.

June 6. Drove round the town in a carriage and pair and into the Chaussee, local Bois de Boulogne, everything so chic and well kept, Bucharest must be the gayest city in Europe and probably the most extravagant one too. Saw King Carol leave his palace in lovely white uniform; all the soldiers look as if they were tin ones straight out of their cardboard boxes, and the officers have pink and white painted faces to match – though the poor things are not allowed to powder their noses on parade.

Got going during the afternoon on beautiful tar-mac roads, which rejoiced Mac's heart and got us to Brasov (Kronstadt) about eight.

We had got to the heart of the oil fields, we could see it oozing from the ground and everywhere there were refineries and oil derricks. Raining hard, so we succumbed to the blandishments of the Corona Hotel and had a sophisticated meal, better-run hotel than at Bucharest.

June 7. The direct road to Sibiu was up, so we had to make a detour of many miles, which was well worth it as it took us over a lovely pass, babbling brooks, burgeoning trees, pines, in fact the whole bag of tricks. After rejoining the main road, flat straight but bumpy roads led us to Hermannstadt, a garrison town with pleasant chestnut avenues and old houses, completely German in atmosphere, which will live in our memory because of cream cakes and coffee which we ate outside a café in front of the entire population. Since going through, the German atmosphere has been explained to me, for it was at Hermannstadt that the Pied Piper of Hamelin came out of the rock followed by the children, who founded a new town on that spot.

We are getting quite used to crowds, sometimes they think we are a circus, sometimes that we are travelling in some patent medicine [sense unclear].

That night we camped at the edge of a wood [possibly Figure 7.13], full of wild strawberry plants, and we made a fire by the light of which we told ghost stories and then to bed with the tree trunks half masking the ghouls and ogres we had conjured up.

June 8. Rows of trees all along the Rumanian roads, acacia, cherry, apple and quince, we had left the realm of folk costumes – tight white trousers for the men with white tunics embroidered in black, wearing fetching pork pie hats – and were finding soberer garb everywhere.

Figure 7.13 Picnic scene, probably in Eastern or Central Europe. In foreground, Ba and Olga. In background, Terry and Mac. Olga Tufnell archive, Palestine Exploration Fund. Courtesy of the Palestine Exploration Fund.

My last camp was late, in a flat marshy plain beyond Arad and near the frontier at Otaka.

June 9. Tedious formalities at Otaka repeated at Gyula for the benefit of Hungary. Good roads most of the way on, culminating in a beautiful concrete Ist class road following the Tizza [Tisza] to Budapest. Got in there as the sun went down behind the hills. The first really western town marked by its slums and rather drab effect. A lovely site, badly handicapped by ultra Victorian buildings which offend the eye after so many clean white-painted homes.

St Gellert Hotel took us in for 7/– a day, old world courtesy, good food and downy bed made one see the town in a better light next day.

June 10. Cooks again and no money. Sudden urge to get home culminated in my borrowing £15 from Terry and we booked sleepers from Buda home via Vienna, Koln – Hook of Holland.

Last continental meal at Vienna at Hartmann's in the Ringstrasse during the two hours' wait for the connection. Met a Dr Werkner Odon (Ugyved) whatever that is (lawyer I believe) on the train, full of information and will show us everything next time. And so ends the diary for on Monday morning at 8.30 I shall be sitting on your bed telling you all about it.

Notes

1   McWilliams 1934.
2   McWilliams 1934, 17. Also see the dedication to McWilliams's book: 'To Mrs Noah, without whom the Ark could never have set forth.'
3   McWilliams 1934, 28.
4   McWilliams 1934, 48–9.
5   This original diary was not incorporated into the Palestine Exploration Fund archive.
6   Davis 2008, 68–70.
7   No further mention is made of a trip to the Amazon, so presumably it did not happen.
8   Three concise volumes were published by the Oriental Institute of the University of Chicago as part of their Oriental Institute Communications series: von der Osten 1927, 1929, 1930.
9   Revelation: an early form of expanding suitcase.
10 In fact the mosaics date to the Umayyad period (early Islamic).
11 Dr Dujardin's Luminous Spectacles: a 1930s invention consisting of a pair of spectacles with four battery-powered lamps and reflectors attached to the frame.
12 A sage plant found in Syria and Palestine: *Salvia triloba L.* 'Miriamiya'. The plant is linked to Arab folklore relating to Lady Miriam (Mary) fleeing from King Herod into Egypt with Jesus while he was still a child. During the journey she rests under a sage shrub which helps revive her spirits, giving it the name 'sage of virtue' (Crowfoot and Baldensperger 1932, 79–81). *Zatar* or *Za'atar* is a generic name for a family of Middle Eastern herbs including oregano, thyme and sage, and is also the name of the condiment made from these dried herbs mixed with salt and sesame seeds as a spice mixture.
13 *Macbeth,* Act I, scene iii.
14 Later comment added by Olga Tufnell.
15 Later comment added by Olga Tufnell.
16 Later comment added by Olga Tufnell.
17 Arthur Rackham (1867–1939), a well-known illustrator of children's books.
18 Arabic, *bakshish* or *baksheesh*, meaning gratuity or tip.
19 Short coats or jackets.
20 See 11 May 1933; either Terry or Pongo.
21 A well-known brand of insecticide powder.
22 The height of this volcano is in fact 12,851 feet.
23 *Develi* means camel in Turkish, though the town of Develi is thought to be named after Devle Bey, a Seljuk commander.
24 'The Gazi' is a term used to refer to Mustapha Kemal Atatürk (1881–1938), revolutionary founder and first President of the Republic of Turkey. *Gazi* means 'veteran' or 'warrior' in modern Turkish.
25 A term used to describe one of the 'Bright Young Things' of the 1920s and 1930s.
26 Later comment added by Olga Tufnell.
27 High-crowned felt or sheepskin cap.
28 *Dabke/dabka*, Arabic. A folk circle or line dance popular throughout the Levant.
29 The house belonging to Daisy, Countess of Warwick. It was demolished in 1937 but the gardens are still open to the public.
30 A harpsichord or hammered dulcimer.

References

Crowfoot, Grace M. and Louise Baldensperger. 1932. *From Cedar to Hyssop: A Study in the Folklore of Plants in Palestine*. London: Sheldon Press.
Davis, Miriam C. 2008. *Dame Kathleen Kenyon: Digging up the Holy Land*. Walnut Creek, CA: Left Coast Press.
McWilliams, Herbert Hastings. 1934. *The Diabolical: An Account of the Adventures of Five People who Set Out in a Converted Ford Lorry to Make a Journey from Palestine to England across Asia Minor and the Balkans.* London: Duckworth.

von der Osten, Hans H. 1927. *Explorations in Hittite Asia Minor: A Preliminary Report*. Chicago: University of Chicago Press.

von der Osten, Hans H. 1929. *Explorations in Hittite Asia Minor 1927–28*. Chicago: University of Chicago Press.

von der Osten, Hans H. 1930. *Explorations in Hittite Asia Minor 1929*. Chicago: University of Chicago Press.

8
Tell ed-Duweir (Lachish): Second, third and fourth seasons, 1933–6

After the experiences of the journey home overland through Asia Minor and Europe, and some time at home, Olga was eager to get back to her friends and life in Palestine. The main company was as before: Starkey as expedition leader, assisted by Harding, Richmond Brown and Inge. Colt had left the expedition in 1933 to work at Sobata and his name was removed from the expedition title. It is apparent that the relationship between Starkey and Colt as co-directors was not sustainable.[1] Sir Henry Wellcome, Sir Charles Marston and Sir Robert Mond were now the main sponsors of the expedition, which became known as the Wellcome Archaeological Research Expedition in the Near East (WARENE).

Although the final excavation reports, prepared largely by Olga, preserve the details and synthesis of the excavation findings, the annual preliminary reports and public lectures published in the *Palestine Exploration Quarterly* provide details of the progress of excavation and key findings season by season.[2] An excellent and accessible overview of the excavations, including an assessment of the main findings by Starkey and the British expedition and many photographs (some also published in this volume), can be found in David Ussishkin's book *Biblical Lachish*.[3] Ze'ev Begin's book in Hebrew *As We Do Not See Azeqa* also presents a history of the expedition, including many photographs. A more critical approach that interweaves the role of Starkey and the expedition team, discoveries relevant to biblical archaeology at Lachish and the colonial context of the Tell ed-Duweir expedition can be found in Billie Melman's book *Empires of Antiquities*.[4]

Olga's work in the second season (1933–4) is only sparsely represented in her correspondence owing to an extended visit by her mother, leaving a sizeable gap in the sequence of letters. During this season, Olga helped clarify the site's outer defensive wall to a greater extent to the south and east sides. Excavation continued on the acropolis with more complete excavation of the 'Persian Residency' and 'Solar Shrine'. Near the northwest corner of the base of the mound, outside and built over the outer edge of the abandoned Middle Bronze Age defences (fosse), were the remains of the Late Bronze Age 'Fosse Temple', excavation of which occupied much of the subsequent seasons (Olga refers to this as 'the shrine' in her letters). The temple was rich in finds including pottery, jewellery, figurine fragments and other exotic goods. Offering pits yielded further rich material, and the famous 'Lachish ewer' featuring a rare proto-Canaanite inscription and a painted motif of two horned animals flanking a 'tree of life' was found close by (Figure 8.1).[5]

Work in the third season (1934–5) continued earlier operations both on and off the mound. Further progress on the Solar Shrine indicated

Figure 8.1   Tufnell with Starkey and the 'Lachish ewer'. Starkey family collection. Courtesy of Wendy Slaninka.

Figure 8.2 Inge with workmen in Cemetery 500, in area of camp buildings. See letter to mother of 29 November, probably 1934. Wellcome-Marston Expedition Archive, Department of the Middle East, British Museum. © UCL Institute of Archaeology, courtesy of the Wellcome Trust and the British Museum.

that it shared architectural elements of the nearby Persian Residency. A major clearance of the saddle area between the mound and the camp-house was intended to provide a new dumping area for excavated soil from the top of the mound. This resulted in the discovery of several Bronze and Iron Age tombs and evidence for ancient quarrying close to the camp itself and roads leading to it. It was becoming clear that the camp-house was constructed directly over an ancient cemetery (Figure 8.2). Other findings off the mound included Bronze and Iron Age tombs on terraces and slopes, as well as evidence for an extensive Chalcolithic to Early Bronze Age settlement.

In January 1935, the most important discovery of the expedition took place – that of the 'Lachish Letters'.[6] In the eastern area of the mound, sixteen fragments of inscribed pottery sherds (ostraca) were found in a burnt layer above a floor of a gatehouse of the late Judaean kingdom that had been destroyed by the Babylonians in 587/6 BC (Level II; Figure 8.3). Following this discovery by Hasan 'Awad al-Qatshan,[7] Olga and Harding carefully searched through all the sherds unearthed in the area, finding two more ostraca.[8] Richmond Brown and a photographer of the Department of Antiquities photographed them,[9] and Harding prepared hand-made copies to aid their decipherment. The inscriptions proved to be parts of letters written in a 'pre-exilic' or 'paleo-' Hebrew alphabetic script using a reed pen and iron-based ink. Significantly, as they were written in ink, the script could have been in common use. To illustrate the potential for widespread literacy in antiquity, Harding, as a joke, taught the alphabet to his illiterate Bedouin workmen, who soon began writing simple notes in Arabic dialect but using the ancient script.[10]

Figure 8.3   Findspot of the Lachish Letters. Court or guardroom (F.18C) in eastern tower adjoining outer gate. Late Judaean period. Discovered after removal of later Persian ruin. Hasan 'Awad clearing burnt deposit in which the Lachish Letters were found. City wall against skyline. Wellcome-Marston Expedition Archive, Department of the Middle East, British Museum. © UCL Institute of Archaeology, courtesy of the Wellcome Trust and the British Museum.

The significance of the 'Lachish Letters' at the time was immense, as these were the earliest examples of personal writing yet found in Palestine.[11] Furthermore, they provided striking parallels in both language and content with passages of the Hebrew Old Testament, in particular the book of Jeremiah.[12] Most of the ostraca were written reports sent from nearby outposts to a commander named Ya'osh stationed at Lachish. Starkey recounted in relation to Letter III (Figure 8.4): 'Towards the end of the letter we are told by the writer that he has heard that the commander of the army, Achbor the son of Elnatan, has passed down to Egypt, taking with him certain men ... a striking parallel with Jeremiah xxvi. 20–23.'[13] Letter IV named Lachish and Azekah, providing an additional piece of evidence helping the

Figure 8.4 Lachish Letter III (reverse side), featuring pre-exilic Hebrew script connected with Jeremiah 26. See letter to father of 29 March 1935. Wellcome-Marston Expedition Archive, Department of the Middle East, British Museum. © UCL Institute of Archaeology, courtesy of the Wellcome Trust and the British Museum.

expedition to identify Tell ed-Duweir as Lachish (see letter of 4 April 1935 below).[14] The Lachish Letters seemed to support Jeremiah 34:7, which states that while Jerusalem was under attack at the hands of Nebuchadnezzar, Azekah and Lachish were the only fortified cities in Judah.

In the fourth season (1935–6) a great amount of spoil could now be removed at a faster rate using a newly instituted rail and chute system paid for through the support of Sir Robert Mond.[15] Starkey focused efforts on the 'Great Shaft', which he believed to be a passage or tunnel into the city akin to the Siloam tunnel in Jerusalem or the great water system at Megiddo.[16] Excavation of the 'Palace-Fort' of the Judaean kingdom period (Level III) included the continued excavation of a mass of 'Lamelakh' storage jars, which Olga referred to in the much earlier letter of 15 March 1933 (see Chapter 6). At the time of excavation, Starkey believed they had found a storehouse destroyed in an earlier Babylonian campaign of the 590s BC, predating the burnt deposit of the Lachish Letters. It was only later in the final reports that Olga redated this level to c. 700 BC, the time of the Assyrian destruction.[17] Associated with this event was a grisly discovery in a chamber found off the mound – a mass of human bones and skulls from several hundred victims of the Assyrian siege and conquest.

The site's importance had already been recognised, attracting visitors of all kinds even before the Lachish Letters discovery. This was important from the perspectives of public and diplomatic relations, interaction with the archaeological community and fundraising. In 1933 the project's sponsor Sir Charles Marston visited together with his wife and two daughters; he came again in 1935 with the manager of his Wolverhampton works (Figure 8.5). Marston wrote popular books on biblical archaeology while sponsor of the Tell ed-Duweir excavations, drawing upon discoveries there and at other sites.[18] Sir Robert Mond also came to inspect the site. Later, Père Vincent came from the École Biblique in Jerusalem with an entourage of priests, followed by the Crown Prince and Princess of Sweden (the former Lady Louise Mountbatten), among others.

After the discovery of the Lachish Letters there was a more constant stream of visitors, especially as news spread following early stories in *The Times* and other newspapers.[19] The visiting archaeologists included Hebrew scholars, archaeologists and dignitaries such as Benjamin Maisler (Mazar) and H.L. Ginsberg (Figure 8.6), Shmuel Yeivin, Prof. Harry Torczyner (who deciphered and published the Letters), John Gray, Mortimer Wheeler (who stayed several days), Guy Brunton, John and

Figure 8.5 Charles Marston and J.L. Starkey at Tell ed-Duweir, from a visit between 1933 and 1935. Reproduced from von Harten & Marston 1979, 138.

Figure 8.6 Dr Benjamin Maisler (Mazar) (left) and Dr H.L. Ginsberg (right) studying the Lachish Letters at the camp-house, February 1935. Mr S. Yeivin, who accompanied them, is not shown in the photograph. See letter of 14 February 1935. Wellcome-Marston Expedition Archive, Department of the Middle East, British Museum. © UCL Institute of Archaeology, courtesy of the Wellcome Trust and the British Museum.

Grace Crowfoot (who came several times), and the Lamons and Geoffrey Shipton from Megiddo. Père Vincent came again with another party of Fathers. Margaret Murray arrived from the Petrie camp at Al-Arish, and again from Ajjul, as did Joan Crowfoot, Veronica Seton-Williams and John Waechter. Gertrude Caton Thompson called in on her way back from the Fayum. The High Commissioner Sir Arthur Wauchope visited, as did Dr Frank Partridge, Bishop of Portsmouth, Peter Johnston-Saint from the Wellcome Museum and John Henry Iliffe from the Palestine Archaeological Museum, Jerusalem.

The division of artefacts is mentioned on a number of occasions, and Olga's hard work and long hours of preparation are evident in several letters. She writes about the large number of objects from the Fosse Temple (referred to in the letters as 'the shrine'). As in previous years with Petrie's summer exhibitions, the Tell ed-Duweir expedition also prepared for the packing of artefacts for shipment and the summer exhibitions in London and accompanying lectures to help raise public awareness.[20]

In 1935 the Lachish Letters were among the highlights of a major exhibition at the Henry Wellcome Research Institute, including film footage from the expedition film 'Lachish – City of Judah', made by Richmond Brown.[21] There are a number of references in Olga's letters about the preparations for this landmark filming, which helped generate publicity for the Wellcome-Marston Expedition and its major discoveries in biblical archaeology, while also encouraging people to visit Palestine.

It should not be forgotten that during these seasons Olga continued to exercise her zest for travel. There were endless opportunities for visiting other excavations or sites of interest, such as Megiddo and Jerash, and innumerable local tells and castles. Nightlife and entertainment feature in the letters frequently, including trips to the cinema in Jerusalem, the Arab music hall in Cairo and a performance by Rina Nokova and her Yemenite dancers in Haifa, an emerging entertainment hub.[22] Olga's visit to Haifa in November 1934 included an invitation to board a British naval vessel made possible through her cousin Commander Tufnell and his wife Evie.

An interesting letter provides some insights into the close relationships with Olga's Arab friends. She takes Taman Salamah to Jerusalem to visit the doctor and do some sightseeing, bringing this 'Bedawy girl' into greater contact with the more rarefied world of the city. During the Eid holidays, when the workmen laid down their tools, Olga and her companions undertook two separate expeditions to Egypt by car (Figure 8.7), crossing the Sinai desert and Suez Canal, travelling to Cairo and beyond. One of the trips provided an opportunity to visit their old friend H.D. Colt and his newly established dig-house at the site of Esbeita in the Negev desert, which, according to its visitors' book, attracted numerous notables – not only many British officials and archaeologists, but also a number of Arab nationalist leaders and educators.[23]

This was still a relatively peaceful time before the impact of the Arab Revolt against the British administration in early 1936, and there are few references to disturbances, although there are more comments about encounters with police officers, perhaps highlighting the increase in the police presence and a heightened sense of security. South-central Palestine, i.e. the Negev, was to become particularly insecure and dangerous during the next two years.

On her way home in 1936 Olga passed through Europe, including Knossos, and visited the scholar Edith Porada, a seals specialist, in Vienna. Two letters to Porada are included below, and continued correspondence between them both, largely concerning scarabs and seals, can be found in the archives of the Palestine Exploration Fund.

Figure 8.7 Crossing the Nile by ferry. Either January 1935 or February 1936. Wellcome-Marston Expedition Archive, Department of the Middle East, British Museum. © UCL Institute of Archaeology, courtesy of the Wellcome Trust and the British Museum.

The final letter in this chapter gives the only indication of Olga's own political activities regarding the Arab cause while staying in London, although no specific details are provided.

Letters of October 1933–May 1936

[8 October 1933; handwritten: PEF/DA/TUF/224]

Tell Duweir.
P.O. Box 23
Gaza
Palestine.

Telegrams
W.A.R.ENE [Wellcome Archaeological Research Expedition to the Near East]
Oct.8.1933

Dearest Mà,
[…] You will be glad to hear that I got through the feat of landing at Jaffa in great comfort. I was neither shot, kidnapped or abducted despite the

fact that all my fellow passengers were of the faith and that I was indistinguishable from them.

The police did not appear to be armed and all was quite peaceful. I got a car at once for Qubeibe,[24] called on the shipping agent to hear if there was any news of the boxes and got here by 11am, where I found everyone busily employed on building operations. All the walls are up of the new storeroom and clinic and it only remains to put the roof on and fill in windows and doors.

During the afternoon I got my room straight and put out all my things so it was difficult to believe I had ever been away. Today I cleared out the storeroom and installed everything in its place, Starks [Starkey] has gone to Jerusalem to get the tests made for his diabetic treatment, so we shall not see him for a couple of days. Shaw, Inge, Gerald [Harding] and I with Mrs Starks and the babies [John and Mary] complete the party.

Went across to the village to see the famous twins born a few weeks ago. This time last year, I was attending the first child of Hamd[25] and his wife, trying despite myself to save it from an inevitable grave. The parents have certainly not wasted much time as the twins are already strong and lusty individuals called Herkomah and Hamdah – can't make out why the former name was chosen, because it means literally translated 'Governess'. [...]

The country looks very dry now, but it will be quite different by the time you arrive. All the Arabs know you are coming so you <u>must not</u> disappoint them. [...]

[Undated letter, probably October or November 1933; handwritten: PEF/DA/TUF/225][26]

Tell Duweir,
c/o P.O. Gaza
Palestine,

Telegraphic address
<u>Warene.</u> Hebron
<u>Or</u> Wellcome Archaeological Research Expedition to the Near East,

Dearest Mà,
We have started work on an outlying spur where those 'cup' marks[27] were which I photographed last year. We do not expect to find much where we are now, but further along there are indications of a very big EB [Early Bronze] settlement.[28]

Today Shaw, Inge and I went again to the sea with usual cheerful escort and bathed solidly all day in limpid blue sea as clear as crystal; it was lovely to get away from the really strong wind which was blowing at home. He [Shaw] has a truck which he bought for £70 in Egypt, it goes like the wind, like a reliable old steamroller with the usual orchestral accompaniment.

The day is most refreshing mentally and physically but I don't know how long we can keep it up as all depends on the weather. […]

My new bed has come and I shall sample it tonight to see if it will do for you – I think it will.

22nd We are having our first shower of rain, so everyone is very damp but extremely elated. You can't imagine how queer it is, living where rain is an unmitigated nuisance most of the year, to find people who walk about soaked to the skin with the same 'spring is in the air' smile which we use for fine sunny mornings in April.

Starks [Starkey] has gone to Haifa to receive the first consignment of goods and the truck. I am still working on the wall and have got round some way.

Very much love from
Olga

[There is a long gap in the letters from this point as Olga's mother visited her, staying in the camp.]

[26 March 1934; handwritten: PEF/DA/TUF/226]

Tell Duweir
c/o P.O.B. 23
Gaza
March 26th 1934

Dearest Mà,
When it came to the point, there was no time for goodbyes or anything so rather belatedly I hope all goes well with you. When the little boat took me away, I got into a bus and was soon on Carmel again, going first to the nuns to see if a letter had come, which it had not. […]

We had asparagus for dinner, one tin, which did not reach as far as me, and a hymn afterwards, then to bed. […]

Imagine my surprise to find Messrs Johnson and Blundell having breakfast when I came down next morning, how they got there or why they were back is still a mystery. However, bedecked with frezias [freesias] and heliotrope I caught the train easily and landed ½ an hour afterwards at Atlit. No one there, but the stationmaster summoned the Government guard who took me round the castle enchantingly jutting out into the sea. He insisted on my seeing everything, even down to the sort of sticky stuff they use to mend pots. Work does not open there till next week. The same applies to Miss Garrod's work in the Wadi Mughrara [sic].[29] I walked there against a fierce wind and was welcomed with open arms by the guard in charge; when we had seen the sites we sat and talked while I ate lunch, which I had remembered to bring, and discussed the archaeologists of our acquaintance.

Meandered back to the station and caught a 3 pm train, 3rd class, to Lud [Lod], which was not so bad as it sounds as I spent the time having tea in a Pullman. There I alighted and found a car which I rather competently snatched from under the nose of a most Seaforthian Englishman who looked a bit bewildered when I made my own bargain and drove off all in a minute or two.

Decided to go back to the Tell and got there by dinner time. Next day being the Aid [Eid al-Adha], I had to feed in the village in the morning and in self-defence I gave a party in the evening in the hosh,[30] which we all enjoyed. A policeman from Beit Jibrin looked in about 10 pm on his round and thought us a huge joke especially when we made him dance a 'dubha' [dabke].[31]

Got on with the drawing today, all very peaceful and pleasant, Pummell[32] had just come back with the truck and so has Diab, so I suppose the holiday is really over.

I am sending this to Brindisi in the hope it will catch you there. […] Various people have asked after you and said they were sorry not to have said goodbye including the man who has his eyes done.

[26 March 1934; handwritten: PEF/DA/TUF/??]

Tell Duweir
c/o P.O.B. 23
Gaza
March 26.

Dearest Daddy,
Very many thanks for yours. […] Mummy had gone when your letter came, but I expect to catch her with some news at Brindisi.

I do think the trip has done her good, she really looked very done in when she arrived, and everyone noticed the change in her, but I think she was more cheerful when she left. We spent the last 3 days away, one night in Jerusalem to collect her visas for Turkey and Greece and the remaining two at a Protestant German Mission Home on Mt Carmel Haifa. We had meant to stay at the R.C. [Roman Catholic] German Hospice, but the driver dropped us at the wrong place which was as well as Princess Mary[33] was taking up all the room in the other place.

You should have seen Mama and I praying at mealtimes thrice daily, but on the evening of the 1st day we got off with 2 men who were also landed there and we were taken to a very good concert in the town.

The sun and the views were quite enough for us the next day and we did nothing but enjoy them, and the following afternoon we went down into Haifa and made our way to the customs. They would not let me on the boat as I had no pass, but I think she will have been quite comfortable. I took her to the side and then had to go straight back in the tender. [...]

[4 April 1934; handwritten: PEF/DA/TUF/227]

Tell Duweir
c/o P.O.
Gaza
April 4.

Dearest Mà,

Just a line to catch the post to tell you that all is well. The season is getting near its end and we expect to have the division round about the 15th and may be leaving here early in May. The Taylors have asked me to stay in Cyprus a few days on my way back and I may do so if nothing more exciting turns up.

Another festival is upon us and 3 days' holiday – the Passover feast really. The weather has been extraordinary, rain and wind unheard of for April, but is clearing now and I hope to start sleeping out shortly.

Various visitors have been, all v. enthusiastic. Mrs McInnes, late Bishop's wife v. amusing about the P. [Petrie] camp.

We had a gay night yesterday, during which I won at vingt-et-un quite heavily – the first and I expect only time we have gambled this year, in fact you would hardly believe, and I know Lady P. wouldn't, how sober we have been compared to last year. The Colonel is now installed and settling down. [...]

[5 April 1934; handwritten: PEF/DA/TUF/228]

Tell Duweir
P.O.B. 23. Gaza
April 5th

Dearest Mà,

I suppose you are now installed once more. [...] Have not had even a p.c. [post-card] from you 'en route', but expect there may be something tomorrow. [...]

Starks [Starkey] says he hopes you will go and see Sir Robert [Mond], we all hope he is all right, though we've not heard a word for months.

Have had an orgy of visitors this last few days, especially over Easter – including visits from Tell Ajjul truants, Weir [?], Peckham both stayed, and Bird (who has been sacked) came down from J. [Jerusalem] though we <u>did not</u> ask him to stay.

Many enquiries after you from the patients, some days ago Hassuna the bride came up with some friends and after much 'humming' and 'hawing' which I thought was a prelude to telling me she was going to have a baby, was however a request that they might be allowed to decorate the outer edges of the door round the ayada [clinic]. I graciously consented and next day they came and drew patterns and trees all over and when I wasn't looking they actually penetrated inside and did a little tree on the wall between the window and the door, anyhow everyone is much impressed with the beauty of it and it makes them more at home.

The shrine[34] is still providing many problems and a formidable collection of bowls, which will be endless to deal with in time for the division, which is taking place after all. We are now working on the Tell, as well, though the far cemetery has closed down and we are easing off week by week.

I have distributed the paint boxes and have had some masterpieces sent in as a result including a portrait of myself administering eye drops which I shall have framed [see Figure 8.8 for photograph of Olga in action – the painting has not been sourced].

All the holiday trips were a great success. Shaw and Charles [Inge] walked across the Arabah to Petra, an 8 hrs trek, and arrived there rather to the astonishment of Cooks' tourists including Mr Morton, with no more luggage than a whisky bottle full of water. Ba [Richmond Brown] is still keen on Umm Baghy [Baqhy? Umm el-Bagh?] and has made out a plan of the castle, which he hopes to restore. [...]

Figure 8.8 Olga Tufnell outside dispensary or clinic with unnamed helpers. See letter of 5 April 1934. Wellcome-Marston Expedition Archive, Department of the Middle East, British Museum. © UCL Institute of Archaeology, courtesy of the Wellcome Trust and the British Museum.

[19 April 1934; handwritten: PEF/DA/TUF/229]

Tell Duweir
April 19th 1934

Dearest Mà,
We have had a busy week, getting ready for the division by preparing the list. On Monday night while we were having dinner, a tousled head shot in through the window and there was Iliffe of the [Palestine Archaeological] Museum who had just come up from Ajjul, having despoiled the Philistines; I believe they have taken all the gold. We expect them to take all the contents of the shrine. Next day Mr Richmond and Zweig the well-known photographer[35] came so we were kept busy. The great day is fixed for next Wednesday, but does not dismay us as Mr I. [Iliffe] is human and reasonable. [...]

Joan du Plat Taylor is coming to stay on Sat. for 2 nights. [...] The 'new boy' [R.M. Cox?] went home last week to start his new term at U.C.

[University College]. I may travel back with Ba, arriving on the night of the 8th, but have not heard about the passage yet; Starks will follow 10 days later.

Shrine or no shrine we will have almost closed down completely, and only 6 men or so are left to finish off. […]

[23 April 1934; handwritten: PEF/DA/TUF/230]

Hotel Fast
Jerusalem
23rd April.

Dearest Mà,

Have had your various letters and am leaving here on Sunday, arriving sometime on the 6th May. […]

We have finished the division list and I came up early this morning with WBKS [Shaw] to present the remaining portion to the Museum. Went and had my hair done where I met Mrs Richmond who asked me to lunch tomorrow and Mr Iliffe has asked me to dine tonight, so I feel quite gay. Met the Esbeita[36] crowd at tea and have to sleep at the French hospice as all the hotels are full. The Rev. Father who received me there had been to T.D. [Tell ed-Duweir] and welcomed me as an old friend. It is fairly noisy but I imagine 'sheep'.

Tomorrow, in the intervals of shopping, I am to see over the new Museum[37] building and hope to fit in a call on Prof. [Petrie] if I can make sure that the M.P. [Lady Petrie] will not be there. We go down somehow tomorrow in time for the division on Wednesday, so I shall only have 3 clear days after it before leaving, and consequently no packing this year.

Travelling on a Messageries boat, to Marseilles, thence by train, by night, home Sunday 6th so this is positively my last letter. […]

[Olga returned to Tell ed-Duweir later that year for the third season].

[8 November 1934; handwritten: PEF/DA/TUF/234]

Windsor Hotel
Haifa, Palestine Nov. 8.
P.O. Box 511

Dearest Mà,

Since I last wrote things have been happening. On arrival at P.S [Port Said] Evie[38] was met by various naval gents and we were all invited aboard the *Ajax* for cocktails. Apparently this is a 'fast' ship in more senses than one, and we spent a hectic half hour trying to avoid drinking gin – Ba had 5 and we all found it difficult to step with decorum onto the launch or 'pinnace' (which by the way is any kind of small launch) on the way back. Evie lunched with an old friend at the hotel, Ba and I at an adjoining table – where we made a plan to get the car sent to Lud [Lod] and transport Evie to Jerusalem for breakfast and then on to Haifa in time for lunch. Various N.O.s [naval officers] were being drafted to Haifa, so the combined luggage made a brave show at Kantara. Dinner at 10 on eggs and beer and then I was lucky to find a carriage 'Ladies' with one other English woman in it, so slept well all the way to Lud. The others had sleepers. No car, so Ba phoned, it had not left Jerusalem so we took a taxi there, and after luxurious bath had a good breakfast. Despite Ba's plans, the tiresome garage people had not told him of new licence regulations, so we could not have the car till that was fixed. Therefore a taxi all the way to Haifa, as Ba anyhow had to collect his gear at the customs.

Desmond [Tufnell] champing up and down at the Windsor Hotel was glad to see us, and the 4 of us lunched here. At teatime we went off to the *Durban*. *Arethusa*, flagship, *Adventure*, *Durban* and *Despatch*, as well as 3 destroyers, are lined up inside the breakwater. We walked along and were taken off to the ship on a dysa [launch]. We made a typical landing, Evie falling over the top step, which upset my gravity, in front of the 'watch' who were standing at attention. Desmond has a good cabin aft next to the captain. He said there was nothing to see on board but we insisted on seeing the bridge and as much as he would show. The ship is antiquated and a sore contrast to the brand new *Arethusa*. Then we had cocktails with the captain in his comfortable chintzy cabin and then back hurriedly to change for dinner. [...] Then we went on to the Evidor cinema (where we heard Schnabel) to a dance recital by Rina Nikova and her Yemenite dancers. First class performance with the Admiral and all the big wigs in attendance. Who should be in the Admiral's box but Lady Downes who beckoned to me, so that I had to go to her, she said she had tried for my address to ask me to stay. Then Keith Roach said surely you are staying for the dance on Sat. I said no, I was off in the morning. Everybody said it was nonsense, and Lady D. said I had better stay with her for it. So that was an idea, it seemed an opportunity and though Ba wouldn't stay, I thought I had better. So I shall go up to

Carmel, after lunch with Evie in the *Durban*, and get back to Jerusalem sometime on Sunday. [...]

[23 November, probably 1934; handwritten: PEF/DA/TUF/235]

Tell Duweir
P.O.B. 23.
Gaza, Palestine
Nov. 23

Darling Daddy,
Tomorrow is your birthday, and I had hoped to get a cable off to you for it to show I'd not forgotten but this has not been possible as there's no car going, so I'm sending a letter instead. [...]

You will want to know about Evie. We all three enjoyed the journey out and the subsequent meeting in Haifa with Desmond. You will have seen in Mummy's letter how we all went to the Yemenite dancers, Ba and I were thrilled to see over the *Durban* and Evie and I lunched with the Captain, all very swanky. [...]

You would love the Downes' garden at Haifa, among the pine woods, she is L[or]d Allenby's sister and therefore quite a person in this country. [...]

Work proceeds steadily and we have the same lot of faces around us. Yesterday most of us went to our old haunt Tell el 'Ajjul and peeked in the Petries' old camp before a bathe in the sea. It was fun to be there again and revive old memories. [...]

[29 November, probably 1934; handwritten: PEF/DA/TUF/236][39]

By my 1st fire.
Tell Duweir.
Gaza
Nov. 29. Palestine.

Darling Mà,
Things have gone very well this week, nothing outstanding either way. I reduced the storeroom to moderate order, since it has been plastered, which should certainly keep it cleaner than it was before.

They are finding tombs under the roadway which leads to the garages so it looks like a miniature Alps round the back. Also Pummell is laying the pipes for the water installation – some game, and I think between you and me and the gatepost, rather unnecessary. The 1st consignment has come and all the gadgets have been unpacked including the refrigerator.

Col. Clarke's gift of the wireless is actually functioning and we got London well last night. There is another piano instead of last year's, I think it has a better tone and Ba is busy struggling with the Dead March.[40]

Tewfiq[41] hit another boy on the head today and so has been sent off to 'Coventry' or 'Jericho' or wherever you like. All of which spites us more than him as we suffer the ministrations of the one who was hit, who will probably have a fit from the awful anxiety he is undergoing.

Did you know that we have Mohammed [el-Kreti] as cook? He had heard nothing from the P's [Petries] so was glad to come and he seems quite happy and says it is heaven and so peaceful. [...]

We have been rather gayer in the evenings so far than last year and have danced and had music several times. The ping pong set and table is also going, so that really things are almost too comfortable. However the roof still leaks, as proved by our first shower of rain last night, so all adventure is not over yet.

[29 November 1934; handwritten: PEF/DA/TUF/237]

Tell Duweir
P.O.B. 23
Gaza
Palestine

Nov. 29. 1934.

Dearest Daddy,
Rather late with my birthday letter I'm afraid this year, it is awful how easily one loses track of dates once one gets out here and there is no excuse, because I had not had time to get really embedded. [...]

It was not possible to say goodbye to his Lordship [unidentified], as he was so full of ire, and said he had 'given me my chance' and so on that I walked out of the room and left him to it.

Hope you [are] getting some shooting. Some very very fine coveys simply waiting for you here, they had made holes for themselves in the dust just under our defence wall and about 8 flew away altogether from under my nose.

Shaw saw a gazelle yesterday about 300 yds behind the house.

We had our 1st shower of rain last night and the roof did a bit of leaking, so we shall be glad when the zinc roofing arrives from London.

My room really looks very nice, yellow plastered walls and a brick fireplace and blinds made of aeroplane silk. Very much love darling and good luck. [...]

Best love
<u>Olga</u>

[14 December 1934; handwritten: PEF/DA/TUF/238]

Tell Duweir.
Dec. 14.

Darling Mà,
We have just finished one of the most hectic days of our career. 2 days ago we were informed that H.E. the Crown Prince and Princess of Sweden[42] and a retinue of 12 were all coming down and they duly turned up soon after midday.

Starks was in excellent form, showed them a tomb behind the house first, then the storeroom, then took them up and round the wall to the well, where a faked bit of work was going on. Then they did the residency and the Temple[43] and then back to the house for lunch. Turkey, plum pudding, fruit and custard went down very well and they were very cheerful all through the meal. H.E. said 'I bring you down into the wilds and you get the best lunch you've had in Palestine'. Later on he said he didn't think Lady P. turned out this sort of meal!

The Princess admired my embroideries just as if she had been opening a sale of work, and I had great trouble getting her to 'minny' [? unclear] as the escort was queuing up for it, and they would play with the signal.

Despite desperate preparations and the non-arrival of the butter, all went well and I think they enjoyed themselves.

That has been enough excitement for one day, Suk day too, so we shall take tomorrow off as a reward.

Poor Gerald has malaria badly and has gone to hospital; we want him to do a cure and get done with it. [...]

[20 December 1934; handwritten: PEF/DA/TUF/239]

Tell Duweir.
Dec. 20

Dearest Mà and Daddy,

Christmas is coming round with horrid haste and the New Year with it. […] Shall look forward to hearing about it.

We have been recovering from the Royal visit and Ba and I composed a few verses to celebrate the occasion. I forgot to say that the Princess wore a grey flannel coat and skirt with <u>brown</u> shoes and a grey hat – just like your suitings [suit fabric] […]

We are finding various tombs with quite good pottery, of an earlier period to the temple which makes for variety, but so far there is nothing sensational.

Gerald is back from hospital, very shaky after the worst bout of malaria he has ever had, I very much doubt if it is malaria, but if so it must be a fresh infection, which will mean more trouble ahead I fear.

The Lasalle, another invalid, has gone to Jerusalem to have a spring mended and is badly in need of new tyres. However Ba loves her so much he would not part with her for pounds.

Elinor [Eleanor] Dyott[44] is really a charming person, thoroughly practical and has had a year's domestic training. Everything is washed, iron[ed] and cleaned to the nth degree and cooking has much improved and there is greater variety in the meals.

Did I tell you Mohammed [el-Kreti] asked very tenderly after you and said that he was in an awful dither when you came into the kitchen at Ajjul one day to ask him how he made the <u>very</u> delicious soup. The M.P. [Lady Petrie] was with you, and he dared not divulge the disgraceful fact that there were onions in the soup, and yet he was terrified that you would guess it. You know onions are anathema in a Petrie camp, and yet Prof. always comments on the excellence of the soup when it is particularly full of the noxious stuff.

I think the P's will have been dining at Govt. Ho. [Government House], as it was almost arranged at the table here, as both said they would like to meet them, so I'm afraid they (the P's) will have to listen to an earful about Duweir and its marvels. […]

We may be thoroughly Christian and go up to Bethlehem on Xmas [Christmas] Eve to see the procession to the church. It is of course impossible to get inside and if you do, you stand a good chance of being bashed on the head.

They are broadcasting the bells again but I don't know who will give the Christmas message. […]

[28 December 1934; handwritten: PEF/DA/TUF/241]

Tell Duweir
Dec. 28. 1934.

Dearest Mà,

[...] Gerald came back much too soon from hospital after his malaria, and the consequence is that he caught a chill and has developed pleurisy and a return of his old kidney trouble. Last night as we were really worried, Ba and I went to Hebron and I came back here with the Dr, who made a thorough examination. He could not say much more than what we've been trying to impress on him [Gerald] since he came back, and now he is to stay in his room and not come out on any pretext. If the kidney trouble does not clear up in 10 days he will have to go into hospital.

Auntie Dora's[45] chincherinchees arrived all right and decorated the Xmas dinner table. We had a cheerful party in the evening in fancy dress, Gerald temporarily better, as an ape, Ba as the local idea of the Crown Prince of Sweden, Shaw very clever as a soldier of Sennacherib, Charles [Inge] as Cleopatra, really most seductive, Elinor very hurriedly turned by me into a Russian peasant and Starks in his usual Bishop's rigout [Figure 8.9].[46] Pummell appeared as Gordon Richards[47] and tried to ride in on Hamas the donkey, who was however not to be persuaded to do anything so rash.

Ba is terribly thrilled because his niece has arrived, I expect you saw it announced in the paper on Xmas Eve. Poor child, it is too bad to be born just then, though it may be useful in later life! We hope it has red hair!

Do you think you could slip a Kestos[48] size 32 into your next letter, and also into a further one a skein of darning? Do you remember those tennis socks I bought, white, blue and yellow? Now of course they are hol[e]y and I have nothing to darn them with. Sometimes you can get variegated skeins which are the nicest I think.

Our new zinc roof is on so we are now leak proof, rather different from when you were here – the chute has arrived and is being installed on the N.W. corner of the mound, it will take sometime to get up but will be noble when it actually functions. [...]

[31 December 1934; handwritten: PEF/DA/TUF/242]

Tell Duweir
New Year's ~~Xmas~~ Eve. 1934

Figure 8.9 J.L. Starkey dressed as a bishop (or other clergyman) with his wife Marjorie dressed as Salome (or other legendary temptress), Tell Fara, 1928 or 1929. Fancy dress parties were popular with Starkey and others at Tell Fara and Tell ed-Duweir. Starkey family collection. Courtesy of Wendy Slaninka.

Dearest Mà,

Just a line to let you know our plans as the Aid [Eid al-Fitr] is upon us and we get a week as it just breaks into the middle so it is decided that we go the whole hog and have the week off. Shaw as you know is leaving to start his Libyan desert trip, so Ba is taking his car and Starks, Charles and I are going with him [to Cairo], Elinor [Eleanor] and McEwen (who is joining the Libyan desert expedition) go in Shaw's car and the 5 of us will have to pack in on the return journey. We can do some Tells on the way and spend some time in the Delta I believe; we get four days, about 2 in Cairo, which should be rather fun. Had a nice card from Mrs Selous, so can look her up. [...]

This is just in case I can't write on Thursday as usual, but will try to get some news in from Cairo. [...]

[6 January 1935; handwritten: PEF/DA/TUF/243]

Victoria Hotel, Cairo
Jan. 6. 1935.

Dearest Mà,

Just got your 2 letters written after Xmas at Beersheba Police Post before setting out across Sinai, without picks!

The night before we had gone up to J. [Jerusalem] to spend the night and I met the Salustous[?] for dinner at the Fast and afterwards we went to the flicks with the result that I did not get to bed till 12.30, which, as you know, is late in these parts. However, felt fresh and ready for anything when we started out at 8.30 next morning. Lovely run to Beersheba where Shaw and Elinor met us in the Ford and after passport formalities we set out for the South. Reached Esbeita[49] about lunch time and had it in the Colt camphouse, which is a good building pleasantly designed. We could not stay long as we wanted to make Hassanah that night as rest houses are scarce in Sinai.

Our road lay through stony country, where the thorniest shrubs struggle for existence in every depression hoping for a drop of moisture. Great banks of hills fantastically shaped on the N.W. and the main pile was the Gebel Halal, which Jarvis says is the Mountain of the Law, rather than the generally accepted Gebel Musa. The country is limestone formation with outcropping chalk, the old land surface is rain eroded, and once upon a time the plains must have been wonderfully fertile. I believe there are flints to be found almost everywhere if one had the patience to look for them.

At Auja ['Auja al-Hafir] they looked at our passports again on official entry into Sinai, and we listened to a telephone conversation, which was worthy of Tewfiq in the dining room at his best [Figure 8.10]. They were trying to find out if the next rest house was empty and we were glad to hear it was so we could share out the 4 beds among the seven of us.

It was dark an hour or so before we reached Hassanah, but we found a lovely fire lighted for us when we did arrive, and beds made with a variety of sheets, some clean, some not.

We had our own food with us and soon had a meal going, which we ate with more than usual relish, and being nearly drunk with sleep turned in soon afterwards, E. [Eleanor] and I getting beds in our status as females and the others tossing for the remainder. Slept peacefully until 6.30, when we got breakfast ready with the help of a willing factotum, for

Figure 8.10 Dining room, with pictures on the wall of sponsors Sir Charles Marston (left) and Sir Robert Mond (right). It is not clear if the person in the photograph is Tewfiq Saleh, referred to in letter of 6 January 1935. Photograph taken in 1934. Wellcome-Marston Expedition Archive, Department of the Middle East, British Museum. © UCL Institute of Archaeology, courtesy of the Wellcome Trust and the British Museum.

an early start, strange to say we left punctually at 8.30, though we'd Starks with us.

From Hassanah to Suez, we passed a man and small girl and five camels, and about the same number of trees braving [and] maintaining their ground against fate.

The hills were more subdued and further off in the south we could see a faint blue range which formed the bulk of the southern mountains. About midday we came to a cathedral-like mass and turned north along it to ascend the Mitla Pass, where a gusty wind blew sand in our faces and gave us a foretaste of what to expect on the other side of the pass. We spent a few minutes on top and I saw my first view of the Red Sea. Then down into a waste of sand, which half covered the road and made going difficult. Soon after, we came upon the low embankment which screens the canal from sight, turned through it and followed along the side of a vivid strip of blue water, almost painful after the drab colouring of the soil we had passed over the last 2 days. We lunched by the canal awaiting the arrival of a steamer to photograph and the *City of Leicester*, Liverpool, duly obliged and we all waved vigorously to the crew on board.

Getting across was a tedious business not without a humorous side. We waited half an hour or more as the tide was too strong to allow the ferry to get over. When she did come and we had embarked, cars and all, we started up and stuck in the middle of the stream, despite the efforts of an 'old salt' in charge, who shook all of us warmly by the hand, and was glad to exchange some words of English.

Suez is a dirty hole, and we were glad to get off, even though it meant leaving the rather lush gardens behind for cold and windy desert. It was arctic all the way and Ba stepped on the gas, which made things more acute for the people in the back. We thought of the glamorous East and the bright posters of a winter in Egypt with some irony, and when the lights of Cairo did appear, we were elated to see streets and shops and electric signs.

As you can see we are staying at the Victoria or New Khedivial which is old fashioned, rather musty but comfortable 50pt. [piastres] a day. Got in by dinner time Sat. 5th and early to bed and no wonder after all that air.

Next day we left Cairo about 11.30 bound for a mystery site in the Delta not far from Zagazig and one of Prof's old haunts, Tell el Yehudiyeh. As we expected all the glowing stories were dust and ashes and false hopes. However we enjoyed a run through green fields along wide canals and past villages where everyone was dressed in their gayest and best for the Aid after Ramadan.

At sunset we managed to get in a few minutes at Tell el Yehudiyeh to see the site of the temple of Onias and the earth bank of the Hyksos fortifications. Scrambling round in the twilight, with only the newest of new moons to guide us, did not give much indication of what was there.

After dinner and champagne we sallied forth to an Arab music hall. I mention the champagne because it may have lent a rose tint to the entertainment. We passed several halls, where thousands of tarbushes [tarbush: brimless felt cap] were literally fighting for admittance and concentrated on a place where the crowd was not so dense and it was to be presumed that the fare was quite respectable. For 16pt we got the best and most secluded box at the back of the hall. It was really a choice position, for just in front was a row of seductive females, all heavily painted, one was munching a sandwich, but put it down when a likely boy-friend appeared.

The hall was heavily decorated and festooned with lights and 2 Xmas trees had positions of honour on each side of the stage. 10 yrs ago Starks says it was very different, plain white walls and hard benches and the girls dressed in cotton chemises tied up with red tape. Now the ladies of the chorus wear the flimsiest of cummerbunds, though a good deal more respectable than the Folies Bergère [in Paris].

CBC[50] would have 10 thousand fits if he could see them hitching up their belts, tripping over draperies, and performing elementary gymnastics with the vast approval of the tarbushes in the audience.

The star was a prize fighter of a woman with a vast row of teeth. Her convolutions and her singing were a bit ponderous, and of course all her jokes were unintelligible. Perhaps it was as well, the comic policeman and the comic tourists also said a thing or two, which set the whole house in a roar. In fact there was a continuous noise, as everyone talked all the time, waiters dashed to and fro with drinks, and in the seclusion of the back rows, the ladies of the chorus got off with fat Effendiat.[51] It was with quite a thrill that we realized that these houris[52] and the row of expectant females were one and the same and interchangeable. When their turn was about due they dashed out, shed the coat they were wearing and tripped onto the stage attired in a few sequins. Then back again to the boy-friend to finish the cup of coffee and take a puff or two at his 'houkkah'.[53]

The show goes on almost non-stop to 1 am, but rather wilted we crept out at 11.30. There was a fine tableau of the Queen of Egypt which sent us home with a final thrill.

Next day up and off by ten to Kom Aushim [ancient Karanis] by the Pyramid road. That was the site of Stark's labours when he worked for Michigan and it was a thrill for him to see his camp and dig and all the changes that have taken place since then. They have electric light, a refrigerator and a garden full of sunflowers and sweet peas, marigolds and nasturtiums.

From K. Aushim we turned northwards along the desert bank of the Birket Qarun [Birket Karun] – the Lasalle took the sand dunes bravely and we roared along, except when Starks thought he saw flints by the wayside, when we all tumbled out of the car and scattered to see what we could find. All those depressions north of the lake were Miss C.T.'s [Caton Thompson's][54] happy hunting ground when she was doing the early cultures of the Fayum. Not long before sunset we got to the mysterious XIIth dyn. [dynasty] temple of Demay [Dime, or Soknopaiou Nesos] built close under a spur of the high desert. No one knows much about it, but it is suggested to be the funerary chapel of the sacred crocodiles probably buried in a valley behind. The sun was nearly down ~~behind the hills~~ when we moved on, <u>not</u> back, to the Roman temple some 2 miles on and it was getting chilly when we reached it and clambered round the great brick temenos wall. We had left the car some way off and literally ran back to it to get away before our own tracks were invisible. The Fayum seems limitless at night and we half wondered whether we should spend the night marooned, as the engine had been giving some trouble. However by judicious cossetting Ba got her back to the main road and we turned towards Cairo. A few hundred yards and ominous pops heralded a breakdown which was one of five stoppages which we had along the way. Ba and Charles performed mysteriously at the back of the car and poured petrol from the back tank into the auto vac. at frequent intervals. We took 8 hrs on a trip of 2 and had a well-earned dinner about 10.30.

Next day we sallied to the Museum in the morning and saw the latest under Guy Brunton's direction.[55] The afternoon was spent seeing a selection of mosques, dusty and dull, also Mohammed Ali's Palace, a decayed mausoleum of unbelievable decrepitude, with a magnificent view. Pottered round the shops and bought some rubbish for the lads – early bed for once.

Wednesday we went out to Saqqara where Mr Quibell[56] took us down into the Blue tiled tomb of Zozer, IIIrd dyn. This is not generally shown as it is not too safe, and the lovely blue tiles in imitation of matting fall off. It is deep under the Sed Hep [Heb-Sed] court, a huge shaft was cut first as well as the approach way and filled up later. Burial was there none, and just recently a mummied foot has been recovered from the chamber under the Pyramid which is thought to be his. A lovely day and we motored home under the new moon via the Pyramids.

Now I am just waiting for the cavalcade to start back home – Shaw has left us to start out for the Libyan desert, but Charles has bought a 2nd hand car, which he hopes to drive to Palestine!

Very much love darling
from <u>Olga</u>

[18 January 1935; handwritten: PEF/DA/TUF/244]

Tell Duweir
P O B 23
Gaza
Jan. 18.

Dearest Mà,
I think my last letter took our adventures up to the moment when we left Cairo on the morning of the 9th. It was 11.30 before we started, not

because we were not up but because Inge had bought a car of elderly lineage the day before and it had to be made to go before we could get on the road. We drove very slowly to Suez to 'run her in' and spent the usual mildly exasperating time at the customs. The ferry got over the canal like a lamb and we found 5 pillar box red Fords on the other side waiting to cross, full of tools and kit bags with a strange assortment of females and chaps in berets. We sniffed round each other but did not speak and we drove on in well-bred silence. By that time, having had no lunch, we had that sinking feeling rather acutely so we lunched at 5 pm sitting in about the same spot as when we went down, next to a canal which had turned muddy grey.

Only our own feckless selves would think of crossing the Mitla Pass after sunset with a car of unknown quantity. It is not the freight that is extraordinary but sand drifts blow up and cover the road at a moment's notice so that it is as impassable as snow or mud. Just on the crest Charles got bogged in one right up to his differential, wherever that is, and we spent a warming and really pleasant half hour digging him out again, scooping sand from underneath with our hands, and congratulating ourselves that it was not mud we were dealing with. At the end of it all when Ba had rushed the danger patch successfully in the Lasalle, we felt glad that we'd had some mild adventure to retail.

Then half across Sinai, we reached Hassanah about 10, where we knocked up the guards and were greeted as old friends. Regardless of our predecessors, who we gathered from the visitors b[oo]k were the Leo Frobenius[57] party going into the Libyan desert, where they will be sure to clash with Shaw, we got into their sheets after a good meal in front of a blazing fire and so thankfully to sleep. We weren't off too early the next morning owing to us females oversleeping when we should have pounded round to make the others feel how late it must be. At Kosseinah [Al-Qosimah?] I was sorry that we had to leave the signpost leading to Ain Gederat (Kadesh Barnea) on our right, but I expect the name is the best part about it. And who could grumble who has spent a day in the Land of Goshen?

The poor Lasalle was very much a lame duck by the time we got to Esbeita and Charles took Elinor and I on, while Starks and Ba crawled on in the other invalid. Camp by 7.30, but after a visit to Esbeita the others did not get in until after midnight.

Perfect harmony surprisingly preserved throughout whole trip; we all came back bronzed and rested from a week's continuous air and motoring. [...]

[30 January 1935; handwritten: PEF/DA/TUF/245]

Tell Duweir
P.O.P. [B.] 23
Gaza.
Jan 30

Dearest Mà,
[…] I had a very good birthday with presents and a marvellous iced cake made by Elinor, the first I've had for 15 yrs!

I believe I didn't get in my letter last week. We went to Jerusalem on Friday last, and I made enquiries about the Pearsalls coming out, and the possibilities of an exhibition. Then we went to Abu Ghosh, an early Crusader church about 8kms from Jerusalem. Lovely solid XIIth cent. building bang on top of a spring set in the floor of the lower church. A very strategical way of acquiring converts. A delightful monk, speaking excellent English, nationality undiscovered but he used such words as 'interstices', showed us round and when we left we were given the monastery wine with biscuits, while we sat round in the parlour.

As Ba's car needed the weekly repair, I came back with Charles. The week has been pleasant, weather unblemished, and the last two days have been enlivened by an excellent discovery of which more anon.

The socks also arrived on my birthday and are already in use, they are excellent, and the wools will do fine.

We are expecting some more drums from Ramleh tonight when Pummell gets back from Jaffa, so I expect we shall make some noise.

Sir Charles [Marston] is due early in February; we are wondering whether he will stay in camp and rather hope not; he is travelling with a friend and they will stay at the King David. […]

[14 February 1935; handwritten: PEF/DA/TUF/246]

Tell Duweir.
POB 23
Gaza.
Feb. 14. 1935

Dearest Mà,
Last Friday we did what we considered a colossal walk to Tell Bornat, beyond Beit Jibrin; it was a perfect day and we felt all the better for it.

On Sat. I went to Hebron to stay with the Forsters,[58] a very pleasant couple with original ideas, good books and a baby and baby Grand, both in good voice. Ostensibly I was to learn how to do injections and attend the Outpatients' Dept. but actually I had a very peaceful time and only worked on Monday and Tuesday morning.

They took me to Dura on Sunday where there is a village school, run on the latest lines, animals, chickens and rabbits to be looked after, carpentry, cobblery and blacksmith's art, and 200 dunams of land to be ploughed and sown. The best thing there, despite all these amenities, was the view, looking right over the Shephelah to the sea; I have already described it once in an article I wrote but never thought anything so inclusive and marvellous could exist in actual fact.

Came back on Tuesday to find the Great Visit [Sir Charles Marston] had not materialised and will not do so till next week, as he is spending some more days in Egypt.

We are having a whole posse of Jewish experts[59] down to look at the inscriptions [Lachish Letters] over the weekend so we should be much wiser afterwards.

Other news is there none. I have bought some seeds and planted them in the back outside the large storeroom door, as a rival to the front garden, edging the path round the rooms, now full of anemones and cyclamen. We are looking quite tidy in preparation and Pummell hopes to get the water laid on. It has just started to rain which is just what I want to start off my garden!

[23 February 1935; handwritten: PEF/DA/TUF/247]

Tell Duweir
c/o P.O.B.
Gaza.
Palestine

Feb. 23.

Dearest Mà,
Our excitement this week was the visit of Sir Charles and his friend Mr Farrer, who is manager of the Wolverhampton Villiers Works.[60] In the end they arrived rather unexpectedly, but we were all tee-ed up and everything went with a swing. I made quite a hit with old Farrer and he left us £10 for a 'treat' for the workmen, so we shall have a great show

next month when the moon is full, with sheep, roasted whole, tons of rice, bonfires and so on. We have got quite an adequate flower border of anenomes [sic], the front courtyard is miraculously tidy now.

The darnings all arrived quite safely, for which many thanks, the bust bodice never came so I suppose the customs found it too intriguing.

Gerald is much better but Goulden has jaundice and has been in bed a week. The work puts it down to the fact that he visited Sheykh Ali's tomb without going through the proper ceremonies of leaving a coin, lighting a candle and having a bath before going in. The only remedy now according to them is to sacrifice a goat there as a trespass offering.

Your trip to Ireland must have been amusing, so glad you got the job done satisfactorily.

I wonder if you will hear rumours of our find [Lachish Letters] through the M.P. We hear that it is said that 1/5 of the Bible has been found, written on potsherds, unfortunately <u>not</u> true, but we have got some interesting letters and we much hope there will be more to come. Sir C. [Charles] is wildly telegraphing news to USA and *Times*.

Mr Wood of the Airways was here yesterday and asked very tenderly after you.

I enclose a photo Ba took, hope you will like it, Tell Bornat in the background. Rain tonight, so shall be able to wash my hair tomorrow!

Very much love
<u>Olga</u>

[28 February 1935; handwritten: PEF/DA/TUF/248]

P.O.B.23.
Gaza.

Feb. 28.

Dearest Mà,
Our week has been enlivened with various visits from experts about the ostraca, and it has done its bit in the way of rain.

Last Friday I walked to Duweir and beyond, and visited some nice troglodytes. Their cave was tidy and clean, a girl was washing in a big tub, the coffee pot was brightly polished and a 'rababah', [a] one-string fiddle, stood in the corner. The lady of the house, having got over her first surprise at seeing me, said she <u>loved</u> English women, and it came out she had once spent a fortnight in the Hospital. So we made friends. It was very muddy going and rained at intervals, but I felt all the better for the walk. [...]

The Crowfoots and Iliffe and Sir Charles Close (PEF [Palestine Exploration Fund]) were down yesterday. She, as enthusiastic as ever, went off with baskets full of flowers and empty ones to collect more in. [...]

We shall have Miss Gardner out on March 5th to start the elephant,[61] so more fun for Starks. He is now in Jerusalem arranging about the house.

Some of them met the P's in the street in J. [Jerusalem] last week, the Prof. most cordial and laughing, looking wonderfully well, but she tried to get him down a side street to avoid the encounter and spent the time scowling in the middle of the street! We think Miss M. [Murray] is coming out but don't know definitely. [...]

[12 March 1935; handwritten: PEF/DA/TUF/249]

Tell Duweir.
March 12.

Dearest Mà,

I sent you such a short note last week that I must try and make up for it now, especially as another Aid [Eid al-Adha] is on us and I am going up north to various sites with Starks and Pummell for 2–3 days. Megiddo, Athlit, Tantara and so on are on the list.

It has been a busy week, and I have been sorting finally the sherds from the Temple and today Mr Ben Dor[62] and I had the satisfaction of throwing all the piles away.

Père Vincent came and asked at once and most tenderly after you, so I said you had already sent him many messages. He was as enthusiastic as ever and thrilled with all our biblical finds. He had about 20 fathers in tow, black, white and khaki!

Today I had an emergency midwifery call to Hudbeh's[63] daughter-in-law, they were getting really anxious as she had been in labour for 15 hrs. when the usual thing is ½ to 1 hr. However my presence seemed to have a moral effect as she performed soon afterwards.

It is getting much warmer now and I am thinking about summer clothes. Shall have to buy a white hat of some sort in Jerusalem.

Ba is going to T.J. [Tell Jemmeh] with Iliffe, Gerald to Gaza, Charles and Goulden to Damascus, and Eleanor is nobly assisting Miss G. [Gardner] at Bethlehem where work is in full swing.

Mohammed [el-Kreti] was thrilled to get yr. letter, you may not remember but he is 'my boy' that M.P. always talked about, and has been the P's cook for 40 yrs.

We hear that the caravan has gone to Sinai. Ba and Gerald were at Ajjul last week and they were very excited, it then turns out that by Sinai they mean Sheykh Zuweideh,[64] the next station before Raffa [Rafah]. [...]

[21 March 1935: handwritten: PEF/DA/TUF/251]

Ard el Hasbun
Bethlehem
Palestine.
March 21.

Dearest Mà,

Here I am at Bethlehem, masquerading as a geologist while Miss Gardner is away with Ba in Egypt. Sounds bad, doesn't it? But Starks wanted her to see the Sinai road. They will be gone 4 days at least and Ba will be bringing back Guy Brunton. We hear Prof. has got his concession for El Arish[65] and will be back under the old auspices of the Egypt. Govt. They expect to look in there on the way back.

Johnston-Saint[66] was here yesterday and at camp and I came up at lunch time with Ba and we met them in Jerusalem and all lunched at the Fast. Then after some shopping came down to take over from Miss G. We have taken a house here which is perfect for summer weather, but distinctly cold and draughty at the moment. It has been drizzling all day and the ground is as slippery as ice. Hope it will soon be better, as I miss my nice warm fire.

Apparently we are to have the Exhib. at the WRI[67] and special apartments have been decorated for our use! J-S. [Johnston-Saint] is lord of all he surveys now that Malcolm[68] has gone and thinks he can 'manage' the old man [Sir Henry Wellcome].[69]

The ostraca are still yielding surprises and I believe they have done the best possible for us – however we shall see.

I think I have still to tell you about the Aid holiday. Starks, Pummell and I went off on Wed. morning from Duweir and reached Nablus (Shechem) in time for dinner at an amusing hostelry. We had seen Ay [Ai] on the way, where Mdme Marquet[70] (who lunched with us once) had been digging, but we spent most of the time there trying to dig up tulip bulbs with our fingers, not very successful.

Tewfiq the proprietor of the only hotel in Nablus is an enterprising man, he has built with his pa's money an enormous block, the lower half to be used as the Ottoman Bank, the upper half as his hotel, h. and c. [hot and cold water] in all the rooms, plugs that pull and so on; how long they will continue to do so I can't say as he seems to have no idea of maintenance or proper staff arrangements.

The cloudburst in Nablus must have been devastating, the damage is still very visible.

Next morning off quite bright and early to Balata (Shechem)[71] where we went round the dig and saw the magnificent B.A. [Bronze Age] wall. From there to Megiddo, where we were given a warm welcome in their palace, which is so perfect that it is to be used as a hotel when the Expedition finally leaves. I was glad to see the site, after all one had heard, and they have every gadget under the sun to work with, still I would rather be where I am.

You will be surprised to hear that we spent the 2nd night at 'Karmelheim', having tried as on a previous occasion to get into the Sisters of St Charles unsuccessfully. To this day I'm ashamed I don't know the name of La Belle Dame, but she sent you many messages, and we bought many plants from the garden, which were confiscated at the agricultural barrier. We had hoped to go south and pick up the Tul Karem [Tulkarem, Tulkarm] road to Jerusalem, but the wadis were impassable and after seeing Athlit caves and Dor we had to retrace our steps. Tantara (Dor) is right on the sea, and you have to search along the shore to reach the ancient site by car from the modern village. Though cold, it was lovely to see the waves dash against the rocks, and the columns of a Hellenistic temple lighted by the occasional gleams of sunshine.

Home through Haifa, dinner in Jerusalem about 9.30 and to Tell D. [Duweir] by 12.45 in pouring rain, we never thought we should get through. [...]

Coming back to the present, [...] the P.s were refused a concession in Syria,[72] which was hard after all they had written and said about the excellent facilities in that country, but they have since got one for El Arish, where I gather they are now. Am going to J. [Jerusalem] tonight to dine (and dance!) at the K. D. [King David Hotel] with Mr Iliffe, so will post this there.

Very much love

Olga

[PS] It is fine and sunny now, so things are brighter.

[29 March 1935: PEF/DA/TUF/252]

Tell Duweir.
March 29th.

Dearest Mà,

Back again after a week at Bethlehem which passed off quite successfully. When I left we had got down 7 metres, leaving 8 metres more to get to the bottom, though we were already finding bone when I went away. Miss G. [Garrod] and Ba returned with Guy Brunton quite according to schedule so I was able to hand over and came back the following afternoon. Now it has turned miserably cold again so I am lucky to be off the hill.

We have had a spate of visitors, G.B. [Guy Brunton] as mentioned, Mr Quibell, Miss Tilly, a friend of his, Donald Brown who was with us one year and has been at Sbeita [Esbeita] with Harris the last 2 seasons and John Richmond who is here more or less to the end of the season, which by the way is drawing near. Starks will find it hard to tear himself away now that the chute is finished [Figure 8.11] and in working order and now that the Residency is destroyed and the plan of the earlier

Figure 8.11 The spoil chute at Tell ed-Duweir, northwest corner of mound. See letter of 29 March 1935. Wellcome-Marston Expedition Archive, Department of the Middle East, British Museum. © UCL Institute of Archaeology, courtesy of the Wellcome Trust and the British Museum.

building slowly emerging. Even the temple has produced a stone plan below the brick benches and a fine serpentine vase has appeared. So it will be difficult to get away! Everything is happening at once, and the ostraca still produce fresh surprises of which you will doubtless read before I do.

The flowers are magnificent just now and at night the whole countryside smells of night-scented stock. The mimosa behind my bedroom is in bloom and in front of it is an enormous anchusa which makes a fine contrast. [...]

I hope it is getting warmer for you, shall hope to be back early in May, when I suppose London will be in pandemonium for the Jubilee.[73] [...]

[29 March 1935; handwritten: PEF/DA/TUF/253]

Tell Duweir
March 29.

Darling Daddy,
It's a long time since I've written but have been thinking of you all the same. [...]

Am just back from Bethlehem where I spent a week looking after Miss Gardner's hole which she is digging in order to look for elephant bones 20,000 yrs old or more. We have hired an empty house on the site, which is lovely in warm weather and simply arctic when wind blows or it rains, as there is not much glass in the windows and too many doors. Bells and clocks strike all day and night as Bethlehem is a very religious place. Saw the first swallows come over and suppose they will soon be getting to you. Also storks some days ago which come in huge hordes and sound like the breaking of waves on a calm day with the beating of their wings.

We have had some good finds of which you may have heard if you have been listening to your wireless industriously. Letters written on potsherds at the time of Jeremiah, just before the invasion of Palestine by Nebuchadnezzar. Some passages are almost word for word the same as the Book, so you can imagine the thrill it is to have something so close to the original document. So far we have 12 letters but hope to get more. Nothing has ever been found like them, as other ostraca (as these written sherds are called) just contained receipts of oil and wine sold and that sort of thing. [...]

[4 April 1935; handwritten: PEF/DA/TUF/268]

Tell Duweir.
POB 23
Gaza.
April 4th

Dearest Mà,

It has been a fairly uneventful week though we have had masses of visitors mostly lured hither by the thought of 'this century's most amazing discovery', which is the worst of going to press so early, though rumours in Jerusalem were getting so hectic it seemed safer to put in something official.

We have got the word Lachish in such a context that there is little doubt of its identification with this site, as well as a host of biblical references and names. One letter almost seems to be the official document on which a passage in Jeremiah is based.[74] Nice for Charlie [Marston], isn't it? We sent off a report today of 16 pages so they ought to have enough to read until the next one goes in.

We had a surprising visit yesterday from 5 armoured cars, who had lost their way. I don't know if we or they were most amazed, perhaps they were to see the Union Jack flying back of beyond and to be spoken to in English on the arrival. Perhaps the beer helped too!

Ba is bringing Miss Murray down tomorrow. She arrived to assist the P's in Syria, but has spent 3 days at El Arish (which was apparently enough) and is now going down to Ajjul to try and clear up the mess and get on terms again with the Department.[75] Not an easy or pleasant task.

I wonder what she will think of this here. Guy Brunton came back from Egypt with Ba and enjoyed himself; he asked after you and Mrs Tit [?].

It is still extremely cold and summer clothes are still a snare and a delusion. Am writing by my fire and feel quite chilly so shall adjourn to bed. [...]

[19 April 1935; handwritten: PEF/DA/TUF/254]

Tell Duweir.
Gaza.
April 19th

Figure 8.12 Party in the courtyard, Tell ed-Duweir. See letters of 19 April 1935 and 21 February 1936. Wellcome-Marston Expedition Archive, Department of the Middle East, British Museum. © UCL Institute of Archaeology, courtesy of the Wellcome Trust and the British Museum.

Dearest Mà,

Though this letter is a bit late and I meant to write one in the middle of the week, I hope it will be a welcome one, as I have practically arranged to sail on the 30th via a Greek boat to Piraeus and Marseilles, arriving at home on the 7th.

When Sir Charles was here (by the way you see he is married again!!!)[76] his friend Mr Farrer left us £10 to have a party with. That was in Feb. I think and since then we have waited in vain for a fine night with full moon. It has been cold and windy all along and it was only last night that we finally got the party going [possibly Figure 8.12].

Naturally there were great preparations beforehand, and for days I was busy dealing out castor oil to those who wanted to be in fine condition. All the countryside heard the news and a troup of 'nuri' gypsies settled nearby in the hopes of providing the entertainment. Vast quantities of food was acquired from Gaza and the 'pièce de resistance' was supplied by Gerald himself in the form of 3 choice specimens from his flock at Tell Jemmeh – a ram with a tail which everyone said must weigh at least 12 lbs and 2 lambs. The transport in the expedition's truck from Gaza was no mean feat and when the joints had duly arrived

– still alive and kicking – we all breathed a sigh of relief, and turned our attention to other things: wood and brushwood had to be collected, dishes and cauldrons had to be borrowed from the village, cooks and butchers had to be enlisted. All was going well on the day until lunch time when the boy who was in charge of the flock appeared to say they were no longer where he had put them. Recriminations were loud and potent, and the culprit leapt on the nearest donkey and scoured the neighbourhood for his lost sheep. As time went on and he did not return with them anxiety increased, others joined in the hunt all overcome with the magnitude of the disaster and prepared to blame the gypsies, who had been seen driving sheep in the vicinity in the morning.

Imagine the general relief when the erring lambs were recovered some miles away, they had merely strayed and been taken charge of by some friendly Bedawy [Bedouin]. To make sure of no further calamity, the butchers got down to their job at once and there was much coming and going and excitement. The work was expertly done and before 4 pm the fires had been lit, and great black cauldrons had been set to simmer, while all the tin baths of the staff were commandeered for the vaste [sic] piles of rice which had to be cooked and kept hot until after sunset. Expectation increased as delicious savours crept round the camp and reached to the workers, still valiantly carrying on their tasks. In seclusion, behind the donkey house the washerwoman and a bevy of maidens were busily baking bread, on circular iron plates inverted over a brushwood fire. Bedawy bread should be as thin as a pancake and about 3 times the diameter, it requires great skill to make and tastes really good, but a little goes a long way, at any rate as far as I am concerned.

By 5 pm a crowd of those no longer on the work was collecting and the evening whistle was blown ½ an hour sooner than usual to allow our own people time to wash and get into their 'glad rags'.

Even before 6 the gypsies had arrived and were established on mats in the middle of the courtyard, with an assortment of musical in[s]truments, drums and pipes, two rather gaudy ladies, and babies carefully chaperoned (at first) by a terrifying beldame and various elderly men who kept up an incessant r[h]ythm on the drums.

It would not be fair on the ladies if they did not receive a fuller description. They were dressed in the height of gypsy fashion in black dresses completely covered with spangles, they wore rather high-heeled shoes (much admired by a small girl of my acquaintance) and glory of glories black woollen stockings, surmounted by heavy silver anklets which jingled. On their heads they had bright handcherchiefs [sic] which were pale indeed in comparison with the vermilion of their cheeks.

Bracelets, bangles and beads added to the general charm and all agreed that they had never seen such lovely females.

We soon learnt that they were enterprising as well as lovely, for custom demands that they should approach each guest in turn, and after singing and dancing to him alone, in the Szigane [tzigane] manner, the guest is supposed to cover the dancer's face with coins, one on the mouth, on the eyes, on the forehead and as many more as they can extract.

A stir went round, and the waiting circle became aware of the procession which was approaching. Men bearing dishes of varying sizes piled high with rice and surmounted by succulent lumps of meat came into the ~~waiting~~ courtyard and distributed their burdens to the different groups, while I made a dash to secure one of the largest portions for the girls. Arab custom decrees that women should feed off the leavings at the end of the feast, but we all thought differently and quite upset some of the more conventional elders by allotting them a dish on their own.

From previous experience we inclined towards a sweepstake on the guests' feeding time of 3–5, the meat off the top goes like a flash, but all their willing efforts made but a slight impression on the mountains of rice, which is in the best tradition as at a generous feast there should always be plenty left over. The women were finished in 3½ minutes and went to wash their hands, the right hand being the only implement required for eating, but the smallest boys stayed on some minutes more in an effort to cram in a bit more food.

There was no doubt that the meal was a success, and after sweets and cigarettes had been distributed the whole company settled down to further appreciation of the dancers. When the meal had settled somewhat various side shows got going, the Southern 'dahiya' with its accompanying verse and refrain, a straight row of men swaying to a double rhythm, was rivalled by the Philistine 'dabka' [dance] led by a miniature Pied Piper of Hamelin.

Spirits rose high and were only damped by a stern brother, who ordered his pretty sister home to bed. I found her in tears going off most reluctantly and after a heated scene with her brother she was allowed to stay, which restored her smiles. I did the heavy 'chaperone' for the rest of the evening. About 10 pm tea was served in kerosene tins and our small supply of cups went round and round, each guest waiting his turn politely. It would be impossible to get such a festive atmosphere in England on tea alone, but here where little pleasures mean much, tea is as potent as champagne. By eleven many of the guests had gone, the gypsies carried on bravely and finished up with the best turn of all, with one of the gaudy ones dancing with a jug of water on her head – most sensational as all agreed.

Gradually the courtyard cleared; voices faded away down the village path, the bonfire died of neglect, and its warm glow gave place to the silver light of the moon.

After effects? Should I mention that the washerwoman was taken ill at her tub this morning, it is not a delicate subject (by Arab standards) but a delicate and subtle compliment to the excellence of the fare which you provided. [...] Needless to say the evening will go down in the annals of the neighbourhood in glowing words, and if you could have been here to see the pleasure that your thoughtfulness gave and if you could have stayed here long enough to get to know our workers, our pleasure would have been complete. [...]

[Olga returned for the fourth season at Tell ed-Duweir.]

[5 December 1935; handwritten: PEF/DA/TUF/256]

Tell Duweir.
P.O.B. 23.
Gaza.
Palestine.
Dec. 5.

Darling Mà,
[...] I've been here a month already so the time is going pretty rapidly. Ba went off to Mach[a]erus last Sunday, though he left when the weather looked most unsettled. It has kept fine so far and it must be lovely up there on the hill, though beastly cold at night. He has to leave the car 3 hrs off and ride the rest, uphill all the way. He seems much better and has been taking a tonic.

We went to Jerusalem last Thursday night. I sped to the hairdresser and we then had dinner at the German Restaurant and then to a cinema, [to see] '20,000 yrs in Sing-sing'. Next morning shopping, Xmas cards and so on and I went to see Iliffe at the Museum. Things are really moving there, boxes are being unpacked and cases arranged; it will be magnificent when finished, they hope to open a gallery next year but nothing will really be ready for about 5 [?]. Card indexes in quadruplicate and all sorts of horrors.

The week has passed quietly enough. Starks has been gone since Monday and we hear he has got to Haifa to see about the arrival of the boxes, let's hope they come soon. [...] Harris arrived in J. [Jerusalem] last week, I saw him at the Fast. Terry [Colt] is by way of coming out next spring and is in Florida with the infant. [...]

[11 December 1935; handwritten: PEF/DA/TUF/257]

Tell Duweir
P.O.B. 23.
Gaza
Palestine
Dec. 11th

Darling Mà,

Your 2 letters of 24th and 1st got here together yesterday, the former having taken 17 days! All the posts seem disorganised so I suppose they are coming through France or by long sea.

I'm sorry there's such bad news of Uncle Herzie,[77] had heard the same from Evie, it will mean a big change for Langleys,[78] but I think not so drastic as Daddy believes; the wild oats (if any) will be finished and done with and Billy[79] will settle down nicely as a country squire. [...]

Mrs R.B. [Richmond Brown] must have been perturbed to write to you, I don't think she knew about the heart attack [presumably of Uncle Herzie] in which [case] she would have been more so. Ba has been gone 10 days now – luckily all of them fine with two windy ones, so it looks as if he'll complete his fortnight after all, he's not got provisions for longer.

I may go to J. [Jerusalem] tomorrow to attend a meeting of the Pal. [Palestine] Oriental Society[80] where all the speeches on the [Lachish] letters will be either in French or German, can get my hair washed (the water here is impossible) and in the evening go to Rheinhardt's [Reinhardt's] *Midsummer Night's Dream* [the film]. Anyhow it is Ramadan so we don't lose any working time.

We had a gay evening on Gerald's birthday last Sunday and danced till midnight, a thing we've not done for ages, all the old beloved tunes came out and we sang the opera.

No news from Sheykh Zuweid,[81] she [Lady Petrie] slept in the truck the night before as it was full of valuables, and was seen riding through Jerusalem on top of the lot when they went south. Much alarums and excursions in the Committee [British School of Archaeology in Egypt] which now consists of Mrs Wheeler[82] (Chairman) elected by Mrs Mackay (who was voted for by Mrs W.) and Miss Murray I suppose. Slight exaggeration perhaps! [...]

[24 December, possibly 1935; handwritten: PEF/TUF/DA/284][83]

Tell Duweir.

Dec. 24.

Darling –
[...] Yesterday it rained for the first time since I've been here, so was able to wash my hair for the festivities – G. [Gerald Harding] comes tomorrow having been held up owing to Sir Arthur's [Wauchope][84] inopportune visit to Aqabah.

We are beginning to find things and are lucky to be in a period which has not so far turned up here – late Ramesside, which will make a change.

I am struggling with Arabic reading in the evenings with Diab and Mustafa – the latter is just beginning and Diab is quite a pundit.

We have had a French Prof. down for some days, talking no English, so Charles and I have had to keep him amused, he is the genial sort and is also a priest, though I doubt if he takes things very seriously.

We have got a chap down with mumps, at least I say so, and have him isolated in a tent. Hope there will be no further cases. [...]

Very much love to you all
Olga

[28 December 1935; handwritten: PEF/DA/TUF/258]

Hotel Fast, Jerusalem
Dec. 28. 1935

Darling Mà,
I wired yesterday's post as we were on the move, so I suppose I must make up for it by a full description of all our doings over Xmas.

On Monday we left camp and proceeded in a leisurely way (as the usual spring was broken) to Jerusalem where the car went into dry dock. After lunch of course I had my hair done and not before it needed it, and then bravely called on the Richmonds. Saw Mrs R. sitting reading but there was a forbidding little card box which said 'OUT' so I duly deposited my pasteboard therein, and went thankfully away.

Early to bed that night. Ba is still feeling the effects of his fortnight at Mach[a]erus, and on the way back he had the misfortune to kill a boy who ran right across the car on a deserted and barren plain miles from anywhere. It would just happen, when you think of the years he has motored in London traffic. No blame to him, but the ordeal upset him and he is feeling the reaction now. All this between ourselves.

Tuesday, I spent the morning at the Ophthalmic [Hospital] picking up scrappy information. Met a Miss Jenes [or Lenes?], who lived at Springfield Place with an aunt for 16 yrs. And knows all the family and friend of Maud Usborn. Early lunch, and afterwards Baramki[85] from the Dept. of Antiquities called for us and we went off down to Jericho to see his dig [Khirbet el-Mafjar], where he is excavating an VIIIth cent. monastery[86] and hopes to find the church which contains (or should do so) the 12 stones deposited by the tribes when they entered Palestine. Sat till it was dark outside his tent watching the stars come up in the still atmosphere of the Jordan valley.

Xmas Eve – it was difficult to realise it, dined at the Fast with the Starkeys and afterwards off to Bethlehem to do the thing in style. Parked the car near the elephant pit and then down to the church, pretty crowded already, got to the front of the crowd, where a British policeman was trying to keep it back. 'Back, back' he kept saying, and then in an undertone to me 'All except you two', so we acquired preferential treatment. Later he beckoned to put us in seats near the pulpit, but a priest came and turned us out again and ultimately we found seats on a bench with the military.

The mass was like any other in the hideous R.C. church, we did not sit it all out, and explored the cloisters and Greek Church which is the lovely Byzantine one, with the shiny columns, deep shadows and chandeliers shrouded in muslin, coloured balls and ostrich eggs hanging from them introduce a ~~witch-like~~ pagan note. The crypt was full of jostling praying people, we did not join them and motored out to the Mt of Olives to see the Mosque of Omar illuminated. Nice discreet lighting, just enough outside [to turn] the dome grey and translucent against the sky. Home to bed.

Xmas Day, we left about 12.30 after various delays for Haifa to see Evie and say goodbye before she left on Friday. Made good way and spent an hour or two at Ta'annek [Taanach] – a fine Tell much mauled by excavation. Reached Haifa 6 or so and found D. [Desmond Tufnell] and E. [Evie] dressing for dinner, we had phoned them before and knew their plans. A quiet evening and the next morning, while Ba slept, Evie packed and we gossiped till lunchtime. D. got off soon after and we motored out with their friend Mrs Tennant to Athlit, where D. did the honours very competently. They are fun to get on with and it was a most successful afternoon. We tactfully left D. and E. together and went to the 7pm house at the cinema – *Gay Divorce* – lovely dancing and nothing much more.

Boxing Day. Got up early to see Evie off, all very sad, D. especially so, at her departure. When I got back to the hotel Ba was stirring and we got off on the q[uie]t trip to Caesarea at 10.30. The road, which is excruciating, goes on past Athlit, turning into the hills at Zichron Jacoub [Zikhron Ya'akov] and then down into the plain to Benjamina [Binyamina] – a Jewish colony and station on the Haifa–Lud line. We have often tried to get there before as a starting point, but the road is impassable after a few minutes' rain and we are now convinced that the only civilised way is to go by train. Left the car at the station, and after some vague directions, started to walk across rolling sand dunes to Caesarea. It took us 1¾ hrs solid going, no path, we saw a green mound on the sea edge and made for that. When we got there we thought 'how disappointing' and sat down to eat rolls and butter, foie gras and marzipan. To the right was a village with red tiled houses, which, as our guide book told us, was inhabited by Bosnians, who were Muslims and had refugeed there in the 80's.

Rocks stuck out into the sea, with battered masonry clinging precariously to them. We made for the city and found ourselves approaching massive walls and a high gateway. So it was Caesarea after all. We went inside and saw a great well head to the left of the gate. Walking towards the sea we came to the harbour, a rock-bounded cove, surrounded by neat stone warehouses, all, I should say, standing as they were left by the Crusaders. A few silent people about who took not the slightest interest in us; we followed the shore, climbing over the loose stone walls put up by the Bosnians to the northern limit of the town, where the wall which is apparently intact juts out into the sea. Regretfully we turned inland, for time was precious, and followed the wall. Every 100 ft or so there was a bastion, protected by a stone talus; built on the walls and flush with the outer face were small houses, many of them I feel, standing from Crusader times [Figure 8.13].

We saw all this in 35 mins. as we had to get out of the dunes by sunset. However we found the path back, cars can't get there through the sand, and we got back to the station in 1¼ hrs. Ba said good going and that I walked as fast as Iliffe, who is considered a bit of a wizard in that line. We enjoyed some Russian tea at the station canteen, and then off to drive to Tulkarm. Really a nightmare drive over the MAIN COAST ROAD

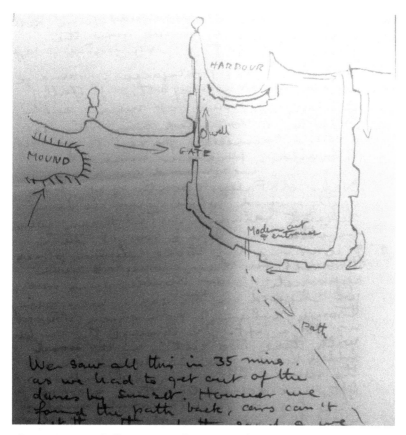

Figure 8.13 Ink illustration of Caesarea, from letter of 28 December 1935. Courtesy of the Palestine Exploration Fund.

Haifa – Jaffa. Plough, holes, precipices, drainage channels and every other pitfall. A storm in front got nearer each minute and [we] expected any minute to find ourselves forced to go back to Haifa. However, cursing and swearing we moved on across Nahr el Faleq, and south of it the battleground where [Richard] Coeur de Lion defeated Saladin. Tulkarm was visible long before we got there and was one of those elusive places that get further away as you approach. Our troubles were over, we stepped on the gas and were roaring through, when 2 policemen stopped us for a lift. On through the night with these two sitting on the folded hood, guns in hand, for all the world like royal flunkeys. After we deposited them we got into fog, and had to crawl. Just as well, as we found a car astride the road, with back wheels in the ditch. As we drew up, a police car arrived from the opposite direction, so we were able to leave them to cope with the drunk driver, who needed 3 men to pull him out of his seat.

Jerusalem by 8.45, and well-deserved dinner at the German Restaurant. Charles got wind that we were there, and his party came round; after much beer, they insisted we should join them at the K.D. [King David Hotel]. We'd walked 10 mls, and driven over 100, all we wanted was bed, but we changed and sallied forth once more to drink and dance till 12.30. Some day, but we enjoyed it.

Tonight back to duty, but Ba has arranged a dinner at the David for our Sirs, 2 military men, he and I, so shan't get home till late.

Tea with the Richmonds, so I must change. Had my ears syringed this morning, not before they needed it.

This boy business[87] crippled us and the plans, as B. [Richmond Brown] could not leave Palestine, and had to keep in touch with the Transjordan Govt. in case complications arose. So taking all in all, we didn't do badly, and it was lovely seeing Evie again. Have asked her to see you and retail all the news.

Very much love darling to you both
from
Olga

[30 January 1936; handwritten: PEF/DA/TUF/259]

Tell Duweir
P.O.B. 23
Gaza. Palestine
Jan. 30. 1936

Darling Mà,
[…] Things have gone well this week. Last Friday I did a marvellous walk to a hill beyond Duweinah with 2 trees on it, which you can see from the camp. Read detective stories all the afternoon in the sun and back to tea. On Sunday Torczy [Torczyner],[88] (your fervent slave, as he put it) came down, he has got over the fireworks of a fortnight ago, so we are back where we started from except for a few minor alterations, which is all to the good. He is sending you his new dictionary when it appears and overflowed with messages for you.

We had a gay evening on my birthday which was also Leslie's [Scott], funny coincidence, and Gerald iced a marvellous joint cake.

At last there are signs of rain and it has been blowing like hell all day. We rather think of going to Sheykh Zuweid tomorrow. The news has come through that they have closed down for a fortnight as everyone is ill owing to under-nutrition (or none at all) though the official explanation given to the workmen is the death of King George.

It was a shock to us, as we had heard nothing till 3 days afterwards, when first we heard we thought it must be George of Greece, could not imagine it was ours. Now what will Edward VIII do? He won't emulate his numerical predecessor in the matter of wives!

Starks and Gerald stayed at Govt. Ho. [Government House] and it all went well, G. [Gerald] has as good as got the job,[89] but it all has to go through the official channels first. The longer it takes the better pleased we shall be.

I hear the new 'head of the family'[90] has already made some changes, but apparently he is rather tied. I suppose death duties will be pretty hefty. [...]

[21 February 1936; handwritten: PEF/DA/TUF/261]

[Tell Duweir]
P.O.B. 23.
Gaza

Dearest Mà,
[...] On Thursday night we had another party of gypsies, less miserable than the last lot, with a better band including 'oudh' (guitar) 'rababa' (one-stringed violin), and 'tableh' (drum). The beauty chorus was more lively too, and one girl wearing a wreath of imitation flowers might well have come from Shuba'd's tomb.[91]

Govt. is making a new road 16m. wide from Gaza to Beit Jibrin, while it is being done there is a fearful morass to go through. The Lamons[92] and Geoffrey Shipton[93] came from Megiddo, had to leave their car at B.J. [Beit Jibrin] and ride out on mules. That night Ba and Charles started out to get to Jerusalem by the old Duweinah[?] road, [and] as they've not come back we presume they got there. Ba is leaving his car in J. [Jerusalem] as he wants to make quite certain of no delay in starting off for Egypt next Thursday. The plan is to motor down as before to Cairo and then continue on up to Tell el Amarna and see the city there. We shall need 8 days, with one spent in Cairo, so it will rather transgress the usual holiday period. Starks, Holbrook Bonney,[94] Leslie Scott are going, I am in two minds, but shall probably succumb in the end, on your principle of not missing any chances, but feel bad about leaving Mrs S [Starkey] alone for all that time, though S. has been most casual about it.

Your letter with *Lit. Sup.* [*Times Literary Supplement*] arrived together, shall have to wait till tomorrow for more news, as Sultan again goes on a donkey through the mud. Gaza has a religious 'urge' and all shops are to be closed in future on Fridays, so market day will be changed to Saturday, and probably our day off with it. [...]

[28 February 1936; handwritten: PEF/DA/TUF/262]

Tell Duweir.
Feb. 28. 1936.

Dearest Mà,
Got your 2 letters of 7th and 12th together after heavy rain had made the roads impassable; Sultan had to go down to Gaza on the donkey and brought post last Monday.

Now we are all keyed up for the Aid Festival, and the flight into Egypt. I tossed up as to whether I should go and luckily it came out right first time, so did not have to toss thrice. Things look doubtful this evening. Ba, Leslie [Scott], Holbrook and I were all going to J. [Jerusalem] this evening to pick up his car and go on from there to Beersheba, Auja and Hassana [Hassanah] for the night. However I got late and had some things to do, so decided to go with Starks and Pummell tomorrow morning via Gaza and Beersheba. Whether I shall ever see the others again remains to be seen, you know what Starks is [like] starting off!

It all sounds nice enough on paper, but Pummell has not arrived back from J. yet with the new truck which has to be licensed and so on. He'll be dead if he had to drive 250 mls [miles] tomorrow too poor chap. Starks is leaving Mrs and the children behind, and has been very casual about it.

We're all most awfully sorry about Miss Murray, poor little thing, I do hope she does not have a long and painful time. I am writing to her tonight. No Petrie news, but I hear she tells all would-be visitors in J. that it is quite impossible for anyone to get down, so they don't encourage people. A Dr and his wife, part of the exped[ition], left after some sort of bust up by plane for Egypt, the wife in tears confided all the horrors of the camp to Mrs Hargreaves. They at any rate insisted on a cook. I can well imagine what they are saying about Mohammed [Osman el-Kreti] and us. Harris [Colt] has made a really sensational discovery of 37 Greek and Arabic papyri,[95] it will be thrilling to know if he gets any lost classics. [...]

[6 March, probably 1936; handwritten: PEF/DA/TUF/263]

Tell Duweir
March 6.

Darling Mà,
Many thanks for yr last 2, Ba says you need not feel that you are not getting <u>all</u> the news, as he always exaggerates in his letters home to make good reading – knowing full well, I suppose, that after maternal editing the result is sure to be striking.

Last week we motored to Tabcha [Tabgha, Galilee] on Friday and back, only a small matter of 320 miles, however the air was lovely and we all came back thoroughly burnt.

On Monday Prof. Torczyner, who [is] doing the ostraca, came down with his wife and small girl, and walking down from the Tell just after the out gate, the former fell. I was sent for and found the poor woman groaning and screaming and a mere touch of the leg revealed that both bones were broken as it [was] floppy above the ankle, so we got splints and bandages, tied her up as best we could, put her on the stretcher and ultimately fixed her up on boards and mattresses in the car. Then it was decided that I should go up with them and a rather nightmare journey ensued, car going at snail's pace and the woman in agony all the time. We got to J [Jerusalem] in 2½ hrs and then started the usual hunt for doctors here, there and everywhere. The last I saw of her was being put under the X ray, which revealed she had a spiral fracture, pretty devilish.

Dinner BATH and bed at the Fast was welcome after that but had to leave at 5am to meet Miss Gardner at Lud. Her train needless to say got in 2 hrs late!

Pummel is going unexpectedly to Gaza so must post. More another day
Love
Olga

[8 March 1936; handwritten: PEF/DA/TUF/264]

Tell Duweir
March 8th 1936.

Darling Mà,
There can be no lack of news this week on my part, as I've the whole Egyptian trip to record. To begin at the beginning –

On the 28th Gerald brought the new Ford Pick-up down by 10.30am licensed and ready for the road at last. He and I and Starks and Pummell went as far as Gaza all together, and after farewell drinks at Spinney's, Starks, Pummell and I set forth to Beersheba rather straightly confined, all three in front. We had hoped to pick up Ba, Leslie [Scott] and Holbrook [Bonney] at Beersheba Customs but they had gone through hours before, so we followed on as far as Auja Hafir, where we came up with them after they had seen the sights. No time for us to stop, so the procession got going for Hassana where we arrived without adventure to find a luxurious resthouse-hotel had been built and furnished by Jarvis, since we were there last year. Our own food was cooked, or more correctly de-tinned, by an efficient 'sufragi' [manservant] and we sat round an immense fire feeling warm and replete. Got away next morning to schedule and travelled merrily on to the Mitla Pass; there we stopped to admire the view and wait for the Ford to catch up. When it did not appear we began to wonder, and finally set out on the way we had come to track them down. We felt they couldn't be far, particularly as S. had seen them, (he alleged) 3 times since we entered the Pass. However we motored an hour and a quarter and found a miserable car and occupants outside the Pass, parked by the road with one wheel leaning against the chassis. Apparently the idiots in J. [Jerusalem] had never tightened the bolts on the wheels and they had been eaten through by the friction of the wheel. They just escaped a nasty accident as they'd slowed down to take a snap. After heated argument it was decided that luggage and all we should get into Ba's car and go to Suez for a fresh wheel and bolts. Ba was just turning to start off again when the angel of the Lord appeared in the form of an Arab driver in survey truck. Of all things he produced a drum extractor, so that we were able to take it in to Suez; he would have done the job on the spot if he had had the bolts. So Starks travelled with him and on we went to Suez. The 'Admiral' was on board the ferry as usual, which lived up to tradition by sticking in the middle for a good 15 min. Customs as inquisitive as usual, so that we didn't get away till 4pm. Tea in Suez and then on over shattering road (which is actually being improved) to Cairo, leaving S. [Starkey] and P. [Pummell] to go back in a hired car to repair the truck. Next day we heard the epic of their adventures – how they stuck in the sand in the effort to help another car similarly stranded – how the garage man swore better than any Arab Starks has known – how they repaired the car by the light of the exposed chests of the garage man's 2 minions, and how they got back to Suez after 2 more sticks at 2.45 am.

We meanwhile were installed at Shepheard's.[96] To me an overrated luxury, no attempt at 'tous qu'il faut pour ecrire' [all you need to write] in one's room, water cold in hot tap and hot in cold, and horror of horrors no place to put the soap in the bathroom and a curved rim so that one had to balance it on one's knee cap or you know where! Next day was dedicated to rest for the drivers, incidentally it was Sunday, so no shops were open. After gargantuan lunch we went out to the Pyramids and actually did the sights inside, which I'd never done before. The great gallery is really impressive, Davidson [sic][97] or no.

Tea at Mena Ho. [House, a luxury hotel] in the haunts of the great, dinner at Finnish Restaurant, recommended to me by the hairdresser at Shepheard's, where we fed on a terrace which adjoined a lane where vendors of all sorts from dirty stories to silver bangles plied their trades. Then for the theatre, we made for the music hall we had visited last year, but actually found ourselves in a full-blown European theatre, next door. A sensational political drama was in progress, followed in breathless attention by the audience. Virtuous young men shot themselves, beautiful daughters gave up all for LUV, and the grand finale was a political meeting where hecklers were distributed among the audience to throw missiles at the hero bravely facing them on the platform. BLUD streams from his head, he falls and dies in the arms of his daughter, who explains all and covers his dead body with the green flag of EGYPT amid roars of applause. Very enjoyable evening and so to bed.

Alarums and excursions next morning as P. [Pummell] had not got his international driving licence, so we didn't get off till 1 pm. Could not resist some minutes at Memphis, which made us even later and then we lost our way among the ditches and canals and had to retrace our steps.

The chain of Pyramids on our right ended with the great pile of Meydum and thence onwards in the failing light we saw little beyond canals and bridges and villages full of children and fields overflowing with succulent greenery and peaceful livestock, contentedly chewing. Ba was very tired by then, and still we went on, our destination, Mellawi [Mallawi], we did not reach till 10.30 and then we tried to get on to the river to cross hook or by crook to Tell el Amarna. However the Omdah [village headman] at Deir Muwas [Mawas] said this was impossible, so we retired defeated to Mellawi's chief hotel, where we spent the night and slept excellently despite all the usual drawbacks plus the early morning celebrations of the 'wagafah' (day before the Aid). Off at a reasonable hour next day, all packed into the Ford, as Ba's was too large for the ferry. Our guide, provided by the Omdah ('Have you been to England? You talk English so well' 'Oh! Yes! I was at Balliol') encouraged us to drive straight aboard, but Ba's native caution distrusted this and we got out to find a felucca [sailing boat] at the edge of a precarious jetty with an eighteen-inch drop down to the deck. This was filled with straw by the men who thought we were making an unreasonable fuss, and ultimately we got aboard. A party of well-to-do ladies were also crossing for the day to visit their dead and they joined in the jubilation and passed round loaves of bread and hard-boiled eggs. With the car balanced athwart the felucca we crossed to our surprise in safety and landed at the village of Tell el Amarna. TILL means bay or depression, AMRĀN is the name of a tribe, pl. Amarnah – there is no actual 'Tell', the word was substituted for Till by early visitors. The green strip of cultivation is very narrow here and beyond the palms we came at once to brick ruins of palaces and temples and the modern cemetery. The Pendleburys[98] have rebuilt an ancient house on its original plan and live there very comfortably I imagine. They had shut down so completely that we couldn't get into more than one room where we cooked and ate dinner, then wrapped ourselves up in coats and rugs and went to sleep in the courtyard. Nothing makes one feel so well in the morning.

Early morning tea was distributed by the Qufti[99] guards at 6 am and we were soon up from the ground. After breakfast we 'did' the temples and palaces; all of brick, plastered over inside originally, both deteri[or]ate quickly and many points are now lost for good. The Palace where the main court was surrounded by aviaries is especially charming and what one would expect of Akhenaten.[100] Everything, sherds, glaze and fragments of inscriptions caught one's eye, so that it was difficult to do things at the required speed to get us to the ferry by 10 am. However we got there by eleven and crossed without any bother. (I find I've left out the most exciting part which was our explorations of the previous day. Now read on.) The Tell el Amarna tombs are all cut in the cliffs which isolate the bay from the high desert. Many were left unfinished when their owners followed Akhenaten's successor back to Thebes, but all had been ambitiously designed, and many still retain scenes of court and daily life which have been reproduced from copies time without number. It is rather discouraging to be unable to recognise many scenes and says much for the Davies' patience and perseverance that they could see as much as they did.[101] Then we acquired donkeys and started up the royal wadi, where Akhenaten's burial place was found in a side valley years ago. The approach up the broad and unusually flat-bottomed valley is magnificent; there is also the same feeling that one is in an enormous domed building, reverberating from the sound of men's voices. Perhaps we rode for an hour, when we came to the obscure side valley which Akhenaten had wisely chosen for his tomb. Pendlebury has trenched it recently but that method has left his chances on a 50–50 basis. It had already transpired that the key for the tomb was not available, so we merely lunched at the entrance and turned back, but not before S. [Starkey] had picked up his usual piece of Akhenaten's carved granite sarcophagus – he already has a good collection and returns them now and again to the EES [Egypt Exploration Society]. Back over the high desert which acts like champagne to me. It was dusk before we reached the plain again and we made our way over to the workmen's village, where many symmetrically planned houses are surrounded by an enclosure wall. Too dark by then to do more and then we rejoined the car, leaving tired donkeys and donkey boys behind us. Dinner was 'al fresco' that night and then to bed as mentioned above.

Mellawi to Cairo next day was uneventful, we made good time leaving M. at 1 pm and getting to Mena Ho. [House] at 8 pm. I found money running short so went on with Ba to Cairo (who was determined to stay at Shepheard's) and I actually slept at Cecil Ho. [House] (bed and break[fast] 6/–) though I did have a very fine dinner at Shepheard's that night, and we were thrilled to find ourselves in the midst of rehearsal for the Russian Ball the next night. There they all were, just such a crowd as we see in London, the flotsam of handsome women and tired men who happened to be cast up in Cairo. They sang all Ba's favourites and were preparing to sing the Boatman's Song[102] when we left, against a background of white paper sails.

I spent the next morning pleasantly in the Museum and then I trammed out to Mena Ho. and met the others for lunch (Ba taking the day off quietly) – the new swimming pool was most tempting and I should have succumbed if we had not had an appointment with Bill Smith to see the Reisner dig.[103] Rather too full of a lavish lunch we set forth but soon forgot all about it in the excitement of those lovely tombs Yenbu, Mor-s-ankh and so on, which I needn't describe to you. We were then conducted to the classic tea and found the room full of ladies, two were good imitations of Lady P. in war paint. Toward the middle of tea (now this is the exciting part) Mrs Smith (Bill's mother) said: 'Was it your mother who came out to see us 2 yrs ago?' I said 'Yes' and she said 'Oh we did so enjoy her.' I thought it pretty good that she should remember you out of all the crowd. Then Bill Smith came over and said 'Oh! that must be why your name is so familiar to me!' You certainly made a great impression in a few minutes. Mrs R. [Reisner][104] I thought very charming, she says I must dine next time I go through – she is a g[rea]t friend of Sir H. [Henry Wellcome] and I am to send her the drawing of our emblem. He [Reisner] did his daily constitutional after tea (46 times up and down the concrete makes a mile) with an admiring bodyguard of his sec.,

Starks, Leslie and I walking in step. Even an imminent dinner party did not prevent him from outlining his theory of early migrations in the Nile valley and he would not let us go till he had finished his song and dance.

Into Cairo that night for dinner at an Arab restaurant, not too inspiring, then the others went on to a music hall show and [I] went back for a marvellous bath.

Actually got off only an hour after schedule next day (6th), reached the canal 1.30 pm to find our usual spring broken.

An army man crossed just ahead of us, saying he was glad we were behind to rescue him if things went wrong. As it happened, when we reached Hassana there was no sign of him, so after waiting an hour we were just ringing up the authorities when he arrived worn out and black from head to foot. He had stuck in a sandhill and burnt out his clutch trying to get out, so that he had to drive on without floorboards, hence the dirt. Hassana to Auja without mishap, and there we stopped to see Harris' dig and the papyri. The latter are spectacular rolls covered with large clear letters partly destroyed by white ants. One of the best texts is the IVth book of Virgil, with crib apparently, it is maddening not to have something more obscure. Both churches are well preserved on the mound and there are many points of interest about the dig. Next yr they intend to settle at Abda, which is inaccessible by car, 4 mls walk every time to get there. Terry [Colt] is due any day now after her visit to Oliver Myers at Armant. The baby is in New York. Had tea with Harris and he motored me as far as Beersheba, so had a chance to hear all the gossip. At Beersheba we all crowded onto the V8 (as Ba was going on to J. [Jerusalem]) and made ourselves most comfortable on top of the luggage. Slept comfortably all the way home. That is the luxurious way to motor, stretched out on mattresses covered by rugs and free to gaze at the stars and the moon.

Work much interrupted by hail storms, quite drastic, but I have plenty to do with patients, skulls, drawing and reports. [...] Miss Gardner comes to do elephant this week, but don't think I shall go to Bethlehem. [...]

[20 March 1936; handwritten: PEF/DA/TUF/265]

Tell Duweir
March 20. 1936.

My Darling Mà,
Your various letters have arrived, including the one containing sound advice to go to Egypt, this was acted upon by telepathy, and your written words were a mere confirmation of what I knew you'd say!

Quite an amusing week. Charles' [Inge's] parents came down on Sat. A charming and typical clerical couple, and his nice young sister stayed a night or two. On Sunday the Garstang family came 'en masse', such visits are always instructive. I always wonder what they say when they go away. Then on Tuesday I went to Jerusalem with Pummell in the new truck, to get my stopping refilled, and made it an opportunity to take Taman Salamah to the doctor and show her Jerusalem. All this without brother's knowledge, who is a bit of a martinet as far as she is concerned.

It was a memorable day and we thoroughly enjoyed it. She'd never even seen Beit Jibrin, so her wonder at Hebron and Jerusalem was great. She clung tightly to me all the time but was not overawed to the extent of failing to enjoy herself, once the rather sinister machinations of the doctor were over. It was difficult to know what to do with her at lunch time so I took her to the Fast and asked Mrs Fast to help me out. Who should we meet there just setting out for Auja but Harris and Terry and their crowd. She was looking just the same, and the cream of the day was to see her and Taman sitting on 2 high stools at the bar gossiping away most merrily. Then one of the Fast minions approached and said 'A table has been reserved for the lady' and we went along to find a table all laid with folded napkin and shiny glass for Taman in the private dinner room. We left her sitting there, looking rather worried by all this magnificence, if I hadn't stopped them they would have served all the lunch, but that would have been too disconcerting, as it was she ate little of the macaroni and beans that they brought her. We took her to the Mt of Olives to see the view and Pummell escorted her to the Suk to buy a coloured handcherchief [sic], to the astonishment of the whole city. The sight of an Englishman escorted [sic – escorting] a Bedawy girl (who clung to his arm all the way!) is rare even in the motley street contents of the Old City.

Went back via Bethlehem where Miss Gardner is already at work and got home by sunset, which enabled Taman to cook brother's dinner, without added reproaches as to its lateness. However he was unexpectedly mild, so a good day was had by all.

The truck is just off, so no time for more. Mrs Garstang asked after you and so did Mrs Richmond, whom I saw in Jerusalem for a few minutes. [...]

[P.S.] I have knitted a cap (passed as wearable by all) and am starting a jumper. Who'd have thought it!

[26 March 1936; handwritten: PEF/DA/TUF/266]

Tell Duweir
March 26.

Darling Mà,

By the time you get this I expect there will only be another fortnight's actual work, then the usual time clearing up and I suppose close down about the end of the month. I expect I shall come home prosaically, as Ba's friend Michael Shaw-Stuart is coming out to travel round and go home with him. It would be good if I could fit in Crete for once. However we shall see.

Ba has gone off to T.J [Transjordan?] today to order the bricks for the house, very exciting, he will get going on it at end of April. Gerald has had a week at Jerash stepping into Horsfield's[105] shoes, he will have to take up the appointment in July, so no G. at the exhibition. Woe unto the Jebusites, I can't realise in the least, after all these years. [...]

Torczy [Torczyner] down today with Mrs, who was brave enough to come again. He asked most tenderly after you and said he had had 2 letters from you in good German. Mr Uribe[106] (one of Sir H's right hand men) is here for the night, he brought me messages from Mrs Reisner. Terry stayed Monday night, in marvellous form quite her old self, we spent an hilarious evening. Mortimer Wheeler[107] is due next week, so we are flooded with visitors. [...]

[2 April 1936; handwritten: PEF/DA/TUF/267]

T.D. [Tell Duweir]
Ap. 2.

Darling Mà,

[...] We went bathing at Askelon [Ashkelon] last Friday, it was marvellously warm, could not help thinking of you all in the cold with pity!

Well, this week brought the long expected visit from H.E. [His Excellency, Sir Arthur Wauchope]. Last Sunday there was a dress rehearsal with an ADC [aide-de-camp] timing things with a stop watch, but his efforts seemed rather feeble to judge by the result. HE and 'guests' were due at 1.30, on Tuesday. We had all got our jobs clear and had plenty to do between our own lunch at 12 and his arrival. At 12.45 I was seeing to the lunch for police escort, when the shout when [sic – went] up 'The cars are coming'; sure enough a string of 5 were on the way, poor Starks nearly had a heart attack, trying to [break][108] exchange his old clothes for clean and appeared with khaki shirt, old, grey flannel coat and waistcoat, (very respectable) brown trousers (most dilapidated) and shoes from Qubeibeh. He told them they were much too early and would have to wait for lunch, which they did, while Gerald and I hurriedly laid the table, just vacated by members of the expedition with their mouths full. They had cold turkey (which had died opportunely the day before), ham, salad, charlotte russe, but Starks forgot about the coffee so they did not have that. Had arranged our best things in the storeroom including the trepanned skulls,[109] so the place looked quite good. The party came through the ayada [clinic] and I was able to ventilate a grievance at length about LIGA's[110] box, a long story like Pandora's not worth entering into here. It was cold and blowy so they made a swiftish survey of the Tell and got off about 3.30, when we all breathed a sigh of relief, and blew the work off for the rest of the day in celebration. Went for a lovely walk with Ba and found strange new flowers.

REM. Wheeler has been here some days, good company, but I still can't quite revise my original impression. J.H. Iliffe with Joan Crowfoot and Miss Seton-Williams,[111] straight from the delights of the Petrie camp spent the weekend. On Saturday night we sang the dear old ballads[112] [...]

[14 April 1936; handwritten: PEF/DA/TUF/269]

Hotel Fast, Jerusalem
Ap. 14.

Darling –
I have at last braced myself up to have my eye done, and go tomorrow at 11.30 for Sir John [Strathearn] to do his worst! Afterwards I shall go straight down to Jericho to take a look at Ba and stay Thurs. night.

To go back to the beginning, spent a hectic last few days finishing off the list, brought it up yesterday and phoned up Iliffe, who met me here and we fixed up dates under the genial influence of 'gin and it'. Dined with them last night, and spent my usual morning early at the hosp[ital] where everyone is terribly nice to me. Museum at 11, where I looked through the new scarab book and gossiped here and there.

Col. Clarke turned up from Jericho with Dr Olga Feinburg,[113] who has Ba in charge, so lunched with them and heard the latest which is still not good. He is not picking up weight as he should and the Dr is not satisfied. 7% more oxygen at Jericho than anywhere else, food is scrumptious there and complete rest, so what is to be done? Shall see how things are myself, but he will have to give up the London Season.

Had Bill and Eleanor [Elinor Shaw] to tea, and afterwards called on the Torczyner's who were full of messages to you. The fourth vol. is now on its way to you of the Bible! They sent me back with roses and 2 detective stories which are always welcome at the Fast.

Starks is by way of coming up tonight with the Bishop of Portsmouth, who stayed 2 nights at Duweir. He is rather wet and still seems oppressed by the fact that he's a Bish. Perhaps he will get over it in time.

All quite quiet and well behaved here – the place full of tourists, largely German, though they don't bring in much grist to the mill. [...]

[23 April 1936; handwritten: PEF/DA/TUF/270]

Ap. 23.

Dearest Mà,
To continue – the eye business was very mild under Strathearn's hands, but have to go back every four days to be douched again down the lachrymeal sac. Went straight off afterwards to Jericho, where I found Ba very comfortable and well looked after. Only other person there was Tulloch of the Dead Sea Concession.[114] Went down to Callia to bathe, the smell (sulphur, I'm told!) is awful and the beach and huts exclusively in use by brawny Jews. However it was cool in the water and pleasant driving back.

Ba took me back to J. [Jerusalem] the next day, and Terry came down with Charles, Holbrook [Bonney] and I to camp in the evening, Ba returning to Jericho. The week has been hectic! Division took place on Sunday night till midnight! And then on Monday, we have again got a very generous share. Tuesday went up for my 2nd treatment and for more work in the Museum. Gerald was up for his lecture to the POS [Palestine Oriental Society] so we dined together. Pere Vincent came down and sent you many messages. He arrived in the middle of the division!

Ba was up with Tulloch on their way to Port Said on Wed. He was very tired indeed and could not do the evening we had planned at the K.D. [King David]. It was disappointing to find him so easily tired after all these weeks. I came down here late that night, and am just off again to Gaza, where we have an awful day ahead. Lunch with Sheykh Abd el Megid, and dinner with Sheykh Freyr – hope to get in a bathe before which will put me in fettle for the festivities!

Shall sail D.V. [God willing] on the 5th spending the night of the 4th at Megiddo if possible, so should be home about 12th. [...]

[8 May 1936; handwritten: PEF/DA/TUF/271]

British School
Athens.
May. 8th.

Dearest Mà,

The last few days in camp were pretty hectic, putting things away and clearing up generally. Luckily I was able to stay till Tuesday, the day of sailing and catch a 10.12 train from Artuf which got me to Haifa soon after 1 pm. The Windsor Hotel man met me, with a note from Desmond [Tufnell], saying how sorry he was that he couldn't come as he himself was sailing for Alex[andria] at the same time. Boutagy at the hotel said there was no time to waste and that I must hurry to the boat, so he came with me and got my ticket and saw me through the customs. Just stepping aboard when I heard a great booming, and there was Desmond looking too devastating in white and <u>covered</u> with medals – ships all in port at Haifa to meet Negus[115] who arrives on Friday.

So we fought our way through crowds of fat Polish Hebrews and found a quiet corner in the 1st Smoking. Heard his side of the Dickson controversy,[116] and talked heartily till it was time to sail and D. left in the Durban launch.

The *Kosciuczynski*, English built, is a good boat, clean and comfortable, but Gawd the people on it had to be seen to be believed. They talk about too many Jews emigrating to Palestine, but what about the ones going out – quite as many it seemed. Their only saving grace was that they sang rather jolly choruses most of the day.

Two days on board, amusing Polish food not at all bad, and arrived at Piraeus by 4 pm yesterday. Drove straight here and called on the Paynes, only to find that he poor man is mortally ill with blood poisoning and is hardly expected to recover. Found they could put me up at the British School, and then called on the Petrocochinos, who were having an identical tea party to one I attended there 6 yrs ago. [...]

Sallied forth with some young man this morning, called at the German School (Mr Karo is travelling to Crete tonight and I may join him) and then on to the Nat. Mus. [National Museum] where who should be walking up the steps but Mrs Horsfield.[117] So we sat on a bench together and I told her how utterly unsuited and useless G. [Gerald Harding] would be for post of Inspector in T. J. [Transjordan] (oh yeah!) and we both said how good it all was. Then we spent the morning going round together and very pleasant it was. At midday went to the tourist office Olympus who had ensnared me on the boat and have booked a return to Crete, leaving tonight and coming back next Thurs. arriving on Friday morning which will enable me to catch an Italian steamer that same night up the Dalmatian coast, to Trieste. Arrive there on the 20th and go on to Vienna where I've had a warm invitation to stay with the von Poradas, and go up to the mountains with them. Too good to miss as it is well on the way home. Home D.V. about the end of the month, rather wicked as there will be much to do.

Everything very cheap here; 520 drachmas to the £1 and a tip of 2 D. [drachma] is quite thankfully received. Shall just take the pig [meaning unclear] to Crete and leave the suitcase at the agency. Shall stay at Villa Ariadne if they've got room. [...]

[12 May 1936; handwritten: PEF/DA/TUF/272]

Villa Ariadne
Knossos,
May 12th 1936. (Heraklion) Crete

Darling Mà,
To continue – I fixed up at the agents before leaving Athens that I would come back to Piraeus on Friday next and leave that same night for Trieste via Corfu and all the funnies up the Adriatic coast. Reach Trieste on the 20th, 7 am and can catch the Vienna express at nine so that [I] shall be in Vienna that night, where my address will be:

c/o Miss Von Porada,[118] (Mrs Barnardo may know what her parents are) Plassgasse 8. Wien IV.

Shall try not to be lured to stay long there as I <u>must</u> get home! Called on Harris Colt but he was out before leaving and got a car down to Piraeus for 120 dr. about 4s/9d, the same man fixed me up and when I said 'can you get me one for 150 dr like last time', he said 'Oh! I think we can manage something cheaper than that now' so he must have thought me rather meshkin [poor]!

People were pouring on to the little cockleshell *Chios* at the port, it seemed miraculous that the ship did not sink under the weight. A miniature saloon and funny wooden bunks with yellow curtains and scarlet blankets. It was easy to pick out Karo and his party and I accosted him, he speaks perfect English and introduced me to his followers and friends, a handsome couple, Baron and Baroness von Stettin, 2 delightful German Protestant sisters Von Bulow and de Bunsen, and his secretary Fraulein Vink, and last BUT NOT LEAST <u>STROPCHEN</u> v. small and elegant, not quite a year old, parents from German Consulate at Corfu but grandparents from Vienna. Was wearing a blue coat, but changed in the chill of the evening to a green one, g[rea]t argument as to which colour suited her best!. [...]

To my astonishment dinner was almost Ritzian, soup, fish, chicken, soufflé, strawberries, coffee, which I ate in rather gloomy silence with teeth-sucking Cretans. But by next meal the Germans had sweetly arranged for me to eat with them. At seven we arrived at Canea [Chania] on the N. coast of the island, and all landed later to look round. Such a joy to see relatively clean houses, what's more women and children were actually sweeping the narrow cobbled alleys with brooms, hard and firmly, as if their lives depended on it. Walked round the Venetian ramparts and penetrated into the fort, lovely mountains behind the town with belated streaks of snow. [Illegible, marked-out words] Coffee by the side of the quay, where salmon coloured caiques alternated with sky blue ones in an orderly row. From the masts floated brown fishing nets, hung out to dry. Rethymno was the next port of call, Venetian castle juts out to sea on a highish crag. Made for it as soon as I landed and climbed up past the prison, where the inmates were singing a melodious chant in no uncertain voice. Inside the ramparts are much ruined buildings, and few hovels where the ladies of the town hang out conveniently close to the barracks. Like the streets they looked clean and nice in white dresses with lavish supply of gold teeth. Dashed down to the boat and got on board by the skin of my teeth. By then the sun was sinking and we glided on a glassy sea past a regular coast line indented like the prongs of a comb. About 7.30 we crept in past the new mole at Heraklion into the old Venetian harbour, beyond which twinkled the lights of the town. A launch full of communists fetched off a leader with much shouting and clenched-hand salute, and soon we heard the cheers of his supporters as he landed. We got off in a leisurely way, I was still under the wing of Prof. Karo, but thought it rather miraculous, when a man accosted me and asked if I was for Villa Ariadne,[119] got into his car and went on to the hotel to see what news had come for Karo about Payne. It was the worst; he had died, and I took the news on to Hutchinson at the Villa, about 5kms outside the town. Drove up a trim avenue to Youlbury between hedges of honeysuckle, overpoweringly sweet. A figure came out to meet me, Hutchinson, of course they thought I was someone else, but welcomed me most charmingly. There is a delightful Miss Eccles here, and Mr H's mother, a most trying old girl, who would drive me mad in a week.

The garden is a mixture of Youlbury[120] and Sidholme sunk garden, lovely palms and pines, great banks of bourgainvillia [sic], and red geraniums! But the honeysuckle takes a lot of beating. The house is solidly Victorian in and out, the builder misunderstood the plans and built in metres instead of yds so it is rather large and money gave out before the 2nd story was built, which is as well as it withstands earthquakes better. The bedrooms are in the basement, nice and cool but dark.

Mr H. gave me the whole morning at the Palace [Knossos], 70 percent is reconstruction in concrete and paint, so that there is a curious effect of unreality. The columns tapering to the base look strange after Egypt, they are painted red in imitation of the wood originals. There is some possibility that the wood used was imported cedar of Lebanon. I can hardly describe the palace in details but suffice it to say that only a fraction has been done of the royal area and nothing at all of the domestic and humbler quarters of the city, which spread over at least two adjoining hills. Only 3 tombs have ever been excavated here, 'Double Axe', 'Royal tomb at Isopata' and 'Temple Tomb', so the marvel is not what has been done but what still remains to do. Trial pits are the rage and originally one sunk on the palace site missed everything as it fell in the middle of the central court.

That night Mr H. went off to Athens to help with poor Paynes's affairs. He was only 32 and very brilliant, they diagnosed his case as rheumatism and massaged his leg. It turned out to be latent blood poisoning and general sepsis set in, he died in under the week. No one has any faith in the Greek doctors, the only ones allowed to practise here.

Yesterday (11th) spent the morning at Candia Museum, quite the gloomiest building, especially now that 3/4ths are pulled down and all cases are squeezed into the remaining 1/4th. Cheered up when I saw some old friends, and had an amusing time looking at the original palace frescoes, which are minute frags. [fragments] of the reconstructed whole, which has been done regardless of probability by Guilléron [Gilliéron].[121] The experts all look on it as perfect scandal, though none dare say anything to Sir A. [Evans]. Met a charming Italian woman Sig. Bendi at the Mus. [Museum] who is doing the Hagia Triada [ancient Minoan site] stuff and had a long talk. She is really employed in the Vatican Library.

After tea was given the keys of the sherd room at the Pal. [Palace] and told to help myself, 'embarras de choix' as the frags are lovely.

Miss Eccles very charmingly bicycled to Candia to arrange about my sharing a car with the Italians to Phaestos [Phaistos], but theirs was full, so providentially the long awaited Argentis turned up with a Mr Nicholls from the Legation, so I am going with them. They are amusing companions and as he is Greek, he'll tackle the driver. More on my return. [...]

Prof. Perrier is an amusing little man, face and figure rather like a clean shaven H.G. [Wells] with a voice uncannily like his, the same little trick of putting in an odd word – in his case – 'qia'. He and Miss Barti showed us the whole site in detail, laying stress on the fact that they had done nothing in the way of reconstruction, only preservation of what was already there. The swing of the pendulum. Plan very like Knossos, situation more imposing. We tried for Hagia Triada, but got lost and the driver became homesick. Went to Cortina [Gortyna] on the way home, and saw the earliest and longest Greek inscription known, the Laws of Cortina, set up in a Roman theatre. V. nice Byzantine church set in cypresses. [Mount] Ida was even more enchanting on the way home, it had rained off and on, bursts of sunlight in the valley and swift veils of white cloud, shrouding the mountain, <u>were magnificent</u>. It had rained heavily at Candia, and we got back to find a general strike fixed for next day in sympathy with Macedonian tobacco pickers. These strikes seem to follow me round! Anyhow it knocked out the possibility of going to Mallia and Gournia, so in the morning I showed the Argentis and Mr Nicholls round the Palace – ha! ha! in the drizzle. Afterwards exasperated by rumours of no boats, no cars, no sights, he and I set off in the rain to walk up Mt Iuktas [Iouktas] (2540 ft) which he did in great style though I got no higher than the 2nd peak. Came home soaked to the skin but full of the virtuous feeling that the afternoon had not been wasted. Next morning the Mayor's car fetched us and went on board the *Acropolis*. The Argentis motored to Canee [Chania] as she is a bad sailor, but I didn't want to take chances of missing the boat at Athens, having forfeited one fare owing to the strike. Quite calm at Canee and we had been invited to dine with the Argentis at Mdme Venizuelos' house, so drove up to a lovely villa in a scented garden outside the town. [...] The housekeeper gave us dinner and then we went back to the harbour and rowed out across it through heavy black water shot with town lights to the ship which looked gay and transformed by the night. Pleasant morning on deck, reached Piraeus 2 pm and went straight to Athens. [...]

The *Rodi* has cancelled its call here, so I have to go ordinary route Brindisi – Venezia – Trieste, v. damnable, leaving tonight at 6 pm. Vienna on Wed. morning. [...]

[22 May 1936; handwritten: PEF/DA/TUF/273]

Plösslgasse 8
Vienna IV.
May 22.

Darling Mà,

[...] I am leaving here on Tuesday at 9.55 am and should be home sometime on Wednesday. Very many thanks for wiring.

Well to go back to where I left off:

Reached Athens under the wing of Jack Nicholls as I told you and went that evening to his wife's cocktail party 'mastica' in a new honeymoonish flat on the slopes of Mt Lycabettus. The most dramatic view of the Acropolis and Hymettus beyond, all Corps Diplomatique ladies talking a variety of languages at the party and a sprinkling of attachés. Walked back to hotel later and to bed. Next morning went up to Acropolis by tram and spent a peaceful morning in the sun moving from point to point just looking without being told anything. So restful. Met a Swiss Prix de Rome[122] girl on the way out and we lunched together. From what I saw of her work she is a good artist – she is on her Wanderjahr [year abroad]. Car at 4 to Piraeus and the usual formalities on to the boat, *Celio*, Lloyd Triestino. Lovely 3 berth cabin to myself (had been De Luxe on Cretan boat owing to Legation wire pulling!) and very few people on board. Young American Jew returning from 9 mths in Zionist Communist Colony had much to say on failure of the system. There was also nice German woman married to a Director of Felt Factory in Brno returning from a visit to her sister in Turkey, who is the wife of Prof Bittel who does the German Govt. excav[ation] at Boghaz Koi [Boğasköy], wheels within wheels you see! Luckily she talked no English so I really had a chance to polish my German and towards the end of the journey I got quite fluent. Enjoyed the few hours in Trieste taking in recent reactions and all mass suggestions it seems to be. Spent comfortable night in train. Side of carriage to myself is all I need, but we got quite hysterical with laughter over the fast recurring frontiers with officials in different uniforms in almost continuous procession. Ate bags of cherries (strawberries, wild and garden on sale all over Trieste at 2 lr a kilo) and was brought hot coffee at 6.30. Arrived Trieste [at] 9 and said farewell to Frau Waldhör who was most anxious I should go on to Brno with her.

Edith [Porada] nobly met me in car and we came here which is a colossal mansion, garden back and trees in front, all among the Rothschild habitations.

The rooms are large with parquet, and brocade, but have not been done up for a long time, which is all to the good as the faded blue silk in my bedroom is far pleasanter than a new one would be. Lots of lovely plumbing all to myself. The household consists of Edith, her sister now away, and her father who returned yesterday from one of his frequent business trips. The mother is I suppose dead and there is a dragon like old governess in musical comedy style, who goes everywhere with Edith in the evenings. The retainers are sweet, a man who waits in white cotton gloves and drives the car, and an attractive housemaid who washes and irons without being told to, and a fat cook whose open strawberry tarts are a dream!

'Papi' is still youngish and energetic with a passion for hunting and 'le sport'; his study is hung with antlers and trophies, and all his spare time is spent up in the mountains.

The first morning we spent at the Museum where the tapestries and objets d'art are unbelievably lovely and actually well shown. It was difficult to do justice to the pictures, but did enjoy the Breughels and the Durers.

Walked at Schonbrunn before lunch and afterwards slept till nearly four. Tea at Demels, supper Gunters[?] and we wandered looking at shops. 26 Austrian shillings to the £ so things are pretty cheap and quite good. Evening to a comedy at Volkstheater, Hans Moser in 'Mein Sohn, der Minister'. Delighted to find I understood quite a bit, enough to enjoy the show, which would do quite well on the English stage, here it is a translation from the French, but the Moser man is really in the front rank.

Thursday was Ascension Day, everyone en fête and lovely warm sun. In the morning Edith took in Cook's Tour of old Vienna, consisting of a French and Swiss youth and myself, it is easy to see the genial ghosts of Schubert and the child Mozart in the clean and tidy alleyways, we looked into echoing country yards with wrought iron gates, we penetrated the empty halls of the old University and tiptoed into many churches where services was on and choirboys singing like larks. The nicest of these was perhaps the church of the fishermen which stands on the brink of the new dry river bed of the Danube. We motored out to Leopoldshof in the woods, where we drank coffee with a thousand others in a terrace, just like the days of Prague. 'Papi' was in to lunch, also the young French man and in the Schwartzenberg Gdns and the Belvedere among the holiday crowds, and I hope I felt Viennese. That evening a cinema and supper afterwards at an Italian restaurant. Friday morning I had my hair done and shopped successfully on my own. Bought a dress and hat (£3, and 12/–), but perhaps on the whole there is not much difference in price. For cheaper clothes, it is only 'exclusive models' that are worthwhile to buy here. [...]

[8 June 1936; typescript copy: PEF/DA/TUF/274]

June 8th, 1936.

Dear Edith [Porada],
I hasten to send you two photographs of the haematite cylinder seal, because we are very curious to have your ideas on the subject. I purposely leave out our suggestions for date to have your independent opinion. Anything that you can tell us as to the symbolism of the various objects and figures, and their frequency in cylinder seal art will be much appreciated. Both Gadd and Sidney Smith have seen the photos and are very vague, Frankfort[123] will be here tomorrow so we shall hear what he has to say.

I have given your name and address to my bookseller who will send you Frankfort's book as soon as published. Meanwhile I shall hear news of it tomorrow.

Can you let me have the Albright pamphlet back soon please? Am not forgetting the other questions to answer but send this at once, as we're thrilled for your reply.

Love to Hilda and Fraulein, in all haste from

[Edith Porada's eight-sided handwritten response, dated 18 June 1936, provides many detailed references and insights on the photographs of the seal in question, and asks a number of specific questions relating to Frankfort's opinions, as well as past findings at Tell el-'Ajjul: PEF/DA/TUF/275].

[2 July 1936; typescript copy: PEF/DA/TUF/276]

July 2nd. 1936

My dear Edith,
My behaviour in not answering your marvellous long letter of information is most reprehensible, but life has really been very hectic and I wanted to be in a position to answer your questions. I have also routed out an old photograph of the 'horse' for your friend.

We were all most interested in what you had to say about the cylinder seal. It was the fullest commentary that we have been able to extract from anyone so far. I will find out from Starks exactly what Frankfort said but was not present when he examined the photos.

You will be sad to hear that his cylinder seal book will not be out till autumn 1937, so you have a long time to wait.[124]

With regard to the (Gaza) horse, which I excavated myself at Tell el Ajjul, photographs are published in Ancient Gaza I, plates VIII–X, though letterpress on that is practically nil.

Miss D.M.A. Bate[125] of the Natural History Museum, South Kensington examined the bones and took certain measurements though she made no definite report. I spoke to her on the 'phone and she kindly says that if Professor Auschler will write to her, she will give him all information in her power, though she does not consider that there is much to say.

As for the actual bones, I believe they are now in the new Archaeological Institute [Institute of Archaeology, London], that is being organized in the recently acquired house in Regents Park. I should think that it will be possible to get access to them in the Autumn.

To go back to Frankfort, he says that the seal should be placed about 1500 BC or just before, and Starks agrees with him in this. Otherwise he did not vouchsafe any further information.

I will send you my own copy of Ancient Gaza I, which you can return at your convenience (that means to say no hurry at all from my point of view) and I am also posting you the Arabic Grammar I promised you and a little word book if I can find one. These latter are for you to keep.

The Exhibition opens on Thursday, and Mr Starkey gave his first lecture here last Friday, so we are all in the midst of things. Besides I am crusading all I can for the Arab cause, which is much misunderstood here, and trying to fit in cocktails and dinners as well. […]

Will you remember me to your father and the hound, and give my love to Hilda and Fraulein. Political situations in Palestine have not so far knocked next season's plans on the head, and naturally we ourselves are all the more keen about it, as it would be really bad policy to desert the district just when things are difficult. So don't give up hope completely just yet:

Love from
[Olga]

Notes

1 Ussishkin 2014, 33.
2 Starkey 1933, 1934, 1935, 1936, 1937a, 1937b; Inge 1938. Preliminary reports have helped identify the year in which some of Olga's letters were composed, as the date written on them sometimes consisted only of the month and day.

3 Ussishkin 2014.

4 Melman 2020, Chapter 4.

5 Sir Charles Marston selected the ewer as the basis for an official expedition emblem. Adaptations of its 'tree of life' symbol were drafted by Olga, and Marston chose the final version. It was embroidered onto an expedition flag by Starkey's sister Olive, and used on the cover of subsequent *Lachish* volumes (Wendy Slaninka, pers. comm., based on Starkey family correspondence).

6 For a full appraisal of the discovery, study, publication and readings of the Lachish Letters, see Zammit 2016.

7 Hasan 'Awad had begun working with Harding on Petrie's expeditions, and became his protégé and lover for nearly two decades (Melman 2020, 143, n. 49). It is somewhat surprising that Olga Tufnell's letters to her mother do not mention Hasan 'Awad. There is, however, a reference to Hasan 'Awad's discovery of the Lachish ostraca in a letter from Olga to Marjorie Starkey: 'The main excitement is the discovery of the ostraca … All from the outer gate tower, Hasan Awad was the lucky finder. Ever since Starks and Gerald have been fiddling about trying to find other fragments …' (letter of 26 February 1935; Starkey family correspondence, courtesy of Wendy Slaninka).

8 Three more inscribed sherds were found in the sixth and final season (1937–8) and were not published in the *Lachish Letters* volume (Torczyner et al. 1938).

9 The other photographer may have been S.W. Michieli, according to unpublished reports (Abigail Zammit, pers comm.), or perhaps S.J. Zweig/Schweig (see note 35 below).

10 Macdonald 2005, 96–7.

11 This paragraph documents the interpretations of Starkey, Torczyner and expedition colleagues, which were not without controversy. Also see Ussishkin 2014, 375–82 for a more recent overview. A reassessment of the ostraca carried out by Abigail Zammit (2016) provides further details on context, reception and new readings.

12 Torczyner et al. 1938, 15–18.

13 Also see Torczyner et al. 1938, 62–73. The reading of 'Achbor' was revised to 'Coniah' by Torczyner in his Hebrew edition of all 21 ostraca in 1940. See Tur-Sinai 1987, 90. For further analysis see Zammit 2016.

14 Despite this linking of Tell ed-Duweir with Lachish through Letter IV, this was not enough evidence on its own to categorically prove this identification (Thomas 1940). A wider assessment of archaeological evidence was required to positively identify Lachish with Tell ed-Duweir (Abigail Zammit, pers comm.)

15 Garfinkel 2016.

16 Starkey 1936, 187.

17 Tufnell 1953, 55. Also see Chapter 6, letter of 15 March 1933 and note 58.

18 For an overview of Marston's interpretations of discoveries at Tell ed-Duweir between 1932 and 1934 (prior to the Lachish Letters discovery), see Marston 1934, 251–62. Marston was quick to include the discovery of the Lachish Letters in his subsequent book (Marston 1937).

19 First published as 'Hebrew inscriptions at Tell ed-Duweir', *The Times*, 18 February 1935, 11. See Zammit 2016, 51–4 for initial publication and media related to the Lachish Letters discovery.

20 According to Olga Tufnell, the London exhibitions for the Tell ed-Duweir expedition first took place at the Palestine Exploration Fund, and then subsequently at the Wellcome Historical Medical Museum (Olga Tufnell interviewed by Jonathan Tubb, transcript of audiotaped interview, c. 1985).

21 Thornton 2017.

22 Hillel 2019.

23 Erickson-Gini and Oach 2019, 20.

24 Qubeibeh, the village by Tell ed-Duweir.

25 Could be Hamid M., one of Olga's workers, photographed in Figure 6.6.

26 A date early in the 1933–4 season is suggested by the mention of the start of rain and the mention of the outlying spur only investigated in the second season. The Expedition was not formally known as WARENE until the second season.

27 Tufnell 1958, 39, pl. 2.3.

28 Tufnell 1958, 30.

29 Dorothy Garrod had been asked by the British School of Archaeology in Jerusalem in 1929 to investigate the Wadi el-Mughara caves on Mount Carmel as they were in danger of destruction by quarrying.

30 Arabic for 'courtyard'.

31 A folk circle or line dance popular in the Levant. See also letter of 19 April 1935.

32 H.W. Pummell, who was in charge of camp equipment, 1933–8.

33 The Princess Royal, Countess of Harewood (1897–1965), daughter of George V.

34 The 'shrine' in this case is the Late Bronze Age 'Fosse Temple'. Tufnell 1958, 48, 59, 61, 141–5.

35 'Zweig' likely refers to Shmuel Joseph Schweig, Curator of the Photography Department at the Rockefeller Museum, Jerusalem. Schweig was responsible for taking many of the photographs of archaeological excavations on behalf of the Department of Antiquities, Palestine, subsequently used in the galleries of the Rockefeller Museum (Fawzi Ibrahim, Curator, Rockefeller Museum, pers. comm.).

36 Es Sbeita or ancient Sobata. Also referred to as Isbeita or Subeita in Arabic and Shivta in Hebrew. Nabataean-Byzantine site in the Negev where Colt excavated between 1934 and 1936 on behalf of New York University and the British School of Archaeology in Jerusalem. The excavation results were never fully published (Negev 1993, 1404–10). Many of the people mentioned in the letters also visited the site, as evidenced by the Es Sbeita visitors' book, including Olga herself (Erickson-Gini and Oach 2019).

37 Proposals for the building of the Palestine Archaeological Museum in Jerusalem were initiated in 1925. It was in the process of construction at the time this letter was written.

38 Evelyn Tufnell (née Hilder) was the wife of Olga's first cousin Commander Desmond Tufnell, the son of Lionel Charles Gostling Tufnell (Olga's uncle).

39 Likely to be 1934 as tombs under the roadway were reported in the third season preliminary report (Starkey 1935).

40 Funeral anthem from Handel's *Saul*.

41 Possibly Tewfiq Saleh, one of Olga's workers, pictured in Figure 6.6.

42 The Crown Prince of Sweden, Gustav Adolf, later Gustav VI (1882–1973), had married (on the death of his first wife) Lady Louise Mountbatten (1889–1965). They were visiting Palestine accompanied by family members.

43 'Residency' here probably refers to the Persian Residency (Tufnell 1953, 48, 58, 131–40); 'Temple' likely refers to the Late Bronze Age Fosse Temple (Tufnell, Inge and Harding 1940), sometimes referred to in Olga's letters as the 'shrine'.

44 Eleanor Dyott was a new arrival to the camp. She was to marry fellow member William Boyd Kennedy Shaw (see Chapter 6, note 38) in 1936. See Erickson-Gini and Oach 2019, 14, for a short biographical note.

45 Dora Davidson, Olga's mother's sister.

46 Starkey's costume may have been related to the Anglican Bishop of Portsmouth, Dr Frank Partridge, a friend of the Starkeys and visitor to Tell ed-Duweir (see letter of 14 April 1936). Olga's reference to 'his usual Bishop's rigout' and the photograph suggest the bishop's costume was reused several times.

47 Sir Gordon Richards (1904–86), champion flat-race jockey.

48 A well-known brand of brassiere.

49 See note 36 above.

50 C.B. Cochran (1872–1951), theatre impresario especially of vaudeville, known for his 'Young Ladies' troupe.

51 Arabic, plural of Effendi: see Chapter 6, note 42.

52 Arabic, a beautiful young woman, or specifically women who will accompany faithful believers in Muslim Paradise.

53 Water pipe for smoking.

54 See letter of 27 October 1930 and related note.

55 See letter of 13 December 1927 and related note.

56 James Edward Quibell (1867–1935), a former student of Flinders Petrie who worked in Egypt at multiple sites. Chief Inspector of the Delta and Middle Egypt 1899–1904, Chief Inspector at Saqqara, 1904–5, Keeper at the Egyptian Museum 1914–23, and Director of Excavations of the Step Pyramid, 1931–5.

57 Leo Frobenius (1873–1938), German ethnologist and archaeologist who worked mainly in Africa.

58 Dr Elliot David Forster (b. 1905), British medic who served in St Luke's Hospital, Hebron.

59 Not specifically mentioned in Olga's letters are Dr Benjamin Maisler (Mazar), Dr H.L. Ginsberg and Mr S. Yeivin, who came to study the Lachish Letters at the camp-house (Figure 8.6). Prof.

H. Torczyner visited in February 1935 and was subsequently tasked with the publication of *The Lachish Letters* (Starkey 1938, 13; Torczyner et al. 1938). Père Vincent was the first visiting specialist to read some of the Lachish Letters (Starkey 1938, 13).

60   Frank Farrer, Chairman and Managing Director of Villiers Cycle Components for Sir Charles Marston.

61   Eleanor Gardner, Research Fellow at Lady Margaret Hall, Oxford (also see note related to letter of 27 October 1930). Gardner was to resume searching for fossil elephant bones near Bethlehem, which were first identified by Dorothea Bate in 1933. In 1934 Starkey, on hearing of the find so near Tell ed-Duweir, had obtained a concession for the site from the Department of Antiquities and persuaded Sir Henry Wellcome to fund the project under the aegis of the WARENE. Dorothea Bate, who had wanted the site to be her responsibility, had no choice but to comply if she wished to continue excavating. The finds were eventually divided among Sir Henry's private collection and the British Museum (Natural History) (Shindler 2005, 244–52), now known as the Natural History Museum. Also see letter of 8 June 1936 for reference to Dorothea Bate.

62   Dr Immanuel Ben-Dor, also known as Emanuel Ben Dor (1901–69), Israeli archaeologist. Worked for the Department of Antiquities, Palestine, as Museum Librarian, 1939–48; subsequently Deputy Director of the Israel Department of Antiquities and Museums (IDAM), founded 1948.

63   Hubdeh, one of the local women who worked for the Expedition (see Figure 6.5).

64   Sheikh Zuweid in Sinai was also the location of a site excavated by Flinders Petrie.

65   A village near Sheikh Zuweid.

66   Capt. Peter Johnston-Saint, collector for Sir Henry Wellcome, and later Conservator (i.e. curator), Wellcome Historical Medical Museum, London.

67   The Wellcome Research Institution in Bloomsbury, London, opened in 1931. It is now the Wellcome Collection, 183 Euston Road. An exhibition there on discoveries at Lachish was being planned for that summer (Thornton 2017).

68   L.W.G. Malcolm, the former Conservator (i.e. curator) of the Wellcome Historical Medical Museum.

69   Sir Henry Solomon Wellcome (1853–1936), born in the United States. In 1880 he established in Britain, with Silas Burroughs, Burroughs-Wellcome & Company, which sold pharmaceutical products. He became a British subject in 1910. He had a passion for archaeology, excavating at Jebel Moya in Sudan for many years. He established an extensive collection of objects related to medicine. Wellcome, alongside Sir Charles Marston, was an important supporter of the Tell ed-Duweir excavations. The Wellcome Trust was created in 1936 on his death (see Wellcome Foundation 1953; Rhodes-James 1994).

70   Judith Marquet-Krause, excavator of et-Tell, commonly identified with biblical Ai.

71   Tall al-Balatah at Nablus, the site of ancient Shechem.

72   Petrie had applied to the Joint Archaeological Committee of Palestine and Syria for a concession to dig at either of two sites, Jebeleh or Tell Ruweiseh. E.T. Richmond (Director of the Department of Antiquities, Palestine) refused his application as Sir Leonard Woolley had already been given permission to dig in northern Syria under the auspices of the British Museum (Drower 1985, 380).

73   Silver Jubilee celebrations for King George V.

74   Letter IV (Torczyner et al. 1938, 75–87) provided reference to the signals of Lachish, enabling the more secure identification of Tell ed-Duweir as the site of ancient Lachish; Letter III appears to be connected with the book of Jeremiah, mentioning a commander of the army and slaves (Jeremiah 34:7). Torczyner writes: 'it is not only the best preserved of the larger ostraca but certainly the most interesting and important document among the Lachish Letters, and may be considered almost as an authentic chapter of the Holy Scriptures' (Torczyner et al. 1938, 62).

75   Petrie had asked Richmond for permission to renew excavations at Ajjul in the forthcoming season and had received a negative reply to the effect that the site had been excavated beyond the terms of the licence and that the list of objects had not been completed. Later a permit was granted with strict limitations including a prohibition on buying antiquities from dealers (Drower 1985, 380).

76   Sir Charles Marston married his third wife, Mary Battey Bonney, in 1935. She was the mother of expedition member Holbrook V. Bonney.

77   Nevill Arthur Charles de Hirzel Tufnell, Olga's uncle.

78 Olga's grandparents' house.
79 Nickname of John Jolliffe Tufnell, who inherited the estate in 1935. He handed it over in 1971 to his niece, Sarah Micklem, granddaughter of 'Uncle Herzie'.
80 Founded 1921 in Jerusalem by a group of Western scholars including W.F. Albright and J. Garstang. Disbanded in 1948 on the partition of Jerusalem.
81 Petrie's new excavation in Sinai.
82 Tessa Verney Wheeler (1893–1936), Sir Mortimer Wheeler's first wife. An innovative archaeologist who helped to train the young Kathleen Kenyon. The Wheelers, as well as Flinders Petrie, played a key role in the establishment of the Institute of Archaeology, London. This letter refers to Verney Wheeler's election as Chairman of the Executive Committee of the British School of Archaeology in Egypt. She had been a committee member since 1927. Wheeler was subsequently frustrated as the Petries often made major financial decisions without consulting the committee. Vice versa, the Petries complained about 'London' being too high-handed. The committee was disbanded later in 1935 (ending Wheeler's role) and replaced with a smaller body in the Petries' home base of Jerusalem (Carr 2012, 130–1).
83 The year this letter was written is unclear. It was initially considered to date to 1936, but this does not match with the report of first rains or reports of findings of Ramesside material, which predated 1936. Therefore, this letter is tentatively ascribed to 1935.
84 Sir Arthur Wauchope, High Commissioner for Palestine.
85 Dimitri Constantine Baramki (1909–84), Palestinian archaeologist. Worked for the Department of Antiquities, Palestine, excavated at Khirbat el-Mafjar (north of Jericho) 1935–48, later with Robert Hamilton. Curator of the Archaeological Museum of the American University of Beirut from 1948, and then Professor, responsible for developing its archaeology programme.
86 1935–6 was the second season of excavations at Khirbat al-Mafjar, later known as 'Hisham's Palace'. At this time, Baramki was convinced he had found a Christian monastery because of an apse-like structure he had discovered (Donald Whitcomb, pers. comm.). The site was later identified as a palace complex assigned to rulers of the early Islamic Umayyad dynasty (eighth century AD).
87 See letter dated 28 December 1935 which indicates that Richmond Brown ran down and killed a boy in Transjordan while driving. In addition to legal repercussions, financial compensation was probably forthcoming to the boy's family.
88 Harry Torczyner/Naftali Herz Tur-Sinai (1896–1973), Professor of Semitic Languages at the Hebrew University of Jerusalem and first to decipher and publish the Lachish Letters (Torczyner et al. 1938; Tur-Sinai 1987). Member of the Israel Academy of Sciences and Humanities and one of Israel's foremost philologists, instrumental in the revival of Hebrew as a modern language.
89 Lankester Harding was appointed Inspector of Antiquities, Transjordan.
90 Presumably John Jolliffe Tufnell (see n. 79).
91 Reference to the Tomb of Queen Shub'ad, later referred to as Puabi, from the Royal Cemetery of Ur.
92 Robert Scott Lamon (1906–75), surveyor and field assistant for the University of Chicago's Megiddo expedition, 1928–36.
93 Geoffrey M. Shipton (1910–87), draughtsman and assistant recorder for the Megiddo expedition from 1928 into the 1930s. He co-edited publications of the Megiddo expedition, focusing on the pottery sequence.
94 Sir Charles Marston's stepson, son of his third wife, Mary Battey Bonney. He was architect at Lachish following W.K.S. Shaw. He is recorded as in charge of the survey at Tell ed-Duweir in the last three seasons and responsible for the plans published in *Lachish IV* (Tufnell 1958, 9). Holbrook Bonney was an American who joined the Royal Air Force in the Second World War as a navigator (Tufnell 1985, 8).
95 Papyri found at 'Auja al-Hafir (Nessana) included a glossary and fragmentary Latin text of Virgil's *Aeneid*, three New Testament pieces and an early version of the St George legend, ranging in date from the early sixth to late seventh centuries AD (Colt 1962, 131–2; Casson and Hettich 1950, vi).
96 The fashionable Cairo hotel, founded in 1845, destroyed by fire in 1952 and rebuilt in 1957.
97 A reference to Davison's Chamber in the Great Pyramid, discovered by English diplomat and writer on Egyptian archaeology Nathaniel Davison (c. 1736–1809).
98 John Devitt Stringfellow Pendlebury (1904–41), curator of archaeological site at Knossos 1929–34. At the time this letter was written he, together with his wife Hilda, was directing

excavations at Tell el-Amarna for the Egypt Exploration Society. During the Second World War he worked for British Intelligence, and was killed on active service in the Battle of Crete, 1941.

99 See pp. 16–17, 25 and 59–61 for information on the Quftis.

100 Ancient Egyptian pharaoh of the eighteenth dynasty (fourteenth century BC). He built a new capital at Amarna (ancient Akhetaten).

101 Norman and Nina de Garis Davies had spent five years copying scenes in the tombs.

102 The Song of the Old Volga Boatmen, a traditional Russian song.

103 W. (Bill) Stevenson Smith was an American art historian and Egyptologist, working with George Reisner who was excavating at Giza for the Boston Museum of Fine Arts and Harvard University.

104 Mary Putnam Bronson Reisner, wife of George Reisner.

105 George Horsfield (1882–1956), Chief Curator and Inspector of the Transjordan Department of Antiquities 1924/6–36.

106 Major J.S. Uribe, a major in the Ecuadorian army who became one of Henry Wellcome's principal assistants (see Rhodes-James 1994).

107 Sir Robert Eric (Rik) Mortimer Wheeler (1890–1976), husband of Tessa Verney Wheeler (see n. 82 above), archaeologist and museum director. Served in the British army in both world wars, reaching the rank of officer. His early scholarship focused on Roman Britain, especially at Verulamium (modern St Albans). Director of the National Museum Wales, 1920–6, and Keeper of the London Museum, 1926–44. Excavated at a range of sites including Maiden Castle in Dorset and Mohenjo-daro and Harappa in modern Pakistan. Alongside T.V. Wheeler and with the support of Flinders Petrie, he helped found the Institute of Archaeology, London (honorary director from 1934). Wheeler also served as Director-General of the Archaeological Survey of India (1944–8). He continued as part-time professor at the Institute of Archaeology, London, 1948–56, and served as President of the Society of Antiquaries, 1954–9.

108 Vertical lines drawn at top of page with added note: 'excuse these hieroglyphs, wrote the front page without looking at the back … PATTERN FOR MY FIRST JUMPER!!!!'.

109 Jack 1937; Tufnell 1953, 405.

110 Possibly the Czech League of Human Rights (LIGA).

111 Veronica Seton-Williams (1910–92), Australian-born archaeologist, introduced to archaeological fieldwork by the Wheelers, and Egyptology student of Margaret Murray. Worked with Petrie at Sheikh Zuweid, Sinai in 1935, with Garstang at Jericho, and John Waechter at Wadi Dhobai. She worked with Joan du Plat Taylor in Cyprus, and with Joan du Plat Taylor and John Waechter at Coba Huyuk (Sakçe Gözü), Turkey. Seton-Williams joined the Tell ed-Duweir expedition in the final season (1937–8), taking over responsibility for photographic records from Ralph Richmond Brown (Tufnell 1958, 9).

112 Such as the favourite camp song contributed by Starkey:

'Not for the greed of gold,
Nor for the hope of fame,
Not for a lasting heritage,
Nor for a far-flung name.
Rather for making history,
And for some lore of old,
This is our aim and object,
Not for the greed of gold.' (Tufnell 1982, 86).

113 Olga F. Feinberg, a doctor who was later to coordinate 'Operation Magic Carpet' (1949–50), which airlifted thousands of Yemeni Jews to Israel.

114 In 1927 Major Tulloch was granted concession of mineral rights of the Dead Sea, having previously founded the Palestine Potash Company in 1925.

115 A title of the Emperor of Abyssinia, Haile Selassie.

116 John Dickson, former Consul-General of Jerusalem (1890–1906). After his death there was controversy over the amount of his widow's pension.

117 Agnes Horsfield (née Conway), wife of George Horsfield, see note 105 above.

118 Edith Porada (1912–94), art historian and archaeologist, born in Vienna, became a United States citizen in 1944. Associate Professor of Art History and Archaeology, Columbia University, New York, 1958–63; Professor 1963–74, then Emerita. Authority on ancient Near Eastern art, especially seals.

119 The mansion that Sir Arthur Evans had built on his own grounds at Knossos, Crete.

120 Sir Arthur Evans's house at Boars Hill, Oxfordshire.

121 Émile Gilliéron (1850–1924), and his son with the same name, were hired by Sir Arthur Evans to create replicas and reconstructions at Knossos, including many of the famous Minoan frescoes.

122 A French scholarship for arts students to stay in Rome for an extended period.

123 Henri Frankfort (1897–1954), Egyptologist, archaeologist, Orientalist and art historian. Director of Excavations for the Egypt Exploration Society, 1925–9; Field Director of the Oriental Institute of the University of Chicago Iraq Expedition (Diyala), 1929–37; Correspondent, Royal Netherlands Academy of Arts, 1931–44; Director, Warburg Institute, London, 1948–54.

124 The volume by Henri Frankfort, *Cylinder Seals: A Documentary Essay on the Art and Religion of the Ancient Near East*, was not published until 1939.

125 Dorothea Minola Alice Bate (1878–1951), pioneering palaeontologist and archaeozoologist who worked in Cyprus, Malta and Crete. In Palestine she worked with Dorothy Garrod at Mount Carmel in the 1920s and Bethlehem in the 1930s. Worked for the British Museum (Natural History) in London and Tring (now known as the Natural History Museum).

References

Begin, Ze'ev B. 2000. *As We Do Not See Azeka: The Source of the Lachish Letters* (in Hebrew). Jerusalem: Yad Izhak Ben-Zvi.

Carr, Lydia C. 2012. *Tessa Verney Wheeler: Women and Archaeology Before World War Two*. Oxford: Oxford University Press.

Casson, Lionel and Ernest L. Hettich. 1950. *Excavations at Nessana Volume II: Literary Papyri*. Princeton, NJ: Princeton University Press.

Colt, Harris D. 1962. *Excavations at Nessana (Auja Hafir, Palestine) Volume I*. Princeton, NJ and London: Colt Archaeological Institute and British School of Archaeology in Jerusalem.

Drower, Margaret S. 1985. *Flinders Petrie: A Life in Archaeology*. London: Victor Gollancz.

Erickson-Gini, Tali and Ami Oach. 2019. 'The Es Sbaita (Shivta) Visitors Book, 1934–1937: Negev Archaeology in British Mandate Palestine', *Michmanim* 28: 9–22.

Garfinkel, Yosef. 2016. 'The Decauville Light Train at Lachish (1933–1938)', *Strata: Bulletin of the Anglo-Israel Archaeological Society* 34: 165–89.

Hillel, Maayan. 2019. 'Constructing Modern Identity – New Patterns of Leisure and Recreation in Mandatory Palestine', *Contemporary Levant* 4(1): 75–90.

Inge, Charles H. 1938. 'Excavations at Tell ed-Duweir, the Wellcome Marston Research Expedition to the Near East', *Palestine Exploration Quarterly* 70: 80–3.

Jack, James W. 1937. 'The Trephined Skulls from Lachish', *Palestine Exploration Quarterly* 69: 62–6.

Macdonald, Michael C.A. 2005. 'Literacy in an Oral Environment'. In *Writing and Near Eastern Society: Papers in Honour of Alan R. Millard*, edited by Piotr Bienkowski, Christopher Mee and Elizabeth Slater, 49–118. New York and London: T&T Clark.

Marston, Sir Charles. 1934. *The Bible Is True*. London: Eyre and Spottiswoode.

Marston, Sir Charles. 1937. *The Bible Comes Alive*. London: Eyre and Spottiswoode.

Melman, Billie. 2020. *Empires of Antiquities: Modernity and the Rediscovery of the Ancient Near East, 1914–1950*. Oxford: Oxford University Press.

Negev, Avraham. 1993. 'Sobata'. In *New Encyclopedia of Archaeological Excavations in the Holy Land*, edited by Ephraim Stern, 1404–10. Jerusalem: Israel Exploration Society.

Rhodes-James, Robert. 1994. *Henry Wellcome*. London: Hodder & Stoughton.

Shindler, Karolyn. 2005. *Discovering Dorothea: The Life of the Pioneering Fossil-Hunter Dorothea Bate*. London: HarperCollins.

Starkey, James L. 1933. 'A Lecture Delivered at the Rooms of the Palestine Exploration Fund, on June 22nd, 1933', *Palestine Exploration Quarterly* 65: 190–9.

Starkey, James L. 1934. 'Excavations at Tell el Duweir, 1933–1934. Wellcome Archaeological Research Expedition to the Near East (Lecture)', *Palestine Exploration Quarterly* 66: 164–75.

Starkey, James L. 1935. 'Excavations at Tell el Duweir 1934–1935. Wellcome Archaeological Research Expedition to the Near East (Lecture)', *Palestine Exploration Quarterly* 67: 198–207.

Starkey, James L. 1936. 'Excavations at Tell el Duweir, 1935–6. Wellcome Archaeological Research Expedition to the Near East (Lecture)', *Palestine Exploration Quarterly* 68: 178–89.

Starkey, James L. 1937a. 'Lachish as Illustrating Bible History (Lecture)', *Palestine Exploration Quarterly* 69: 171–9.

Starkey, James L. 1937b. 'Excavations at Tell ed-Duweir, the Wellcome Marston Research Expedition to the Near East (Lecture)', *Palestine Exploration Quarterly* 69: 228–41.

Starkey, James L. 1938. 'Discovery', in H. Torczyner et al., *Lachish I: The Lachish Letters,* London and New York: Oxford University Press, 11–14.

Thomas, D. Winton. 1940. 'The Site of Ancient Lachish: The Evidence of Ostrakon IV from Tell ed-Duweir', *Palestine Exploration Quarterly* 72: 148–9.

Thornton, Amara. 2017. 'Filming a Biblical City', *History Today*, 4 October 2017, https://www.historytoday.com/miscellanies/filming-biblical-city, last accessed 10 August 2020.

Torczyner, Harry, with Gerald L. Harding, Alkin Lewis and James L. Starkey. 1938. *Lachish I: The Lachish Letters.* London and New York: Oxford University Press.

Tufnell, Olga. 1953. *Lachish III: The Iron Age.* London: Oxford University Press.

Tufnell, Olga. 1958. *Lachish IV: The Bronze Age.* London: Oxford University Press.

Tufnell, Olga. 1982. 'Reminiscences of a Petrie Pup', *Palestine Exploration Quarterly* 114: 81–6.

Tufnell, Olga. 1985. 'Reminiscences of Excavations at Lachish: An Address Delivered by Olga Tufnell at Lachish on July 6, 1983', *Tel Aviv* 12: 3–8.

Tufnell, Olga, Charles H. Inge and Gerald L. Harding. 1940. *Lachish II: The Fosse Temple.* London: Oxford University Press.

Tur-Sinai, Naftali H. 1987 [originally published 1940]. *The Lachish Ostraca: Letters from the Time of the Prophet Jeremiah.* Jerusalem: Jewish Palestine Exploration Society.

Ussishkin, David. 2014. *Biblical Lachish: A Tale of Construction, Destruction, Excavation and Restoration.* Jerusalem: Israel Exploration Society.

von Harten, Marjorie, and Marston, Melissa. 1979. *Man of Wolverhampton: The Life and Times of Sir Charles Marston.* Cirencester: Coombe Springs Press.

Wellcome Foundation. 1953. *Sir Henry Wellcome: A Biographical Memoir.* London: Wellcome Foundation.

Zammit, Abigail. 2016. *The Lachish Letters: A Reappraisal of the Ostraca Discovered in 1935 and 1938 at Tell ed-Duweir.* Unpublished D.Phil. dissertation, University of Oxford.

9

Tell ed-Duweir (Lachish): Fifth and sixth seasons, 1936–8

No sooner was Olga back in camp in December 1936 than she was off again to Syria with Richmond Brown, visiting Damascus, Kadesh and Ras Shamra, as well as Byblos in Lebanon. This travelling partnership was set to continue the following year, as she and Richmond Brown journeyed back overland across Europe and down the Dalmatian coast, staying briefly in Athens and exploring the surrounding countryside. They then parted, Richmond Brown (who was not well) returning to England, and Olga travelling on to Haifa. Such travels were considerable diversions from the troubles related to the rise of fascism in Europe, as well as issues resulting from the Arab Revolt (1936–9) in Palestine, which was ultimately to result in tragedy for the expedition.

Sir Henry Wellcome died in July 1936 and Sir Charles Marston increased his support of the expedition to a half-share of all the expenses. Thus the expedition became known as the Wellcome Marston Archaeological Research Expedition to the Near East. Other changes included the absence of Harding, who had departed earlier that year. With Richmond Brown staying behind in the winter of 1937–8, the atmosphere may have been somewhat different, at least socially, during this final season, as remarked by Veronica Seton-Williams: 'Tell ed-Duweir had a curious atmosphere and was not a happy camp ... Only at Christmas when Gerald Harding, who had been appointed Director of Antiquities, came over from Trans-Jordan was there any attempt to get together; otherwise, we all seemed to live separate, isolated lives.'[1]

Work in the 1936–7 season included continued progress on the city gate and exposure of the roadway, as well as a Roman road found close to the site (presumed to be that which Eusebius recorded in relation to Lachish). Middle and Late Bronze Age tombs, containing large numbers of scarabs, were also excavated. Olga also refers to a seal featuring a

Hebrew inscription ('for Shefat[.]yahu Asyahu'),[2] indicating her attempts to decipher the script (letter of 5 March 1937). The 'Great Shaft' now reached a depth of 75 feet and proved a great danger to life and limb for the expedition staff and workforce, yet it failed to lead to a spring or secret passage as Starkey hoped. He suggested it was unfinished. It is now thought to have been a quarry for stone used to build structures of the Judaean kingdom levels.[3]

Late Bronze Age (1550–1200 BC) finds began to appear on the mound for the first time in significant quantities, albeit from disturbed fills. These included Mycenaean sherds and Egyptian-style bowls featuring hieratic inscriptions of the late Ramesside period. These apparently related to the nearby 'Acropolis Temple', which had been partially exposed in the sixth and final season of 1937–8.[4] Work continued on Bronze and Iron Age tombs (including those close to the camp-house), and Late Bronze Age houses and the Fosse Temple beyond the city walls.

However, the successful progress of the expedition was shattered by Starkey's murder in January 1938, a hugely significant and shocking event. In 1936 and 1937 the security situation in Palestine had deteriorated owing to the tensions of the Arab Revolt, which was a hazardous and tense period for Arabs, Jews and the British alike. The Arab Revolt was largely for Arab independence and against Jewish immigration to Palestine. It started mainly as a peaceful general strike in May 1936, though there was the trigger of armed action against Jewish and British interests by Arab rebels. The British engaged in counter-insurgency measures, including curfews and the arrest and execution of Arab rebels.[5] Jewish paramilitary organisations expanded at the same time, either alongside the British, or as offshoots conducting counter-attacks on Arabs.

The expedition apparently experienced very little in the way of harassment, yet its members were well aware of the need for caution owing to the increase in attacks and looting. There had been an incident in early October 1936 in which the camp was attacked and its guards beaten and robbed by a gang of armed Arabs before the excavation team had returned, as communicated by Diab Basham to Olga.[6] Yet despite the risks, the work continued. It is also apparent that there were attempts at downplaying the dangers. An incident involving two expedition members (Cuming and Pummell) in December before Starkey's murder was not shared with Sir Charles back in England for fear of causing worry.[7] Of course, Olga's letters home are filled with reassurances about the security situation at Lachish. She did not wish to alarm her mother, and presumably wished to prevent any possibility of being summoned home at a crucial moment. Olga's letter to her mother on 16 December 1937 seems almost prescient, however: 'Incidents still continue in Jerusalem but they are nearly always at night or twilight and people now don't go about much on the roads after dark. But all this does not affect us in our backwater.'

Starkey was late in starting out on that fateful evening of 10 January 1938 for Jerusalem, as was his habit (see letter of 12 January 1938). He was on his way to attend the opening of the new Palestine Archaeological Museum in Jerusalem. At dusk, the car was stopped by a group of 'Arab brigands' on the Beit Jibrin road northwest of Hebron. Starkey, having identified himself as British, was ordered out of the car. The driver was told to drive on to Hebron without Starkey, and as he did so he heard the fatal shots being fired.[8] This was apparently in spite of the driver trying to explain that Starkey was a friend to Arabs in the area. It is also thought that those who had stopped the car believed Starkey to be a Jew because of his beard.[9] According to John Starkey, J.L. Starkey's son, his mother Marjorie used to insist on his father shaving whenever she was at the camp (Figure 9.1). She remarked afterwards that the tragedy

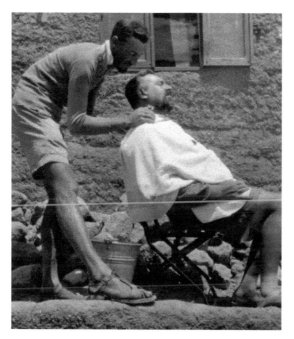

Figure 9.1   G.L. Harding as camp barber with J.L. Starkey, probably at Tell Fara. Olga Tufnell archive, Palestine Exploration Fund. Courtesy of the Palestine Exploration Fund.

might have been averted had she been present at the time.[10] It has been suggested that Starkey's murder took place due to a long-standing grudge concerning the withholding of payment for use of agricultural land being excavated and built upon at Tell ed-Duweir.[11] In addition, a degree of distrust is noted between Starkey and the local community of Qubeibeh when he was requested to provision armed guards for the expedition in 1936 after the October raid (see above). He specifically excluded the option of guards coming from the local village.[12] The grudge theory cannot be proven, however, and an attack by a gang based in the vicinity of Hebron remains the most likely explanation of the incident, given that this area was a hotbed of insurgency during the Arab Revolt.[13] The ringleader accused of his murder was apprehended and sentenced to death.[14] As shown extensively in the letters presented in this volume, there were longstanding and close relationships fostered between the expedition team and the people of Qubeibeh. Despite these local tensions, as well as within the context of the backdrop of the ongoing Arab Revolt, it would still make such a plot to murder Starkey unlikely.

There was public outrage at news of the murder. Large numbers attended his funeral the following day in Jerusalem (which Olga had to arrange), where 'archaeologists of all faiths mingled with bearded scholars and civilian notables in the congregation' (Figure 9.2). That evening Harding delivered a tribute to Starkey, prepared largely by Harding and Olga, through the Palestine Broadcasting Service.[15] A memorial meeting took place the next day at the Hebrew University, with addresses by Professors Torczyner, Mayer and Sukenik.[16] Obituaries followed, paying tribute to his archaeological accomplishments and strength of character, while drawing attention to the sad and premature end to his life and career.[17] Charles Inge and Olga compiled a report based on the sequence of events and information that had been gathered on the murder for the Wellcome Trustees in London.[18] Following these tragic events, there was considerable confusion over the future of the expedition and the risk to personnel. Inge, who was temporarily put in charge, wrote to Sir Charles Marston with a list of priorities for the expedition. Marston was anxious to continue its work, and finish excavations in key areas such as the temples and cemetery, while giving up on the Great Shaft. Marston indicated his continued interest in finding inscriptions. He believed that the Palace Fort may have contained further archives, but was aware this may have been too big a job to tackle.[19] In the weeks that followed the murder, six Palestinian police and a truck were placed in the camp for the protection of team members.[20] Sir Robert Mond also wanted the work

Figure 9.2 J.L. Starkey's funeral, 11 January 1938. Protestant cemetery, Mount Zion, Jerusalem. Olga Tufnell, Gerald L. Harding and John H. Iliffe stand in the centre next to the tree. Behind them to the right of the picture is Père Vincent. See letter of 12 January 1938. Starkey family collection. Courtesy of Wendy Slaninka.

to carry on and provided a wireless station for the camp in case of emergency. By March it was decided that work should continue and Harding was given leave from his post with the Department of Antiquities in Transjordan to take over supervision of the excavation, with Inge as his assistant. A 'temporary' closure was recommended at the end of the season to allow for publication.[21]

At the end of the 1938 season it became obvious that there would be little hope of returning to Tell ed-Duweir for a long time; the situation in Europe was becoming ominous. Olga took up duties in London and thereafter concentrated on publishing (see the Epilogue).

Following the loss of Starkey and the outbreak of the Second World War, the expedition at Tell-ed-Duweir was never to reassemble. Due to the tragic circumstances surrounding the end of the expedition, Sir Charles Marston even later suggested that 'the powers of evil' had cursed efforts to find archaeological evidence to confirm the scriptures.[22] Other expeditions suffered as well, with Petrie's expedition house in Gaza being burned and its contents destroyed in September 1938, and the Colts' expedition house in Esbeita meeting a similar fate just a month later as British forces temporarily lost control of parts of Palestine.[23]

Olga later wrote with respect to Tell ed-Duweir: 'the grove, the garden and the house did not long survive the closing of the camp in 1938. The local guards left in charge … were powerless to withstand attack from a marauding band, and when part of the buildings were burnt in a second raid, their position became untenable. The railway equipment was sold at the time of Rommel's advance to Egypt, and the villagers cleared all that was left of stones and equipment.'[24]

Her next visit to the site did not come until 1972, where she observed: 'the barren slopes were clothed with spruce and fir already well-grown, motor roads encircled the mound and the fellah village we knew on an adjoining spur had disappeared without a trace. How much can happen in one lifetime!'[25] The village's inhabitants were displaced and the village was destroyed during the Arab–Israeli war of 1948 by Israeli forces following armed action that led to the defeat of Egyptian forces.[26] Several years after the area came under Israeli control, a moshav (agricultural settlement) was established adjacent to the site of the village.

As mentioned in Chapter 1, Olga visited Lachish for the last time in 1983 as a guest of the Lachish Expedition, which was under the direction of David Ussishkin of Tel Aviv University. She enthusiastically shared her memories of past archaeological work, mentors, friends and colleagues, and also reflected upon how much things had changed since the 1920s and 1930s. The lecture, which was later transcribed and published, is a fitting testament to her memory.[27]

Letters of December 1936–April 1938

[7 December 1936; handwritten: PEF/DA/TUF/280]

SS *Mongolia*,
Nearing Port Said.
Dec. 7th 1936.

Darling –
We get in tomorrow at 7.30 and I shall have to spend the usual dull day at Port Said, where I shall get my hair washed to pass away the time. Shall towel up with some women from the boat, Mrs Lightbody and Mitchell both wives of Govt. officials, so shall be in sound hands?

The whole boat is shaking with the Simpson affair,[28] to most on board it was a complete bombshell, but certainly things have been pushed into the open with disastrous effect, they could I suppose hardly ignore the continental press any longer, if they had only kept quiet the whole thing would have followed the course of others.

As you can imagine I can't contribute any news, the perfect weather has continued all the way and I have I believe put on stones from the colossal meals I've been eating.

Competitions are in full swing for which it is no good entering so we no longer get much chance to play deck tennis and ping pong.

Very much love darling, more when I reach camp on Wednesday morning –
Olga

[14 December 1936; handwritten: PEF/DA/TUF/281]

Orient Palace Hotel
Damas [Damascus]

Dec. 14. 1936.

Darling –
This may surprise you somewhat – arrived in camp on Tuesday as per schedule. Had two busy days settling in and getting my jobs going and now have set forth with Ba [Richmond Brown] into the blue. He has been very ill – the mutt drove to Jerusalem sitting on a wet seat and got pleurisy which nearly led to pneumonia and he only got to camp the day before me. As a very strenuous general trip had been arranged to Akaba [Aqaba] and Petra it seemed mad for him to attempt it, so we are doing this instead. Plans uncertain but we have to be back Friday night.

Left camp late on Friday, and spent the usual night at the [Hotel] Fast [in Jerusalem], where everyone seemed pleased to see us. Next day we got our visas, where a bit of diplomacy was needed to pull it off without waiting. Got going by eleven and came through Nablus and Nazareth to Tiberias. All along workmen were busy repairing the blown-up bridges, nearly every one had been damaged. Still a good many troops about, but no regular patrols.

There is an incongruous café-restaurant dance hall now on the lake-side where we had tea to the strains of Strauss waltzes and then on to Tabcha [Tabgha]. Had a cheerful dinner with people on leave, RAF, Engineers and Police, and then to a chilly bed. The wind very cold

Figure 9.3 Synagogue at Capernaum. No date given. Olga Tufnell archive, Palestine Exploration Fund. Courtesy of the Palestine Exploration Fund.

but dazzling sun next morning when we side tracked to Capernaum [Figure 9.3]. A very creditable Jewish effort for the period, much to Ba's annoyance. The car has been her noble self up to now – one puncture, when we were helped by two unknown Englishmen, one loose wheel remedied by Ba and so far nothing else. Had a quick glance at Hazor, under the slopes of Hermon, a delight to us the whole way from Tiberias to this place. Not much snow on her now but perfect lines of purple shade in the folds. Negotiated the frontier, Ba got off with a customs officer, with whom he is going to America, saw Tell Benat Jacoub, where we did not succeed in finding the early pottery which should have been there.

Damascus by 5pm where this very palatial hotel caught our eye, so we have deserted the Omayad and are here – very new, very French, very heated – which is what we want after the rigours of the road.

Well I suppose this must do duty as a Xmas letter – we are really whicked [sic] to be gallivanting so soon after arrival, but it's in a good cause. [...]

Ever your loving
<u>Olga</u>

[18 December 1936; handwritten: PEF/DA/TUF/282]

Windsor Hotel
Haifa, Palestine

Dec. 18. 1936

Darling –
Damascus seems far away now but must transport myself back to fill in the story – it was desperately cold and the only thing we did there was to scour the suks [markets] to find a pair of gloves for Ba. The streets were full of holidaymakers massed round the sweet stuff sellers, the photographers, and the cinemas. So we were glad to take the road north to Homs. Soon the gardens of Damascus were left behind and we found ourselves moving up and up onto the arid plateau of Djeroud [Jayrud]. Backward glance showed the shiny slopes of Hermon between breaks in the hills. We stopped for lunch at the 1400 metre level, nearly 5000 feet, and sat under singing telegraph poles in the hot sun eating biscuits, figs, chocolate and preserved fruit, which has been our usual fare at midday, washed down with a tot of brandy. Most unconventional! During the afternoon we drew level with the great block of grand anti-Lebanon, the marshy lake of Homs, fed by the Orontes, which we have seen at its source as a sparkling spring, releases the pent up waters of the river, which flows west of Homs, is crossed by the road at Rastan and becomes a wide and tranquil servant of man by the time it reaches Hamah [Hama].

Round the lake itself, Tells stand up like mushrooms, great Kadesh to the south, where the Egyptian and Hittite power was measured in 1282 BC and eight other sites can be seen from the road, while in front lay the citadel of Homs. The great pile of debris, rising some 200 ft above the plain, is now topped by the Turkish fort, now occupied by the French Foreign Legion. Though we couldn't go inside, we had a few words with the men lounging at the gate, who told us that a compatriot called

'Lovibond' was with them. If he hadn't been transferred to Damascus I'm sure we should have ended up at a pub together. So we consoled ourselves by walking round the slopes, searching for sherds and this and that.

Hotel Raghdan advertised 'tout conforts' including central heating, private bathrooms and all. Radiators yes, but no 'chauffage' in them, so instead we had lovely charcoal braziers, and enjoyed a good meal in the dining room full of 'Effendiat' celebrating the Aid [Eid al-Fitr] in araq, which we drank, the experiment for me was none too good, aniseed makes me feel sick – however I survived.

[undated letter, perhaps continuation of above letter, PEF/DA/TUF/282. Probably late December 1936, missing p. 1; possibly to Beauchamp Tufnell, due to repetition: PEF/TUF/DA/323]

Played 'demon' patience in the heavily upholstered lounge and then to bed.

Off reasonably early next day 9.30, after I had walked in the market before breakfast through high arched street displaying a curious mixture of home produce and cheap importations, each shop warmed by old fashioned braziers, or their modern equivalent – half a kerosene tin. Bought 6 bananas for 1/9d so I wept for Walton's, though it was only my stupidity and objection to haggling which was to blame.

Homs to Hamah is a straight road, over barren ground. The only deviation in its course occurs at Rastan, ~~where~~ a great Tell rises from the plain, where the Orontes swings east across the road. The break in the plateau, caused by the river, is an emerald strip in the surrounding land, the fields are watered by the great 'norias' (water wheels) driven by the current, they hum as they rotate and are to me the nearest approach I can imagine to the music of the heavenly spheres. This was familiar ground, for it was down in a small valley close to the river banks that we had camped with Terry [Colt] on our journey home. Much as we should have like[d] to dally there to call on our late host Bekyr Barazi, we did not dare spend the time, and we climbed regretfully onto the plain to pursue our way.

Our road continued almost due north, while the river make[s] a great bend and cut[s] more and more deeply into the smooth surface of the plain. Hamah is almost completely concealed in the hollow, and the ancient mound rises from it, flanked by the river bed, to almost the same height as the surrounding country.

The houses fill every available spot in the valley, but seem strangely reluctant to debouch onto the plain; the bottled heat in summer is, I suppose, preferable to the tearing winds of winter.

Gay people were hurrying across the stone bridge intent on festivity, the great wheel sprayed them as they passed, and the brick pedestal was suitably adorned with icicles gleaming in the sun.

We spent an hour or so on the Tell, where a Danish Exp[edition] has been working. Their guard showed us round and we did our best to work out the significance of what we saw. A large building of black basalt, split to fragments by fire, concealed under temporary cairns a pair of monumental lions and a huge statue of a man. Many trial pits had been dug and we peered hopefully into them, but without guidance we were not much advanced in knowledge.

From Hamah we turned west making for the coast, soon the plain led us to stony foothills and we began a steady climb. Massyaf [Masyaf], castle of the Hashishyn (Assassins) guards the approach to the Naisere[?] [Nusayriyah] Mountains, it overlooks the plain from its stony eminence, its walls rise from the rock and are virtually intact, pierced now and again by narrow iron barred weir dams – Roman columns, millstones and any old material was used to pile them up, yet the miscellaneous collections in the village took the shape of valleys of ebot[?] in the market place and as the key could only be obtained from the Town Clerk we projured[?] to leave them to it.

Up into the hills, 600, 700, 800, 900 meters, the cold was intense, the streams were all frozen over and to complete the situation a cutting wind whistled over the pass, one of the steepest and most sudden I've ever negotiated. Qadmous, Oillaqa, and Kahf are all Assassin castles finally in the hands of the Knights Templars, each one beckoned to us from their hills but we pushed on deaf to their wiles for it was nearly dark. […]

[23 December, probably 1936; handwritten: PEF/DA/TUF/283]

Tell Duweir
POB. 23
Gaza.

Dec. 23.

Darling –
To continue – where had I got to? Hamah, I think, anyhow we saw the Tell there, very fine position on the bank of the Orontes, where it has cut a great gorge for itself in the plateau. The buildings on the Tell were mainly basalt, split into fragments by the fires of the final destruction. Apparently

2 basalt lions and the torso of a man lie buried under cairns of stones so we did not see the pièce de resistance. The midday sun saw us on our way again across the plain and up into the most barren and bouldered foothills I've ever seen. After an hour or so the forbidding walls of Massyaf came as a relief, set on a hill against a background of the Naisiri Mountains. We lunched at the edge of a quarry looking onto the castle and the square walled enclosure around it. The castle was the first foothold that Rachid ed din es Sinan [Rashid al-Din Sinan] otherwise 'The Old Man of the Mountains' gained in Syria, where his eaters of Hashish 'Assassins' soon had everyone in fear for their lives.

The village notables, including the holder of the castle keys were all celebrating the Aid by firing volleys in the square, so we knew it was hopeless to hang round trying to get them.

Up into the hills and within 15 minutes we had climbed a colossal series of hairpin bends to a height of 900 metres. The hills were green with shrub oak which had turned yellow and as we reached the top we found the streams frozen over. Over the pass our troubles began, an icy wind whistled round us and we pressed on, praying that we should escape punctures or other mishaps. Qadmous [Al-Qadmus] guarded our road to the left, and within sight were 2 other castles, Qalaat el Kahf [Qala'at al Kahf] and Oilaqa [Ulayqah] whose history was controlled by the fortress of Massyaf. It was relief to get within sight of the sea and the grandest castle of all, Marqhab [Margat], controlling the road along the plain. The sun was just setting, so that all we saw was the ser[r]ated silhouette against the sea. Crusader stronghold, Marqhab held out against the Saracens almost to the end.

Once on the coast at Banyas, we turned north and followed a fine tarmac all the way to Latakia. It was dark when we arrived, we threaded our way through the strolling crowd to the sea and the Casino-Palais Hotel, where we found all the élite playing bridge. Frenchmen and their wives, the Bank Manager, officers from the garrison and Europeanised 'tarbushes' [fez-like cap] sat in a beautiful warm fug wrapped in festoons of smoke, just the atmosphere we were longing for. Tea and toast pulled us together, and we found our rooms boasted all the conveniences including bidets and radiators, both of which were more ornamental than useful.

Next morning when I had carefully washed in the water from my hot water bottle, I found that the taps were steaming hot, so they had the laugh on me after all.

On the road by 9.30, towards Ras Shamra,[29] which we found without much difficulty. The guard was a policeman in charge of a gang of some 5 men busily laying a railway line at the angle of the Giant Racer [rollercoaster] at Wembley, so anything may befall when it gets going.

We saw what we could, including the tomb chambers of the early merchants it is suggested, who were buried in finely cut tombs inside the houses. Perhaps they felt less lonely among their own people than they would have buried outside the walls in a strange land.

Minet el Beda [Minet el-Beida] was the port on the shore itself, the whole was a prosperous trading centre until the XIXth dynasty.

We retraced our steps all the way to Banyas, and on past Marqhab which we would dearly have liked to explore. Tartarus [Tartus] our next stop, a perfectly preserved Crusader town with the basilica of 'Our Lady of Tortosa' in its midst. The first church dedicated to her, it has no apse and a square exterior, flanked by 2 towers. Again luck was against us, as we could not spare the time to wait for the keys, as the guardian had gone to visit his mother or aunt on the outskirts in the usual tiresome way.

Lunch to the strains of Ba's harmonica by the sea, the unusual sounds soon brought a row of listeners, like the Pipes of Pan. For the second time on our journey we sat among crocuses, not the mauve kind, which are spread over the hills of Palestine, but a deep golden yellow flower.

We passed through Tripoli and sped on to reach Byblos, now Djebil, before nightfall. We sent in cards to the Director, Maurice Dunand,[30] and he came straight out and gave us a most intensive round. At the risk of boring you I will put it all down, for it may be useful to me for reference.

First know, O! Mama, that Byblos is probably the oldest city in the world (with the exception of Tell Duweir of course!).

Seriously, Eneolithic-chalcolithic man was buried there in the sand dunes which overlay the rock, in itself no more than a consolidated dune. Adults and many children lay crouched in half a large jar, with a bowl or two, a few carnelian beads and occasionally metal (silver rings). Above these burials were two town levels, the foundations of houses built in rough stone and mud. The walls of the lower layer run under the massive town wall, an elaborate construction of stone and earth [Figure 9.4], but it is in the third building level that alabaster jars from Egypt occur, bearing royal names from Ka-Sekh-em-mui [Kasekhemwy] of the IInd–IIIrd dyn to Pepy of the Vth, so that puts the two earlier towns close to the predynastic period in Egypt.

Figure 9.4 Ink sketch by Olga Tufnell of wall and rampart at Byblos, from letter of 23 December 1936. Courtesy of the Palestine Exploration Fund.

Building technique as represented in the IIIrd level showed a mastery in dressing and handling stone, which could only have been acquired after centuries of experience. Therefore, M. Dunand feels sure that the builders were not mere nomads of Semitic origin – he favours a western home for them. The whole city was destroyed in the universal debacle at the end of the Old Kingdom Period. Two roads of the IInd Bronze Age meet at the city gate, one brought travellers from inland and the other brought trade and traders from the harbour. Up this road once came Wen-Amon, an Egyptian envoy sent to buy timber, who recorded his adventures and misfortunes in a papyrus which has come down to us (1100 BC). He tells in naïve ill spelt sentences how the prince of Byblos interviewed him, sitting in an upper chamber of his palace, 'leaning his back against a window, while the waves of the great Syrian sea beat on the shore behind him'.

A temple of the 17th cent. BC is full of interest and some few similarities with ours, and another one of the Old Kingdom lies beneath it. Images of a god were cut from a flat gold sheet, scratched with eyes, nose and mouth and deposited in the temple, and as with us disused equipment or offerings were buried in the floors.

We saw besides a statuette in bronze covered in gold in the style of the great copper statue of Pepy, though here the features are quite un-Egyptian.

It was quite dark and there was a long way to go so reluctantly we tore ourselves away after an absorbing hour. Beyrouth that night, all the comfortable hotels full for the Aid, so we had to content ourselves with a mediocre affair, no bath and smells. Ba had a Turkish bath which revived him, I had no more than a lick and promise.

Next morning we set off for the Museum accompanied by a comic character in Rabalaisian [sic] style, who suddenly cried: 'Stop! Stop! There is the Prince, the Director of the Museum.' So a nice young man lifted his hat and spoke to us with the result that we spent the whole morning with him, first at his office, then at the old Museum and finally at the new building in course of construction. So we were able to ask questions and came away full of information.

Through lovely gardens and olive orchards [we drove], within a stone's throw of the sea, which was tranquil again – Tyre, Sidon, we passed, with a nod and a glance, and came at last regretfully to the frontier, Ras en Nakoum, set on a headland, just a rock barrier between the two countries – Carmel under a load of cloud, clearly before us.

Trouble at the customs – Ba's harmonica was too much for them. It had no seal on it from the previous customs, anyhow it seemed like a deadly weapon. Ba was taken off to higher authority and I did not know what had befallen [him] until I heard familiar strains issuing from some sanctum, and I knew that peace had been made.

Before we reached Haifa, it was raining, our lights were low and we crawled into the Windsor [Hotel] about five. Our last day took us to Megiddo, where everyone was away, so we side-tracked later on to Shiloh, where there are good mosaic floors, though the place is more famous as Joshua's sanctuary. Negotiated the whole road without mishap or hold-ups – of course we were longing for some bandits and had our scheme of approach all worked out.

Tea in Jerusalem where we met the whole Akabah [Aqaba] party, who had got in the night before. It had been freezing there, without any accommodation and icicles held [sic – hang] by the wall[31] all down the Wadi Rhum [Wadi Rum]. Gerald [Harding] and Miss Murray had been with them.

There rumours reached us of disasters in camp, and we found on arrival that the terrific gale which had nearly blown us out of the car in Syria had quite blown off my roof and the storeroom roof at Duweir! So I am still camping in the office, while extensive repairs are undertaken, these are much held up by rain!

All proceeded smoothly to Xmas Eve, when Starks [Starkey], Ba, Holbrook [Bonney] and I went up to do some shopping. Left at 4.30, arrived in time to get my hair washed, where my Viennese hairdresser gave me a warm welcome. Dinner at the Fast, and then well oiled and lit we went and sang carols outside the Iliffes' house, who were pleased to see us and then outside the Shaws', who pretended not to hear! So home past Bethlehem, cold but bright, by half past twelve.

Slept it off next morning and found Gerald had arrived for Xmas. Ate largely, and then prepared for the usual fancy dress dinner. Gerald sinister in black as a Vampire, Starks, a keeper of the harēm in Imperial Stambul [Istanbul] – Ba a cossack – Warren Hastings – Flora Mac. the pride of the pack. Mrs H – a witch. Barbara Parker[32] – the Spirit of Minny or the house with the sign! The others rather indefinite. I went as Rashid ed Din as Sinan the old man of the mountains – smoking Hashish. All very cheerful till nearly two am.

Mercifully it rained next morning, so we slept again, but, except for a break on Sunday, when Gerald left, it has continued to do so ever since, everything soaked and the wadi pouring down under the bridge which may get washed away at any moment. So can't guarantee when you will get this!

Enclosed are the photos, rather scrappy considering the amount we saw, but there it is.

Very much love
Olga

Tell L. that the pudding was very good, particularly liked the cherries on top.

Very many thanks for all your Xmas mail, which arrived on the right day. Punch is also most welcome.

[31 December 1936; handwritten: PEF/TUF/DA/285]

Tell Duweir.
P.O.B. 23
Gaza.
Dec. 31. 1936

Darling Daddy,
Well another year has gone, and as I seem to have been very remiss about Christmas letters, I am sitting down now to wish you everything of the very best in the New Year. May the birds lay, the people buy eggs and pay for them afterwards, may 'Mexico cities' soar into the clouds and rain down golden guineas, and may Mrs Nash's shoot be swarming with pheasants and partridges.

Over here I have been doing very well, you will see my letters to Mama with all the details of the Syria trip, which was a great success. The country up north is lovely, along the coast it is much more fertile than

Palestine and many more remnants remain of the great forests which used to supply wood for Egypt and for the building of Solomon's Temple. I still have not seen the famous cedars of Lebanon, but imagine that the one at Waltham House[33] is probably bigger and better in every way.

The Crusader castles are magnificent, it is marvellous what these people did, representatives of many races, travelling thousands of miles, mostly on foot, and then they put up buildings which are almost as firm and complete as on the day that they were built. Time did not allow us to stop long at any one, but we were able to get a general impression.

Everywhere both the natives and the French were very nice to us, of course we had to speak it or Arabic all the time, and we made some nice acquaintances among the archaeologists.

Gerald came for Xmas, I think he is rather at a loose end at Jerash, because there is no money for him to do things with, but I expect he will settle down and make work for himself. We all dressed up for Xmas and had a gay time. I don't think we shall celebrate this evening, as we shall have to do so on Stark's birthday on the 3rd.

Do let me have a line from you to say how you are getting on. Ate Helen's Xmas pudding with no ill effects [...] much wonder how the Xmas festivities 'en famille' went off. Do tell me all about them. [...]

[9 January, probably 1937; handwritten: PEF/TUF/DA/286]

Tell Duweir
P.O.B. 23
Gaza.
Jan. 9.

Darling Mà,
This week has been uneventful after all the excitements of the Aid. I don't think anything has happened worthy of note. We had some more rain not before we needed it, even now I fear the crop on high ground has dried too much to benefit. Our garden is doing well, the cyclamen are coming out in all the wall crevices and my pots are full of anemones and narcissi. The trees have grown out of all recognition and now that the courtyard wall is finished we have put in a row of cypresses which will look nice in about 30 yrs time when we are being wheeled round in Daddy's proverbial bathchair.

The Levinskaya wedding party must have been very funny. [...] When I met Sir Ronald [Storrs] there some yrs ago he said 'I don't know how I got here, where am I and who is she?' or words to that effect. [...]

Work is going along well, everything is very much mechanised, I suppose things do get done more quickly; all the bit between garage, house and lavatory has been done and for weeks we have been walking to and fro along a sort of precipice with all the work looking on and more or less timing one's sojourn inside [the lavatory].

Several enquiries after you and Mohammed [el-Kreti] insisted on writing you a letter, which he will be delighted if you will answer. I translated it verbatim which makes pleasanter reading. The P's [Petries] have not written for him, and he has not heard from them. We hear that they think him too old now for work in the 'desert'; whether that is the real reason or not I don't know. A woman in Qubeibeh, talking about her small daughter who is going to hospital said 'Couldn't she stay the night with your mother in Jerusalem'. I had to explain you were a little further off than that! [...]

[14 January 1937; handwritten: PEF/TUF/DA/287]

P.O.B. 23
Gaza
Jan. 14. 1937.

Darling –
[...] Quite the wettest season so far, a good crop may make for a quieter spring if the Commission[34] does something good, it was quite a good move to get the last say with the Commission, but we haven't heard with what results.

Am still busy with all sorts of things, it is rather funny being the 'doyen' of the Exp[edition] apart from Starks, have to sit up and take notice and supply information about sherds and so on to the new boys which is very good for me. Am also learning to do serious photography under Ba's tuition, which is very exciting, as it is still sub rosa and we will produce the fait accompli for Stark's benefit. As quid pro quo, I'm teaching him about pottery. Charles and Ba got caught by rain in Jerusalem, but arrived this evening on horses from Beit Jibrin, as they couldn't get the cars any further. So we shall hear some news of the great world this evening.

The P's have found water at Sheykh Zuweid, so they have left for Jerusalem – more recent gossip I know not, probably you know much more.

Figure 9.5 The Great Shaft during excavations at Tell ed-Duweir, with unidentified worker. Wellcome-Marston Expedition Archive, Department of the Middle East, British Museum. © UCL Institute of Archaeology, courtesy of the Wellcome Trust and the British Museum.

I'm glad the Xmas festivities went off well, as you say it is an improvement on last year and I expect conversation now flows more easily. I did not realise that the aunts were ill, poor dears, Xmas without the regulation visits is not Xmas at all. [...]

[21 January 1937; handwritten: PEF/TUF/DA/288]

P.O.B. 23.
Gaza

Jan. 21. 1937.

Darling,
It has been reasonably fine all this last week and we have got on nicely in all directions. The great shaft and tunnel [Figures 9.5 and 9.6] are getting quite exciting, 70 ft deep[35] we have come on the bottom, or is it only a ledge of rock? Starks is revelling in all sorts of theories about secret exits and passages. There was a similar affair at Megiddo – of course we hope ours is bigger and better in every way. You get down by a series of ladders, rope and otherwise, and have a drop at the bottom to reach the horizontal cut:

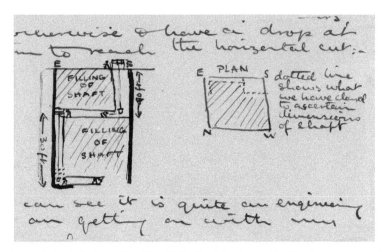

Figure 9.6 Ink sketch by Olga Tufnell of the Great Shaft being excavated. Letter of 21 January 1937. Courtesy of the Palestine Exploration Fund.

As you can see it is quite an engineering feat! I am getting on with my knitting and shall hope to finish next month. Meanwhile Ba's stockings are finished and I only have to await the 26th before I have the pleasure of wearing them!

It is possible that Ba and I may go to stay with Gerald for the next festival which falls towards the end of February.

So Vivian's life has had a sensational close, there was much about him and his film star in the papers this Summer. Ba knew his 2nd wife well and was brought up with her in Wales. According to him plain and stupid but nice. I suppose she was a reaction after the soignée Mary.

I enclose a nice letter I had from the woman I met on the boat, funnily enough her name is Wallis! A visit to Omdurman would be fun.

[…] May probably go to Tell Beit Mirsim tomorrow if fine, it is up in the hills beyond Duweinah where Albright worked.

Arab calendar for this month which I try to translate as follows:

The old woman says, 'thank God'

Shubat (name of the month) has passed and has taken from me neither goat nor grandchild.

Shubat [February] says: 'Oh Dar [Ahdar/Azar – March]! (the following month) my nephew,

Three from you and four from me (days)

And I will make all the wadis sing. (with the rainwater)

With very much love
Ever yours
Olga

[29 January, probably 1937; handwritten: PEF/TUF/DA/289]

Tell Duweir.
Jan. 29.

Darling,
[In pencil] NO! I am not ill but can't find my pen. As a matter of fact I have had a stiff neck this week owing to quickly following extremes of hot and cold, but am now <u>quite</u> all right and pursuing all my usual vocations.

Very many thanks for your most dashing birthday present, though it is hardly camp wear it will make a colossal splash in Jerusalem. Your letter and Daddy's both came very well to time. We had a tea party and fun and games afterwards, I wearing my yellow self-knitted cap, the completed socks by Ba and half the jumper I am now making. [...]

Much more rain this last week, 2 days solid and there has been snow in the hills and roads impassable.

Starks has started night shifts in the tunnel which I hope will <u>not</u> last long. I am manoeuvring against it, Ba and Charles have both got colds from it and it is mad. Starks is down there himself tonight.

I hear from Daddy that the grape fruit have reached him safely, so hope you have the oranges. [...]

I don't think there is any more news. I am getting down to drawing now that things are coming in from the cemeteries. We are quite a happy party and there are no misfits this season! [...] Towfiq [Tewfiq Salah?] sends his Salams!

Yours ever
<u>Olga</u>

[5 February 1937; handwritten: PEF/TUF/DA/290]

Tell Duweir.
Feb. 5. 1937

Darling,
Another rainy week, but not so cold. Ba got another severe chill by spending the night in the tunnel on night shift (as I told Starks he would!) so he has been in bed all the week. Was afraid of bronchitis and all sorts of complications, but luckily his temp. kept down. I have to write a sedative letter to his mother after this, as she is likely to hear of it from a mutual friend in Jerusalem.

Have done some photos this week and finished the drawing of the Tell pottery. Things are beginning to come in from the cem. [cemetery] so I am well ahead.

Would you very kindly look in my bookshelf and abstract a book by L[or]d Avebury called I think *The Pleasures of Life*. It belongs to Prof. [Petrie] and I really must return it next time I'm in J. [Jerusalem]. He once asked me for it, and I couldn't find it but it has since appeared. I suppose it is better to confess now than not at all.

Will see Strathearn when I'm next up, probably about the 20th if we go to Gerald, but it is possible that Ba may go to Luxor, though I think the journey and violent transitions to heat and then back to cold would not be beneficial.

The Iliffes came down last week and have been almost our only visitors this year, for which the Lord be praised. Weather and political uncertainty has kept them all away! I shall be going up to the Museum to do a couple of days work on our pottery later on.

Blowing up as I write for more rain, so we are likely to be cut off again by road. [...]

[25 February 1937; handwritten: PEF/DA/TUF/292]

Hotel Fast, Jerusalem
Feb. 25. 1937

Darling –
Just on the way back from a week with Gerald at Jerash [Figure 9.7]. The Hastings and I made it in a day from camp taking a car on from Jerusalem. Crossing the Zerka [Zarqa] River was quite an event as a car had stuck there earlier in the day and we had to paddle across while the car made a dash for it empty except for the driver. Arrived at Jerash in the dark just as I had done before, the house is much the same as in Horsfield's day, Gerald has not done all he intends to do yet. His piano looks nice and sounds really well in that high room.

Went for a walk next morning much further than I'd meant to, lovely day and warm enough to sit and read at intervals. [...]

Under Miss Murray's impetus, Gerald has started sketching, so together we made various efforts with the help of a paint box between us. I did the spiral staircase on a wet day and 2 outside bits.

On Sunday we went to Ajjlun [Ajlun], a Saracen castle high on a hill, where we scrambled round. It was done up by Horsfield and will stand many a century in its present state.

Figure 9.7 Ruins of Jerash (Gerasa), Transjordan, looking south. See letter of 25 February 1937. Olga Tufnell archive, Palestine Exploration Fund. Courtesy of the Palestine Exploration Fund.

Next day not so fine, but we were well occupied splodging on paint, followed by tea at Miss Butler's, who is a marvellous and amusing old bird. A wealthy woman, she lives at Jerash all winter and spring in a native house in the middle of the village, superintending school work. She has nursed all her life in the east. Then in June, she makes tracks for home and has a flutter at the tables at Monte [Carlo] on the way. She lives alone and has a fund of comic experiences to talk about.

On Wed. we started out early to Mafraq on the edge of the eastern desert, with the idea of getting back to lunch, but from Mafraq we were lured on to Um Gemal [Umm el-Jimal], a practically intact Byzantine town built of basalt. A square tower still stands dominating the flat plain, which stretches endlessly, just now it is covered with short green turf, and as we motored across we put up literally thousands of sand grouse – nice fat birds, so tame that many did not bother to move for the cars, how Daddy would have loved to have been there, complete with gun, the air was just black with them.

Um Gemal has lovely stone doors to the houses, roofs made of slabs of basalt thrown together like an ill-made card house, but the general effect might be that of a mediaeval Italian city, Assisi, Ravenna – in fact it is really the same influence and period at work in very different surroundings.

It was hot exploring deserted churches, khans and stables, so when we saw a large reservoir delightfully full of water most people thought they would like to bathe – First our Arabs went in (4 of them were among the house party!) and then Alice and I had it to ourselves and had an invigorating swim without bathing dresses or towels, so we dried off in the sun afterwards.

Turned back to Jerash and got there famishing at 3 pm. It was too late to start for home that night. This morning I finished my third sketch and after an early lunch Gerald drove us to Amman, where we found a car to bring us right here.

The Wadi Shaib [Shu'ayb] is marvellously full of flowers just now – white broom, gorse, lupins, asphodel, wild peas, stocks and a dozen others. Our driver, a friendly nice man, stopped whenever we shouted at him and helped us dig them up with screwdrivers and spanners.

Back here we found Ba, who has been at Dr Olga Schweinskopfe (or some such name)[36] clinic at Jericho, he looks better and fatter and has been well fed, he went back almost at once for another week – the longer he stays there the better.

Shall be back in camp by this time tomorrow, much better for the change, with a lot ahead to get done, considering that there's only six weeks to go before the technical end of the season. [...]

[5 March, probably 1937; handwritten: PEF/DA/TUF/293]

Tell Duweir.
March. 5.

Darling –
[...] You'll never believe it but I am now the proud possessor of a cabuchon [sic – cabochon] sapphire, which when mounted will make a marvellous ring.[37] A boy brought it from B-J [Beit Jibrin], and luckily I was the first to see it. Despite our contracts (nothing whatsoever must be acquired in any way etc etc) and the Government, Starks has v. kindly presented

me with it, though he hankered for it himself. It is extremely rare to find sapphire at all, especially when engraved, as this one is, with a head of a man it is Hellenistic, I really am thrilled with it.

We had the same old gypsies dancing last night, rather boring, now that one is used to them.

Tewfiq has gone after a series of rows with Alice [Hastings] who is inclined to nag and is apt to wear our patience, though she is thoroughly well-meaning.

In one tomb we have 75 scarabs, all late Bronze.[38] They take time to draw, and I've only done a third to date, so shall have to hurry to get the division list done in time! Only a month to go.

We have a Mr Grey [John Gray][39] staying here, who is a Hebrew scholar, so he is going to help me through the Grammar. We have some more nice Hebrew seals and one inscribed gem. [...]

[10 March, probably 1937; handwritten: PEF/DA/TUF/294]

Tell Duweir.
March 10th

Darling,
[...] Ba came back last Sat. very much better for his fortnight at Jericho and has put on half a stone. But I don't think he is quite right yet and he must go slow. He has had 'adhesions' in the lung after bronchitis. Dr Olga Feinberg looked after him well and they are fed there like fighting cocks.

Weather wonderful after a short shower 2 days ago which freshened up the green. It will mean good crops for all which may help to keep things peaceful. Everything quiet today in Jerusalem, despite the murder at the Wailing Wall, which was, I suppose, on all your posters long before we heard about it.

We have only another six weeks to go, but it seems very doubtful if any passages will be available at any time before the Coronation [of King George VI]. Do you think it worth making an effort? I should anyhow be back in the following fortnight. Ba is taking his family in £10 seats! Personally I think one will see more at the cinema and I can't help being disappointed that it's not Edward.

Miss Gardner and Miss Bate start at Bethlehem next week and hope to finish the pit this year. It has certainly been going on long enough.

Sir Charles [Marston] has asked if he can use information from my notes on Lachish in his forthcoming book 'Lachish and the Bible'.[40] I am very nervous as to what it will be like and wish we had first innings with the official account. It is sure to give a wrong impression. He is not coming out this year, but is sending the Bishop of Portsmouth to look us up! [...]

[19 March 1937; handwritten: PEF/DA/TUF/295]

Tell Duweir.
March 19th 1937

Darling –
We had a pleasant day at Askelon [Ashkelon] last week bathing and sailing Ba's collapsible boat with the assistance and hindrance of dozens of small boys who swam round there and are usually a nuisance. They were so excited by the boat that they were quite amenable for once and though they broke the mast and had to be fought off when they tried to board the craft, a good time was had by all.

Just like flies they hung on to the car when we left and we shed them at intervals all along the road to Migdol.

Mr and Mrs Crowfoot spent a night here to see Joan at the end of the Hellenic cruise, he had been lecturing and they had met Usborne. Mr C. with his usual venom thought U. behaved disgracefully about Mrs [Usborne] and never took her on the shore excursions! [...]

We had a nasty accident on the work yesterday, a boy fell from the rope ladder down the shaft 25 metres, and was picked up more or less whole at the bottom – they telephoned to the house, Pummell went down to the bottom and strapped and roped him to a seat and we hauled on the pulleys at the top. Got him straight onto a stretcher and did not move him again till he was put to bed in Hebron. The journey in the truck took us 3 ¼ hrs, they gave us dinner in Hebron.

No doubt there are flaring headlines in the papers about the situation here. We see little of it. There has been a curfew but everything is well in hand! You know more about it than we do! [...]

[25 March, probably 1937; handwritten: PEF/DA/TUF/296]

Tell Duweir
March 25.

Darling,
Weather still perfect, and not too hot. I am working up for the division, but can't draw 170 scarabs in the time. Have done 80 and the rest will have to be photographed, it is a record group from one tomb, and there

are many kings' names.[41] We have another inscribed bowl just turned up,[42] which will be the subject of more letters to the *Times*. Charlie [Marston] sends wild wires about his book and is evidently in great pain about it. He is not coming out this year.

Ba went off to Mach[a]erus on Monday for a fortnight. He was not too grand when he left, but was determined to go. However Gerald will keep an eye on him, and he hopes to get to Petra to see Miss M. [Murray] for a few days. He is building his house of bricks. Things are beginning to dry up now and the crops have a faint yellow tinge. The anebusas are a marvellous sight and yellow daisies and poppies have taken the place of anemones and cyclamen. The evening air is perfumed by sweet-scented night stock, which is so strong that it penetrates to me here sitting in my room.

I will do whatever you say about coming back for the 12th though it may not be possible to get the division done in time, it would mean leaving here on the 9th or thereabouts and boats are said to be full.

Please thank Daddy very much for his letter, which I will answer next week and hope there will be more news then.

Miss C. T. [Caton Thompson] is coming up from Egypt, did I tell you? Next winter she goes to the Hadhramaut with Freya Stark,[43] they ought to make a good pair. She is concentrating on learning better Arabic.

Very much love
from
Olga

[1 April 1937; handwritten: PEF/DA/TUF/297]

Tell Duweir.
March, no April Ist

Darling –
Easter brought us a spate of visitors – the Megiddo crowds, who looked over the site and pottery very professionally, the Richmonds, who will soon be packing up and go home for good, and a nice German professor, Lirchow [?] from Bonn, who came straight from the pages of 'Fleig und die Blatte' [sic][44] goodness knows if that's right!

Gerald came yesterday and has just gone – he did a hard day's work deciphering the bowl inscription which is very faint, but has more signs in the early script than we have seen together before. Now Miss Caton-Thompson is here, after her successful Fayum trip, and she is going on to

Jerash later. Starks is taking her south to Fara [Far'ah] tomorrow. She seems very well and looks just as spick and span as in the Albert Hall M[illegible]!

I am busily working up for the division, and shall hope to get through before long. We have very little pottery, rather to my relief, only the 190 scarabs weigh rather heavily on my mind! [...]

Easter crowds in J. [Jerusalem] were as great as usual, so I suppose every one for the moment is feeling more flush and less prone to make trouble. People seem to think things will go quietly until after the Commission's Report, which will not be published until after the Coronation. [...]

[P.S.] Mohammed [el-Kreti] will be very hurt if he does not receive an answer to his letter, which I hope you received safely!

[7 September 1937; typescript copy: PEF/DA/TUF/302]

VON PORADA [handwritten]

Marston

Institute of Archaeology,
Regent's Park.

September 7th, 1937.

My dear Edith,
Very many thanks for your postcard, glad you are having a good time. Here we have been very busy, the Exhibition took up much time and energy, but we had a good attendance of over 2000 people. Now we are clearing up and trying to get on with proofs of the book about the Lachish Letters, of which I enclose a prospectus for your amusement.

As I promised you, I now send a print of the three and only cylinder seals that we found this last season. They all come from a triple-chambered tomb, No. 4004, below the north-east corner of the Tell. The contents had been thoroughly plundered, turned over, and smashed and finally the residue had been deliberately burnt, as the condition of the rock roof and walls show. We collected 192 scarabs and seals from this group, surely the largest lot found together in Palestine. Among them are many royal names, mostly Pharaohs of the XVIIIth Dynasty, but there are two of Pepa or Shesha, the Hyksos ruler, and one of an overseer of the palace, which by the style must be XIIth–XIIIth dyn. In fact a large proportion of the design scarabs are certainly Hyksos. By the pottery we get a series ranging from late Hyksos to early Ramesside, so I'm afraid the dating point for the cylinders can be spread over 400 years. However perhaps you may have some remarks from the photographs. We shall be interested to hear what you have to say.

You now have a rival in your field, there is a girl here called Barbara Parker who has taken up cylinder seals too, but she is specialising on those from Palestine, which will, I suppose, be a much smaller show.

As usual, we are all uncertain about our plans for next winter, no decision has really been made yet about Palestine, and everyone is still on tenderhooks [sic]. Hoping to hear from you soon, and with love to Hilda,

Yours ever,
[Olga]

[Olga returned to Tell Duweir for the sixth and final season, 1937–8, with Ralph Richmond Brown as travelling companion.]

[16 and 26 November 1937; handwritten: PEF/DA/TUF/303]

Greece,
nearing Athens.
Nov. 16. 1937.

Dearest Mà,
We found ourselves nearly the only passengers on this boat, in comfortable little cabins. It is all nicely miniature but well run. The first night out was fairly choppy but by next morning we were in calm grey seas with clouds gathering in. Our first stop was Split which we got to in the late afternoon, dusk and a strong wind blowing. We went ashore and wandered, the best way of seeing things, so that we came on the Cathedral – Diocletian's mausoleum quite unexpectedly – in its frame of great columns. Metrovich's colossal statue (at least I only guessed it was his) loomed up against the tall houses, so black and nebulous that it took a moment to take it in, as a solid mass of stone. We were lucky to get into the Cathedral: the guardian, always on the look-out for a tip, took us in by a side door into the black interior behind the high altar. He found the light switch and flooded the domed building with light. Lovely pulpit as you know, but XVIIth century alterations have disguised to some extent the charm of the original.

Nov. 26. Athens – Haifa.

When we came out the threatened storm broke and we sought abris [shelter] in a café but were nevertheless drowned rats when we got aboard. Next stop – Dubrovnik [Figure 9.8], about 10 am, and we had till 12 to do the Sights. A tram to the town and then a breathless hour

Figure 9.8 Rooftops in Dubrovnik. See letter of 16 November 1937. Olga Tufnell archive, Palestine Exploration Fund. Courtesy of the Palestine Exploration Fund.

darting up steps and down passages and through doors enthralled with everything. It is all so untouched by modernity, so clean and fresh, as for the battlements and the views therefrom – well you know it all, so I need not add more.

But Koter [Kotor] was the best of them all, the long journey inland through creeks lit up by the placid moon, penetrating further and further into a strange haven protected by great cliffs rising sheer from the water, then the town itself, walled, and flanked by a rushing torrent, solid stone buildings and a lucky entry into the Basilika of St Tryphon also after hours, completed the illusion of enchantment – the treasure ornamenting rather grisly relics, the conscious theatricality of the décor, especially the steps leading to the Reliquarium, with the huge candles on either side at every four steps, the marble angels and the iron grille through which one sees a ceiling of gold stars on blue. Night of course adds something but I should like to go there again.

It proved impossible to land at Bar, and we had to be content with an hour or so at Durazzo [Durrës], such a contrast to Yugoslav prosperity. Proportionally it is the richest country in the world and I suppose its neighbour Albania is one of the poorest, though they are striding ahead under King Zog.

No further stops but a continual panorama of isles and mountains until Corfu where we only waited half an hour. Athens the next day at midday, straight up to the city and a lovely afternoon on the Acropolis. Next day we went up to Mt Parnes with the hope of staying there, but nothing but a small restaurant and no place to sleep, so the chauffeur suggested a hotel in the woods which we could see far below us and there we went [to] VARIBOPI [Varympompi] and just perfect it proved to be. Meals at an estaminet where you chose your own food in the kitchen before it was cooked under your nose. Delightful personnel of the simple sort and in the evenings great blazing log fires. The hotel is used by Airways for their passengers but we had it entirely to ourselves and had only to ask for to receive. Two large rooms with balconies apiece 80 drs. a day, roughly 4/–. Tatorio [Tatoi] the king's estate is at the hotel's gates and for miles in all directions stretch pine forests brightened just now by 'koumara' bushes on which a red berry grows rather like a strawberry and very good to eat. Many autumn crocuses around. These woods are in a hollow between the range of Parnés and the Mt Pendaylis [Pentelicus], where the marble for the Parthenon and all Athens comes from. Even then Varibopi is 1000 ft above the sea and looking out the whole of Athens is spread out below, topped by Lycabettus and over a glimpse of the Acropolis is visible.

We did long walks and went by bus to Oropos on the coast opposite Euboeus. Hoped Ba would stay there but I had to catch this boat and he had caught one 4 hours after mine back up the Dalmatian coast to Venice. Then I hope he will be meeting a friend and going straight to Arosa,[45] he threatens going home for Xmas, but I hope he won't. This is a large and rickety Roumanian vessel, but I have a IInd Class 4 berth cabin to myself so nothing else much matters. Arrive Beyrouth Sat. morning and Haifa that same evening.

Called on the Petrocchinos [Petrocochinos?] and the Horsfields came down from the flat above to meet us, so we had a pleasant meeting, though I had to tell the P's about the aunts [? – illegible].

Doubt if you can read this – it gives some indication of the energy of the screw in this part of the boat! More anon –

Olga

[20 November 1937; handwritten: PEF/DA/TUF/304][46]

Acropole Palace Hotel
Athens, Greece [Letterhead]

Nov. 20. 1937.

Darling –
This is just a line to let you know that we are at Athens after a really lovely journey – Good weather nearly all the time. Got soaked at Spalato [Split] but sun stayed out to let us catch a glimpse of Dubrovnik. I have started a fuller account which is now packed at the bottom of my suitcase so it will have to follow [see above letter].

Yesterday we got here from the boat in time for lunch having flourished the 'laissez passer'. Things went smoothly as usual. After that we spent the afternoon on the Acropolis wandering and drawing a bit and came down when they shut at sunset. Ba has a good knowledge of the lower haunts of Athens and we had a look round, and supper on the slopes below Lycabettus at a beer hall – really only a trattoria, sitting out under the vines. Ended up at the cinema – *The Pearls of the Crown* – done at such speed that the voices squeaked and the words were almost unintelligible. This morning glorious and we are off to Parnes but whether we can stay there remains to be seen.

The little boat was a success – we had about 400 sheep as fellow-passengers and a dozen water buffaloes, but they were well-behaved and docile and only emitted a pleasant rural effluvium. Three young Americans on their wanderjahr [year abroad] and a man with a foldboat[47] who was going up the Danube in the spring had to find space among the sheep – we were alone in glory in the First Class. Ba put in some practising on the piano, such as it was.

The Yugoslav captain seemed very pro-English, largely because he can only express his opinion of the Italians by expectoration. He says if England and Italy do fight, Cattaro [Kotor] will be our naval base. I said we had put up with a good many slights, but he said the English don't talk they just stay quiet and then act. [...]

[4 December 1937; handwritten: PEF/DA/TUF/305]

Hotel Fast, Jerusalem
Dec. 4. 1937.

Darling Mà,
Got to Haifa at 6 am on the 28th but 2 hours did not suffice to allow me to catch the 8 am train to Lydda. Customs strict and slow nowadays. Had breakfast at the Windsor with the Polish journalist from the boat and then just filled in time till the train at midday. Talked to Cameroon [sic – Cameron] Highlanders in the train – braw Scots fra' Glasgow, who naturally don't think much of Palestine, though they all prefer the Arabs to the Jews.

At Lydda Hamil Yallouk met me and we went straight to camp, where everything was going on as usual. Room soon put clean and straight, also clinic, office and storeroom.

Of course hardly had I settled in but it was the Aid Festival. I didn't want to go to Egypt en bloc – Starks with most of the crowd, but Charles suggested going over to Gerald for a couple of nights, so we took three of the chaps and went in his car. Lovely weather, and Gerald very well, but getting a little bored with rather an empty existence – he is more or less an architect or foreman builder as the work just consists of putting stone on stone at Jerash and there is no money to do more. Came back here today and Gerald comes over too, so we may have a party tonight at the K.D. [King David Hotel]. [...]

Everything in Jerusalem seems quiet, all the shops open and people going about just as usual. T-J [Transjordan] quite peaceful, we saw the Emir [Abdullah] twice dashing along in his cream coloured car. [...] Still no news as to who will succeed Richmond. The P's have put in for concessions in T-J [Tell Jemmeh] and Ajjul, but at the moment, owing to their own lack of tact, it looks doubtful if they've got either. However Miss Murray and Mackay[48] are strong assets....

[10 December 1937; handwritten: PEF/DA/TUF/306]

Tell Duweir.
Dec. 10. 1937.

Dearest Mà,
I don't think there is much news, when I last wrote I had just started with the dentist. He has done an elaborate filling, amalgam, he said, was all wrong where the nerve was so nearly dead so he has fixed it with cement and protected the whole cavity with a gold filling; he says it should last 10–15 yrs! All this fun and games cost £3.15.0 and £7 altogether by the time I'd finished with the hotel.

Gerald came down to Duweir with us for a night and then we all trailed back for further sittings as poor Charles is also dentisting.

Spent some time at the Museum on Tuesday and went to the Hamiltons[49] for cocktails later; he is Acting Director until a new one is appointed, charming little wife and 2 babies.

Got back to camp about 10.30, but the party from Egypt did not get back till the next night, though Starks came up by train. They had had a strenuous time seeing everything possible in a short time. [...]

Heard from Ba who has gone straight back to England despite everything and will not be starting at Arosa until after Xmas. With all the accounts in the papers of bad weather it does seem silly. However —

I suppose this is in the nature of a Xmas letter. [...] I send a cheque for £3 – one for each of the staff (if still in your employ!) as I did nothing about them before leaving. Give them my best wishes. [...]

[16 December 1937; handwritten: PEF/DA/TUF/307]

Duweir.
Dec. 16. 1937.

Darling Mà,
[...] We seem to have settled down into the usual routine after the Aid excursion. The next thing will be Xmas when Gerald comes again, but I expect we shall celebrate on Xmas Eve and do the dressing-up. As always I am devoid of ideas till the last minute. [...]

How are the papers in London treating Palestine at the moment? I suppose you are getting the usual large headlines. Incidents still continue in Jerusalem but they are nearly always at night or twilight and people now don't go about much on the roads after dark. But all this does not affect us in our backwater. I had quite a welcome from the village on arrival and an embarrassing attendance for the first few days, but now it has dropped to the normal thank goodness. There is quite a lot of eye trouble around which keeps me busy. […]

We are expecting a French Professor here next week, also a Chinese student[50] and we have already a Jerusalem girl called Nina Cummins [Cuming],[51] whom we have known since she was 'so high'. Just seventeen, very thin and frail, but has an excellent opinion of herself. She may quieten down later! […]

[17 December 1937; handwritten: PEF/DA/TUF/308]

Tell Duweir.
Dec. 17. 1937.

Darling Daddy,
This is just a line to wish you as many orders as you have pheasants and as many pheasants as you have orders in the New Year and death to the foxes by fair means or foul.

You will have heard about the trip in Greece from Mama; only 10 miles out of Athens there is the king's country estate Tatoiu and for miles around as far as the east coast of Greece there is nothing but marvellous pine woods with a few firs and occasionally an enormous oak tree. There must be a lot of game about, but though I did several long walks I did not see anything. Just now the 'mock strawberry' tree, a small bush with brilliant red berries like strawberries, is in fruit and people pick large baskets of them, they cheer up the look of the country when there is nothing much in flower, except patches of heather on the hill tops. They are still quarrying marble from the great quarries on Mt Pendeles where the stone for all the famous buildings of Athens came from and I suppose now that most of it is exported.

The country people was all very nice and I met one of the king's game keepers, […] who was very amazed […] to see me and went through all possible nationalities till he discovered I was English, when my presence was quite explained. Greece is used to the mad English since Byron's day.

Work is in full swing here, but it is our Sunday today (Friday) so I am off on a duty visit to Gaza to see about the young wife of one of our workers who has gone blind. Not owing to my ministrations, I'm thankful to say!! Shall also get in a bathe with any luck, so we are still pretty warm here. […]

[30 December, probably 1937; handwritten: PEF/DA/TUF/309]

Tell Duweir.
Dec. 30.

Christmas has come and gone quite successfully. We worked last Friday, so that we could have Sunday off instead to recuperate after the binge.

Gerald got here on Friday evening having given HE [His Excellency, Wauchope] the go-bye who had also asked him for Xmas at Petra. Mr Fast sent a Xmas tree from Germany and it was duly decorated, but it seemed rather a waste without the Starkey children.

Costumes were varied and amusing. Starks came as the God Serapis, Gerald as a wizard who was transformed later in the evening to a Greek youth of some kind, I was a Botticellian, the one which was 'dusted down by Auntie Nellie' referred to by the classic Douglas Byng.[52] I wore <u>both</u> nightgowns, the famous red and the flowered one I bought this year and various weeds dispersed around me in garlands. There were also various emperors, a cowboy and suchlike. The due[?] of the evening was undoubtedly Diab[53] who came, unexpectedly, as Lady P. [Petrie] and after a marvellous impersonation he then took Starks off to the life so there was no respect of persons!

The usual dancing and to bed about 1 am. G. [Harding] stayed over Sunday and went off reluctantly on Monday again. We have been busy with the pieces of a pottery coffin, inscribed in characters which are probably local hieroglyphs.[54] It will make a nice addition to our bits of writing. It probably has the name of the owner on it. The storeroom is beginning to fill up and I have my work cut out even if we find nothing more at all, so I don't know what it will be like by the end of the season!

Pummell will be going to Gaza tomorrow, so I expect there will be news of you. Glad you saw Ba, I suppose he was looking much as usual and no doubt the effect of Greece, (if any) had quite worn off by the time you saw him. […]

[7 January 1938; handwritten: PEF/DA/TUF/310]

Tell Duweir
Jan. 7 1938

Darling –

Your nice long Xmas letter reached me last night, as we had an extra run to Gaza and the post was collected a day sooner than usual. The Punches[55] come most regularly and are much appreciated by all, as they go the rounds. I'm sure I nearly always refer to your letters, but if I don't it is not from lack of appreciation. [...]

It is very comic L's[56] reason for not feeding with you over Xmas. You might retaliate by say[ing] that some object to meeting those 'living in sin'!![57]

[...] could you look in the top of my cupboard, in a white Granny cardboard box and extract a few of the plainest handcherchiefs [sic] and put one in your letters as you write, I came out with a meagre supply, and if I should catch a cold I should be lost.

The week was enlivened by Stark's birthday celebrations followed by dancing and snapdragon. The weather has definitely broken, chilly and cloudy now. The P's start digging at Ajjul in 10 days with Mackay in charge, there have been rumours of their coming to Tell Sandahannah (where we went to see the caves and painted tombs!) but as they would have been working with the Hebrew Univ.[58] it would have been madness to introduce the Jewish element into a district. [...]

[12 January 1938; handwritten: PEF/DA/TUF/311]

Hope you got my wire.

Hotel Fast, Jerusalem [Letterhead]
Jan. 12.

Darling –

As you know the unbelievable has happened. Even now I can't realise it, though we had always feared for his imprudence at travelling at night or in the dusk. As I said in a recent letter that is the danger in these times.

The first we knew was when the Gaza police came up to say he had been slightly shot in the leg. That was on Tuesday morning – shortly after Gerald arrived, for as luck would have it he, like Starks, had also to be in Jerusalem for the opening of the New Museum.[59] It was decided that work should go on as usual with Charles in charge and that Gerald and I should do the Jerusalem–London end. We got up by 11.30 and he put calls through to Trustees and Marston and we tracked down Sir Robert [Mond] in Cairo. So by that evening we knew that personally each was in favour of continuation to the end of the season, as we feel is essential.

It is no longer a personal matter, it is something that we must do, not only for Stark's memory but for the morale and peace of south Palestine.

It happened on the bend of the road 3km out of Hebron just where you turn back to look at the best view in the country. There is little doubt that the hold up was the work of the notorious bandit whom everyone has been out to catch for months for repeated crimes of a similar nature. So you can put your mind at rest that there is anything personal about it, it would have happened to any non Moslem travelling on that road so late.

If we take reasonable precautions – and we shall – and avoid all unnecessary excursions, there should be no danger, but even if there were we cannot and do not intend to chuck in our hand now.

Spent this morning with the Police and heard there of your wire. As usual I must pay a tribute to your invariable knowledge of whom to write to, but it was a very <u>naughty wicked</u> Ma as the last thing to have in this country is a Police Post. However H.E. [Wauchope] has insisted for the moment.

Everyone has been very helpful and our path will be made as easy as possible. The funeral was simple and impressive – the pall bearers with palms, HE and the Govt., the Bishop and best of all a queer mixed bag of every race and creed in the city, Pere Vincent, Torczyner, Mackay, Lady P. among them. We spent the time before and after preparing a broadcast appreciation which G. delivered at 9.25.[60] We both felt and still do horribly numb but there is a good deal to do which will keep us going.

This is all I can do for the moment, expect to be back at the Tell tomorrow and hope to sit fast there without gallivanting.

of future plans later

All my love to you and Daddy
from
Olga

[19 January 1938; handwritten: PEF/DA/TUF/312]

Tell Duweir.
Jan. 19. 1938.

Darlings –
Both your letters of the 11th arrived together on Monday, as we had sent a special messenger down. Actually I believe you must have known in London before we did down at Duweir, we knew nothing till about 8.30

and then the Gaza police came and told us Starks was slightly wounded in the leg. It was not till Gerald got here after 9 that we knew the worst. Your letters were a great help and comfort and I have had many more from all sorts of people. The whole thing is still so unbelievable, it is the only thing which helps us to carry on. Everything is continuing perfectly normally in camp, except that we have a guard somewhere about, but I will say this for them one never sees them and they are as distressed as anyone. The whole countryside is miserable, Gaza, Khan Yunis, Feluja [Faluja], they all know they have lost a friend, and the women in Qubeibeh wept bitterly.

We are still awaiting the final word from the Trustees and Sir C. [Charles Marston]; we hope they will not gainsay our earnest hope that we may carry on. (PRIVATE – From HE [Wauchope] downwards everyone feels, as we do, that it would be disastrous to British prestige in south Pal[estine] (or to such of it as remains) if we closed down suddenly). With reasonable precaution things should be quite all right and we have promised to keep off the Jerusalem road as much as possible, where the activities of these rival bandit gangs make the roads unsafe at dusk or after dark. This gang of lawless thieves are just taking advantage of the times to stage these hold-ups, they have already accounted for 7 Arab lives before they got Starks. We haven't heard the result of the troops' activities, you probably know more.

Gerald went back to clear up in T-J [Transjordan] on Sunday, and then comes back here for a week or two – I expect you will have been at the service yesterday. I'm afraid Starks would have loathed it, but it was very nice of everyone to think of it and carry it out. I don't suppose there is anything one can do for Mrs S. Sir C. is looking after her I know. I wrote her a full account by the last post. Thank you both for all that you said and try not to worry, I will be very careful. [...]

[26 January 1938; handwritten: PEF/DA/TUF/313]

P.O.B. 23.
Gaza.
Jan. 26. 1938

Darling –
Your 2 letters with enclosures of 15th and 16th came this evening with another large lot of letters from all sorts of people. Including a very nice personal one from Sir C. Glad you have been in touch with him. Gerald is actually in charge of the outfit from now on, with Charles nominal charge

so please don't let people think that I am. Uncle B. [Bertie] who writes a sweet letter evidently rather thinks so. Gerald and I had a beastly day yesterday going through and listing all the contents of Starks' rooms, it is all the little knick nacks that make it so painful, and today we have got off all his personal papers to Mrs S. Now, we have to make a financial statement for the Trustees, they have not been very definite in their decision as to what we're to do, but we understand from the papers that we're to carry on! Anyhow that suits us all right. We still have our police here and they give no trouble and are enjoying their rest cure away from Hebron. If you could send me the *D.* [*Daily*] *Telegraphs* for the next few weeks it would be rather nice, as all the newspaper subs. stopped on S's death and we get no news at all until we can book new subs. which we don't want to do until we are surer of the future. I expect Sir C. was rather astonished at Richard – we have had several kind offers in the same line. My 'nephew' is also keen to come up, shall he bring rifles, revolvers or what?

It is still raining more or less which means one can get on with things in the house without being swamped by outside staff. I really don't think there is much news. As you say my birthday has not been very bright, but many thanks for all your wishes and for the noble birthday present. [...]

P.S. I should have no cause to go to J. [Jerusalem] now till end of season, so please don't worry that I am on the roads.

[1 February 1938; handwritten: PEF/DA/TUF/314]

Tell Duweir.
Feb. 1st 1938.

Darling –
Charles is going to Jerusalem today so I am sending this line a bit earlier than usual. Everything continues smoothly here; it has been raining almost without a break for the last fortnight but now we have a fine spell again and can get on.

There is really very little news – I had a lot of letters which I am still answering, everyone writes so nicely but it is a sad job. I enclose one from Sir C. [...]

Very many thanks for all your communications and cuttings and handcherchiefs [sic]. All kinds of news is very welcome. Gerald is here till the end of the week when he returns to T J [Transjordan] and will come back at the end of Feb. for a bit. [...]

[6 February 1938; handwritten: PEF/DA/TUF/315]

Tell Duweir.
Feb. 6. 1938.

Darling –
Just a line to thank you for your 2 letters of the 22nd and 27th Jan. with all the cuttings and headlines. Gerald left on Friday, when Charles returned, to stay with HE [Wauchope] for 2 nights who announced that he was coming down on Sat. We were all togged up and cleaned and ready but he did not come, though he wired but needless to say that didn't arrive till much too late. Then when we'd given him up the next day, he did arrive with Gerald about 2.30 and did a lightning tour in ¾ hr. It was a noble gesture to come at all as it is his last month in Palestine. I thanked him as he left and he said he wished he were leaving all Palestine in as good an order as we were. He has done, and is doing everything possible to help us.

We have now got round again to the Aid holiday, this year it is rather a problem and I am all for staying here but people think it would look bad if I did alone so as others are going to Jerusalem I suppose I shall have to also, Gerald suggests Jerash and I may do that.

Rather worrying that I've had no word from Ba, his last letter was 4 days after arriving at Arosa, I see his brother represented him at the service, which he had spent in bed, and I do hope he is all right. He wrote cheerfully then but said the doctors had told him he would have to be careful! I seem to have heard those words before. [...]

[11 February 1938; handwritten: PEF/DA/TUF/316]

German Hospice
Haifa
Feb. 11. 1938.

Darling –
There is plenty to record since my last letter from camp. I left there on Monday after all with the convoy. Mr Evans Assistant District Commissioner, and Flt Lt Cuming, came down (Nina's father) with 2 cars and we went up to Jerusalem via Migdol and Jaffa which is a longer way but quite safe. I stayed with the Cumings for 2 nights and spent a busy time. The first evening I dined with Mr Keith Roach (District Commissioner)[61] whom you remember I met in Haifa some years ago and

heard from him of the steps he was taking for the better security of the Hebron district. He is the man who has done so much to make Haifa content and he had just been transferred to Jerusalem (which includes Hebron) as he is such a good administrator. He was very helpful and concerned for our welfare.

Charles and I had thought of availing ourselves of Lady Downes' old invitation to go there for a rest if ever I or any colleagues wanted one. He rang up for us but she couldn't manage it, so we are sta[y]ing a night here instead.

The following day, Tuesday, we lunched with Harry Iliffe and had pâté and champagne at the King David with Holbrook, I did not dare the oysters which were the reason of the meeting.

I called on Eleanor [Elinor Shaw] at the hospital to see her new baby, a girl, just like Bill Shaw [W.K.S. Shaw] who you remember meeting and had the evening meal with the Cumings.

Next morning early Charles and I went to Bethlehem to make arrangements about the pit, and then to the Bank where the Manager Mr Clarke has done much to help us. We then took the road for Haifa, virtuously travelling again to Jaffa and then up the coast, now a nice safe route. We arrived at Megiddo where we'd arranged to stay a night at teatime and spent 2 most pleasant days there, despite wind and rain, seeing the site, the finds and generally relaxing. They are a delightful crowd, ½ English, ½ American and of course the camp is the height of comfort. Just been to call on the Downes who asked tenderly after you, they both look just the same and the house is as nice as ever. Tomorrow […] we hope to get through to camp though I doubt if the roads will be passable. We may have to hang round till the next day. The change has been a good thing and we both feel fresher for it. […]

[P.S. at top of letter] Your letters will be awaiting me from Gaza when I get back. Had a nice one from Garstang, from Jeffries and from Prof. Hooke for whom I have to write a memoir for the PEFQS [Palestine Exploration Fund Quarterly Statement] of which he is Editor.

[17 February 1938; handwritten: PEF/DA/TUF/317]

Tell Duweir.
Feb. 17. 1938.

Darling Mà,
A letter of yours came yesterday for which many thanks and also 2 copies of the 'DT' [Daily Telegraph] and a 3rd had already got here. It is nice to

have them if not too much trouble. We reached camp on Sunday with an armoured car trailing along as escort. Weather is fine at the moment, so we're getting on. Did you see the awful bit in the *Evening Standard* by Charlie [Marston] about the coffin inscription. One chap to whom we sent the drawing sent his version to Charlie direct and of course he rushes into print.

Charles R. B [Richmond Brown] will be thrilled about the son and Ba equally so for it removes any necessity for him to produce a future baronet! I heard from him yesterday but my letter was the first indication he'd had that Starks had gone. He has not been too well which is disappointing.

Gerald's dog 'Lachish' is staying here till his return at the end of the month which I find very pleasant, as he sleeps in my room and keeps the cats out who tend to have petting parties on my premises about this time of year. He is a large but lovely mongrel who likes being brushed and combed but objected when Diab and [I] bathed him last week. He barks fiercely at strangers and the Arabs are terrified, so that he makes an excellent watch dog.

The Ps are at Ajjul with Miss Murray and Mr Mackay and have just started digging. Charles with Father Hennequin think of going there tomorrow but I think I will follow up with a visit at the end of the season. [...]

[10 March, probably 1938; handwritten: PEF/DA/TUF/318]

Tell Duweir.
March. 10.

Darling,
Very many thanks for your last with Punches and D.T. [*Daily Telegraph*], much appreciated by all.

Gerald has been here but had to leave again yesterday as he had to spend £150 on works before April! We are doing very well on finds in all areas – even ostraca – (between you and me) and it now looks as though the rains are over.

Tomorrow we rather expect Keith Roach and Sir C. Tegart[62] down with their various satellites. Lachish (the dog) is still with us and is sweeter than ever, I get a lot of pleasure out of having him.

I send you a snap taken as Charles and I came away from Megiddo and faced an imposing battery of the expedition's cameras [perhaps Figure 9.9]. It is perhaps more amusing than flattering!

Figure 9.9 Olga with Charles Inge during a visit to Megiddo. Undated, possibly 10 March 1938. Olga Tufnell archive, Palestine Exploration Fund. Courtesy of the Palestine Exploration Fund.

There is a lot to do in the storeroom and the clinic goes on much the same. We have now got the writing down to normal proportions and continue the usual fortnightly reports.

I have asked Ovenden (sec. of the PEF) to send you a proof of my memoir on Starks[63] for any corrections, commas and so on that may be needed. I hope it will be all right.

Under separate cover you will receive a letter from Mohammed el Aneti [Kreti?] (in Arabic!) to which please send an appropriate reply as he much appreciates his annual letter. Special messages from DIAB ARCHAM [Brahim? or Diab Basham?] in it and that they are all very sad about the death of Starks. [...]

[16 March, probably 1938; handwritten: PEF/DA/TUF/319]

Tell Duweir.
March 16.

Darling –
Another week has come round and brings us to the middle of March. [...]

    Mr Cuming came twice last week to see his daughter; he is Intelligence RAF and supposed to be behind the scenes in most things and he has no hesitation in leaving Nina here – his one ewe lamb though after 18 yrs there is now another on the way! Mrs comes from Colchester or thereabouts and is very Essex. [...] Nina's puppy came down on approval with her father and clicked so wholeheartedly with Lachish that he was allowed to stop. Now they do everything together and have a marvellous time and keep us all much amused with their antics.

    We have a little heathen Chinese[64] with us – a student of Glanville[65] and Wheeler, who is really very sweet and most intelligent, much more human than our Japs. [...]

    I hear from Ba that he goes back to England on March 25th, <u>much</u> too soon again, he really is wicked just when he is getting well again, and the Swiss doctor says he is all right if he doesn't do too much. He has enjoyed himself out there and got on well skying [sic – skiing] but no Poulenc. [...]

[25 March, probably 1938; handwritten: PEF/DA/TUF/320]

Tell Duweir.
March 25.

Darling –
Just a line to say all goes well here – it is now lovely fine weather and we can get on. No particular excitements all this week but today has been very gay and busy as we've had 3 visitors. Charles brought Geoffrey Shipton down from Jerusalem yesterday – He is from Megiddo and did the honours to us there when we stayed, so we are having fierce pottery discussions again. Then Nina's father came to take her up to Jerusalem for a few days, full of the various news and scandal of the city. Also John Waechter[66] arrived to spend the night, so really we feel quite in the world again.

    Much doing if I'm to get the division ready in time, but the sooner it's done, the sooner we can get closed down. I can't promise at the moment that it will be any earlier than usual but will try to make it so. Anyhow when we do shall come straight home as there will be much to settle in London.

Lachish is in very good form and continues to be a most pleasurable companion. He does like eating shoes but otherwise has no faults.

[...] The Austrian situation is most sinister and I'm particularly sorry for Betty starting off in that atmosphere and only hope the family is pro-Nazi for her sake. I daren't think what will have happened to the Poradas.[67] The D.Ts [*Daily Telegraphs*] really do help to keep us in touch and are read from cover to cover by all. [...]

[P.S.] Special messages from Mustafa M. [...]

[1 April, probably 1938; handwritten: PEF/DA/TUF/321.1]

Tell Duweir
April 1st.

Darling Daddy and Ma,
April Fool has been duly observed here today and Hasan the carpenter[68] caught me nicely by saying a gold scarab had been found in the Temple! Several workers are going home [Figure 9.10] so it looks as if we are slowly closing down, though I doubt if we shall actually leave before the usual date at the end of the month – we have had several visitors, including Mr Evans, the Assistant District Commissioner, who is in Hebron to keep an eye on the Arab in charge I suppose.

I hope to have finished the division list by the beginning of next week and shall take it to Jerusalem about the 10th. Shall come straight home via Egypt and Marseilles I expect as Austria is certainly out of the question now. What about Betty will it make a difference to their plans? I'm afraid the Poradas will be in the soup. [...]

I don't think I have written since Miss M's [Murray] visit last Friday. She came up in the Petrie car with Pape[69] and A.N. Other in attendance. She was in marvellous form wearing a solar topee under which she was almost invisible. She climbed about all over the Tell and refused all help at negotiating huge stones. They are doing wonderfully well at Ajjul; we hear of the masses of gold through the workers though of course we were much too polite to speak about anything more than potsherds! It is still definitely cool here which from my point of view is all to the good.

Figure 9.10 Workers leaving Tell ed-Duweir, 1938. Olga Tufnell archive, Palestine Exploration Fund. Courtesy of the Palestine Exploration Fund.

[14 April 1938; handwritten: PEF/DA/TUF/321.2]

Tell Duweir
April 14. 1938

Darling Mà,
Have had quite a hectic week getting the list ready or rather the first instalment of it, as we are still finding things and interesting early pottery. On Sunday Pummell took me up and we found Gerald waiting at the Fast. Called on the Cumings and after dinner he and I went to the PBS [Palestine Broadcasting Service] to listen in to his song 'Weep no more sad fountains' sung by Margery Iliffe to the accompaniment of Elizabeth Posten [Poston].[70] She is a most striking and unusual girl who composes and plays – she has been staying with G. [Harding] at Jerash and has been encouraging and criticising his tunes. Her brother was HE's Sec. and he is now a Director of the PBS. [...] I enclose a cutting of the musical criticism in the *Pal. Post*.

Next day I paid a visit to the Hosp[ital] to say how do you do and farewell and spent the rest of it at the Museum doing this and that and going through photos with Gerald. Drinks with the Shaws and then to dinner with the Iliffes, Mrs Gluek [Glueck?][71] and the Poston brother and sister. She played most of the evening, v. good Early English and modern, excellent style and appreciation but cannot quite manage big things which I expect she realises. [...]

Harry I. [Iliffe] picked me up at 8 am next morning and we came down here for the division which went off very well and to our satisfaction. Gerald is also down for a week and tomorrow we go to call at Ajjul! Wonder what we shall be shown if anything.

Robert Hamilton, Acting Director is staying here tonight so we've had quite a varied time.

Lachish is very bad with distemper at the Animals' Hosp. [and we] are very worried that he may be left with nervous complications. I saw him all wrapped up and looking thin and miserable poor darling. I do blame myself for having kept him here but who could tell.

Enclose 2 snaps for your amusement – the group from L. to R. – Veronica Seton Williams, Alice Hastings, Charles, O., Mr Keith Roach, Holbrook Bonney, but of course not everyone is in it, taken by Col. Perowne.

Tried to see about boats in J. [Jerusalem] but could not decide anything definitely, hope to get finished here by the end of the month but there will be more than usual to do if we have to shut down bearing in mind the possibility of not coming next year.

[21 April, probably 1938; handwritten: PEF/DA/TUF/322]

Tell Duweir
April 21.

Darling Mà,
Your letter from Christchurch got here in the middle of the week as there was a special visit to Gaza mainly to get enough old newspapers to pack with, here again the D.T.s [*Daily Telegraph*] are proving their value! [...]

Last Friday, Gerald, Charles and I went down to Ajjul and got in a bathe before calling on the camp. We had already seen the familiar topee poaked [sic] round the door as we sped past and it was the first thing to meet our eye as we returned. We found Prof. in the Library, writing, looking well and plump but very shaky about the legs. He was pleased to see us and tea was ordered. We talked of this and that, of the importance of prompt publishing, he has now reached the point when he seriously advocates printing the plates before the division. After tea and biscuits we were allowed to see the storeroom, pots laid out but no gold or scarabs visible, though Prof. could not resist saying that 20% of wages had been spent on bakshish.[72] Mackay is pretty fed up with everything but hopes to call here on his way back. Miss M. [Murray] and the others Pape and Caralfi we had met in Gaza where they had gone to sketch. They've had a 9 wks season. Lady P. enquired tenderly after you and made various remarks about C-S [Czechoslovakia]. Both her feet were bandaged up, perhaps cheaper than socks? The row of pails were in position and the cat not far off.

Two nights later we had our annual party with the Sheykh of the Ajjulyn[73] – a windy hot night and a longest walk to the tent, exceptionally full of life human and insect, the usual mutton and rice was safely negotiated and after polite converse till 10 pm we all went home, had a drink and deloused – total bag next day 72, unusually high total chiefly due to sheep sharing camping ground.

I don't see much chance of getting away before about May 6, there is much to be done as I must clear the storeroom before leaving and everything must be divided in case we don't come next year. [...]

Notes

1 Seton-Williams 2011, 77.
2 Starkey 1937a, 177.
3 Starkey 1937b, 233–35; Ussishkin 1993, 906.
4 It was later excavated by David Ussishkin in the renewed excavations at Lachish by Tel Aviv University and the Israel Exploration Society (1973–83).
5 Segev 2000, 415–33; Cohen and Kolinsky 1992; Hughes 2010.
6 Handwritten letter in pencil from Diab Basham, site guard (*ghaffir*) at Tell ed-Duweir, to Olga Tufnell, dated 7 October 1936: 'I beg to inform you that since 3 days some of the Palestine Revolutionests [sic] men 25 nearly with their rifles attacked the camp. They asking for Benzine and Kerosene to fire the Company. But they did not find. At last then beated us and striked us. Then they took our money our watches and other things which coasts [costs] more than five pounds that all what the company looses: they were about to kill us but God save us from them – give salutation to father, mother, and all friends … yours obediently' (PEF/DA/TUF/277). The police report of this event, indicating some slight variations to Diab Basham's account, is published in Garfinkel 2016, 94–5. A letter from Hilda Petrie to Olga Tufnell, dated 10 October 1936, also highlights concerns about safety and looting: 'You – or some of you – should be finding out from some reliable source in Palestine whether there is a likelihood of being able to work next season? From all I hear, the answer would be NO. So do persuade your spokesman, whoever it is, to make reliable enquiries. I suppose you have seen that yr premises and ghaffirs have been molested by insurgents: I think in Palestine Post of 6th, 7th or 9th [...] The notion here is that even if the shooting and p'ercer [?] of the acts are suppressed, there must continue to be marauding gangs going about looting. Blackmail holding up for gain, and house looting are the present order of the day already – first Jews, then police and military, then British, now looting!' (PEF/DA/TUF/279).

7   A letter to Sir Charles Marston from expedition member Holbrook Bonney suggested that a gang had been operating in the vicinity of Hebron 'for months' before the murder. There had been a previous attempt to stop the expedition vehicle, as well as shots fired at the car, just a month prior to the murder very close to Hebron. The incident was reported to police, but not to Sir Charles for fear of worrying him. 'Copy letter received from Mr Holbrook Bonney from Tell Duweir. 24/1/38', folder WA/HSW/AR/Lac/B.13, 'Report re murder of J.L. Starkey, 1938', Wellcome Collection, London.

8   'Murder of British Archaeologist', *Palestine Post*, 11 January 1938.

9   'His Beard Cost Him His Life', *Palestine Post*, 13 February 1938; 'Extra-ordinary report II, 31 January 1938; Re Murder of J.L Starkey on Jan 10th. 1938', signed C.H. Inge and Olga Tufnell, folder WA/HSW/AR/Lac/B.13, 'Report re murder of J.L. Starkey, 1938', Wellcome Collection, London; excerpt from District Commissioner's report, published in Ussishkin 2019, 152.

10 John Starkey, pers. comm., 2007.

11 Garfinkel 2016. Also see Seton-Williams 2011, 78–9.

12 Melman 2020, 152, n. 77.

13 Ussishkin 2019, contra Garfinkel 2016. Also see Melman 2020, 152–3.

14 'Arab Admits Part in Starkey Murder', *Palestine Post*, 21 January 1938; 'Prisoner Acquitted by Jerusalem Military Court', *Palestine Post*, 28 January 1938. It was later admitted that the real murderers of Starkey were not successfully apprehended, as stated by Keith-Roach, the District Commissioner of Jerusalem, and also suspected by Inge and Tufnell (Ussishkin 2019, 153). The perpetrator of the murder is currently thought to have been a member of an armed group within the Hebron district led by Issa Al-Hajj Suleiman Battat (Melman 2020, 153, n. 80).

15 Letter of 12 January 1938; for a history of the Palestine Broadcasting Service, including its important role during the Arab Revolt period, see Stanton 2013.

16 'Noted Archaeologist Buried in Jerusalem', *Palestine Post*, 12 January 1938. This article contains a thorough list of the notable attendees and the edition contains tributes to J.L. Starkey from Flinders Petrie and Harry Torczyner. Also see Ussishkin 2014, 49–53 and Melman 2020, 125–7.

17 For example: Murray 1938; Murray et al. 1938; Tufnell 1938.

18 'Extra-ordinary report II, 31 January 1938; Re Murder of J.L Starkey on Jan 10th. 1938', signed C.H. Inge and Olga Tufnell, folder WA/HSW/AR/Lac/B.13, 'Report re murder of J.L. Starkey, 1938', Wellcome Collection, London.

19 Letter from Sir Charles Marston to Charles Inge, 1 February 1938, folder WA/HSW/AR/Lac/B.13, 'Report re murder of J.L. Starkey, 1938', Wellcome Collection, London.

20 Also see Garfinkel 2016, 95–6 and Seton-Williams 2011, 79.

21 Folder WA/HSW/AR/Lac/B.13, 'Report re murder of J.L. Starkey, 1938', Wellcome Collection, London.

22 'Bible Search is "Cursed" Says Scientist', *Daily Express*, 9 May 1939.

23 Erickson-Gini and Oach 2019, 11–12.

24 Tufnell 1953, 32. Also see Garfinkel 2016 for remaining traces of the rail and chute system at Tell ed-Duweir.

25 Tufnell 1982, 85. The 'fellah village' means the villager farmers of Qubeibeh.

26 See Abu-Sitta 2010, 36, which cites a population of 420 as of 1945. Abu-Sitta also cites the destruction of machinery, killing of farm animals and burning of houses and granaries by Israeli forces in October 1948 (2010, 95).

27 Tufnell 1985.

28 King Edward VIII's proposal of marriage to Wallis Simpson, an American divorcée, caused a scandal and ultimately led to his abdication on 11 December 1936.

29 Site of the ancient city of Ugarit.

30 Maurice Dunand (1898–1987), French archaeologist who excavated Byblos between 1924 and 1975.

31 'When icicles hang by the wall': Shakespeare, *Love's Labours Lost*, V.ii.

32 Barbara Parker (1908–93), archaeologist and Assyriologist. Sir Max Mallowan's epigrapher at Nimrud, Iraq, and a founding member of the British School of Archaeology in Iraq (1932), becoming its secretary-librarian. Married Mallowan soon after the death of his crime-novelist wife Agatha Christie in 1976.

33 Olga's former home in Essex.

34 The Royal Commission of 1936, headed by Lord Peel, proposed a plan for the partition of Palestine. It intended to transfer the Arab population from land intended as a Zionist homeland to other areas. The plan was rejected by Arabs, as well as by Jews, who considered the territory offered them too small and not including Jerusalem (Segev 2000, 401–4).

35 Tufnell 1953, 158–60; pls 25, 26.

36 Olga Feinberg: see letter of 14 April 1936 and related note.

37 A letter to Olga Tufnell dated 12 May 1939 (PEF/DA/TUF/385) from Ogden, a jeweller's in London, indicates the mounting of an intaglio gem, which is probably this one.

38 Tufnell 1958, 92–110.

39 John Gray (1913–2000). Old Testament scholar introduced to archaeology by J.L. Starkey at Tell ed-Duweir, probably during a year of travel on scholarship. Became Chaplain to Palestine Police, 1939–41. Lecturer, and later Reverend Professor of Hebrew and Semitic Languages, University of Aberdeen, 1953–80.

40 Published as *The Bible Comes Alive* (Marston 1937).

41 Tufnell 1958, 62–92, 129–30.

42 Inscribed 'ration' bowls in Egyptian hieratic of the New Kingdom period; see Tufnell 1958, 129–30.

43 Dame Freya Madeleine Stark (1893–1933), explorer and travel writer. The first Western woman to travel through the Arabian Desert (Hadhramaut).

44 The *Fliegende Blätter* (Flying Pages), a German weekly illustrated humour and satire magazine.

45 A Swiss resort. Pure air in Switzerland was considered beneficial for tuberculosis or any other disease of the lungs.

46 This letter overlaps with letter of 16 and 26 November 1937.

47 A collapsible kayak made of rubberised canvas.

48 Ernest John Henry Mackay (1880–1943), archaeologist trained by Petrie in Egypt, 1907–12, working on Theban tombs, 1912–16; Custodian of Antiquities, Palestine, 1919–22. Assisted Beth Shan excavations in 1922; Field Director of archaeological excavations for the Joint Oxford–Field Museum expedition to Kish, Iraq, 1923–5; Field Director, Mohenjo-daro, Indus Valley, 1926–31, and subsequent excavations. Mackay worked with Petrie and Margaret Murray at Tell el-'Ajjul in the final 1938 season.

49 Robert William Hamilton (1905–95), Chief Inspector of Antiquities, Palestine, 1931–8; Director of Antiquities, Palestine, 1938–48; Senior Lecturer in Near Eastern Archaeology, Oxford, 1949–56; Keeper, Department of Antiquities, Ashmolean Museum, Oxford, 1956–72; Keeper of Ashmolean Museum, 1962–72.

50 Nai Xia (1910–85), in expedition list as 'N. Shiah'. Student of Stephen Glanville at UCL. Completed doctoral thesis on 'Ancient Egyptian Beads' (1946). Became one of China's most distinguished archaeologists (Director of the Institute of Archaeology in China, 1958–82).

51 Nina Cuming joined the expedition for this final season.

52 Douglas Byng (1893–1988), cabaret star famous for female impersonations.

53 Presumably Diab Basham, who appears to have served in multiple capacities on the expedition as assistant as well as an unarmed guard (also see note 6 above).

54 Tufnell 1958, 130–2.

55 *Punch* (1841–1992), illustrated magazine of humour.

56 Louis, Olga's younger brother.

57 Perhaps a reference to the separate lives of Olga's parents and to Louis's lifestyle.

58 The Hebrew University of Jerusalem, opened 1925.

59 The Palestine Archaeological Museum, built with funds from John D. Rockefeller Jr., was opened to the public on 13 January 1938.

60 'An appreciation of James Leslie Starkey, Broadcast by Lankester Harding on Palestine Broadcasting Service, January 11th 1938 at 9.25 p.m.' Typed transcript in folder WA/HSW/AR/Lac/B.13, 'Report re murder of J.L. Starkey, 1938', Wellcome Collection, London.

61 District Commissioner of Jerusalem, 1938–43.

62 Sir Charles Tegart was an expert on counter-terrorism and worked to restore security in Palestine from December 1937.

63 Tufnell 1938.

64 Nai Xia; also see letter of 16 December 1937 and note 50 above.

65 Stephen Ranulf Kingdon Glanville (1900–56), excavated Tell el-Amarna for the Egypt Exploration Society. Edwards Professor of Egyptology and Philology, UCL, 1935–46.

66   John Waechter, prehistorian. Worked with Petrie and Seton-Williams at Sheikh es-Zuweid, as well as Wadi Dhobai, Transjordan, and Jabbul Plain, Syria, in the late 1930s. Collaborated with Seton-Williams and du Plat Taylor on projects in Cyprus, Syria and Turkey. Lecturer, then Senior Lecturer, in Palaeolithic Archaeology at the Institute of Archaeology, London, during the 1950s–70s.

67   In March 1938 Hitler's army had invaded Austria, which was then annexed to the German Reich. At the urging of friends in Long Island, New York, Edith Porada and her sister left Austria for the United States that year. She later became established as a leading scholar of ancient Near Eastern art and archaeology at Columbia University (Pittman 1995).

68   Hasan Khalaf was a carpenter for the expedition.

69   Carl Pape, architect. Worked with Petrie at Tell el-'Ajjul.

70   Elizabeth Poston (1905–87), English composer, writer and pianist who edited and collected folk songs.

71   Probably Helen Ignauer Glueck (1907–95), haematologist and wife of Nelson Glueck, American rabbi, academic and pioneer of biblical archaeology. Nelson Glueck served as the Director of the American School of Oriental Research, Jerusalem, 1936–40, and worked at Khirbet el-Kheleifeh, Transjordan, 1938–40.

72   Arabic, *bakshish* or *baksheesh*, meaning gratuity or reward payment. In this context *bakshish* was for intact finds reported and presented to Petrie. The method was employed by archaeologists to discourage theft of finds by workers, and encourage a rapid pace of work while maintaining careful excavation of the artefacts.

73   Presumably Sheikh Suliman el Ajjulyn of the Amarin tribe of Bedouin. For related reference, see Garfinkel 2016, 89.

References

Abu-Sitta, Salman H. 2010. *Atlas of Palestine: 1917–1966*. London: Palestine Land Society.

Cohen, Michael and Martin Kolinsky, eds. 1992. *Britain and the Middle East in the 1930s: Security Problems, 1935–39*. London: Palgrave.

Erickson-Gini, Tali and Ami Oach. 2019. 'The Es Sbaita (Shivta) Visitors Book, 1934–1937: Negev Archaeology in British Mandate Palestine', *Michmanim* 28: 9–22.

Garfinkel, Yosef. 2016. 'The Murder of James Leslie Starkey near Lachish', *Palestine Exploration Quarterly* 148: 84–109.

Hughes, Matthew. 2010. 'From Law and Order to Pacification: Britain's Suppression of the Arab Revolt in Palestine, 1936–1939', *Journal of Palestine Studies* 39(2): 6–22.

Marston, Sir Charles. 1937. *The Bible Comes Alive*. London: Eyre and Spottiswoode.

Melman, Billie. 2020. *Empires of Antiquities: Modernity and the Rediscovery of the Ancient Near East, 1914–1950*. Oxford: Oxford University Press.

Murray, Margaret A. 1938, 'James Leslie Starkey: 3rd January, 1895–10th January, 1938', *Man* 38: 42–3.

Murray, Margaret A., Gerald A. Wainwright and Kenneth de B. Codrington. 1938. 'Starkey, J.L., 1895–1938', *Palestine Exploration Quarterly* 70: 75.

Pittman, Holly. 1995. 'Edith Porada, 1912–1994', *American Journal of Archaeology* 99: 143–6.

Segev, Tom. 2000. *One Palestine Complete: Jews and Arabs under the British Mandate*. London: Little, Brown.

Seton-Williams, M.V. 2011. *The Road to El-Aguzein*. London and New York: Routledge.

Stanton, Andrea L. 2013. *'This Is Jerusalem Calling': State Radio in Mandate Palestine*. Austin, TX: University of Texas Press.

Starkey, James L. 1937a. 'Lachish as Illustrating Bible History (Lecture)', *Palestine Exploration Quarterly* 69: 171–9.

Starkey, James L. 1937b. 'Excavations at Tell ed-Duweir, the Wellcome Marston Research Expedition to the Near East (Lecture)', *Palestine Exploration Quarterly* 69: 228–41.

Tufnell, Olga. 1938. 'James Leslie Starkey: An Appreciation', *Palestine Exploration Quarterly* 70: 80–3.

Tufnell, Olga. 1953. *Lachish III: The Iron Age*. London: Oxford University Press.

Tufnell, Olga, 1958. *Lachish IV: The Bronze Age*. London: Oxford University Press.

Tufnell, Olga. 1982. 'Reminiscences of a Petrie Pup', *Palestine Exploration Quarterly* 114: 81–6.

Tufnell, Olga. 1985. 'Reminiscences of Excavations at Lachish: An Address Delivered by Olga Tufnell at Lachish on July 6, 1983', *Tel Aviv* 12: 3–8.

Ussishkin, David. 1993. 'Lachish'. In *New Encyclopedia of Archaeological Excavations in the Holy Land*, edited by Ephraim Stern, 897–911. Jerusalem: Israel Exploration Society.

Ussishkin, David. 2014. *Biblical Lachish: A Tale of Construction, Destruction, Excavation and Restoration*. Jerusalem: Israel Exploration Society.

Ussishkin, David. 2019. 'The Murder of James Leslie Starkey: Addendum to the Paper of Yosef Garfinkel.' *Palestine Exploration Quarterly* 151: 146–54.

Epilogue

This Epilogue presents a summary of what came next for Olga after her time in Palestine and the end of the Tell ed-Duweir expedition, drawing largely from obituaries, tributes and biographical accounts.[1] It briefly assesses her longer-term legacy, and offers closing thoughts on potential future directions for research into Olga Tufnell and her contemporaries.

As described in Chapter 9, Olga's fieldwork was cut short. She returned to London in 1938 to focus on publication efforts with the support of the Wellcome Trust, specifically to work on the excavation reports for Lachish, volumes II, III and IV, covering the Fosse Temple, the Iron Age and the Bronze Age respectively. At this time she was based at St John's Lodge at the Institute of Archaeology in Regents Park, where artefacts and field records were gathered for restoration and study. She was not alone in this period. Among others, she was assisted in the restoration of many ceramic vessels by Olive Starkey, the sister of the late expedition director J.L. Starkey.[2]

During the Second World War, Olga served as an ARP (Air Raid Precaution) warden and censor, and was subsequently recruited to join the BBC Arabic Service (in Aldenham) because of her knowledge and experience. She was offered a post in Baghdad by the Middle East Office, but she refused on account of the climate of Iraq. Olga could have continued with the BBC after the war, but was committed to the completion of the publication, with the encouragement of Wellcome Trustees. Whereas volume II was largely completed before the outbreak of the Second World War and published in 1940, volumes III and IV were completed in 1953 and 1957 respectively (with assistance from Ros Henry from 1955).

This major effort of publication is testament to Olga's patience, thoroughness and attention to detail, collaboration with others, and, quite simply, hard work. As any user of the volumes will attest, they are an exemplar of archaeological publication for the time, with clear organisation, presentation of data and objects and specialist reports. The drawings, which had largely been done by Olga and Harding in the field, are simple but effective, and augmented by high-quality photography. As indicated by David Ussishkin in his later excavations and research on Lachish (see Chapter 9), although methods employed in the 1930s would be viewed as outmoded today, their findings and overall interpretations based on the excavations remain relatively solid. This stands in contrast to other large-scale expeditions of the time, such as Megiddo, which suffered from multiple changes of director and diverse interpretations of chronological sequences and findings.

In 1951, Olga was particularly pleased at being elected a Fellow of the Society of Antiquaries, as proposed by John Garstang. Hinting at the gender imbalances that continued in archaeology in the post-war period, she anticipated some male opposition that was not, however, forthcoming. She declared that becoming an FSA was one of her proudest moments. Olga apparently neither sought nor was offered an academic post or teaching opportunities. She later modestly claimed that she had 'no status in the academic world'.[3] She 'retired' from the Institute of Archaeology when it moved to its new location in Gordon Square in 1957, even though she had only recently turned fifty. She never truly did retire, however, and many people continued to seek her advice and benefited from her wide-ranging knowledge. Olga gained respect and admiration for the Lachish volumes and numerous articles she published.

Olga continued her zest for travel and new experiences. She participated in excavations at Nimrud, Iraq, in the mid- to late 1950s. Reminiscences about Olga from this time are scarce, though a published letter by archaeologist Robert Hamilton, written when they spent a season together at Nimrud in 1955, shares his candid impressions of her: 'Olga is an admirable woman, very unselfish and kind; rather solemn about potsherds and archaeology, but quite ready to laugh at other things, and always being as nice as possible to everyone, including the horrid little cat we had for a time, which has now been sent back to the village.'[4] She stayed in Yemen in 1959, where she studied traditional pottery techniques. This period of her life is well represented in letters and photographs in the Palestine Exploration Fund archives, which have been studied and presented in lectures by archaeologist Carl Phillips.

Olga also continued her interests in Palestinian folk traditions and costumes, collaborating with Violet Barbour on the Palestine Folk Museum in Jerusalem in the early 1960s. Olga's work with museums and exhibitions continued that decade in her co-ordination and promotion of the centenary exhibition of the Palestine Exploration Fund at the

Victoria and Albert Museum in London in 1965,[5] which travelled to other parts of Britain as well as Lebanon, including with the help of her old friend Gerald Lankester Harding, who identified the floral specimens for the exhibition. Olga also took the opportunity to give lectures in America and the Middle East during this time.

In the 1960s she continued her academic research on scarabs and seals, collaborating with the American Egyptologist William Ward of the American University of Beirut. Olga's research on the scarabs from Lachish had begun back in the 1930s, as shown in her correspondence with Edith Porada. It was pursued with the publication of the Lachish volumes in the 1950s, and her continuous search for parallels expanded her knowledge of Palestinian and Egyptian scarab seals considerably. This led to continued efforts to find synchronisms that would tie Egyptian and Palestinian chronologies more closely together for the second millennium BC. The desire to gain greater clarity on the Hyksos era, the Second Intermediate Period, was particularly important here, an interest that she had acquired when working under Petrie. An important study was published by Tufnell and Ward on the Montet Jar in 1966, and subsequently two 'Studies on Scarab Seals' volumes, one published by Ward in 1981, and the other by Olga in 1984. She also began to explore the use of computers in studying the typology of scarab seals as late as 1985, the year of her death.

Olga returned to visit Tell ed-Duweir in Israel in the late 1970s and early 1980s, and developed close relations with the new excavators of this important site, including David Ussishkin, whom she met again at a public lecture in London soon before she passed away. Jonathan Tubb of the British Museum conducted an oral history interview with Olga and edited a memorial volume dedicated to her in 1985.

The value of Olga's letters and photographs of the 1920s and 1930s for future research is difficult to quantify as they refer to many people, places and events that will continue to be of interest to a range of scholars – not only archaeologists, but also historians, sociologists, geographers and biographers. Some directions for research based on this volume relate to insights gained into Olga's career as an 'amateur' archaeologist. Even though she never saw herself as an 'excavator',[6] she was as skilled and knowledgeable as any archaeologist of the time with a doctoral degree. As archaeology became increasingly professionalised, Olga found her own niche, which was inextricably linked to the collections she spent decades studying and publishing, as well as the social skills, connections and friendships she cultivated over many years. It was through these networks that she was able to build her scholarly and professional profile within the Middle East, Europe and the United States. She became a significant contributor to the field, being held in high regard, despite not having formal qualifications. It is hoped that her story can be more fully integrated alongside those of other influential women archaeologists of the twentieth century.

What may be of future interest to researchers is a prosopographic study of biographical networks of connections between people, not only using the Olga Tufnell archive, but including other sources to explore the social, political and scholarly networks of the Mandate period and beyond. Olga's letters are filled with references to friends, relatives, colonial officials, academics and workforce members, situating individuals at specific places and dates. There are also interesting dimensions to archaeologists' responses to political and security disruptions in this colonial era, notably their desire to continue work in the face of impending dangers. This volume has relied mostly on a single archive, and focused on a single person – yet future studies may explore wider connections through other archives and publications, including those geared more to public audiences.

Another fascinating area of research is the intersection between public health and archaeology in the Mandate period. Olga's voluntary activities running the clinics at Fara, Ajjul and Tell ed-Duweir attest to her charity and generosity of spirit, as well as the important role that this played in building relationships with local communities. Further work should be done to identify the individual members of Petrie's and Starkey's workforces, incorporating their names and identities into excavation histories and acknowledging their contributions to knowledge creation.

The photographs taken by Olga, as well as others referred to and reproduced in this volume, also attest to the importance of cultural heritage documentation – as archaeological sites, historical places and settlements change or disappear over time. The film footage from old excavations conducted by Olga and her contemporaries is in need of digital preservation and dissemination, building on the success of the *Filming Antiquity* project at UCL. It is hoped that through continued digital preservation and online dissemination of archives and publications, Olga's story can live on well into the future.

Notes

1   See Chapter 1, note 67.
2   Slaninka 2018.
3   Olga Tufnell interviewed by Jonathan Tubb. Transcript of audiotaped interview, *c.* 1985.

4 Letter of 16 April 1955, published in Hamilton 1992, 163.
5 Victoria and Albert Museum 1965; Fraser and Thornton 2015.
6 Olga Tufnell interviewed by Jonathan Tubb. Transcript of audiotaped interview, *c.* 1985.

References

Fraser, Adam and Amara Thornton. '2015. Our First Hundred Years (and Fifty More)', *Palestine Exploration Fund Blog*, https://www.pef.org.uk/blog/our-first-hundred-years-and-fifty-more/, last accessed 25 August 2019.

Hamilton, Robert W. 1992. *Letters from the Middle East by an Occasional Archaeologist*. Durham: Pentland Press.

Slaninka, W. 2018. 'Olive Starkey: A Lady of Lachish', *Filming Antiquity*, https://www.filmingantiquity.com/blog/category/olive-starkey/, last accessed 11 August 2020.

Tubb, Jonathan N., ed. 1985. *Palestine in the Bronze and Iron Ages: Papers in Honour of Olga Tufnell*. London: Institute of Archaeology.

Tufnell, Olga. 1984. *Studies on Scarab Seals, Volume II: Scarab Seals and their Contribution to History in the Early Second Millennium BC*. Warminster: Aris & Phillips.

Tufnell, Olga and William A. Ward. 1966. 'Relations between Byblos, Egypt and Mesopotamia at the End of the Third Millennium BC: A Study of the Montet Jar', *Syria* 43: 165–241.

Victoria and Albert Museum. 1965. *World of the Bible: Centenary Exhibition of the Palestine Exploration Fund in Co-operation with the British School of Archaeology in Jerusalem*. London: Victoria and Albert Museum.

Ward, William A. 1981. *Studies on Scarab Seals, Volume I: Pre 12th Dynasty Scarab Amulets*. Warminster: Aris & Phillips.

Biographical index

Abd el Megid, Sheykh
23 April 1936; PEF/DA/TUF/270

Abu Shareik, Sheykh Ahseyr?
14 February 1932; PEF/DA/TUF/192

el Ajjulyn, Sheikh Suliman
21 April, probably 1938; PEF/DA/TUF/322

Albright, William Foxwell
4 January 1929; PEF/TUF/DA/124

Ali, Salman
25 January 1933; PEF/DA/TUF/210

Allenby, Edmund
17–18 November 1927; PEF/DA/TUF/90

Atatürk (Kemal, Mustafa)
8 May–10 June 1933; PEF/DA/TUF/223 –
    May 23 1933

Avi-Yonah, Michael
5 December 1928; PEF/TUF/DA/122

Baramki, Dimitri
28 December 1935; PEF/DA/TUF/258

Basham, Diab
30 December, probably 1937; PEF/DA/
    TUF/309
17 February 1938; PEF/DA/TUF/317
10 March, probably 1938; PEF/DA/TUF/318

Bate, Dorothea
8 June 1936; PEF/DA/TUF/276
10 March, probably 1937; PEF/DA/TUF/294

Ben-Dor, Immanuel
12 March 1935; PEF/DA/TUF/249

Bin Al Hussein, Abdullah (King Abdullah I)
25 January 1931: PEF/DA/TUF/305

Bonney, Holbrook V.
21 February 1936; PEF/DA/TUF/261
8 March 1936; PEF/DA/TUF/264
23 April 1936; PEF/DA/TUF/270
23 December, probably 1936; PEF/DA/
    TUF/283
14 April 1938; PEF/DA/TUF/321.2

Breasted, Charles
15 April 1930 and later; PEF/TUF/DA/166

Broome, Myrtle
17–18 November 1927; PEF/DA/TUF/90
probably 19 December 1927; PEF/DA/
    TUF/98.2
18 December 1927; PEF/DA/TUF/100
8 March 1928; PEF/TUF/DA/111

Brown, Donald
26 December 1932; PEF/DA/TUF/206
29 March 1935: PEF/DA/TUF/252

Brunton, Guy
13 December 1927; PEF/DA/TUF/97
6 January 1935; PEF/DA/TUF/243
21 March 1935; PEF/DA/TUF/251
29 March 1935; PEF/DA/TUF/252
4 April 1935; PEF/DA/TUF/268

Cafferata, Raymond Oswald
4 February 1931; PEF/DA/TUF/178
19 February, probably 1931; PEF/DA/
    TUF/181
28 February, probably 1931; PEF/DA/
    TUF/182
13 March, probably 1932; PEF/DA/TUF/195

Carter, Howard
18 December 1927; PEF/DA/TUF/100

Caton Thompson, Dr Gertrude
27 October 1930; PEF/DA/TUF/169
6 January 1935; PEF/DA/TUF/243
25 March, probably 1937; PEF/DA/TUF/296
1 April, probably 1937; PEF/DA/TUF/297

Colt, Harris Dunscombe, Jr. The following
    letters include reference to 'the Colts', i.e.
    H.D. Colt Jr. and Teresa Strickland Colt.
    For specific reference to Teresa Strickland
    Colt, see below.
27 January 1929; PEF/TUF/DA/127
11 February 1929; PEF/TUF/DA/131
8 March 1929; PEF/TUF/DA/135
11 January 1930; PEF/TUF/DA/151
27 October 1930; PEF/DA/TUF/169
10 December 1930; PEF/DA/TUF/174
19 December, probably 1930; PEF/
    DA/TUF/175

25 January 1931; PEF/ DA/TUF /177
4 February 1931; PEF/DA/TUF/178
14 February, probably 1931; PEF/DA/
 TUF/180
19 February, probably 1931; PEF/DA/TUF/181
28 February, probably 1931; PEF/DA/
 TUF/182
24 March, probably 1931; PEF/DA/TUF/184
3 January 1932; PEF/DA/TUF/190
8 January 1932; PEF/DA/TUF/191
14 February 1932; PEF/DA/TUF/192
24 February 1932; PEF/DA/TUF/193
13 March, probably 1932; PEF/DA/TUF/195
11 April 1932; PEF/DA/TUF/198
19 April 1932; PEF/DA/TUF/199
29 November 1932; PEF/DA/TUF/200
3 December 1932; PEF/DA/TUF/201
26 December 1932; PEF/DA/TUF/206
4 January 1933; PEF/DA/TUF/207
25 January 1933; PEF/DA/TUF/210
4 March, probably1933; PEF/DA/TUF/215
15 March, probably 1933; PEF/DA/TUF/
 217
7 April 1933; PEF/DA/TUF/220
12 April 1933; PEF/DA/TUF/221
6 January 1935; PEF/DA/TUF/243
28 February 1936; PEF/DA/TUF/262
12 May 1936; PEF/DA/TUF/272

Colt, Teresa: *see* Strickland Colt, Teresa.

Crowfoot, John Winter, and Grace (and
 daughter Joan)
5 December 1928; PEF/TUF/DA/122
4 January 1929; PEF/TUF/DA/124
8 March 1929; PEF/TUF/DA/135
7 March 1932; PEF/DA/TUF/194
13 March, probably 1932; PEF/DA/TUF/195
10 December 1932; PEF/DA/TUF/202
13 December 1932; PEF/DA/TUF/203
17 February, probably 1933; PEF/DA/
 TUF/213
28 February 1935; PEF/DA/TUF/248
2 April 1936; PEF/DA/TUF/267
19 March 1937; PEF/DA/TUF/295

Clarke, Col.
10 December 1931; PEF/DA/TUF/188
26 December 1932; PEF/DA/TUF/206

Cuming, Nina
16 December 1937; PEF/DA/TUF/307
11 February 1938; PEF/DA/TUF/316
16 March, probably 1938; PEF/DA/TUF/319
14 April 1938; PEF/DA/TUF/321.2

Davies, Norman de Garis, and Nina de Garis
21 November 1927; PEF/DA/TUF/91
8 March 1936; PEF/DA/TUF/264

Dunand, Maurice
23 December, probably 1936; PEF/DA/
 TUF/283

Dyott, Eleanor (*also see* Shaw, Eleanor)
20 December 1934; PEF/DA/TUF/239

30 January 1935; PEF/DA/TUF/245
12 March 1935; PEF/DA/TUF/249

Engelbach, Reginald
21 November 1927; PEF/DA/TUF/91

Evans, Sir Arthur
28 December 1929; PEF/TUF/DA/146
12 May 1936; PEF/DA/TUF/272

Farrer, Frank
23 February 1935; PEF/DA/TUF/247
19 April 1935; PEF/DA/TUF/254

Feinberg, Olga F.
14 April 1936; PEF/DA/TUF/269
25 February 1937; PEF/DA/TUF/292
10 March, probably 1937; PEF/DA/TUF/294

Forster, Elliot David
14 February 1935; PEF/DA/TUF/246

Frankfort, Henri
June 8 1936; PEF/DA/TUF/274
July 2 1936; PEF/DA/TUF/276

Freyr, Sheykh
19 April 1932; PEF/DA/TUF/199
23 April 1936; PEF/DA/TUF/270

Frobenius, Leo
18 January 1935; PEF/DA/TUF/244

Gardner, Eleanor W.
27 October 1930; PEF/DA/TUF/169
14 November, probably 1930; PEF/DA/
 TUF/171
28 February 1935; PEF/DA/TUF/248
12 March 1935; PEF/DA/TUF/249
21 March 1935; PEF/DA/TUF/251
29 March 1935; PEF/DA/TUF/253
8 March 1936; PEF/DA/TUF/264
20 March 1936; PEF/DA/TUF/265
10 March, probably 1937; PEF/DA/TUF/294

Garrod, Dorothy
17 February, probably 1933; PEF/DA/
 TUF/213

Garstang, John
24 March, probably 1933; PEF/DA/TUF/218
3 May 1933; PEF/DA/TUF/222
20 March 1936; PEF/DA/TUF/265
11 February 1938; PEF/DA/TUF/316

El Gerzawy, Mohamed Hasan
Undated, probably November 1927: PEF/DA/
 TUF/0105
5th–9th December 1927; PEF/DA/TUF/95
Undated; November or December 1927

Gjerstad, Einar
11 January 1930; PEF/TUF/DA/151
4 February 1930; PEF/TUF/DA/154
Undated; probably 9–12 February 1930;
 PEF/TUF/DA/155

10 March 1930; PEF/TUF/DA/161
Undated, possibly 16 March 1930; PEF/TUF/DA/162
15 April 1930 and later; PEF/TUF/DA/166

Glanville, Stephen Ranulf Kingdon
16 March, probably 1938; PEF/DA/TUF/319

Glueck, Helen Iglauer
14 April 1938; PEF/DA/TUF/321.2

Gray, John
5 March, probably 1937; PEF/DA/TUF/293

Gunnis, Rupert Forbes
31 December 1929; PEF/TUF/DA/147
5 January 1930; PEF/TUF/DA/149
11 January 1930; PEF/TUF/DA/151
Undated, probably 9–12 February 1930; PEF/TUF/DA/155
25 March 1930; PEF/TUF/DA/163
15 April 1930 and later; PEF/TUF/DA/166

Guy, Philip Langstaffe Ord
13 March, probably 1932; PEF/DA/TUF/195
17 February, probably 1933; PEF/DA/TUF/213

Hamilton, Robert William
10 December 1937; PEF/DA/TUF/306
14 April 1938; PEF/DA/TUF/321.2

Harding, Gerald Lankester
10 December 1927; PEF/DA/TUF/96
Undated, November or December 1927
Undated, probably 19 December 1927; PEF/DA/TUF/98.2
18 December 1927; PEF/DA/TUF/100
23 December 1927; PEF/TUF/DA/106
26 December 1927; PEF/TUF/DA/107
13 January 1928; PEF/TUF/DA/108
1 February 1928; PEF/TUF/DA/109
8 March 1928; PEF/TUF/DA/111
23 March 1928; PEF/TUF/DA/114
7 February 1929; PEF/TUF/DA/129
8 February 1929; PEF/TUF/DA/130
8 March 1929; PEF/TUF/DA/135
22 October 1930; PEF/DA/TUF/168
27 October 1930; PEF/DA/TUF/169
1 November 1930; PEF/DA/TUF/170
14 November, probably 1930; PEF/DA/TUF/171
21 November, probably 1930; PEF/DA/TUF/172
30 November, probably 1930; PEF/DA/TUF/173
10 December 1930; PEF/DA/TUF/174
19 December, probably 1930; PEF/DA/TUF/175
25 January 1931; PEF/DA/TUF/177
4 February 1931; PEF/DA/TUF/178
14 February, probably 1931; PEF/DA/TUF/180
19 February, probably 1931; PEF/DA/TUF/181

12–13 March, probably 1931; PEF/DA/TUF/183
24 March, probably 1931; PEF/DA/TUF/184
3 January 1932; PEF/DA/TUF/190
8 January 1932; PEF/DA/TUF/191
24 February 1932; PEF/DA/TUF/193
23 March 1932; PEF/DA/TUF/196
7 April 1932; PEF/DA/TUF/197
11 April 1932; PEF/DA/TUF/198
19 April 1932; PEF/DA/TUF/199
3 December 1932; PEF/DA/TUF/201
10 December 1932; PEF/DA/TUF/202
6 February, probably 1933; PEF/DA/TUF/211
23 February 1933; PEF/DA/TUF/214
8 October 1933; PEF/DA/TUF/224
14 December 1934; PEF/DA/TUF/238
28 December 1934; PEF/DA/TUF/241
23 February 1935; PEF/DA/TUF/247
12 March 1935; PEF/DA/TUF/249
19 April 1935; PEF/DA/TUF/254
11 December 1935; PEF/DA/TUF/257
24 December, possibly 1935; PEF/TUF/DA/284
30 January 1936; PEF/DA/TUF/259
8 March 1936; PEF/DA/TUF/264
26 March 1936; PEF/DA/TUF/266
2 April 1936; PEF/DA/TUF/267
23 April 1936; PEF/DA/TUF/270
8 May 1936; PEF/DA/TUF/271
23 December, probably 1936; PEF/DA/TUF/283
31 December 1936; PEF/TUF/DA/285
21 January 1937; PEF/TUF/DA/288
5 February 1937; PEF/TUF/DA/290
25 February 1937; PEF/DA/TUF/292
25 March, probably 1937; PEF/DA/TUF/296
1 April, probably 1937; PEF/DA/TUF/297
4 December 1937; PEF/DA/TUF/305
10 December 1937; PEF/DA/TUF/306
16 December 1937; PEF/TUF/DA/307
30 December, probably 1937; PEF/DA/TUF/309
12 January 1938; PEF/DA/TUF/311
19 January 1938; PEF/DA/TUF/312
26 January 1938; PEF/DA/TUF/313
1 February 1938; PEF/DA/TUF/314
6 February 1938; PEF/DA/TUF/315
17 February 1938; PEF/DA/TUF/317
10 March, probably 1938; PEF/DA/TUF/318
14 April 1938; PEF/DA/TUF/321.2
21 April, probably 1938; PEF/DA/TUF/322

Hastings, Alice
10 December 1931; PEF/DA/TUF/187
10 December 1931; PEF/DA/TUF/188
23 March 1932; PEF/DA/TUF/196
25 February 1937; PEF/DA/TUF/292
14 April 1938; PEF/DA/TUF/321.2

Hastings, E.F. Warren
10 December 1931; PEF/DA/TUF/187
10 December 1931; PEF/DA/TUF/188
14 February 1932; PEF/DA/TUF/192

23 March 1932; PEF/DA/TUF/196
23 December, probably 1936; PEF/DA/
TUF/283
25 February 1937; PEF/DA/TUF/292

'Hofny/Hofney/Hofni/Hophni' [probably
Hofny Ibrahim]
5–9 December 1927; PEF/DA/TUF/95
10 December 1927; PEF/DA/TUF/96
18 December 1927; PEF/DA/TUF/100

Horsfield, George
26 March 1936; PEF/DA/TUF/266
8 May 1936; PEF/DA/TUF/271
25 February 1937; PEF/DA/TUF/292
16 and 26 November 1937; PEF/DA/TUF/
303

Ibrahim, Hamid M.
8 October 1933; PEF/DA/TUF/224

'Hajji Ibrahim'
17 February, probably 1933; PEF/DA/
TUF/213

Iliffe, John H.
15 March, probably 1933; PEF/DA/TUF/217

Inge, Charles H.
26 December 1932; PEF/DA/TUF/206
5 April 1934; PEF/DA/TUF/228
28 December 1934; PEF/DA/TUF/241
31 December 1934; PEF/DA/TUF/242
6 January 1935; PEF/DA/TUF/243
18 January 1935; PEF/DA/TUF/244
30 January 1935; PEF/DA/TUF/245
12 March 1935; PEF/DA/TUF/249
24 December, possibly 1935; PEF/TUF/
DA/284
21 February 1936; PEF/DA/TUF/261
20 March 1936; PEF/DA/TUF/265
23 April 1936; PEF/DA/TUF/270
14 January 1937; PEF/TUF/DA/287
29 January, probably 1937; PEF/TUF/DA/
289
4 December 1937; PEF/DA/TUF/305
10 December 1937; PEF/DA/TUF/306
12 January 1938; PEF/DA/TUF/311
26 January 1938; PEF/DA/TUF/313
1 February 1938; PEF/DA/TUF/314
6 February 1938; PEF/DA/TUF/315
11 February 1938; PEF/DA/TUF/316
17 February 1938; PEF/DA/TUF/317
10 March, probably 1938; PEF/DA/TUF/318
25 March, probably 1938; PEF/DA/TUF/320
14 April 1938; PEF/DA/TUF/321.2
21 April, probably 1938; PEF/DA/TUF/322

Keith-Roach, Edward
8 November 1934; PEF/DA/TUF/234
11 February 1938; PEF/DA/TUF/316
10 March, probably 1938; PEF/DA/TUF/318
14 April 1938; PEF/DA/TUF/321.2

Khalaf, Hasan
1 April, probably 1938; PEF/DA/TUF/321

Kraemer, Casper John Jnr.
13 March, probably 1932; PEF/DA/TUF/195

el-Kreti, Mohammed Osman
22 November 1927; PEF/DA/TUF/92
25–29 November 1927; PEF/DA/TUF/94
5–9 December 1927; PEF/DA/TUF/95
30 November, probably 1930; PEF/DA/
TUF/173
29 November, probably 1934; PEF/DA/
TUF/236
20 December 1934; PEF/DA/TUF/239
12 March 1935; PEF/DA/TUF/249
9 January, probably 1937; PEF/TUF/DA/286
1 April, probably 1937; PEF/DA/TUF/297
10 March, probably 1938; PEF/DA/TUF/318

Kuesevich
23 December 1930; PEF/DA/TUF/176
28 December 1931; PEF/DA/TUF/189

Lamon, Robert Scott
21 February 1936; PEF/DA/TUF/261

Mackay, Ernest John Henry
4 December 1937; PEF/DA/TUF/305
7 January 1938; PEF/DA/TUF/310
12 January 1938; PEF/DA/TUF/311
17 February 1938; PEF/DA/TUF/317

McWilliams, Herbert Hastings
10 March, probably 1933; PEF/DA/TUF/216
7 April 1933; PEF/DA/TUF/220
3 May 1933; PEF/DA/TUF/222

Markides, Menelaos
31 December 1929; PEF/TUF/DA/147

Marston, Sir Charles
29 November 1932; PEF/DA/TUF/200
10 March, probably1933; PEF/DA/TUF/216
15 March, probably 1933; PEF/DA/TUF/217
24 March, probably 1933; PEF/DA/TUF/218
30 January 1935; PEF/DA/TUF/245
23 February 1935; PEF/DA/TUF/247
19 April 1935; PEF/DA/TUF/254
12 January 1938; PEF/DA/TUF/311
19 January 1938; PEF/DA/TUF/312
26 January 1938; PEF/DA/TUF/313
1 February 1938; PEF/DA/TUF/314

Mayer, Leo Aryeh
19–22 March 1929; PEF/TUF/DA/136
3–4 April 1929; PEF/TUF/DA/138.1-2

Mond, Sir Robert
15 March, probably 1933; PEF/DA/TUF/217
24 March, probably 1933; PEF/DA/TUF/218
12 April 1933; PEF/DA/TUF/221
5 April 1934; PEF/DA/TUF/228
12 January 1938; PEF/DA/TUF/311

Murray, Margaret Alice
13 December 1927; PEF/DA/TUF/99
Undated; probably 9–12 February 1930; PEF/
TUF/DA/155

1 December 1931; PEF/DA/TUF/186
19 April 1932; PEF/DA/TUF/199
29 November 1932; PEF/DA/TUF/200
28 February 1935; PEF/DA/TUF/248
4 April 1935; PEF/DA/TUF/268
11 December 1935; PEF/DA/TUF/257
28 February 1936; PEF/DA/TUF/262
23 December, probably 1936; PEF/DA/
    TUF/283
25 February 1937; PEF/DA/TUF/292
25 March, probably 1937; PEF/DA/TUF/296
4 December 1937; PEF/DA/TUF/305
17 February 1938; PEF/DA/TUF/317
25 March, probably 1938; PEF/DA/TUF/320
1 April, probably 1938; PEF/DA/TUF/321.1
21 April, probably 1938; PEF/DA/TUF/322

Myers, Oliver H.
30 November 1928; PEF/TUF/DA/121
18 January 1929; PEF/TUF/DA/126
27 January 1929; PEF/TUF/DA/127
1 February 1929; PEF/TUF/DA/128
14 February 1929; PEF/TUF/DA/132
8 March 1929; PEF/TUF/DA/135
5 January 1930; PEF/TUF/DA/149
8 March 1936; PEF/DA/TUF/264

Newberry, Percy Edward
18 December 1927; PEF/DA/TUF/100

Parker, Barbara
23 December, probably 1936; PEF/DA/
    TUF/283
7 September 1937; PEF/DA/TUF/302

Parker, Dr G.
10 January 1929; PEF/TUF/DA/125
18 January 1929; PEF/TUF/DA/126
2 March 1929; PEF/TUF/DA/134
23 December 1930; PEF/ DA/TUF/176

Partridge, Frank (Bishop of Portsmouth)
April 14, 1936; PEF/DA/TUF/269
March 10 1937; PEF/DA/TUF/294

Payne, Humfry
23 December 1929; PEF/TUF/DA/144
8 May 1936; PEF/DA/TUF/271
12 May 1936; PEF/DA/TUF/272

Pendlebury, John Devitt Stringfellow
8 March 1936; PEF/DA/TUF/264

Petrie, Prof. Sir William Matthew Flinders
5–9 December 1927; PEF/DA/TUF/95
13 December 1927; PEF/DA/TUF/97
18 December 1927; PEF/DA/TUF/100
30 November 1928; PEF/TUF/DA/121
5 December 1928; PEF/TUF/DA/122
4 January 1929; PEF/TUF/DA/124
27 January 1929; PEF/TUF/DA/127
1 February 1929; PEF/TUF/DA/128
7 February 1929; PEF/TUF/DA/129
11 February 1929; PEF/TUF/DA/131
14 February 1929; PEF/TUF/DA/132
2 March 1929; PEF/TUF/DA/134

8 March 1929; PEF/TUF/DA/135
19–22 March 1929; PEF/TUF/DA/136
23 December 1929; PEF/TUF/DA/144
11 January 1930; PEF/TUF/DA/151
23 February 1930; PEF/TUF/DA/157
25 March 1930; PEF/TUF/DA/163
27 October 1930; PEF/DA/TUF/169
14 November, probably 1930; PEF/DA/
    TUF/171
30 November, probably 1930; PEF/DA/
    TUF/173
Typed document: PEF/DA/TUF/3206
10 December 1930; PEF/DA/TUF/174
19 December, probably 1930; PEF/ DA/
    TUF/175
Olga's draft article, probably March 1931;
    PEF/DA/TUF/3207
4 February 1931; PEF/DA/TUF/178
19 February, probably 1931; PEF/DA/
    TUF/181
12–13 March, probably 1931; PEF/DA/
    TUF/183
3 January 1932; PEF/DA/TUF/190
8 January 1932; PEF/DA/TUF/191
14 February 1932; PEF/DA/TUF/192
24 February 1932; PEF/DA/TUF/193
13 March, probably 1932; PEF/DA/TUF/195
23 March 1932; PEF/DA/TUF/196
11 April 1932; PEF/DA/TUF/198
19 April 1932; PEF/DA/TUF/199
10 December 1932; PEF/DA/TUF/202
15 March, probably 1933; PEF/DA/TUF/
    217
12 April 1933; PEF/DA/TUF/221
3 May 1933; PEF/DA/TUF/222
12 May 1933; PEF/DA/TUF/223
30 May 1933: PEF/DA/TUF/223
4 April 1934; PEF/DA/TUF/227
23 April 1934; PEF/DA/TUF/230
23 November, probably 1934; PEF/DA/
    TUF/235
29 November, probably 1934; PEF/DA/
    TUF/236
20 December 1934; PEF/DA/TUF/239
6 January 1935; PEF/DA/TUF/243
28 February 1935; PEF/DA/TUF/248
21 March 1935: PEF/DA/TUF/251
4 April 1935; PEF/DA/TUF/268
9 January, probably 1937; PEF/TUF/DA/286
14 January 1937; PEF/TUF/DA/287
5 February 1937; PEF/TUF/DA/290
4 December 1937; PEF/DA/TUF/305
7 January 1938; PEF/DA/TUF/310
1 April, probably 1938; PEF/DA/TUF/321.1
21 April, probably 1938; PEF/DA/TUF/322

Petrie, Lady Hilda Mary Isobel
21 November 1927; PEF/DA/TUF/91
13 December 1927; PEF/DA/TUF/99
18 December 1927; PEF/DA/TUF/100
5 December 1928; PEF/TUF/DA/122
4 January 1929; PEF/TUF/DA/124
7 February 1929; PEF/TUF/DA/129
14 December 1929; PEF/TUF/DA/140
Undated, probably 9–12 February 1930;
    PEF/TUF/DA/155

23 February 1930; PEF/TUF/DA/157
10 March 1930; PEF/TUF/DA/161
15 April 1930 and later; PEF/TUF/DA/166
14 November, probably 1930; PEF/DA/
    TUF/171
30 November, probably 1930; PEF/DA/
    TUF/173
10 December 1930; PEF/DA/TUF/174
19 December, probably 1930; PEF/ DA/
    TUF/175
23 December 1930; PEF/ DA/TUF/176
4 February 1931; PEF/DA/TUF/178
14 February–13 March, probably 1931;
    PEF/DA/TUF/180-183
1 December 1931; PEF/DA/TUF/186
28 December 1931–23 March 1932; PEF/DA/
    TUF/189-196
11 April 1932; PEF/DA/TUF/198
19 April 1932; PEF/DA/TUF/199
10 December 1932; PEF/DA/TUF/202
15 March, probably 1933; PEF/DA/TUF/
    217
12 April 1933; PEF/DA/TUF/221
4 April 1934; PEF/DA/TUF/227
23 April 1934
23 November, probably 1934; PEF/DA/
    TUF/235
29 November, probably 1934; PEF/DA/
    TUF/236
20 December 1934; PEF/DA/TUF/239
23 February 1935; PEF/DA/TUF/247
12 March 1935; PEF/DA/TUF/249
4 April 1935; PEF/DA/TUF/268
11 December 1935; PEF/DA/TUF/257
28 February 1936; PEF/DA/TUF/262
9 January, probably 1937; PEF/TUF/DA/
    286
14 January 1937; PEF/TUF/DA/287
4 December 1937; PEF/DA/TUF/305
30 December, probably 1937; PEF/DA/
    TUF/309
7 January 1938; PEF/DA/TUF/310
12 January 1938; PEF/DA/TUF/311
21 April, probably 1938; PEF/DA/TUF/322

du Plat Taylor, Joan Mabel Frederica
22 January 1930; PEF/TUF/DA/152
Undated; probably 9–12 February 1930;
    PEF/TUF/DA/155
23 February 1930; PEF/TUF/DA/157
6 April, probably 1930; PEF/TUF/DA/165
19 April 1934; PEF/DA/TUF/229

Porada, Edith
8 May 1936; PEF/DA/TUF/271
12 May 1936; PEF/DA/TUF/272
22 May 1936; PEF/DA/TUF/273
8 June 1936; PEF/DA/TUF/274
2 July 1936; PEF/DA/TUF/276
7 September 1937; PEF/DA/TUF/302
25 March, probably 1938; PEF/DA/TUF/
    320
1 April, probably 1938; PEF/DA/TUF/321.1

Poston, Elizabeth
14 April 1938; PEF/DA/TUF/321.2

Pummell, H.W.
26 March 1934; PEF/DA/TUF/226
29 November, probably 1934; PEF/DA/
    TUF/236
28 December 1934; PEF/DA/TUF/241
30 January 1935; PEF/DA/TUF/245
14 February 1935; PEF/DA/TUF/246
12 March 1935; PEF/DA/TUF/249
21 March 1935: PEF/DA/TUF/251
28 February 1936; PEF/DA/TUF/262
8 March 1936; PEF/DA/TUF/264
20 March 1936; PEF/DA/TUF/265
19 March 1937; PEF/DA/TUF/295
30 December, probably 1937; PEF/DA/
    TUF/309
14 April 1938; PEF/DA/TUF/321.2

Quibell, James Edward
6 January 1935; PEF/DA/TUF/243
29 March 1935: PEF/DA/TUF/252

Reisner, George Andrew
21 November 1927; PEF/DA/TUF/91

Reisner, Mary Putnam Bronson
8 March 1936; PEF/DA/TUF/264
26 March 1936; PEF/DA/TUF/266

Reynolds (couple)
26–29 April 1928; PEF/TUF/DA/117
3–4 April 1929; PEF/TUF/DA/138.1-2

Richmond, E.T.
19 April 1932; PEF/DA/TUF/199
10 December 1932; PEF/DA/TUF/202
4 December 1937; PEF/DA/TUF/305

Richmond, Mrs
12 April 1933; PEF/DA/TUF/221
1 April 1937; PEF/DA/TUF/297

Richmond Brown, Ralph
30 November, probably 1930; PEF/DA/
    TUF/173
19 December, probably 1930; PEF/ DA/
    TUF/175
25 January 1931; PEF/DA/TUF/177
4 February 1931; PEF/DA/TUF/178
14 February, probably 1931; PEF/DA/
    TUF/180
19 February, probably 1931; PEF/DA/TUF/181
12–13 March, probably 1931; PEF/DA/
    TUF/183
24 March, probably 1931; PEF/DA/TUF/184
1 December 1931; PEF/DA/TUF/186
3 January 1932; PEF/DA/TUF/190
8 January 1932; PEF/DA/TUF/191
24 February 1932; PEF/DA/TUF/193
7 March 1932; PEF/DA/TUF/194
23 March 1932; PEF/DA/TUF/196
19 April 1932; PEF/DA/TUF/199
10 December 1932; PEF/DA/TUF/202
4 March, probably 1933; PEF/DA/TUF/215
24 March, probably 1933; PEF/DA/TUF/218
7 April 1933; PEF/DA/TUF/220
3 May 1933; PEF/DA/TUF/222

8 May–June 10 1933; PEF/DA/TUF/223
5 April 1934; PEF/DA/TUF/228
19 April 1934; PEF/DA/TUF/229
8 November 1934; PEF/DA/TUF/234
23 November, probably 1934; PEF/DA/
TUF/235
29 November, probably 1934; PEF/DA/
TUF/236
20 December 1934; PEF/DA/TUF/239
28 December 1934; PEF/DA/TUF/241
31 December 1934; PEF/DA/TUF/242
6 January 1935; PEF/DA/TUF/243
18 January 1935; PEF/DA/TUF/244
23 February 1935; PEF/DA/TUF/247
12 March 1935; PEF/DA/TUF/249
21 March 1935: PEF/DA/TUF/251
29 March 1935: PEF/DA/TUF/252
5 December 1935; PEF/DA/TUF/256
11 December 1935; PEF/DA/TUF/257
28 December 1935; PEF/DA/TUF/258
21 February 1936; PEF/DA/TUF/261
28 February 1936; PEF/DA/TUF/262
6 March, probably 1936; PEF/DA/TUF/263
8 March 1936; PEF/DA/TUF/264
26 March 1936; PEF/DA/TUF/266
2 April 1936; PEF/DA/TUF/267
14 April 1936; PEF/DA/TUF/269
23 April 1936; PEF/DA/TUF/270
14 December 1936; PEF/DA/TUF/281
18 December 1936; PEF/DA/TUF/282
23 December, probably 1936; PEF/DA/
TUF/283
14 January 1937; PEF/TUF/DA/287
21 January 1937; PEF/TUF/DA/288
29 January, probably 1937; PEF/TUF/DA/289
5 February 1937; PEF/TUF/DA/290
25 February 1937; PEF/DA/TUF/292
10 March, probably 1937; PEF/DA/TUF/294
19 March 1937; PEF/DA/TUF/295
25 March, probably 1937; PEF/DA/TUF/296
16 and 26 November 1937; PEF/DA/TUF/303
20 November 1937; PEF/DA/TUF/304
10 December 1937; PEF/DA/TUF/306
30 December, probably 1937; PEF/DA/
TUF/309
6 February 1938; PEF/DA/TUF/315
16 March, probably 1938; PEF/DA/TUF/319

Risdon, D.L.
18 December 1927; PEF/DA/TUF/100
26 December 1927; PEF/TUF/DA/107
1 February 1928; PEF/TUF/DA/109
11 March 1928; PEF/TUF/DA/112
30 November 1928; PEF/TUF/DA/121

Risdon, Mrs
18 December 1927; PEF/DA/TUF/100
23 December 1927; PEF/TUF/DA/106
26 December 1927; PEF/TUF/DA/107
13 January 1928; PEF/TUF/DA/108
11 March 1928; PEF/TUF/DA/112
23 March 1928; PEF/TUF/DA/114
18 January 1929; PEF/TUF/DA/126

Rogers, Prof. G.F.
15 April 1930 and later; PEF/TUF/DA/166

Salamah, Taman
20 March 1936; PEF/DA/TUF/265

Scott, Norman
14 November, probably 1930; PEF/DA/
TUF/171
19 December, probably 1930; PEF/ DA/
TUF/175
4 February 1931; PEF/DA/TUF/178

Seton-Williams, M.V. (Veronica)
2 April 1936; PEF/DA/TUF/267
14 April 1938; PEF/DA/TUF/321.2

Shaw, Eleanor (*also see* Dyott, Eleanor)
23 December, probably 1936; PEF/DA/
TUF/283
11 February 1938; PEF/DA/TUF/316
14 April 1938; PEF/DA/TUF/321.2

Shaw, W.B. Kennedy
26 December 1932; PEF/DA/TUF/206
17 February, probably 1933; PEF/DA/
TUF/213
3 May 1933; PEF/DA/TUF/222
23 December, probably 1936; PEF/DA/
TUF/283
14 April 1938; PEF/DA/TUF/321.2

Shipton, G.M.
21 February 1936; PEF/DA/TUF/261
25 March, probably 1938; PEF/DA/TUF/320

Sitwell, Osbert and Sacheverell
15 April 1930 and later; PEF/TUF/DA/166

Sperrin-Johnson, John Charles
10 December 1931; PEF/DA/TUF/188
19 April 1932; PEF/DA/TUF/199

Stark, Freya Madeleine
25 March, probably 1937; PEF/DA/TUF/296

Starkey, James Leslie
23 December 1927; PEF/TUF/DA/106
26 December 1927; PEF/TUF/DA/107
13 January 1928; PEF/TUF/DA/108
1 February 1928; PEF/TUF/DA/109
23 March 1928; PEF/TUF/DA/114
27 March 1928; PEF/TUF/DA/115
5 December 1928; PEF/TUF/DA/122
18 January 1929; PEF/TUF/DA/126
8 March 1929; PEF/TUF/DA/135
19–22 March 1929; PEF/TUF/DA/136
27 October 1930; PEF/DA/TUF/169
1 November 1930; PEF/DA/TUF/170
14 November, probably 1930; PEF/DA/
TUF/171
21 November, probably 1930; PEF/DA/
TUF/172
30 November, probably 1930; PEF/DA/
TUF/173
10 December 1930; PEF/DA/TUF/174
19 February, probably 1931; PEF/DA/
TUF/181
10 December 1931; PEF/DA/TUF/188

14 February 1932; PEF/DA/TUF/192
24 February 1932; PEF/DA/TUF/193
19 April 1932; PEF/DA/TUF/199
3 December 1932; PEF/DA/TUF/201
10 December 1932; PEF/DA/TUF/202
13 December 1932; PEF/DA/TUF/203
23 February 1933; PEF/DA/TUF/214
15 March, probably 1933; PEF/DA/TUF/217
8 October 1933; PEF/DA/TUF/224
Undated, probably October or November
    1933; PEF/DA/TUF/225
5 April 1934; PEF/DA/TUF/228
19 April 1934; PEF/DA/TUF/229
14 December 1934; PEF/DA/TUF/238
28 December 1934; PEF/DA/TUF/241
31 December 1934; PEF/DA/TUF/242
6 January 1935; PEF/DA/TUF/243
18 January 1935; PEF/DA/TUF/244
28 February 1935; PEF/DA/TUF/248
12 March 1935; PEF/DA/TUF/249
21 March 1935: PEF/DA/TUF/251
29 March 1935: PEF/DA/TUF/252
5 December 1935; PEF/DA/TUF/256
28 December 1935; PEF/DA/TUF/258
30 January 1936; PEF/DA/TUF/259
21 February 1936; PEF/DA/TUF/261
28 February 1936; PEF/DA/TUF/262
8 March 1936; PEF/DA/TUF/264
2 April 1936; PEF/DA/TUF/267
14 April 1936; PEF/DA/TUF/269
2 July 1936; PEF/DA/TUF/276
23 December, probably 1936; PEF/DA/
    TUF/283
31 December 1936; PEF/TUF/DA/285
14 January 1937; PEF/TUF/DA/287
21 January 1937; PEF/TUF/DA/288
29 January, probably 1937; PEF/TUF/
    DA/289
5 February 1937; PEF/TUF/DA/290
5 March, probably 1937; PEF/TUF/DA/
    293
1 April, probably 1937; PEF/DA/TUF/297
4 December 1937; PEF/DA/TUF/305
10 December 1937; PEF/DA/TUF/306
30 December, probably 1937; PEF/DA/
    TUF/309
7 January 1938; PEF/DA/TUF/310
12 January 1938; PEF/DA/TUF/311
19 January 1938; PEF/DA/TUF/312
17 February 1938; PEF/DA/TUF/317
10 March, probably 1938; PEF/DA/TUF/318

Starkey, Marjorie Rosaline
23 December 1927; PEF/TUF/DA/106
26 December 1927; PEF/TUF/DA/107
13 January 1928; PEF/TUF/DA/108
23 March 1928; PEF/TUF/DA/114
30 November 1928; PEF/TUF/DA/121
19–22 March 1929; PEF/TUF/DA/136
1 November 1930; PEF/DA/TUF/170
21 November, probably 1930; PEF/DA/
    TUF/172
24 March, probably 1933; PEF/DA/TUF/218
8 October 1933; PEF/DA/TUF/224
28 December 1935; PEF/DA/TUF/258
21 February 1936; PEF/DA/TUF/261

19 January 1938; PEF/DA/TUF/312
26 January 1938; PEF/DA/TUF/313

St Barbe Baker, Richard
5 December 1928; PEF/TUF/DA/122
27 January 1929; PEF/TUF/DA/127
1 February 1929; PEF/TUF/DA/128
7 February 1929; PEF/TUF/DA/129
8 February 1929; PEF/TUF/DA/130
11 February 1929; PEF/TUF/DA/131
2 March 1929; PEF/TUF/DA/134
8 March 1929; PEF/TUF/DA/135
23 February 1930; PEF/TUF/DA/157

Storrs, Sir Ronald Henry Amherst
31 December 1929; PEF/TUF/DA/147
11 January 1930; PEF/TUF/DA/151
25 March 1930; PEF/TUF/DA/163
9 January, probably 1937; PEF/TUF/DA/286

Strickland, Kitty
7 March 1932; PEF/DA/TUF/194
13 March, probably 1932; PEF/DA/TUF/195
23 March 1932; PEF/DA/TUF/196
11 April 1932; PEF/DA/TUF/198
29 November 1932; PEF/DA/TUF/200

Strickland Colt, Teresa (Terry). Referred to
    with her husband as 'the Colts' in several
    letters (see Colt, Harris Dunscombe, Jr).
    References below relate to Teresa Strickland
    Colt specifically.
25 January 1931; PEF/ DA/TUF /177
14 February, probably 1931; PEF/DA/
    TUF/180
19 February, probably 1931; PEF/DA/
    TUF/181
24 February 1932; PEF/DA/TUF/193
11 April 1932; PEF/DA/TUF/198
29 November 1932; PEF/DA/TUF/200
6 February, probably 1933; PEF/DA/
    TUF/211
4 March, probably1933; PEF/DA/TUF/215
24 March, probably 1933; PEF/DA/TUF/218
7 April 1933; PEF/DA/TUF/220
Enclosure, Memorandum of Understanding;
    PEF/DA/TUF/219
3 May 1933; PEF/DA/TUF/222
8 May–10 June 1933; PEF/DA/TUF/223
5 December 1935; PEF/DA/TUF/256
8 March 1936; PEF/DA/TUF/264
20 March 1936; PEF/DA/TUF/265
23 April 1936; PEF/DA/TUF/270
26 March 1936; PEF/DA/TUF/266
18 December 1936; PEF/DA/TUF/282

Sweden, Crown Prince and Princess of
14 December 1934; PEF/DA/TUF/238
20 December 1934; PEF/DA/TUF/239

Tewfiq (possibly Tewfiq Saleh – could refer to
    one or more than one individual)
29 November, probably 1934; PEF/DA/
    TUF/236
6 January 1935; PEF/DA/TUF/243
29 January 1937; PEF/TUF/DA/289]

Tegart, Sir Charles Augustus
10 March, probably 1938; PEF/DA/TUF/318

Terazi
22 November 1928; PEF/TUF/DA/120
22 October 1930; PEF/DA/TUF/168
3 December 1932; PEF/DA/TUF/201

Torczyner, Prof. Harry / Tur-Sinai, Naftali Herz
26 March 1936; PEF/DA/TUF/266
14 April 1936; PEF/DA/TUF/269
12 January 1938; PEF/DA/TUF/311

Vernon, J.G.
14 November, probably 1930; PEF/DA/
    TUF/171
19 December, probably 1930; PEF/ DA/
    TUF/175
4 February 1931; PEF/DA/TUF/178
19 February, probably 1931; PEF/DA/
    TUF/181

Vincent, Louis-Hugues ('Père Vincent')
23 February 1933; PEF/DA/TUF/214
12 March 1935; PEF/DA/TUF/249
23 April 1936; PEF/DA/TUF/270
12 January 1938; PEF/DA/TUF/311

Waechter, John
25 March, probably 1938; PEF/DA/TUF/320

Wainwright, Gerald Avery
21 November 1927; PEF/DA/TUF/91
23 December 1927; PEF/TUF/DA/106

Wauchope, General Sir Arthur Grenfell
24 December, possibly 1935; PEF/TUF/DA/
    284
2 April 1936; PEF/DA/TUF/267
30 December, probably 1937; PEF/DA/
    TUF/309
12 January 1938; PEF/DA/TUF/311
19 January 1938; PEF/DA/TUF/312
6 February 1938; PEF/DA/TUF/315

Wellcome, Sir Henry Solomon
21 March 1935: PEF/DA/TUF/251
8 March 1936; PEF/DA/TUF/264

Wheeler, Sir Robert Eric Mortimer
26 March 1936; PEF/DA/TUF/266
2 April 1936; PEF/DA/TUF/267
16 March, probably 1938; PEF/DA/TUF/319

Woolley, Sir Charles Leonard and Katharine
    Elizabeth
15 April 1930 and later; PEF/TUF/DA/166

Xia, Nai
16 December 1937; PEF/DA/TUF/307
16 March, probably 1938; PEF/DA/TUF/319

Index of places